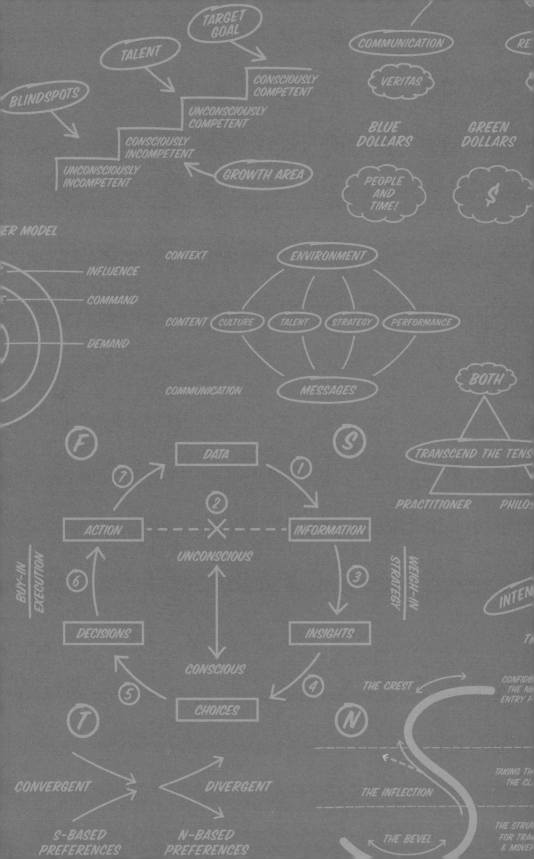

LEADERSHIP RIGOR!

LEADERSHIP RIGOR!

BREAKTHROUGH
PERFORMANCE & PRODUCTIVITY
LEADING
YOURSELF · TEAMS · ORGANIZATIONS

ERICA PEITLER

Circle Takes the Square Publishing
Morristown, New Jersey

© 2014 Erica Peitler

All rights reserved. No part of this book may be reproduced or transmitted in any form or by any means, electronic or mechanical, including photocopying, recording, or by any information storage and retrieval system, without permission in writing from the publisher.

Published by
Circle Takes the Square Publishing
Morristown, New Jersey

Publisher's Cataloging-Publication Data
Peitler, Erica.

Leadership Rigor! Breakthrough Performance & Productivity Leading Yourself, Teams, Organizations. – Morristown, N.J. : Circle Takes the Square Pub., 2014.

p. ; cm.

ISBN13: 978-0-9815124-2-6

1. Leadership. 2. Teams in the workplace. 3. Organizational effectiveness. 4. Management. I. Title.

HD57.7.P45 2014
658.4092—dc23   2014939597

Project coordination by Jenkins Group, Inc.
www.BookPublishing.com

Cover and interior design: Eric Tufford

Printed in Singapore

18 17 16 15 14 • 5 4 3 2 1

This book is dedicated to three groups of people with whom I have had the pleasure of enjoying amazing experiences:

To the Canadian Consumer Care Division of Bayer Healthcare (1999–2005), you challenged me to quickly become a consciously competent leader on both an operational and organizational level, and I will be forever grateful for the learning and growth our time together created!

To the members of Vistage CEO Board #3497, you are a great source of insight into the practical challenges leaders face today in the entrepreneurial world!

To everyone at The Hampshire Companies, thank you for embracing these concepts and becoming the "first" organization to role model **Leadership Rigor.**

Contents

PART 1
LEADING YOURSELF

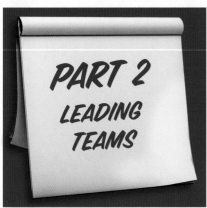

PART 2
LEADING TEAMS

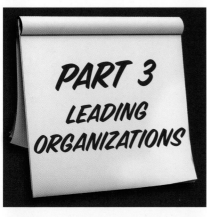

PART 3
LEADING ORGANIZATIONS

Foreword

The fact that you have opened this book suggests that you, like me, are seeking insights or perhaps even a road map for how to be an excellent leader.

My hope is that you will embark on the journey called **Leadership Rigor.** If you do, your understanding of how you impact and influence others will be transformed. You will become a mindful leader, which will enable you to build nimble, adaptable, productive teams and a high-performance organization.

2008 marked the fifth year of my tenure as CEO of The Hampshire Companies. At the time, I felt stale in terms of my personal leadership and in my leadership of the organization as a whole. Nonetheless, my overriding objective was to create an environment of empowered, integrated individuals and teams in order to drive performance. We made progress, but I had the gnawing feeling that we were just scratching the surface.

Earlier in my career, I had been introduced to various leadership concepts, but I was struggling to put some of these ideas to work within our organization. I was also searching for how to be more intentional in this process.

In my experience, being aware that you are struggling is the first step. The second step is to begin searching for answers. The third step is to be open to possibilities. When you are in this state, critical people can enter your life.

Just such an encounter took place when Erica Peitler walked into my office. I soon realized this was the right moment and the right person to help me lead a transformation at The Hampshire Companies.

A short while later, in February 2009, I brought the senior people of Hampshire together to embark on what has been an incredible journey of personal, professional, and organizational growth for all of us.

Introduction

Leadership Rigor is both *a practice and a philosophy* designed to accelerate your leadership performance and productivity. Already gaining traction and momentum with an emerging group of cutting-edge companies and executives who have been exposed to these concepts and the breakthrough experiences that can result from its use, **Leadership Rigor™** is *becoming a movement,* a no-nonsense approach aimed at learning how to lead yourself, teams, and organizations. The publication of this book is well timed for (3) compelling reasons.

> *First, in March 2014, Bersin by Deloitte published their latest Global Human Capital Trend Survey that captured the insights from (2,532) business leaders across (94) countries stating that:*

"Building leadership capability is by far the most urgent need for companies today... and that companies see the need for leadership at all levels, in all geographies, and across all functional areas. In addition, this continuous need for new and better leaders has accelerated."

> *Second, whether you are an aspiring leader or a current CEO, you and your organization are facing unprecedented pressure to find innovative ways to fuel growth and improve profitability. "Innovation" is defined as:*

"The action or process of introducing new ideas or methods; changing, altering, transforming, or creating a breakthrough."

Leadership Rigor offers innovation in leadership through its unique signature models and straightforward approaches for transforming the way you lead. The simple truth is that "how" you lead is the precursor to "what" you can successfully achieve as a leader, yet it is often underestimated, dismissed, or not a conscious consideration.

Surprised by the boldness of this statement?

Introduction

Consider the reality organizations face today with respect to growth. Most executives and their leadership teams struggle with the question of how to achieve growth and mistakenly lunge into strategy sessions to assess their priorities and create their action plans. If you listen carefully to them, their real challenge centers around how to actually lead the growth process across their organization.

This is because many organizations lack the environment, culture, and most importantly the "ready now" talent they need to capitalize on the growth opportunities that are right in front of them. *They are stuck in a battle with themselves,* holding on to underperforming employees for extended periods of time or long-standing employees in critical "blocker positions" of leadership who keep the organization running operationally at its current level but are not capable of leading their teams through the necessary changes to reach higher levels of performance and growth.

Whether the root cause is employee reluctance to evolve their work style to meet the changing organizational conditions and requirements or a lack of the required capabilities because employees have not received the essential development needed to advance their skills quickly enough or even simply because they were a bad hire, the problem is significant.

How do you get out of this stuck system if you are a team leader or CEO? Even more importantly, how do you lead yourself as an individual with talent to ensure you are consciously and continuously nurturing your personal "readiness" for what is next? The answer is, you **Rigor it!**™

Fundamentally, *Leadership Rigor* suggests (2) considerations all CEOs and up-and-coming leaders must understand with respect to growth (both personal and business):

- **You first must be ready for it**
- **You must then decide how best to go after it**

Introduction

One of the concepts **Leadership Rigor** focuses on is the importance of *sequencing*. The order in which you do things matters! Most leaders get the sequencing wrong when it comes to growth. They skip the "being ready for it" part and unabashedly leap into action, falsely assuming they can make the adjustments needed along the way. Being ready, however, cannot be underestimated as it includes creating an environment for growth, a well-defined culture, and securing the appropriate talent with both the leadership and the technical skills needed to execute on the opportunities. All of this involves behavioral expectations that are not likely to occur without an investment of time and effort. Measure twice and cut once, or you will be wasting your resources on continuous *delays and do-overs,* an unfortunate yet frequent occurrence that is pointed out throughout **Leadership Rigor.**

Being ready for growth also requires that you appropriately anticipate the changes you will need to make and the risks you will need to take. The trajectory of your growth, both in business and personally, will depend on the choices you make as well as your sense of timing.

Leadership Rigor is focused on creating *"change-ready" leaders.* These leaders can openly embrace ambiguity, chaos, and complexity because they have tools, models, frameworks, and language to quickly assess, structure, discuss, and collectively facilitate the decision-making process, resulting in aligned actions. They also have the mindset and emotional skill sets needed to effectively lean into the uncomfortable change process. By innovating on this preparedness first, these "change-ready" leaders are far better equipped to realize the growth they are seeking for their teams and organizations.

Unfortunately, those leaders who underestimate what is required to be ready, not to mention what is at stake, will ultimately find themselves constrained and falling further behind in terms of marketplace competitiveness, placing their organizations at increased risk for missing the opportunity to create both scalability and sustainability. In small to mid-sized businesses, this reality is all too common and far too real.

> *Third, Leadership Rigor addresses the fact that it has never been more important to be able to communicate and build relationships in the workplace than it is today. Thanks to multiple generations interfacing together, changing workspace dynamics, the pervasiveness of technology platforms that are transforming how we engage and socialize information, the globalization of business requiring cross-cultural collaboration, and the increasing complexity and speed of the business world, the day-to-day challenges of working together are immense.*

Throughout **Leadership Rigor,** the focus is on working with and through people. As leaders, we quickly come to learn that the reality of being in this people business means that we need to understand and empathize with a wide range of emotional needs. We also come to appreciate, by comparison, that the business itself is often the relatively straightforward part of our challenge.

Most leaders excel at either communication or relationship building and typically struggle with the other. To lead at your highest level, and certainly if you aspire to lead at the team or organizational level, you must become a master of both. **Leadership Rigor** refers to *communication and relationships* as the (2) currencies of leadership and discusses how to develop these skills at each progressive level of your development journey.

Introduction

Why I Wrote *Leadership Rigor*

I am a *technical scientist,* a pharmacist by training who has always been intrigued by the "mechanisms of action" of how and why drugs work. Scientific rigor has always been a familiar concept.

Today, as a professional leadership performance coach and experienced facilitator, I bring this same curiosity and passion to my coaching practice by creating models and frameworks that help to explain how leadership works and why it works that way. Understanding and incorporating the concepts presented in this book can greatly assist you if your goal is to develop yourself as a leader as well as to build a future generation of leaders versus randomly hoping that either you or they will spontaneously appear one day equipped to lead.

Today's team and organizational leaders need to have a sincere desire to engage and develop others and to be genuinely curious about "how people work." This requires a significant investment of your time and energy; it isn't merely something you squeeze in after your day job is complete. In fact, as a leader, it is the priority role you must play.

Absolute brilliance, in case you haven't already received the email, text, or tweet, is no longer the reason individuals get the "big jobs." Instead, being emotionally intelligent is the ticket to high-level leadership roles because the skills that emotional intelligence requires enable individuals, teams, and organizations to reach their highest levels of performance and productivity. Whether you are a leadership performance coach, a CEO, or an aspiring team leader, you need to become a *social scientist* if you want to achieve leadership success today.

Introduction

Who This Book Is For

This book was written with (3) audiences in mind. The primary audience is the small to mid-sized CEO/business owner or divisional president of a large corporation. The second is the aspiring leader who wants to advance into senior executive roles as a functional area or business unit team leader, and the last is the ever-curious, enlightened leader who is looking to learn new techniques to apply on the ground in his or her evolving leadership practice.

▪ Small to Mid-Sized CEOs/Business Owners

Small to mid-sized company CEOs and business owners who are looking to take their firms to the next level of growth are the first audience for this book. This primarily includes entrepreneurial leaders who are approaching or have hit a wall in their trajectory of success. They pride themselves on building or expanding upon the foundation they and their families/predecessors have established, but their bandwidth may be tapped out and their ability to grow may be becoming exponentially more challenging or difficult for them personally as well as for their organization. They may have loyal employees but simultaneously lack the talent needed to take the company forward to a new breakthrough level of growth and success. Wanting to move forward but lacking clear plans, these leaders often grab at whatever they can as it crosses their paths, thereby running into two challenges, working out of sequence and at the wrong altitude.

For these individuals, *Leadership Rigor* can be a road map for evolving their organizations from being entrepreneurially driven to being run more like an enterprise with transparent processes and practices that maintain the essence or spirit of what has built their success so far. There will be choices to make here that involve risk and change. These decisions will be difficult, but the path to growth depends on courageous choices.

Introduction

The goal in **Leadership Rigor** is to balance creativity and the entrepreneurial spirit while providing enterprise structures and frameworks to the process so that the work can be appropriately executed as well as replicated across the organization. This philosophy of *"freedom within structure"* is a prescription for accelerated growth with rigor!

■ Aspiring Corporate Executives

The second audience for **Leadership Rigor** includes aspiring executives who are members of large corporations or divisions and who want to lead at the functional team/organizational level. These ambitious leaders have set their sights on a leadership role and are looking for a transparent road map to chart the course of their careers.

If you are an aspiring executive who wants to know what it takes to lead at the highest levels, **Leadership Rigor** can be the ticket to successfully developing yourself as a high-performance individual contributor, a high-performance team leader in your current role, or for developing a career-building platform for orchestrating your next several promotions if you take on the challenge and work through the process.

■ Enlightened Leaders Seeking New Insights

The third audience for **Leadership Rigor** includes enlightened leaders who are students of themselves and the architects of their evolving leadership practices. These lifetime learners want to stay at the top of their games and are looking to obtain new innovative insights they can test out and apply on the ground.

Introduction

What Is the Value Proposition in Leadership Rigor?

Leadership Rigor is a philosophy of conscious discipline you relentlessly practice, resulting in breakthrough performance and productivity that can be realized at the level of leading yourself, leading teams, and leading organizations.

A "philosophy" is fundamental knowledge, beliefs, or attitudes held by a person or organization that act as guiding principles for behavior.

A foundational belief expressed throughout *Leadership Rigor* is that high-performing leaders are consciously competent. This means they know what they are doing, how they are doing it, and why they are doing it. Consciously competent leaders are performance focused;

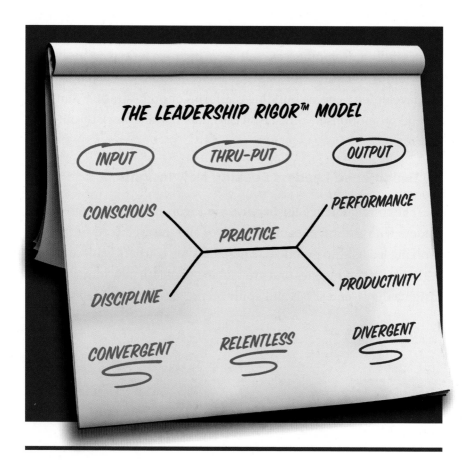

they understand that what they do and how they do it are equally important in achieving their outcomes. They also understand and communicate why they are doing it so they establish context, perspective, and meaning for their audiences.

A convergent focus on conscious discipline provides a powerful engine of *"input"* energy that drives leadership development toward those skills and behaviors that are known to produce performance and productivity, or the divergent *"output."* This assumes, of course, an ability to relentlessly practice these skills on a consistent basis with *"through-put"* energy.

As an example, consider (2) golfers. The first is a (2)-times-a-year sales conference hacker who wants to have a great round. With intense muscle and might, he throws everything he has into his drives off the tee, only to find his ball sailing off the fairway and into the woods. This individual is focused on the output, which is distance, and has not paid attention to the input or "through-put" pieces.

Compare this individual to the seasoned player who practices the fundamentals regularly, consciously considers her swing, and focuses on the input to the stroke, leaving the output out of her mind. This individual's swing is long and straight into the middle of the fairway and results in a playable ball.

Serious athletes as well as business and leadership professionals know that being strong performers at the top of their games requires focus, fundamental skill building, and relentless practice. They, and you, must **Rigor it!**

Introduction

A Life Cycle Approach to Leadership Development

Leadership development needs to be a journey with a road map rather than a black box mystery! In service of this philosophy, *Leadership Rigor* takes a life cycle approach across the evolution of your career development and advancement. You cannot give to others what you do not have, so learning to lead yourself is the first step.

Armed with knowledge and insights about yourself as well as fundamental leadership skills and capabilities, you might decide to pursue the challenge of leading a team. You will be cautioned, however, to choose this path only if you have a true desire to coach and develop others. If you are simply chasing money, a title, or a perceived increase in power or authority, you will ultimately fail as a team leader while stalling the growth of those entrusted to your leadership role.

Do you want to develop and lead a strong talent bench while orchestrating the architectural development of culture, strategy, and performance on an enterprise level? Or, alternatively, do you want to further dive into the expertise of your profession and become a functional area or technical thought leader? These are choices you must thoroughly understand and be ready to rigor.

Mastering the team leader role can provide you with the potential opportunity of leading at the organizational level. Here, your ability to maintain extreme discipline and to focus *on* the business versus *in* the business will be significantly pressure tested.

One of the game-changing concepts presented in *Leadership Rigor* is playing at the right altitude. Different levels of play exist within each leadership role, and the expectation of "where you need to play" dramatically shifts in emphasis as you advance from an individual contributor to a team leader and ultimately into organizational leadership roles. As a leader, you must understand what these shift requirements are and how to appropriately play the role you are in at the right altitude so you can provide lift to your team/organization and avoid dropping into the space of others, causing compression.

> *This is often a surprising revelation for many leaders, who come to understand that they have been stifling the growth of their teams/organizations as well as themselves by playing the roles of other people rather than the roles they are supposed to play and, often, the role that only they can play.*

Throughout my career as both a business leader and coach, I have been amazed at how unclear and/or unexpressed the process of leadership development is in most organizations. As a result, individuals often invest years of time doing what they think will advance their careers only to be surprised, disappointed, and confused when they are passed over for promotions or terminated.

These are, quite frankly, instances of *"leadership malpractice."* Team and organizational leaders need to appropriately set expectations and coach their talent for performance so surprises of this kind do not occur along the way. Accordingly, **Leadership Rigor** outlines how to raise the bar across your enterprise community in terms of what is expected in performance-based organizations!

Technical proficiency, for example, is no longer the primary reason why an individual might be given an expanded role that requires supervising others. Today, enlightened organizations are embracing a more selective approach to promotions into leadership roles based on willingness and capabilities to perform their primary responsibility: building the talent bench for the future. This shift reflects that leadership is now viewed as a skilled profession and not merely an extracurricular activity you occasionally engage in a few times a year in high-profile settings! Being entrusted with the organization's most valuable asset, its talent, requires a new level of expectation in the leadership ranks.

Introduction

The organizations at greatest risk for falling behind are those without defined leadership teams or those with underperforming leadership teams. While time ticks, the skill sets of employees either stagnate or decline.

Let me be clear that there is a time value to talent. It is an asset that either appreciates or depreciates. Many companies fail to act quickly enough in this area and are surprised when they ultimately realize the time and effort it takes to move the needle forward with the skills and behaviors that are required for individual, team, or organizational success. In fact, many companies give themselves "double bogeys" right out of the gate by consciously hiring people they believe are good for the next year or two but not for the long term. The time and effort invested in the on-boarding and development process is wasted when, a few years down the road, the organization must once again hire someone new to take the organization to the next level. Of course, some companies hold on to their underperforming talent, avoiding the discomfort of change and choosing instead to stifle the growth of their teams/organizations.

> *These are huge, value-destroying decisions that not only affect performance and productivity today but jeopardize the scalability and sustainability of your future.*

Unfortunately, this general inertia is often imperceptible to those who don't realize what is happening or what is at stake. For these individuals, *Leadership Rigor* can serve as a loud and clear wake-up call to get into action quickly!

Even still, many leaders will not immediately see or likely believe that their situation is that bad in their personal career, team, or organization because of their blind spots and/or lack of receptivity to the feedback they may be receiving. This is why *Leadership Rigor* is best combined with team/organizational coaching so that high impact facilitation and conversations can create the context for change in real time with an aspiring leader or intact leadership team. This combination can often create the breakthrough that is needed to reach the next level of performance.

What This Book Is Not

Leadership Rigor is not another book designed to debate the age-old questions of what leadership is, what the differences are between leaders and managers, and whether leaders are born or made.

The premise of *Leadership Rigor* appreciates that *you already have the initiative and ambition you need* to create either a thriving career or a thriving business. You are currently in or are soon to be in a leadership position, and you aspire to either more expansively fill that role or advance further into new roles.

What This Book Is

Leadership Rigor provides you with a *comprehensive set of tools* that will help accelerate your leadership performance and productivity while navigating the challenging dynamics of your environment as you advance your career. More specifically, it will help you understand that:

- The positions you hold are meaningless; what really matters is *how you choose to play* your leadership role.

- Leadership is learnable, emotional, and in service of others; you either *buy into* and embrace these (3) core principles or you don't.

- Leadership skills are built and developed over time. Though some of you may have talents that give you a legitimate fast start, you are not necessarily assured of a strong finish, so *don't coast* or count on your capabilities to magically appear!

■ The skills/capabilities that are required at each level of leadership (i.e., leading yourself, leading teams, and leading organizations) *change and escalate,* so you must dedicate yourself to practicing your skills in increasingly complex circumstances and reaching the conscious competency required at these various progressive stages.

■ Leadership has its own language, not unlike law, medicine, and business. If you want to be a leader, you must speak the language of leadership *fluently.* This includes utilizing tools like **The Accountability Conversation**™ that is presented in *Leadership Rigor.* This unique dialogue is a straightforward negotiation that encompasses both role and process clarity, thereby helping you focus on performance and productivity while simultaneously assisting you in expressing your leadership voice.

■ Leadership roles can take several paths, and you will need to choose yours. Leading the development of others requires *will and skill,* so it is not an appropriate choice for everyone. The alternative of independent subject matter expertise (SME) or thought leadership is an often overlooked approach that many would be well served to consider early in their careers to avoid a mismatch that results in a *lack of true fulfillment* and pursuing a role that is not really right for them. This book will challenge you to determine your optimal path.

Introduction

How This Book Accelerates Leadership Development

■ The Fundamentals

Leadership Rigor introduces concepts and frameworks that are fundamental to developing your leadership skills at progressive stages as represented by the book's (3) sections:

- Part 1—*Leading* Yourself
- Part 2—*Leading* Teams
- Part 3—*Leading* Organizations

Each concept and framework is a building block for current and future use as it sets the context and provides the content for your development work. Your progress will be determined by your behavioral awareness, acceptance, and alignment with the material. Learning to use these concepts and frameworks in real time and placing them on the ground (OTG) is the ultimate goal for leading with rigor!

■ Signature Models

Each of *Leadership Rigor's* (3) sections also contains a signature model designed to help make your thinking visible and to increase your influence as you accelerate the skill development of others working with you:

- Part 1 *Signature* Model—The Progressive Mindset™
- Part 2 *Signature* Model—Analytical Rigor™
- Part 3 *Signature* Model—Organizational Excellence™

These signature models provide you with practical techniques for focusing on communication, decision making, and mapping out your organizational action agenda for change and growth.

While you will be exposed to many models and frameworks throughout *Leadership Rigor,* the signature models are enduring tools that you will continuously use to enhance and accelerate your team, organization, or your own forward progress.

At the team and organizational level, these signature models will also provide you with elements for creating your own unique cultural dynamics of "how we do things around here." Again, if relentlessly practiced with conscious discipline, the output will be breakthrough performance and productivity!

Tensions to Resolve

As you progress in your leadership development journey, you will occasionally come upon a "speed bump" that causes you to slow down. In *Leadership Rigor,* these are referred to as "tensions to resolve." Each stage of development contains a critical choice or challenge for you to work through and ultimately embrace or transcend:

- **Part 1 *Tension***
  Crossing the Knowing-Doing Gap

- **Part 2 *Tension***
  Becoming a Practitioner and a Philosopher

- **Part 3 *Tension***
  Being an Entrepreneurial or an Enterprise Leader

Each tension describes the challenge/choice you face as well as a methodical approach to working through the resolution process so that you can advance to the next level, if you choose to do the work.

Rigor Alerts

Finally, the book includes a number of Rigor Alerts and sidebars that offer practical advice, stories, and cautionary tales.

Demonstrating Both Veritas and Gravitas

Leaders who are passionate advocates for an idea or belief often demonstrate both veritas and gravitas. They understand their issues and their audience. Not afraid to say what needs to be said and fiercely serving the needs of the collective "we," these leaders frame the context of their communication so that it can be intellectually listened to while empathetically connecting to the emotional needs of their audience so that it can be heard.

How to Use This Book

Leadership Rigor can be used as a reference, resource, or road map. You can read it through cover to cover or target the areas you believe you need to focus on right now. My personal advice is to start at the beginning so you can fill in the gaps or blind spots you may not know you have, but the choice is yours, and each of the book's (3) individual sections can stand solidly on their own.

In my own leadership development journey, I have read several books over and over, writing in the margins and making notes to myself. I hope *Leadership Rigor* inspires that same initiative and desire in you.

Read the book, write in it, and wear it out! It is meant to be part of your growth forward, a companion that, perhaps along with some experiential add-ons including individual or team coaching, can make a transformative impact in your leadership development and your life.

If this sounds inspiring to you, let the rigor begin!

"Three things are extremely hard: steel, a diamond, and to know one's self."

– Ben Franklin

PART 1:
LEADING YOURSELF

If you are genuinely interested in pursuing a leadership role, you must first be a student of yourself. Without a curious and disciplined approach to discovering the truth about who you really are, not the image you project (your ego) and want others to buy into, you will be challenged in authentically connecting with other people.

This is not about being self-centered or self-absorbed; it is about being anchored in knowing and understanding yourself for the purpose of building and being in healthy relationships.

To put it bluntly, if you want to lead others, you must first develop an intimate relationship with *yourself*.

Such a statement may sound obvious and even a bit silly, but the fact is that many people do not understand themselves. As a result, they are not capable of building strong relationships with others, which means they cannot lead them.

As a leadership performance coach, I often see extreme examples of this. Most people proudly believe they know themselves very well, claim to be highly self-aware, and categorize themselves as strong performers in their professional roles. Only a brave few openly admit they probably have a lot to learn.

You will face many challenges in your leadership journey, and they all begin with knowing yourself.

In the first part of *Leadership Rigor*, you will learn how to create the foundation for your own personal leadership development journey. Once you have created this foundation for yourself, you will be introduced to the first signature model of *Leadership Rigor*, **The Progressive Mindset**. This versatile tool will give you a structure for developing and delivering communication messages that can move your projects and team initiatives forward with confidence.

As a closing step to Part 1 of *Leadership Rigor*, you will be asked to resolve the first of (3) tensions on your leadership journey, crossing the knowing-doing gap. Here you will need to choose whether leadership is merely an interesting concept for you or something you want to be a skilled professional at by applying yourself on the ground and in real time to practicing it!

Ready to embrace the rigor required to be a student of yourself? Let's begin!

The Fundamentals of Leading Yourself:

CHAPTER 1:
Creating Your Leadership Mindset

CHAPTER 2:
Creating Your Leadership Practice

CHAPTER 3:
Creating Your Leadership Voice

"A pervasive lack of self-awareness—90% of managers think they are in the top 10% of performers in their workplace."

– Business Week

CHAPTER 1:
Creating Your Leadership Mindset

"Getting your head around" exactly what you are signing up for in your leadership journey is important for ensuring that you will be inspired, not frustrated or disappointed. As we explore the fundamentals of what this means, you might actually be surprised to find that the expectations for leading yourself are quite different from what you initially thought.

Creating Your Leadership Mindset Starts with Understanding and Embracing (3) Principles:

    I.   Leadership Can Be Learned

    II. Leadership Is Emotional

    III. Leadership Is in Service of Others

I. Leadership Can Be Learned

Being a lifetime learner is the cost of entry for the journey called **Leadership Rigor**. Whether you are an aspiring leader or a seasoned veteran, one fact you can take comfort in and seek inspiration from is that leadership absolutely can be learned!

While many love to debate the question of whether leaders are born or made, the reality is that leadership is a skilled profession. Natural aptitude may give you a head start, but it will only take you so far. The rest is the result of hard work.

Leadership has a language, models, tools, and styles of approach that can all be broken down, understood, and applied at a high level of competency with discipline and practice. Unfortunately, for most of us, this is not a quick or easy process. In fact, it might be one of the most challenging initiatives you ever take on. Nonetheless, for the true leaders among us, it will be an incredibly fulfilling lifetime journey.

As is true with most professional roles, the skills you will be required to demonstrate escalate as you advance in your career. Understanding the fundamentals of leading yourself is the critical first step, so get ready to **Rigor it!**

Learning Agility

The word "agility" describes the ability to quickly learn from your experiences and then wisely apply that learning to new and different circumstances. Not surprisingly, learning agility is an emerging area that is fast becoming a determinant for identifying individuals who can successfully advance into leadership roles. It is a measure of current potential and therefore a predictor of future performance.

Throughout *Leadership Rigor*, you will be introduced to concepts, frameworks, and models that can be used in a variety of circumstances. The test of your own learning agility will be to see when, where, and how to apply them. There are no absolute right or wrong answers, just better choices and good judgments, so let's start learning to **Rigor it!**

The Mindful Leadership Model

> *The first goal of* **Leadership Rigor** *is to prepare you to be a consciously competent leader.*

Have you ever wondered how it is that certain people come to be in their leadership positions? They appear to be only concerned about themselves, are oblivious to their impact on others, and are seemingly unaware of the chaos or disruption they cause in the environment.

On the flip side, have you ever admired the graceful ease with which certain leaders enter a room, give a compelling presentation, and then comfortably interact with the participants? If you were to take one of these leaders aside and ask how they learned to speak so persuasively and they replied, "I don't really know; it just comes naturally to me," what would your reaction be?

As these two examples demonstrate, leaders need to be mindful about what they do and how they do it. The Mindful Leadership Model outlines the different stages of consciousness and competency that you need to be familiar with as a leader. The first example represents a state of being *unconsciously incompetent.* Those who are unconsciously incompetent move through the world unaware of how they impact the space around them or the performance of their colleagues. I call these individuals "Mr. and Ms. Magoos" after the cartoon character from the 1970s. They march to their own tune, are out of sync with others, and leave a multitude of disturbances and frustrations in their wake.

They have significant blind spots and unfortunately "don't know what they don't know." They demonstrate no self-awareness regarding their own behavior and will likely continue on this trajectory unless they are given direct feedback that strongly encourages a change.

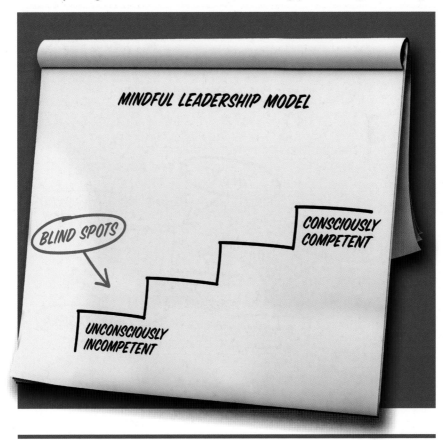

When a blind spot is revealed through feedback, these individuals move into a phase of being *consciously incompetent* in that area. This can be both uncomfortable and enlightening, since they are now perhaps painfully aware that one of their behaviors is either not working or is having a negative impact. This *gift of feedback*, if acknowledged and accepted, can transform a blind spot into a growth area. These leaders now have something *known and visible* they can consciously choose to work on to improve their performance. Doing so, however, will require both *discipline and practice.*

Let's go back to the leader with poise and grace who effortlessly gives an inspiring talk and claims that it comes naturally. Such individuals are *unconsciously competent.* They have a personal innate talent but are unable to consciously break down and share how they

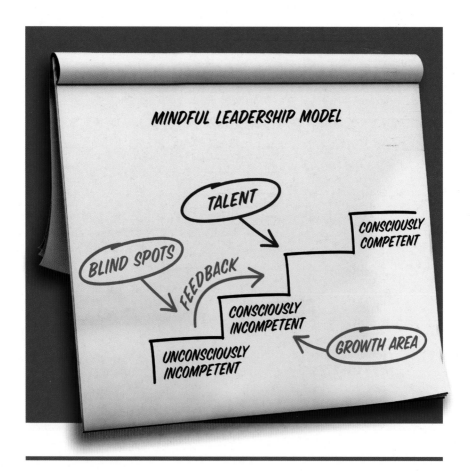

do what they do with others because they don't honestly know. This is also a leadership development challenge!

Unconsciously competent leaders need to take the time to stop and think about what they are doing and find the language that communicates it in a simple, straightforward way. If you aspire to a team or organizational leadership role, you must be able to express what you do and how you do it so that you can coach and develop the skill sets of others.

You lead at your personal highest level when you are consciously competent, aware of what you are doing, how you are doing it, and why you are doing it. This is the first step for leading yourself with rigor!

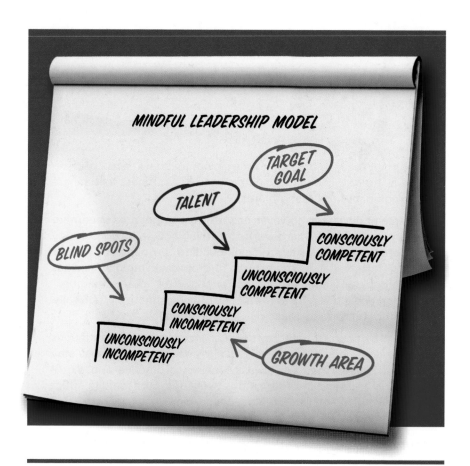

How Athletes and Leaders Differ on the Consciousness Model

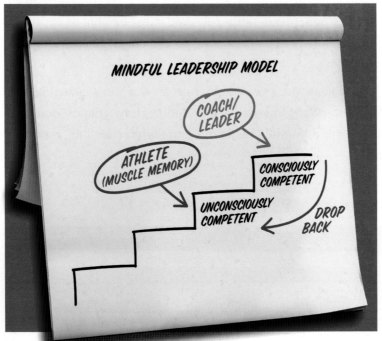

Given their focused attention on training, feedback, and coaching to be at the top of their respective "games," business leaders are often compared to great athletes.

One area of deviation, however, occurs in the target area of competency. Athletes do the hard work of learning how to be consciously competent through structured skill building (despite their natural talents), but they allow themselves to drop back into unconscious competency, or what might be better known as "muscle memory." They practice a skill until they can perform it instinctively, naturally, and without having to consciously think about it.

Leaders, by contrast, need to develop and maintain a continuous level of conscious competency. Like a coach, leaders must stay constantly alert. They are always looking to practice and modify skills in real time in order to positively and purposefully affect performance. When leaders "go unconscious," the learning and growth slows down or stops around them.

The Gift of Feedback

To reach your potential as a leader, you must continuously learn about yourself by asking for feedback. You need people to share with you what you can do better as well as what is working well. To receive this valuable feedback, you must proactively demonstrate your desire for it and then gracefully accept it.

In workshops I facilitate as a leadership coach, team members often struggle with naming the unproductive behaviors of their colleagues. What I encourage them to consider is that not providing feedback or sharing their observations is the equivalent of saying, *"I don't care enough about your growth and development to tell you what you need to hear; I am consciously choosing to let you stay stuck by not helping you move forward."*

When put in this context, the perspective in the room dramatically shifts, and the courage required to give the feedback is called forth, so rigor it with feedback!

A Fast Start Is Not Always a Leadership Advantage

Young leaders who have natural unconscious talents in communication and relationship building can get early attention and a fast start to their careers by impressing senior executives, especially when they are high-performance individual contributors. Often designated as **"fast trackers"** who get promoted quickly and surprisingly to their colleagues, given their lack of experience in overseeing the performance of others, these individuals can be set up for future failure when put into their first supervisory roles where they must break down their skills for others to learn.

To be a consciously competent leader, it is important to understand what you are doing and how it contributes to your success so you can continuously replicate it and not just leave it to luck or chance. This requires training, development, time, and practice.

Leadership is less about a fast start and more about a strong and consistent showing over time of skills that are consciously and deliberately applied. Being able to share your learning and insights to build skills in others is the goal of the team or organizational leader.

The (2) Currencies of Leadership

The quality of your communication enhances the quality of your relationships. For this reason, a foundational concept utilized throughout **Leadership Rigor** is the importance of mastering what I refer to as the (2) currencies of leadership: **communication** and **relationships.**

Everything leaders are involved with, and I do mean everything, moves through these (2) currencies. The term **"currencies"** is used because each represents *a comprehensive set of value creating skills* and capabilities that leaders must master over time.

As important as these (2) currencies are, most leaders genuinely struggle with them throughout their careers because the expectations for both continuously evolve as leadership roles escalate and advance.

You will likely be stronger in one area than another initially, but make no mistake—communication and relationships are equally important. Learning to master these (2) currencies will determine the degree and extent to which you will achieve success as a leader, so let's take a closer look at how they work.

The Currency of Communication

The ability to *listen, write, and speak* in a clear and concise way is a basic requirement for all leadership roles. If you are challenged in any of these areas, seek training or coaching as soon as possible. The importance of communication skills increases exponentially as you progress in your career, which means these skills can either propel you forward or abruptly limit your advancement.

Rigor Your Communication with (3) Building Blocks:

- Develop a Clearly Framed Message

- Deliver a Credible Message

- Demonstrate *Veritas*

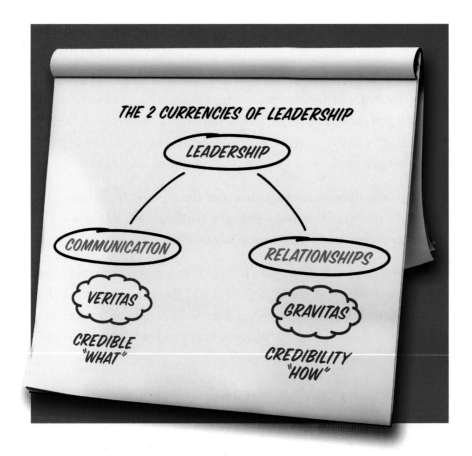

▶ **Develop a Clearly Framed Message**

A clearly framed message first and foremost **establishes the context** of why this communication is important and grounds your audience for appropriate engagement in the discussion. Leaders must understand that their role in communicating to an audience is to ensure that **the message is both delivered and received!** Simply getting the message out is only half the work.

In my first general management role running Bayer Healthcare's consumer care division in Canada, I was surprised when members of my leadership team would dive into specific content details within (10) seconds of starting a discussion. I would immediately *"stop the action"* and request that they take a step back and *"frame the topic."* I wanted to know where we were in the process, when we last discussed this issue, what had changed since then (bringing us to where we were today), and where they were now proposing that we go.

Simply put, failing to establish the broader context and therefore shape the expectations for the content discussion wastes time and causes frustration. The result, as my leadership team experienced, is frequent interruptions with multiple questions as the audience struggles to get oriented.

> *The unfortunate consequence for the presenter is not only a disrupted message delivery sequence but damage to his or her leadership credibility as well.*

As a leader, be sure that you always take a moment to intentionally frame the context of the topic you will be discussing, regardless of how basic or well understood you personally believe it to be. This ensures that your audience is ready to listen and productively engage in the content with you.

▶ Deliver a Credible Message

Framing a clear message is the first step; ensuring that the message is credible comes next. Take the time to do your homework and make sure that what you are bringing to the table is researched, organized, and appropriately reflects the knowledge, needs, and experiences of your audience. Leaders often make the mistake of trying to impress people with how smart they are and include more information than they need to make their points. *Don't fall into this trap; communication is about the audience, not you!*

For example, you would not review the basic science of a new drug when presenting to a team of cutting-edge researchers in the field, but you certainly would when addressing your marketing or sales team.

Being seen and heard as a communicator with credibility requires that you have a credible message appropriately targeted to the audience!

Communication Is an Illusion

Throughout my corporate career, I was reminded that communication is often an illusion. While it frequently appeared that someone was speaking and someone else was listening, an aligned experience was exceedingly rare. As a result, I became increasingly curious about how communication and messaging actually work.

While launching and leading the marketing efforts of heavily advertised consumer healthcare brands, I began to notice that our television commercials received higher scores for message retention and impact when visual messages on screen accompanied the verbalized messages delivered by the actors. In other words, *"Say it and show it"* was more effective than just "Say it."

The essence of **Leadership Rigor** is a "Say it and show it" approach in which concepts, frameworks, and models visually reinforce the messages of the content being presented. Impact, comprehension, and recall are greatly enhanced as a result.

When you communicate a request, either verbally or in writing, do so clearly, as in "Here is my request." If you are looking for follow-up, make the clear statement, "I would like to have you follow up with me tomorrow."

Don't let communication be an illusion. Make sure you have an aligned takeaway on what is said, what is heard, and the actions that will result from your communication exchange. *Confirming that the message lands is the leader's responsibility; failing to confirm this is the leader's mistake.*

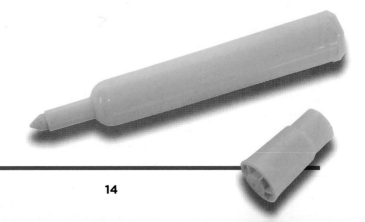

▶ Demonstrate *Veritas*

Veritas is the ability to speak truth to power. ***Veritas*** takes courage, conviction, and an ability to maintain composure. As a leader, you need to express the truth of what you see, hear, and feel even though you may be concerned about the risks or consequences of challenging peers or senior executives. Perhaps you have been told to get alignment up front or to take something off-line as opposed to bringing up "sensitive issues," especially in an open forum. ***Bold as it may sound, this may not always be the best advice to take.***

While you never want to be rude or obnoxious, expressing a strong point of view, posing a challenging question, or raising a realistic concern about what you hear is the essence of communicating with *veritas.* Leaders are expected to raise the real issues so they can be dealt with effectively.

> *At some point, you will have to tell the emperor that he or she is not wearing any clothes if you want to be a leader! And if the "emperor" is also a true leader, he or she will be open to learning and growth, your perspective will be acknowledged, and you will be thanked!*

Nonetheless, it is always wise to get advice on how best to apply *veritas* within your organization's culture. Not all leaders possess the ability to demonstrate *veritas*, so in seeking advice, make sure you ask the people you believe ***do*** clearly demonstrate it to assist you. What

Demonstrating Both Veritas and Gravitas

Leaders who are **passionate advocates** for an idea or belief often demonstrate both veritas and gravitas. They understand their issues and their audience. Not afraid to say what needs to be said and fiercely serving the needs of the collective "we," these leaders frame the context of their communication so that it can be intellectually listened to while empathetically connecting to the emotional needs of their audience so that it can be heard.

you are saying will be less of an issue than how you choose to frame and express it. Step into your *veritas* and **Rigor it!**

The Currency of Relationships

Today, all work involves engaging and collaborating with others. This is why relationships are not only critical but in fact are the second leadership currency you must master. If relationships are a problem for you, your leadership plans will most definitely derail. Be attentive and ensure that your relationships are built on solid foundations and that you continually nurture them over time.

Rigor Your Relationship Currency with (3) Building Blocks:

- **Establish Credibility**

- **Be an Authentic Messenger**

- **Demonstrate *Gravitas***

▶ **Establish Credibility**

Relationships in business are often first established in forums where technical topics are discussed. Asking insightful questions, listening attentively to what others have to say, validating someone else's viewpoint with your own experiences, and sharing useful information will start to establish your credibility. These behaviors also signal your sincerity to **build mutually beneficial relationships** versus engaging in superficial conversations with either no agenda or in which your own personal agenda is emphasized.

> *Making a positive first impression through interactive engagement is an entry point that can lead to a shared interest in investing more time in building deeper relationships.*

Building personal credibility is an ongoing process that is facilitated by your sincere, consistent, and service-oriented behaviors to share your knowledge and expertise.

Why Relationship Building Is Hard

If you struggle with relationships, try to take a realistic look at why. Uncovering the essence of this challenge can make a big difference in how you address your personal learning and development process.

For example, *being introverted* may limit the number of relationships you build because your preference is for fewer, more intimate, connections. For other individuals, being disconnected from their own feelings may make them insensitive to the feelings of others, inhibiting their ability to empathize and therefore create meaningful connections. Still others may fear not being accepted or, worse, rejected, which may make them reluctant to proactively engage in the relationship-building process.

Being self-absorbed, needing to be the smartest person in the room, or being so focused on tasks that the people you are working with don't even cross your mind are additional reasons why relationships may elude you.

Find the root cause and challenge yourself to consciously address it with a coach or mentor. Seek feedback on how to change your approach so that you gain more comfort and achieve greater success with this critical leadership currency.

If relationship building *simply does not seem important to you*, you may have a choice to make with respect to your leadership aspirations. As you progress in your professional career, your technical skills will start to matter less and your interpersonal skills will matter more. If you aspire to team or organizational leadership roles, relationship building is mandatory. If you can't or won't address this vital area, you simply will not advance in your career!

▶ Be an Authentic Messenger

Authenticity requires being real in expressing who you are to others. To gain followers, you must be authentic, because people want to genuinely connect with, trust, and believe in their leaders.

> *Being our authentic selves naturally serves as a magnet to attract others into relationships with us.*

Being an authentic messenger means that you honestly understand how you feel about a given topic and communicate your perspective in a way that conveys both your intellectual and emotional points of view on it. When you are an authentic messenger, you are able to build deeper relationships because you are connected to yourself and therefore transmit an emotional connection to others. *Authentic connections establish intimacy beyond transactional information sharing; they build trust and confidence.*

▶ Demonstrate Gravitas

Having established both credibility and authenticity creates the conditions for you to now demonstrate that you are a leader with *gravitas*.

While many find it difficult to describe, people look up and actively turn attention to the individual who has this desirable quality.

> *Gravitas is similar to charisma in that it captivates us, but it is less about how you physically show up and attract attention and more about how you compel others to lean in and listen with extreme interest to what you have to say because it is expected to be insightful and is delivered with meaningful wisdom.*

Being recognized as a leader with *gravitas* is a highly regarded distinction. These leaders build powerfully intimate relationships. They have authentic credibility and magnetism on steroids!

The Leadership Performance Framework

Delivering results is no longer all that matters in business. In today's progressive organizations, how you behave while delivering those results is equally important!

Leadership Rigor seeks to enhance performance. This is a higher order and integrated expression of both results (what you do) and behaviors (how you do it). What you will find is that positive behaviors, if appropriately demonstrated, will set the stage for delivering outstanding results.

In learning to lead yourself, it is important to take a balanced approach and be careful not to focus exclusively on becoming a technical expert who simply delivers results. You must be equally conscious about developing and demonstrating your interpersonal skills and leadership behaviors early in your career if you aspire to be a team or

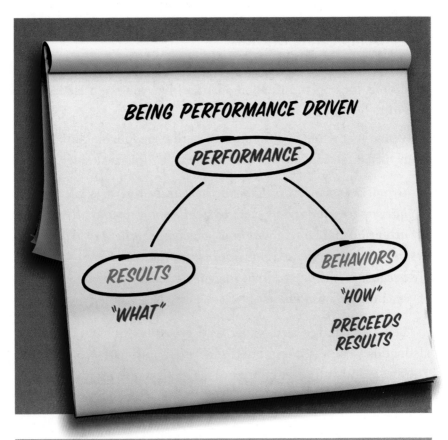

organizational leader. If you fail to consciously do this, you might find yourself prematurely limited to an individual contributor or subject matter expert (SME) role.

Most companies have documented behavioral values they expect to be "actively demonstrated and lived" in their unique cultures. In organizations where talent management is a priority, for example, competency models detail the progressive behavioral expectations and capabilities required for each advancing level of leadership. These competencies form the organizational blueprint for talent development as well as for promotional advancement and career development.

Beyond their expressed desire to lead, *potential team leader candidates* in performance-based organizations might be required to demonstrate the following behaviors:

- ☑ Resourcefulness
- ☑ Active listening skills
- ☑ Ability to take initiative
- ☑ Learning agility
- ☑ Openness to receive and ability to provide feedback
- ☑ Ability to build healthy relationships
- ☑ Strong verbal and written communication skills
- ☑ Ability to hold self and peers accountable
- ☑ Ability to engage in productive conflict
- ☑ A desire to coach and develop others
- ☑ Willingness to demonstrate vulnerability
- ☑ Strong emotional intelligence
- ☑ Ability to demonstrate **veritas** and **gravitas**
- ☑ Leadership presence

While this is only a short list of sample behavioral competencies, notice that it focuses on *how business gets done* and *how individuals show up* through their interpersonal and behavioral skills.

Intellectually knowing what behaviors are expected is important, but what really matters is putting them "on the ground" (OTG) and into action. You need to be able to cross what will be discussed later in the tension section as the "knowing-doing gap" in order to advance as a leader.

Whether you seek to lead a team, division, global function, or organization, you will need to demonstrate critical capabilities and to have acquired specific experiences in order to be considered for certain roles (in large corporations) or for success in the roles you are given (in small to mid-sized corporations). *Leadership Rigor* provides insights on how to proactively navigate your career and leadership development regardless of organizational type, size, or challenge.

RIGOR ALERT!

Is Your Organization Practicing Performance-Based Principles?

Behavioral competencies are increasingly being integrated into organizational performance management processes. Many corporations now use a 50/50 split in terms of their percentage emphasis on both technical and behavioral performance criteria. As an aspiring leader, you need to understand the behaviors your performance evaluations will be based upon and proactively work to develop them.

In performance-based organizations, talent management, leadership development, and succession planning are priority initiatives. Understanding what your specific leadership goals are will provide you with more choices for co-creating your career development path with your employer. It will also ensure that you have the time to acquire the skills and experiences required for you to participate in the leadership roles to which you aspire.

Being Identified as a "High Potential" Leader

Throughout my career, I was identified by the organizations I worked in as being a "high potential" leader. While definitions vary by organization, these individuals are generally recognized as demonstrating consistently strong performances in their current role(s) and showing early signs of having the ability to advance into targeted senior leadership positions, assuming the trajectory of their learning and growth continues.

Being identified as high potential created exciting opportunities as well as challenging choices. I was asked to participate in special training programs, to take on multiple high-visibility projects with increased exposure to senior leaders, and to rotate through various assignments, including some with extreme travel commitments or requirements to live outside of the country for a number of years to give me broader exposure to cultural, strategic, and operational leadership challenges.

In accepting these challenges, I had to be open to my organization's objectives for talent deployment into the specific growth or need areas it was targeting as well as its commitment to accelerate the development of my professional skill sets on a certain timetable. This was a co-creation process and partnership, and it worked as long as my personal goals and the goals of the organization were aligned.

Make sure your personal goals and the goals of your organization are aligned, or you will find yourself taking on assignments that do not contribute to your true aspirations and personal life goals. Once you are on a track for being a high potential, your career path can take on a life of its own, so rigor it with conscious career planning.

Learning How You Are Hardwired

We each have natural preferences. We are early birds or night owls; we like chocolate ice cream or we prefer vanilla; we are left handed or right handed. Some preferences are strong while others are more flexible.

We also have different learning styles. Many of us learn by reading or hearing, others visually, and some of us prefer to learn kinesthetically through touch, feel, or experience.

Preference variability also holds true in our professional lives. We are each hardwired with specific preferences for how we communicate, organize our lives, make decisions, and collect information as well as for how we approach change and conflict.

Consciously understanding your personal style preferences is critical as a leader and can guide your behaviors in the following ways:

- It *provides* you with the perspective to balance your openness, objectivity, and flexibility while working with others who are different

- It *allows* you to appropriately apply your talents and self-manage your time, energy, and moods so your work is completed in a productive way

- It *enables* you to learn how to appropriately time and frame your communication so that what you say is heard and how you say it is appreciated by your audience

- It *facilitates* your understanding of how to leverage the inclusion of different personality styles so that everyone's contributions to the work process are maximized

Working consciously with your own style preferences will clarify the type of discipline you will need to apply in order to manage your time, be comfortable with information, organize yourself for productivity, and manage how you are "showing up" as a leader.

Create Your Own Authentic Style

Be mindful about emulating someone else's style as a perceived shortcut to success. Consciously learning to work with your own style preferences allows you to lead from your authentic strengths, which is the better way to go.

It is not uncommon to join a company, assess how others (including the leader) operate, and try to fit in by copying their approach. While this can work for a while, if it isn't aligned with your natural preferences, it will be exhausting and ultimately unsustainable.

It is also unwise for leaders to expect team members to have styles or work preferences similar to their own and then use this expectation as a means for evaluating performance or promoting advancement.

For example, an early bird leader who is extremely neat might look at the messy desk of an employee who arrives on time and think, "Hey, John will never make it in a leadership role at our company."

John may be a strong performer who works best in the latter part of the day and despite his lack of visible organization can readily locate any information requested of him. While the leader's comments are neither fair nor accurate, this type of observational bias based on style comparisons can and does happen frequently.

This leader may try to "fix" John and suggest to him how to organize his workspace as well as encourage him to arrive earlier by calling early morning meetings.

From my perspective as a coach, it is important to remember that people are not broken and, more importantly, that we cannot fix them. If a lack of organizational skills and time management practices are inhibiting performance and productivity, coaching can be an appropriate next step.

If performance and productivity are not an issue, acceptance of style diversity is required. We need to seek to understand where and how individuals are different and what the flexible and negotiated requirements are for successfully working together.

As a leader, evaluate your employees based on their performance and productivity, not their work-style preferences.

Extroverts, typically energetic and outgoing personality types, may call more attention to themselves, especially early in their careers. They actively reach out in social settings and easily engage in conversations, often projecting personal confidence. This can, rightly or wrongly, signal a natural propensity for being comfortable with or skilled at communication and relationship building.

Introverts, typically more quiet and reserved personality types, may have to work harder at establishing their leadership presence early in their careers. Because they are often actively thinking about or reflecting on what is happening, introverts are less likely to find or take advantage of natural entry points into conversations. Potentially misunderstood or often underestimated, introverts may not appear on the surface to be great communicators or relationship builders, though still waters often run deep. Also, being introverted does not necessarily mean an individual is shy. Often, breakthrough business insights and opportunities for building personal friendships are missed because leaders are not skilled at appropriately creating space and actively bringing introverts into more discussions.

Introverted leaders are just as prevalent and successful as extroverted leaders; what is different is how each needs to work at showing up and creating the impact he or she desires.

Other differences in style preferences present challenges, too. When making decisions, some prefer objectivity, consistency, and the lens of "black and white" logic as they think about their choices. On the other end of the spectrum are individuals who prefer a more subjective view that integrates their heartfelt feelings, personal values, and an assessment of how the decision will affect others in the specific situational circumstances they are navigating. Neither approach is right or wrong, yet without mutual understanding, it's easy to imagine the potential gap that might exist between two people on the far ends of this continuum.

In business, we deal with a lot of information. How we each go about *managing the intake and organization of that information* varies significantly. Some of us are big-picture, conceptual thinkers who rely in part on our intuition to see how all the information fits together. Others need to get a tangible sense and understand the information from the ground up, anchoring themselves in the details and specifics. Most of the conflicts, challenging debates, frustrations, and misunderstandings that occur in business center around the basic differences in how we each prefer to gather information and make decisions.

Interpersonal relationships can also become strained when two people have starkly different styles in *managing their planning approach toward work.* Some people are organized and structured planners while others are more likely to have a more informal approach and go with the flow. Whether you have a preference for

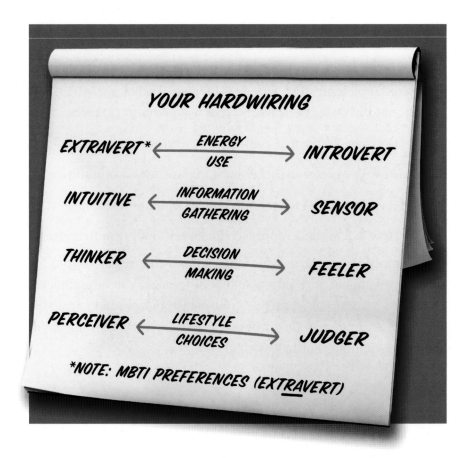

linear project management and a comprehensive to-do list or desire the freedom to work on multiple projects with spontaneous creativity as the mood hits you, we are all different. In the workplace, however, we need to acknowledge that these differences, if not consciously understood and managed, will result in stress, frustration, and resentment, especially if timelines are missed, constant reminders need to be given, people feel harassed or micromanaged, or work is consistently completed at the last minute.

In my coaching practice, I use multiple tools and diagnostics to assist individuals and teams in learning how they are hardwired in order to provide a foundation for appreciating how others are different. The insights that result become the starting point for taking team building and performance to a higher level as individual players learn how to communicate, productively challenge each other, make decisions, and manage through the complexities in the business more productively with each other.

One of the tools I use for understanding preferences is the Myers-Briggs Type Indicator*. Based on Jungian psychology, MBTI, as it is referred to, assesses personality types by looking at (4) areas:

- How you prefer to use energy (introvert or extravert)

- How you prefer to gather information (sensor or intuitive)

- How you prefer to make decisions (feeler or thinker)

- How you prefer to approach life/work (judger or perceiver)

Diagnostic tools can provide language and contextual insights for securing alignment with others so that differences can be embraced, understood, and used to drive performance and productivity. This can make a game-changing difference, so rigor it by learning about and understanding your hardwiring!

Note: For more information on MBTI, you can refer to the Myers and Briggs Foundation or the cpp.com website.

II: Leadership Is Emotional

Creating your leadership mindset involves embracing the fact that leadership is emotional and people are messy, including you. As I often tell my coaching clients, "The business is relatively straightforward to deal with; what's really complicated are you and your colleagues!"

> *Like it or not, in performance-based organizations, your behavioral soft skills will make or break whether you advance in your career, get left behind, or even get fired.*

Some of you might dismiss this perspective and claim it is nonsense, while others will be intrigued and want to learn more about how to acquire these softer skills. Wherever you are on this spectrum, understand that:

- Research is clear that emotional intelligence (EQ) is a greater predictor of leadership success than IQ or technical skills.

- Corporations are increasingly focused on soft behavioral skills for selecting and developing their talent for leadership roles.

- Choosing to embrace these facts will help you become a better leader, parent, friend, life partner, and all-around happier person!

People's egos; career aspirations; and desires for power, recognition, and respect as well as their access to decision makers are not rational considerations; they are all emotional. Pursue a leadership role, and you will be in the middle of sociology, psychology, and reality TV right along with the technical aspects of your business discipline.

If you aren't up for this challenging dynamic, if the complexity of moods and emotions sounds like nonsense to you, or if you believe we should all just "get over it and get to work on the real operations of the business," please choose to be an individual subject matter expert (SME) and not a leader of others!

The Emotional Intelligence Model

Having a high IQ and the intellectual ability to learn and problem solve is no longer enough for success in today's complex world. We must be able to understand ourselves and connect with others in healthy and productive ways. We must have emotional intelligence.*

One additional compelling fact regarding emotional intelligence: emotional intelligence is a learnable set of skills and behaviors that you can *continuously strengthen* throughout your career.

The (4) general areas of emotional intelligence include:

- Self-awareness

- Self-management

- Social awareness

- Relationships

Self-awareness and self-management are personal competencies for leading yourself. Social awareness and relationships are competencies that impact your ability to effectively engage with others.

Individuals with high emotional intelligence typically have healthy relationships. Given that relationships are one of the (2) currencies of leadership, you can see how vital it is to build your emotional intelligence skills if you wish to reach your potential as a leader!

*Note: For more information check out Daniel Goleman's *Emotional Intelligence* (New York: Bantam, 1995) and Travis Bradberry's *Emotional Intelligence 2.0* (San Diego: TalentSmart, 2009).

Self-Awareness

Earlier, when presenting the Mindful Leadership Model, I highlighted the fact that being a consciously competent leader is the first goal of **Leadership Rigor**. A consciously competent leader tends to be emotionally intelligent and, not surprisingly, has a high level of self-awareness.

Being self-aware means that you clearly understand your hardwired preferences and seek to uncover your blind spots through continuous feedback while actively embracing and working on your known and visible growth areas. You also know the *triggers* that can and do pull you out of your emotional balance, causing you to have impulsive reactions or mood swings that may disrupt your personal productivity and performance or that of your colleagues.

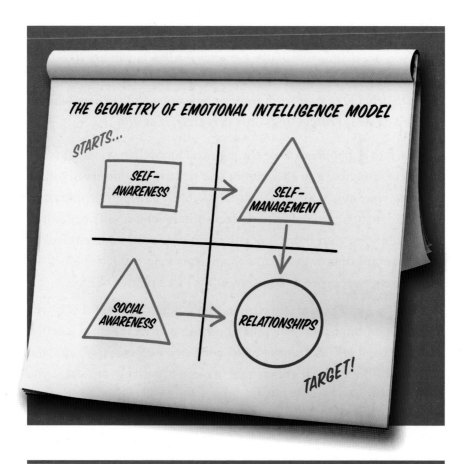

The challenge for increasing your self-awareness is genuinely believing and accepting that a change in your current behavior is necessary. Others can point to how your behaviors hold you back, but if you don't agree or embrace this feedback, you will not make the necessary adjustments. As a result, neither your self-awareness nor your performance will improve.

Perhaps you believe that you are already highly self-aware and that you do openly accept feedback. Maybe you like your behavioral style and don't want to change it, or perhaps you don't respect the people giving you the feedback so you dismiss it as irrelevant or discount its value.

Just understand that this perspective is the equivalent of saying, "I don't care how my behavior affects you or others; it is more important for me to feel good about who I am than to worry about how I am affecting you...You are just not that important to me."

If you are dismissive of one person's feedback, you are likely dismissive of most feedback you receive, though you may patiently listen to it from some people more than others while voicing your real feelings only privately, if at all.

The fact is, people can see through you more than you might care to believe, and how you show up in one situation is, more often than not, how you show up in all situations. While your relationships may appear to be functional on the surface, others may simply be temporarily tolerating your behaviors either out of fear or a current lack of understanding of how to address them. How long will it be before the real consequences reveal themselves? It's just a matter of time.

Whether you care or are curious enough to find out if this is true for you is an important personal choice in your leadership journey. Building your self-awareness takes *curiosity and courage*, and you must be willing to hear things that are constructively critical if you want to grow as a leader. Take a moment and reflect on what has not worked for you in other relationships. If you're honest, you might find some recurring themes.

Increasing your self-awareness is the first step to improving your overall emotional intelligence, and you must genuinely embrace this to grow into being a consciously competent leader. Without an ongoing commitment here, you are either going nowhere or you will find yourself plateauing quickly in the leadership world.

Self-Management

With self-awareness comes increasing visibility and clarity into the behavioral challenges you face.

Self-management requires *"being with"* your emotions and behavioral challenges in real time, working to consciously regulate your responses so you can avoid slipping into an unconsciously reactive or impulsive state.

Self-management *does not mean* clenching your fists, casually dismissing others with your body language, or mentally distracting yourself so you can ignore those who irritate you. That is self-control, and it will last only as long as your willpower can fend off an eventual explosion.

Self-management *does mean* finding ways to appropriately own and express your feelings as well as being clear about what you may emotionally need from those with whom you are interacting.

An example might be that an executive starts yelling in your team meeting. Instead of shutting down and withdrawing from the interaction or escalating the situation, you self-manage and say, "This discussion is starting to feel uncomfortable for me. You appear to be upset, and I am concerned that we will not hear each other effectively if you raise your voice. I understand that you are frustrated, and I want to work through your concerns. Should we reschedule for another time or take a short break before we continue?"

Another example of self-management might focus on your tendency to interrupt people in meetings. Instead of impulsively indulging yourself, jot down notes while your colleague is speaking. Make a hand gesture or lean forward, indicating through your body language that you would like to comment. When the speaker finishes, acknowledge that you were actively listening by restating a point that resonated with you and then present your ideas. This is respectful of the person speaking and demonstrates self-management in how you appropriately enter and productively engage in the conversation.

Self-awareness and self-management help us to *master our own behaviors*, a foundational requirement for establishing healthy relationships with others.

Social Awareness

Social awareness is the ability to sense and respond appropriately to the environmental dynamics that surround you. Reading *body language* is a large part of social awareness since facial expressions, posture, hand gestures, and other *nonverbal cues often reveal the true conversations under way*. Without this emotional leadership skill, you may miss the risks and opportunities that present themselves, which may result in significant consequences.

Leaders must be master communicators. If you cannot read and effectively transmit communication both verbally and nonverbally, you will not maximize your opportunities for intimately connecting with others.

> *Social awareness skills in business often relate to timing. Being able to "read the room" and sense when to close a conversation, open up a challenging topic for discussion, or let the dialogue continue without restriction all relate to your social awareness skills.*

Even knowing when to adjust the thermostat in a room or call for a break represents a practical utilization of emotional intelligence through social awareness.

Relationships

The ultimate prize of emotional intelligence is strong and healthy relationships, one of the (2) leadership currencies. People always remember how you make them feel and can sense whether you are attentive and compassionate or distracted and dismissive. If you think you can fake it, you're probably wrong, but if you can fake it and do, you are a master manipulator, not an authentic leader.

The quality of our relationships is related to the amount of time and energy we invest in shared experiences and things that matter. Taking a sincere interest in others and learning what is important and motivating to them helps us create the conditions for successfully building a working relationship together.

In certain relationships, you get what you tolerate. How often do you ask your kids or partner to participate in sharing home responsibilities only to hear excuses about why they can't or don't? Frustrated or disappointed by their response, you either stop asking and do it yourself (their preference) or occasionally blow up (after trying to exert self-control versus self-management).

The same holds true in business. Have you ever not delivered on an expectation for someone and then noticed how this individual stopped including you on projects or ceased to engage in casual conversation with you? These are subtle but telling ways in which relationships erode because of unresolved disappointments.

> *Your relationships are a combination of what you create and what you tolerate.*

Being aware of how you show up, self-managing behaviors that can be counterproductive, and appropriately reading and responding to the surrounding dynamics you are engaged in all contribute to building healthy relationships. If you ignore this, you will erode your relationships, whether you see it clearly, are willing to admit it, or are ready to deal with it. Ultimately, there will be consequences. The only questions are, when will they come, and how severe will they be?

Don't let your leadership career aspirations be compromised by a lack of emotional intelligence. This is something you can consciously improve with discipline and practice. In addition to making you a better professional leader, it will add value to the quality of your relationships with family and friends, so **rigor it** with emotional intelligence!

Vulnerability: A Leadership Skill That Builds Trust

At the start of a new coaching engagement, I often ask my client, "What does vulnerability mean to you?"

Nine out of ten times, the answer I receive expresses something negative or horrifying. Occasionally, I get an answer that nails vulnerability as "The ability to ask for help or say that you don't know the answer to something."

Yes! Vulnerability is actually a leadership skill. Asking for help, having the self-confidence to say "I don't know," or expressing an apology are impactful ways that leaders demonstrate vulnerability.

As a leader, you create two powerful conditions when you openly express vulnerability. First, you *create a safe environment* in which others can also admit that they don't know the answers, can ask for help, or apologize. Second, your vulnerability *creates space around you* so that others can step up and play their roles in bigger ways. For example, stating, "I need you and the team to help me collectively be our best," will drive team commitment, cohesion, and bonding.

Creating safety and space, however, is secondary to the most important impact vulnerability has: *building trust.* When you are vulnerable, people see your authentic self without you hiding behind your power or ego. Expressing vulnerability draws others into closer, more intimate, relationships with you.

Inspiring trust as a leader is critical because you will frequently need to ask people to stretch, grow, take risks, and change. These are uncomfortable requests. If you are not trusted, others are unlikely to proactively follow or even reluctantly come along with you, which inevitably holds back progress.

While trust takes significant time to build, it takes only seconds to lose. If you make a mistake that threatens the bond of trust, act immediately to repair it and be prepared for potential resistance to rebuilding that trust again, at least initially. If you are sincere, apologize quickly and commit to not repeating the same mistake, your relationship will likely grow stronger as a result.

In fact, *the strength of your relationships can often be measured by how quickly you express your vulnerability and apologize.* If the relationship is healthy, you will do it immediately. If the relationship needs work, you might find yourself more reluctant to apologize. Take both of these messages as calls to action to protect and build—or rebuild—your relationship currency.

Are You a Giver or an Earner of Trust?

Is your natural preference to give trust to others or to have them earn your trust? How do you personally prefer to be treated regarding trust?

If your preference is to have your trust earned, your risk is that people will not know where they initially stand with you, causing them to act with less confidence. After all, having to prove yourself worthy of trust can be unsettling. Even more challenging is the question of how you both will know if or when trust has been earned. If a mistake is made after a long process of earning your trust, what then?

Inspiring leaders give trust. They consciously build confidence in their relationships by letting people know up front that they trust them to do the right thing. If a mistake is made, and it will be, inspiring leaders treat it as a *learning experience.* They talk it over, determine what went wrong, and discuss how to prevent it in the future. They are willing to forgive and move on, giving their trust again. If a similar mistake is repeated, they address it as a *problem.* This time, they choose to either trust again with a consequential warning or they decide they cannot trust again.

The choice is yours. Keep in mind, however, that to take on the risks that are necessary for growth and learning, it is important to feel safe and supported. Trust and confidence have a significant impact on performance and productivity!

Let Them Love You

As leaders, we often feel compelled to project strength under all circumstances, not letting the personal realities of life visibly impact our professional performance. The truth is, terrible things happen to all of us. Leaders need to be open to and accepting of being loved and cared for by others, especially when they suffer personal challenges, tragedies, and losses.

Relationships are two-way streets. Sometimes we need to create space for others to express their empathy and compassion for us even if we want to pretend we don't need it. They need to give it to us, and we need to let them. **Rigor it** with accepting their love!

Aligning Your Intention and Impact

Two words serve as powerful anchors for calibrating how we choose to show up as leaders: *intention* and *impact.*

In leading yourself, you must take ownership and accountability for your actions as well as their emotional impact on others. You might have an intention in mind of how you want a situation to play out, but in real time you may find that it goes very differently than you expected.

Perhaps you completely and inappropriately lose your temper and someone calls you on it. You may be defensive and start explaining yourself by saying, "I did not mean that...What I meant was blah, blah, blah..."

> *The critical takeaway for leaders is that if your impact is bad, your intention does not matter!*

You can only apologize, take accountability for your actions, and work to do better the next time. As a leader, you must own your impact. Don't leave things to chance. Consciously think about the

Carefrontational Feedback

A concept related to aligning your intention and impact is delivering feedback in a "carefrontational" manner. This approach requires looking through the lens of seeing another person's potential for greatness and growth. You courageously give them the direct and constructive feedback they need to hear on what it is like to be with them (their impact) so they can gain perspective on being a better leader (their intention).

Being able to appropriately frame and deliver feedback is a leadership skill. It is related to your up-front preparation and clarity (your intention) as well as your compassionate and purposeful delivery (your impact).

impact you want to have up front and then align this with your intention around how you will show up and presence yourself. Use your emotional intelligence skills of self-management and social awareness to increase your probability of success.

The consequence of having a negative impact is that you risk damaging your relationships, so **rigor it** by aligning your intention and impact!

Tools or Weapons?

In applying the concepts of *Leadership Rigor*, be mindful about whether you are using them as tools for the greater good or as weapons for your own agenda.

For example, when receiving constructive feedback on your performance, ducking behind a statement like "The impact you are having on me is negative" does not negate the fact that there is something to understand about yourself, even if the delivery is not, in your view, appropriately carefrontational.

Likewise, remember to always demonstrate respect for the individual when giving feedback. Feedback is a gift meant to help, not hurt. It is not appropriate to give feedback under the guise of help if you are really just trying to "take a jab" at someone.

Another watch-out here concerns your personal communication style and how it needs to flex and reflect the alignment of your intention and impact. For example, you may prefer to be direct and straightforward, yet this approach can be hard on others and not appropriate in all circumstances. Your communication messages must serve a purpose, which means they must be heard, understood, and utilized by others. Otherwise, you are egotistically talking to yourself and using your role to wield weapons against, instead of tools in service of, others and their learning. **Rigor it** with tools, not weapons!

The Power Model

Power and influence are highly sought after yet are often dramatically misunderstood by ambitious aspiring leaders. Many mistakenly believe the size of their budget or direct report team, the loftiness of their title, whom they report to, and whom they know or have access to are signs of their power and influence. They are not!

Let's look at this concept of power and the (3) types available to us:

1. Position Power

Early in life, we learn about position power, the first of the (3) powers at play in our world. The classroom has a teacher, the school has a principal, the town has a policeman, the team has a coach, and

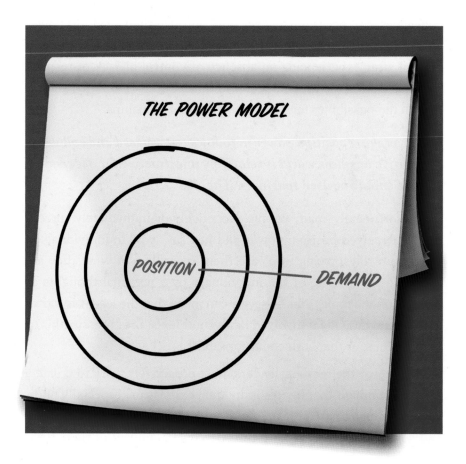

so on. *Authority figures,* we learn, are to be feared and/or respected because their *position power can have an imposing and consequential impact on us.*

At the start of your career, the position power phenomenon continues. You have a boss, your boss has a boss, and the company has a CEO who also has a "boss" called the board of directors.

Given its pervasiveness, you might be surprised to learn that position power is the weakest form of power. This is because it is only temporarily attached to a person in a specific position of authority; it is only relevant as long as that individual holds that position or has the jurisdiction over you to exert that power.

In business, individuals who struggle with their self-confidence, have difficulty being heard, or who feel overpowered by domineering colleagues will occasionally "act out" and use their position power with direct reports or outside suppliers in an effort to feel more in control after experiencing an absence of control or lack of respect. This can cause resentment, decrease this leader's credibility, and diminish the possibility for healthy ongoing relationships.

> *Leveraging position power in today's team-based and collaborative business world is relatively unattractive for a leader and should be used sparingly, if at all.*

Unfortunately, many people proactively or immediately surrender to perceived position power and just say "yes" to individuals in leadership roles, trying to please them regardless of what they are asking for or in spite of the individual's own personal thoughts or feelings on the topic. This behavior can mean that the leader is intimidating, the individual involved lacks confidence in expressing his or her opinions, or that both conditions exist.

Whatever the reasons, leaders must proactively work to create a safe environment that invites individual expression, especially of diverse opinions that can promote progress. They must be self-aware and self-manage to eliminate the "perceived" impact of their position power that may be holding people back from openly expressing themselves and limiting their valuable contributions.

Early in your career, you can mistake your job title and the perceived position power you believe it holds as something "real" that validates your self-worth. This is an illusion, a temporary mantle you can mistakenly become attached to causing problems as you develop an unhealthy relationship with your position power (which is temporary) instead of with your true self (which lasts forever). *The reality is, the genuine power of a leadership role does not lie in any formal position or title.*

2. Expertise Power

The second power we have access to is expertise power. Unlike position power, expertise power is associated with the enduring

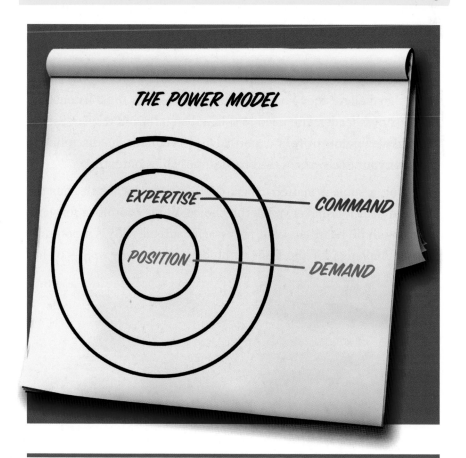

knowledge, experience, and skills that an individual has worked diligently to acquire. Our doctors, lawyers, accountants, or mechanics who are technically proficient and can professionally navigate through the challenges we know little or perhaps nothing about have expertise power. We implicitly trust their education and experience, often without a second thought, though this extreme is not always wise.

> *In the business world, you must be careful not to automatically accept expertise power without first asking clarifying questions, especially from highly confident experts.*

Expertise conveys a deep, often specialized knowledge, but business decisions contain complexities that require more than an understanding of the technical facts. There are conditions and risks to be considered as well as people and a broader environmental context to be mindful of, so expertise is often only an aid to judgment in business.

Here is where potential tensions can arise. Experts want to be right, they believe they know best, and they expect to be listened to. As a business leader, you need to solicit, listen to, and respect the insightful viewpoints of your expert advisors yet have the discipline to consider your decisions in the broadest possible context.

Being a subject matter expert (SME) is a critical role, but the ultimate decision maker holds the choice on how to move forward. Learning to be heard and not necessarily agreed with is a potential growth challenge for the leader who depends heavily on his or her expertise power.

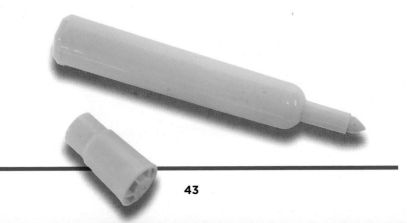

3. Personal Power

The third power we have access to is personal power, which is our ability to engage and connect with others in ways that are both meaningful and influential. *This is the only power with a truly level playing field at all times.* This is also the only power we can seek to master through how we show up and what it is like to be with us because *it is based completely on our behaviors and emotions!*

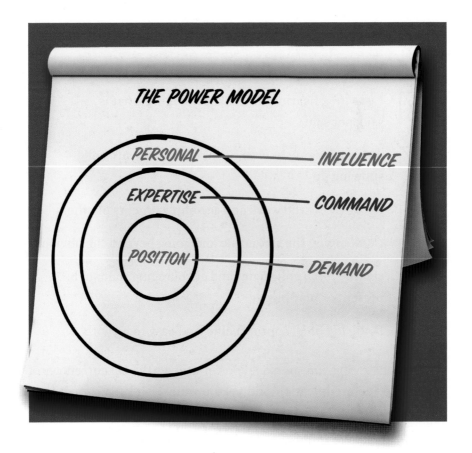

Expressing your personal power is your greatest asset as a leader at any time, in any situation, at any level you operate on.

Effectively utilizing your personal power brings out the best in everyone while influencing and navigating progress in service of your team or enterprise initiatives. Behaviors that demonstrate your personal power include:

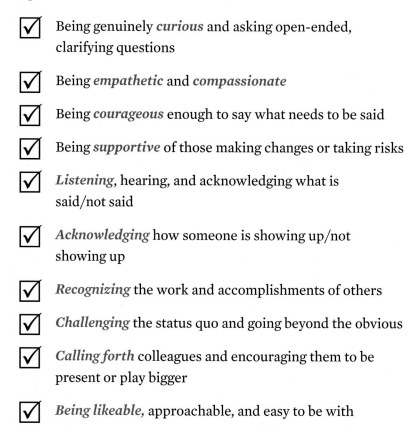

- ☑ Being genuinely *curious* and asking open-ended, clarifying questions

- ☑ Being *empathetic* and *compassionate*

- ☑ Being *courageous* enough to say what needs to be said

- ☑ Being *supportive* of those making changes or taking risks

- ☑ *Listening*, hearing, and acknowledging what is said/not said

- ☑ *Acknowledging* how someone is showing up/not showing up

- ☑ *Recognizing* the work and accomplishments of others

- ☑ *Challenging* the status quo and going beyond the obvious

- ☑ *Calling forth* colleagues and encouraging them to be present or play bigger

- ☑ *Being likeable,* approachable, and easy to be with

Demonstrating your personal power utilizes the (2) currencies of leadership (communication and relationships) and your emotional intelligence in a consciously competent way.

You are able to influence others through the use of your personal power because you establish an authentic connection with them. They will feel not only your encouragement but also your advocacy for them and will therefore place trust in you and be influenced by you, so rigor it with your personal power!

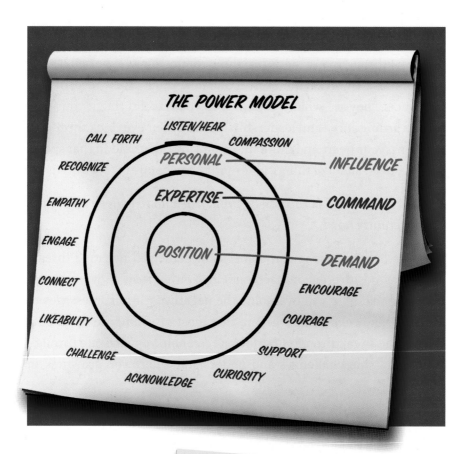

"The key to successful leadership today is influence, not authority."

– Kenneth Blanchard

The Breakthrough Framework

Breakthroughs are new insights, connections, experiences, or possibilities that reveal themselves and take you to a new level of performance. They are what you pursue as you travel through your personal learning curve and leadership journey. Your eyes look through a new lens, your heart and mind find a new opening, and in that space, you see, hear, and feel things differently than before.

> *A breakthrough is the newly found freedom to believe and act differently now!*

Your breakthroughs can come from perceived negative threats as well as positive encouragements, but either way, *they are game changers* that help you overcome the negative self-talk, messages of sabotage, and relationship drama that most of us impose upon ourselves. The Breakthrough Framework can help you navigate through your leadership challenges and understand where you are stuck in the process.

Barriers: Your Self-Talk Messages of Sabotage

Whether you are consciously aware of it or not, self-talk is constantly running through your head. Ideally, your self-talk consists of empowering and encouraging messages that fortify you to take on your challenges with courage and conviction. What tends to be more common, unfortunately, is sabotaging self-talk that creates a barrier to your success and sounds more like, "I am really not good at public speaking," "I will never be comfortable challenging senior executives in a meeting," or "I am not comfortable with office politics where I have to brownnose with senior executives, so I will never advance here."

Creating your leadership mindset means breaking through barriers and getting your self-talk to work for you by positively aligning your thoughts and feelings. If you say to yourself with passionate energy, "I believe I am going to achieve all of my professional goals and enjoy the process of getting there as an exciting learning adventure,"

THE BREAKTHROUGH FRAMEWORK

SABOTAGING SELF-TALK

BARRIERS

you establish the expectations for the experience you will now have. As a consequence, you literally create this reality.

Self-talk is incredibly powerful. Use it to make what you desire manifest itself; don't allow it to manifest what you fear, which is a common mistake we all make until we understand how this dynamic works. You will create what you consistently think about, so break through your self-imposed barriers and rigor your thinking and feelings to align to the outcomes you want.

Baggage: Relationship Drama and the Hurt You Carry

Relationships that challenge you often conceal lingering, unresolved issues. Perhaps someone violated your trust, embarrassed you publicly, behaved unethically, threw you under the bus to avoid personal accountability, or was completely over the top with unjustified

THE BREAKTHROUGH FRAMEWORK

UNRESOLVED
RELATIONSHIP DRAMA

BAGGAGE

criticism. The baggage associated with carrying around the resulting hurt or disappointment **holds you back and slows you down.** In business, and especially on teams, you need to talk it out and clear the air. This is hard, but appropriately expressing yourself using your emotional intelligence and a self-management/relationship focus gives both parties the opportunity to resolve the outstanding emotional issue and move forward with a new appreciation and understanding of each other—*creating a breakthrough!*

In some cases, the breakthrough is finally choosing to let go and accept that a particular relationship is not going to be what you wanted or expected it to be. Perhaps you need to *forgive and stop punishing someone in your mind* and/or holding a grudge for something they already apologized for. Forgiveness and acceptance allow you to

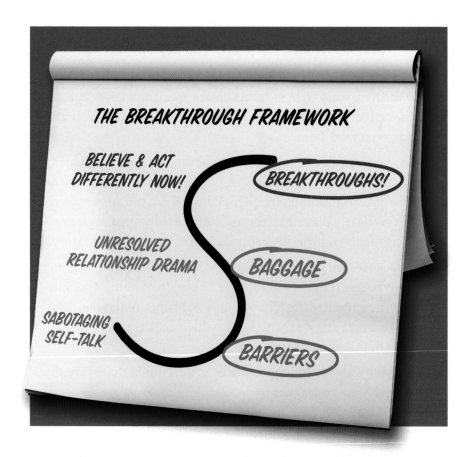

THE BREAKTHROUGH FRAMEWORK

BELIEVE & ACT
DIFFERENTLY NOW!

BREAKTHROUGHS!

UNRESOLVED
RELATIONSHIP DRAMA

BAGGAGE

SABOTAGING
SELF-TALK

BARRIERS

move on and not be held prisoner by unresolved emotions. Resolve or accept, but break through and let go!

To lead yourself, you must continuously look for opportunities to overcome barriers, let go of baggage, and drive toward your next breakthrough. You will meet a variety of personalities along your journey that will be challenging to work with. While understanding your differences and working with these individuals will be your goal, you are not going to emerge unscathed without some difficult and painful skirmishes. *You must stay alert and find ways to build and repair relationships as you go forward.* This takes conscious discipline, but it is worth the effort, as each relationship breakthrough creates forward momentum on your personal leadership journey. **Rigor it** with breakthroughs!

The Old Story and the New Story

In my coaching practice, I use the concept of the old story and the new story to help teams create space and new expectations for their relationships with each other so that meaningful change can take place.

When you have baggage with another person, you usually have an "old story expectation" about how you believe he or she will behave or make you feel. This comes from your past experiences and is usually reinforced and kept alive by ongoing conversations that reconfirm this individual's reputation or "old story."

Because you come to expect these behaviors, you look for them whether they actually appear or not. In so doing, you minimize the potential for change and hold this individual back with your old story expectations, which means your relationship with this person stays stuck.

If you want to grow personally as a leader and provide the space for your colleagues to grow, you need to create new story space by getting rid of old story baggage. Expect change and growth. This is a leadership mindset challenge!

STORY DYNAMICS

NEW STORY — CHANGE IS HARD

OLD STORY

1. STOP THE DOWNSLIDE
2. ACKNOWLEDGE A SLIP
3. CHOOSE TO CHANGE

Skillfully Applying Your Emotions as a Leader

You can start to apply what you have learned about the emotional impact of leadership on the ground in (3) ways:

1. Create moments

2. Share memories

3. Tell stories

Create Moments

Life is full of experiences that cause spontaneous and unconscious reactions. For example, a colleague may be emotionally triggered in a conversation and lose her temper. This event can be an entry point for you to "create a moment" by being a consciously competent leader and expressing your personal power in service of this colleague.

You may use your curiosity to ask questions about what she is experiencing that caused her reaction, challenge her to self-manage with a more balanced response, or ask that she articulate what she is expressing with her body language. Leadership is emotional, and being with her as she experiences her emotion without judgment but with empathy and support is your goal. In assisting this colleague through this process and toward a positive outcome, you utilize your personal power to connect and create a stronger relationship. Whether in the moment or later, after reflection, your colleague will appreciate your support.

Share Memories

Relationships are initially built through shared experiences and then nurtured over time by reflecting on the memories you have created together. We can all remember someone at a business event saying, "Remember when Jeffrey said...and then we all..."

Sharing memories of your challenges and breakthroughs creates emotional bonding moments for having been there together to see, hear, and feel it. Share your experiences, laugh until you cry, and create memories that last!

Tell Stories

Using your currencies of leadership and personal power to tell stories of recognition about colleagues in a way that showcases the context of their challenge, how they persevered, and how proud you are of their contribution is something you can never do enough of as a leader. Through your stories, you create the living legacy of your colleagues and their professional journeys. You give witness to and validate their struggles and successes in a way that both honors them and humbles you. This is absolutely priceless, and it is utterly emotional.

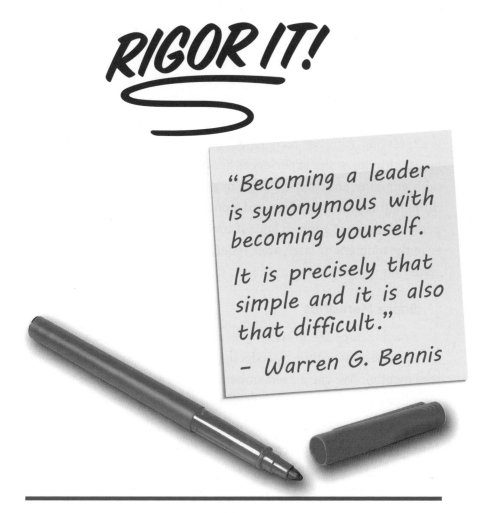

RIGOR IT!

"Becoming a leader is synonymous with becoming yourself.

It is precisely that simple and it is also that difficult."
– Warren G. Bennis

III: Leadership Is in Service of Others

Creating your leadership mindset includes recognizing and appreciating that leadership is a service. Specifically, it is "in service of others" and not really about you, the leader, at all!

As a leader, *your role is facilitating the growth and development of ideas and people.* Once again, you will need to make choices, understand the dynamic complexities under way, and be clear that this is a role you in fact want to play. Assuming you do, you will need to embrace that:

1. You Are an Instrument

2. Leadership Is a Being State, Not a Doing State

3. You Need to Be "We" Oriented Versus "I" Oriented

4. You Must Choose How You Will Serve as a Leader

You Are an Instrument

The description "a well-oiled machine" implies that something is running smoothly. As a leader, you need to care for yourself as though you are a finely tuned instrument so that you are running smoothly and can bring your best self into your leadership role.

Here are (3) questions to ask about your "instrument":

- How does it work?

- How do I effectively use it?

- How do I renew, recharge, and revitalize it?

How Your Instrument Works

The physical, mental, and emotional energy it takes to be a leader in business today *requires a disciplined approach to your health and well-being.* If you are not in great shape, you simply won't be able to perform at your highest level.

This starts with your quality and quantity of *sleep*. Without this foundation, you are physically and emotionally out of balance at the start of your day. A disciplined approach also includes a *healthy diet, exercise,* and some form of *spiritual connectivity.* This can be helping individuals you work with reach their highest potential or perhaps serving a cause greater than your company.

> *As a leader, being focused on creating purpose and meaning for the work you and your colleagues as well as your organization engage in is as important, if not more important, than merely creating shareholder value.*

The meaningful connections you create within the community of your organization will inspire performance and productivity that naturally delivers shareholder value. You must learn to focus on and serve the greater good as a leader.

Effectively Using Your Instrument: Time and Energy

Leading yourself requires that you master your personal resources. Throughout your leadership development journey, the most critical challenge you will face is how to manage your most precious resource, your time.

Managing time is difficult because it is a hardwired lifestyle preference. Some of us are hardwired to be rigidly time focused while others are more casual about time management.

You need to understand your natural hardwiring on this spectrum to determine how much self-management and discipline are required for optimizing your performance and productivity.

▶ Managing Your Time

Early in your career, your natural work preferences start to form and become visible. Your supervisors initially watch to see whether they need to play a direct role in helping you to focus and prioritize your responsibilities or whether you appear to be self-initiating and self-sufficient in terms of delivering quality work on time.

You may find yourself working with a micromanaging boss who has an intense relationship with time or a supervisor who is completely undisciplined and consistently misses deadlines. Reporting directly to either individual, you might be lured into mirroring their approach, which may or may not be comfortable or optimal for you.

> **You need to understand your own natural preferences with respect to time and pay attention to how your own instrument works best.**

As an example, perhaps you plan your schedule weeks in advance, knowing exactly what you are committed to do each day to accomplish your goals. You are disciplined about staying on track and don't let interruptions derail your focus. If something urgent comes up, you reprioritize a more realistic approach given the changing dynamics.

The challenge for you is to be *flexible* and not get emotionally out of balance if your original plan must be adjusted or if you don't accomplish everything you planned. You may feel compelled to work evenings or weekends to complete the original book of work you committed to and may harbor frustration about the additional workload or the inefficiency of colleagues who did not deliver what you needed on time. *Self-management (and mood management) will be important for you* as you evolve in your leadership role if this describes your relationship with time.

Alternatively, you may be relaxed in your approach to time and how you work. Perhaps you have general priorities but choose to work on a variety of projects simultaneously and wait until a deadline is looming before kicking into gear. You may or may not hit your original deadlines because you are waiting for additional information, have not yet crafted the right approach, or have decided you don't have enough time to do a quality piece of work. This time management approach can be frustrating to others downstream who are depending on you to deliver your work product so they can complete their projects.

If this describes you, be mindful of your credibility and the reputation you will build based on your approach to time. Are you an effective team player? Are you aware of the emotional impact your late starts and deadline misses have on the overall project deliverables and individuals involved? Are you self-serving, or are you being of service to others?

> *In both examples, time management requires discipline and practice to ensure that everyone's needs are considered and addressed so that emotional frustration does not affect relationships in the long run.*

Managing time well is a requirement for successfully leading yourself and becomes even more critical when leading at the team and organizational level. Without proficiency here, the stress will be overwhelming. What's more, you will be a menace to those you work with, causing chaos, resentment, and ultimately damaging your relationships.

We all have the same (24) hours each day. Understanding your natural relationship with time and appreciating its effect on others will serve you well as you learn to lead yourself at a high level of performance and productivity.

▶ Managing Your Energy

When you get to the point of having no more hours in the day and your bandwidth is totally tapped out, you need to consciously move into energy management (assuming you aren't already there), which can increase your productivity and improve your performance while utilizing the same amount of time or less.

Each of us has a *diurnal (2)-peak pattern of energy* in any given (24)-hour period with a strong energy peak and a moderate peak. My personal high peak time is 5:00 to 7:00 a.m. In these (2) hours, with disciplined focus, I can experience a threefold lift in my productivity. In other words, these (2) hours are worth (5) to (6) hours of time. I fiercely protect these hours so I can focus on writing proposals, reviewing research, or planning workshops.

My second peak period occurs during the hours of 4:00 to 7:00 p.m. It is slightly less productive, but I can get a 50% increase in productivity, which means these (3) hours of focus can be the equivalent of (4½) hours of time.

People often wonder if this productivity is based on the fact that these periods simply contain uninterrupted time. As a small business owner, I can choose uninterrupted time at any point during the course of my day. After conscious experimentation, I have learned that I am far more productive at these (2) time periods than any other time.

Find your high productivity energy time slots and protect them!

Renewing, Recharging, Revitalizing Your Instrument

Having a strong work ethic is great, but not at the expense of your health and wellness. Early in the process of learning to lead yourself, program into your thinking the importance of taking regular breaks to renew, revitalize, and recharge your instrument.

Concentration breaks every hour during the day, shutting down your smartphone at night, a weekend getaway during the busiest time of the year, and regularly planned vacations with your family are all important to your well-being. Your instrument will perform at its best and you will be less likely to become emotionally imbalanced if you give yourself revitalizing experiences as often as possible.

Today's leaders are role models for balance and good habits!

"It is one thing to praise discipline and another to submit to it."

– Miguel de Cervantes Saavedra

Leadership Is a Being State, Not a Doing State

The first homework questions I often give my new coaching clients are reflective inquiries asking them to ponder (2) questions for a few weeks:

These questions accelerate personal insights into self-awareness, self-management (intention and impact), social awareness, and relationships while awakening my coaching clients to the critical fact that leadership is a state of "being" and is not about doing!

> *When you reflect on these (2) questions, you will start to notice what you are doing to distract from or contribute to your effectiveness as a performance-based leader.*

Are you primarily listening, talking, or interrupting conversations? Are you asking open-ended questions, or are you telling people what they should do, what they should think, or what you think? Are you challenging what you see and demonstrating the courage to speak truth to power by asking the hard questions? Are you holding yourself and your peers accountable?

Leadership can be expressed in any moment. It is a way of being in a circumstance, situation, conversation, and interaction. You are playing an architectural role in creating experiences through the structure or conditions in which the work gets done.

Regardless of what you do for a company, organization, or association, always be conscious of cultivating your being state; it is the infinite source of your leadership. It bears repeating that people will remember the experience of being with you and how you make them feel (both about you and themselves) more than what you can ever accomplish through doing things.

As a leadership coach, I have the opportunity to work with many types of leaders. They range from being ambitious to reluctant, reflective to impulsive, practical to conceptual, and include a cross-section of those who are merely surviving to those who clearly excel in their roles.

> *It is important in your leadership journey to calibrate and strike the right balance between being the best leader you are now and the one you ultimately want to be.*

Leadership Rigor is about consciously designing your own approach to leadership development. You are being presented with various tools and concepts to consider applying in this process, yet everyone is different and will pursue their own path forward.

Read the following leadership descriptions, see which resonate, and assess what type of leader you are right now so that you have a clear foundation from which to grow:

- [ ] I'm a reluctant leader; I will be there if/when you need me.

- [ ] I'm an impulsive leader; I need to be in constant action.

- [ ] I'm a seemingly natural (unconsciously competent) leader.

- [ ] I'm a knowledge-seeking leader; I need to learn and be seen as smart.

- [ ] I'm a let's-just-get-things-done leader; I like less talking and more doing.

- [ ] I'm a give-me-a-new-tool-to-implement-today leader.

- [ ] I'm a self-reflective, curious leader; I don't mind waiting to do something.

- [ ] I'm an I-want-to-be-the-best-I-can-be leader.

- [ ] I'm an I-am-doing-my-best-with-what-I-have-to-work-with leader.

- [ ] I'm a slow-to-change leader; things seem to be working okay now.

- [ ] I'm an everything-is-great leader with no worries at all.

- [ ] I'm an I-want-to-build-other-leaders leader; it's about the future and talent bench.

What kind of leader are you right now? What kind of leader do you want to be? Understand where you are starting from and commit to move forward from here. It is not where you start but where you finish that matters most. Make your decision and **Rigor it!**

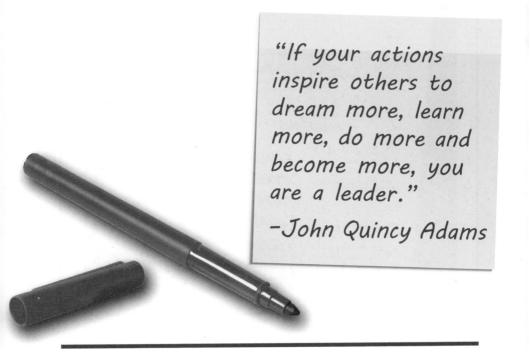

"If your actions inspire others to dream more, learn more, do more and become more, you are a leader."

-John Quincy Adams

Are You a Winner or a Loser with Relationships?

Individuals may hold titles or positions, but they will never play their leadership role of being in service to others if they are arrogant, ignorant, or self-righteous. As leaders, we must avoid being caught in any of these (3) areas, as they separate us from using our personal power and destroy our relationship currency.

Being arrogant means you think you always know the answers or are above it all. You project an aura of self-importance that suggests you believe you are the smartest, most important, or most sophisticated person in the room. Your lack of interest in others' viewpoints is evidenced by your dismissive body language. Others seldom seek relationships with you because you appear aloof or because it feels like you are in service only to yourself.

Being ignorant means you confidently and passionately assert your personal point of view as the best choice while simultane-

ously demonstrating that you are uninformed about viable alternatives. This limits your relationships because few individuals want to associate with someone who is narrow minded or uneducated in important areas yet exerts a pompous opinion.

Being self-righteous means you adamantly assert your political, religious, or personal views in an imposing way. Your beliefs are unwavering and you demonstrate no real tolerance for diversity or new thinking. You are self-serving, dismissive, and disinterested in the needs or concerns of others if they are different from yours. Being in a relationship with you is only possible for those who share the same moral viewpoints on almost everything.

Instead of being a loser, choose to be a winner with relationships. Winners are authentic about who they are and what they believe. They are open minded, open to feedback, and open to working collaboratively with others. Most importantly, they are flexible about working with other peoples' styles and preferences, which allows them to effortlessly connect with and get the best out of those with whom they work.

You Need to Be "We" Oriented Versus "I" Oriented

Learning to lead yourself requires being able to demonstrate that you can balance your "I" versus "we" orientation. If managed well, this can identify you early in your career as a potential team leader.

Sequentially, you first need to learn to establish your "I" position to effectively presence yourself as a leader through expressing your personal point of view and then seamlessly transition into more of a "we-based" orientation that consistently serves your team and organization.

There are two types of "I" positions, and understanding their not-so-subtle differences is a game changer in learning to lead yourself:

- *I-imposing*

- *I-presencing or I-voicing*

I-imposing means coming across as self-centered and self-absorbed, having to prove your intelligence and requiring your own personal information needs to be met first and expeditiously so that you can do your job. It may also reflect an excessive use of your expertise power. The energy of I-imposing feels oppressive, negative, and "all about you."

I-presencing or I-voicing means strongly expressing your point of view while acknowledging that your perspective is just one of several potential considerations being brought forward. While projecting a firm position, you remain open to engaging in a dialogue around other possibilities. I-presencing and I-voicing *create inclusive space and welcome a collaborative discussion with productive debate.*

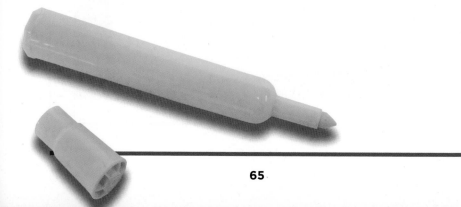

There are also two types of "we" positions:

- *We:* Speaking for the group

- *We:* Speaking with an enterprise-first perspective

Sometimes, in the mistaken belief that others share our feelings, we take the liberty of expressing ourselves and speaking for the group. In doing this, we risk being wrong as well as demonstrating potential arrogance and ignorance in front of our colleagues. Others in the room with strong personal power will likely voice opposition, partly out of frustration at this generalized assumption but also to open up the room to the diverse perspectives that more likely exist. *Always speak for yourself only!*

A hallmark characteristic of emerging leaders is that they quickly gravitate toward assuming an "enterprise-first perspective" that transcends both their individual and team priorities. *This perspective represents the big-picture view of what their organization is collectively trying to accomplish* and seeks to ensure that everyone is aligned and working together.

Evolving into the "we-based" enterprise mindset and understanding the dangers of I-imposing versus I-presencing or I-voicing is a signal of your maturity as well as your potential leadership capabilities. This is the mindset and service orientation that leaders need to have!

You Must Choose How You Will Serve as a Leader

We can serve in any moment from any role because we are all leaders with personal power! As you consider your career progression, however, you will want to make certain choices early and proactively. The first is, do you want to be a leader of people or a thought leader who focuses more exclusively on your own technical expertise, deal making, or innovative ideas?

Each option involves different passions and skill sets. Be mindful not to jump to what you believe is "the right answer" or to sound arrogant and/or ignorant by proclaiming you want to do both. One is a *generalist* and the other is a *specialist,* and to be good at either you need to be skilled and disciplined.

For example, a lawyer may choose to be a solo practitioner and not the managing partner of a firm. A practicing physician may not want to be the chief of surgery. A financial analyst may want to oversee a portfolio of assets but not a team of investment managers.

It might be unthinkable for you not to see yourself as a leader of others, at least initially. How will you get to work on the more meaty projects without a team of direct reports getting the basic work done for you? What would it look like to your peers if you did not have a team reporting to you?

Leadership first and foremost is about service to others. Do you have a passionate desire to coach and develop colleagues, team members, and direct reports? Do you get excited watching others grow? Do you have the patience, persistence, and desire to invest your time in helping others learn and develop as an integral part of your job, not just as something that you do when you have a free hour for lunch or when your day job is complete?

Dishonesty here will lead you astray and be painful in the long run. You may initially be hired into a team leadership role, but if you don't have the skills or passion to do it well and if your organization keeps you in that role (in large organizations, this won't happen for long; it's more likely to occur in small to mid-sized private companies depending on the CEO/owner), the real losers are your direct reports and the future of your organization.

How you will serve as a leader is a choice you must rigor!

For many, being a subject matter expert (SME) and thought leader is where the real action is. These individuals relish the knowledge, the kill of the deal or transaction, and advancing ideas. They prefer to be right in the middle of the action, leading the charge forward themselves. Developing the capabilities of others, coaching performance, and engaging in team- or organizational-level planning initiatives feels like wasted time and an energy drain for the thought leader.

You must follow your heart and ask yourself which leadership path is best suited to your talents and desires. There is no right or wrong answer, just a path that is more or less energizing and fulfilling for you. *You must embrace your authentic self and choose.* Of course, the truth will ultimately reveal itself, either through an ineffective performance or a low-energy experience if you chose the path that is not optimal. Make an early and proactive choice that helps your career take flight versus a reactive one that causes you and others continuous turbulence. This topic is further developed in the tension section of Part 2 that discusses becoming both a practitioner and a philosopher.

RIGOR IT!

"There is no coming to consciousness without pain."

– Carl Jung

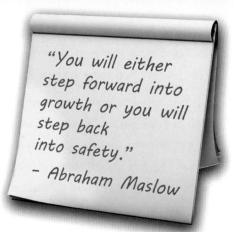

"You will either step forward into growth or you will step back into safety."

— Abraham Maslow

CHAPTER 2:
Creating Your Leadership Practice

Playing a leadership role is not a casual or part-time undertaking; it requires conscious discipline and the consistent application of professional skills.

Leadership Rigor requires creating a personalized leadership practice that will become the arsenal of tools, models, frameworks, philosophies, and approaches you come to passionately believe in and attempt to master as you continue to learn and develop as a leader. It will also define the signature elements of your behavioral style that you will bring to your various leadership roles over the course of your career. The material in *Leadership Rigor* will guide you in creating a practice that is focused on performance and productivity for leading yourself now and, later, for leading teams and organizations.

To begin creating your leadership practice, you need to be able to speak the language of leadership, develop leadership presence, and navigate the field you are playing on at the right altitude.

Accordingly, This Chapter Focuses on (3) Areas:

I.   The Language of Leadership

II. Leadership Presence

III. Leading at the Right Altitude

I. The Language of Leadership

Like medicine, business, or law, leadership has a language. While the organization you are a part of will likely have its own unique leadership dialect as part of its culture, the basic principles are similar across industries, sectors, and companies. Utilizing a common language along with tools and models increases performance and productivity by minimizing the time required to secure up-front clarity and alignment. It also lowers the risk of wasting resources because of misunderstandings, which is why it is so highly valued by organizational leaders. In short, *having clarity on and fluency with the language of leadership will position you to be an influential leader both within and outside your current organization.*

Being able to speak a language, whether it is French, science, or leadership, requires a baseline vocabulary. For our purposes, understanding fundamental leadership terms and using them properly is the first step. *Leadership Rigor* highlights both vocabulary and concept building to give you a strong foundation for establishing your fluency in the language of leadership.

But language is more than just words and concepts. It includes symbols, pictures, tools, stories, and gestures that help you convey and deliver a broad spectrum of messages.

Being proficient in the language of leadership with conscious competency will require you to understand and demonstrate:

- **The Language of Listening**
- **The Language of Observation**
- **The Language of Appropriate Response**
- **The Language of Leadership Styles**
- **How to Clarify Your Intentions**
- **How to Socialize Ideas for Traction and Momentum**
- **Naming Your Values and Philosophies**
- **Using Specific, Targeted Language**

The Language of Listening

Listening means *actively paying attention*, using your eyes and ears to receive messages and being alert to what is *not* said as much as to what *is* said.

Listening and understanding *what is going on "over there"* with the other person is the most critical part of initially learning the language of leadership. **You communicate with your listening that you see, hear, and care.** The language of listening conveys to the person you are with that he or she is important and that this conversation matters.

The Language of Observation

There are *always two conversations going on*, the one you are having with your words and tone of voice and the one your body is projecting. Your body language always validates your truth in a conversation because it is most genuinely aligned with your emotions, regardless of the words you use.

What you physically see and socially read in the person you are communicating with offers insights into what matters most and how that individual really feels. If you want to connect, engage, and influence as a leader, you must be observant, using your social awareness skills and knowing when to ask, "What is going on here for you right now?" The conversation will then go where it needs to go versus you being oblivious and plowing ahead with your predetermined agenda.

> *You may also observe or sense confusion when communicating with someone. When facilitating workshops, I often make the comment, "I see a bubble over your head that is saying..."*

This observation provides *an entry point for the conversation* to go where the participant wants/needs it to go, and I can clarify or change direction as needed in real time. This is emotional intelligence at work through social awareness and the language of observation!

The Language of Appropriate Response

Listening and observing are powerful tools for determining how to communicate effectively with appropriate responses. As a leader, *you need to demonstrate agility and flexibility* by applying a variety of leadership styles as well as understanding how to select the best choices for the specific circumstances you face.

For example, if you observe or hear anxiety in a conversation, don't just move forward and ignore it. Choose to pause and acknowledge the feelings you sense and, if appropriate, take a moment to empathize with the individual. This will foster trust and credibility as you build your relationship.

If you observe or hear impatience, stop and ask a few questions that allow these feelings to be brought to the surface and openly expressed. If the individual is simply time sensitive, you might ask if he or she wants to do this at a different time or whether he or she even needs to be a part of this work at all? *Veritas* at work!

Finally, *mirror (and match) your body language or style approach* to the other person's in order to foster connectedness. Because we communicate most effectively when we connect with others, mirroring increases the likelihood that we will be listened to and heard.

For example, perhaps the person you are talking to is walking around the conference room during your discussion. You might choose to stand and walk over to the window, matching this approach. Alternatively, you might be engaging with bottom-line communicators who speak in short sentences and headlines. While your natural style preference might be more relaxed, you are best served to tighten up your cadence and flex to their style so that your communication is on their wavelength.

An even *more sophisticated leadership approach* is to listen for personality preferences and to respond similarly. For example, you might observe that someone is interested in facts and details so you spend considerable time here versus rushing into your personal preference of talking about the big-picture possibilities and implications. Or, if you sense that you are speaking with an introvert, you might consciously pause and let silence sit for a few extra seconds, giving the individual a chance to take advantage of an entry point in the conversation, gather his or her thoughts, and have the space to actively contribute to the discussion.

The Language of Leadership Styles

Later in **Leadership Rigor,** I will cover the following (6) interpersonal leadership styles in greater detail. Below is a preview of the language of leadership associated with each of these styles to give you insights into how to incorporate them in your mirroring activities.

1. Directing

This approach is straightforward and **to the point.** Leaders who have a dominant directing style speak in short sentences and headlines. They may write in bullet points and phrases. If you want to speak this individual's leadership language, you might succinctly summarize back in bullet points what you hear and agree to.

2. Coaching

This approach is heavily guided and **influenced by questions** as well as patience and space. An open-ended, curiosity-based question typically starts the process; as answers unfold, a coaching style probes deeper into an area or two by following a thread.

The focus is predominantly on revealing and discovering insights and learning. Asking the individual to capture and articulate back to you the content that was (un)covered and the connections that were made during the exchange is important at the end of a coaching conversation.

3. Pace-Setting

This style feels similar to directing, but the emphasis is more on **specific targets with timelines and milestones.** Playing back your understanding of the targeted goals and dates for the agreed-upon deliverables will ensure a leadership language connection with the individual using this style.

4. Visionary

Here the language of leadership is likely to be in **pictures and stories**. Visionary leaders paint a picture of the future they see and include vivid descriptions of others being there with them in a starring role so they can all emotionally connect to the experience. The stories created may tell of the struggle to get there or the feelings upon arrival. This style of leadership is highly emotionally engaging. The best way to communicate back in this language is to acknowledge, appreciate, or even share in the excitement of the vision described and how being a part of it makes you genuinely feel.

5. Affiliative

The language of affiliation is flush with **empathy and compassion.** Understanding how the other person feels, verbalizing it, and sharing your own personal emotional experience with the situation at hand are all parts of the affiliative leadership approach. The challenge with this style is to avoid getting stuck in the emotional connection phase, which can lead to a downward spiral of emotion depending on the situation at hand. The language of affiliative leadership needs to anchor emotionally in being with others in the moment and then utilize the emotional energy that is present to move forward into action (**"connect and go"**).

An example of this style may sound like, "The financial challenges we are facing will require us to let go of the hard work and passionate efforts we have all put forth on this initiative. It is incredibly disappointing for those of us who have invested years in the research here, and I know it will take some time to emotionally let go. I am, however, energized about and grateful for the opportunity to pursue an alternative initiative in the new year, which will offer us another chance for a breakthrough success in this area, and I am anxious to get the team refocused as soon as possible."

Effectively using this style requires both self-management and social awareness skills to ensure appropriate time is applied to both the "connect" and "go" parts of this style.

6. Participative or Facilitative Leadership

The language of participative or facilitative leadership is energetic, action oriented, and ***focused on creating experiences together.*** This approach uses language such as, "I have some thoughts, but I would like to hear what you guys have to say about this first" or "Let's discuss ideas on how to plan our next national meeting together."

The key to communicating with a participative/facilitative leadership style is shared engagement. Co-creating an outcome or plan as well as noting the input and ideas from all involved is the best way to mirror this leadership style.

How to Clarify Your Intentions

Good drivers use their *blinkers* to communicate where they are going on the road. The same is true in business and leadership.

Here are some examples of how to overtly use your language of leadership to signal the direction you that are heading in as a leader:

> *I would like to talk about how we are progressing in building trust together as a new team. I am concerned that we may not be asking each other for help, and no one needs to be a hero; we are all in this together. Remember that vulnerability shows strength. We need to be able to rely on our collective resources and not just have broad shoulders ourselves.*

> *I am concerned that we may be getting into a situation where we are stretching ourselves too thin. This is budget planning season, so let's be disciplined with our cross-functional partners to ensure priorities are set, expectations are clear, deliverables are agreed to, and required resources are appropriately lined up and available.*

As we approach year-end, let's take a look at the behaviorial and technical goals we initially developed. In our next one-to-ones, I would like to discuss where you have made significant progress and where you need to put additional focus either on your own or with my help. Please bring your individual development plans so we can review your progress and your commitments.

Notice how each of these examples articulates the leadership concept, offers a general explanation of what the leader is looking for, and makes a specific action request. By putting your blinkers on and clearly stating what you are looking for, you increase the potential for both better performance and greater productivity.

How to Socialize Ideas for Traction and Momentum

This heading might be confusing if you don't understand the language of **Leadership Rigor**! Not surprisingly, my clients are often amazed, or perhaps more likely amused, at the language of leadership I use to coach them. What does "socializing an idea" look like? In the context of leadership, what are traction and momentum?

"Socializing an idea" means exposing people to it in different forums and seeing if it resonates or "lands" with them. *When you socialize an idea, you look to create a groundswell of dialogue on it and acceptance around it.* The key here is that you are open to shaping and molding the idea with additional input and perspective versus *"floating an idea"* you actually want accepted as is. Without a doubt, social media makes socializing ideas easier than it's ever been before.

What do traction and momentum have to do with the language of leadership? A great deal, as it turns out. *Traction* means you have done the preparatory work and are appropriately grounded in the data, facts, or environmental conditions of a project you are working on and therefore will not waste time or effort "spinning your wheels" without direction, in essence going nowhere.

You always want to make sure you have traction before you put your foot on the gas and accelerate your efforts, especially when resource investments are involved. An example would be learning to lead yourself as a way to get traction before being promoted into the role of leading a team or organization. If you move too quickly, you will not have the required skills to do the job well, and you will spin your wheels in frustration and have limited success.

Momentum is the ability to create forward action that builds upon itself and becomes self-sustaining. In building a leadership practice, you demonstrate momentum as you increase your performance and productivity through the consistent and appropriate use of skills and models as well as by helping others learn, thereby creating traction and momentum in their own respective leadership practices.

▶ Will It "Stick," or Is It Just "Shtick"?

Language concerns both comprehension ("Do I understand it?") and application ("Do I feel comfortable utilizing it?"). Without *relevance and resonance*, language quickly drops into the "shtick" category, cute phrases that may initially sound catchy but are not memorable and therefore do not have long-term staying power in your leadership practice because you either don't know how to or feel uncomfortable using them.

Look to avoid "shtick" and to maximize "stick" as you learn about models, processes, and tools that will enhance the performance and productivity of your leadership practice. *Remember, all that matters is putting your learning on the ground (OTG), not in your memory or files.*

Naming Your Values and Philosophies

Think for a moment about what it means to you to have a great day. Have you ever paused and reflected on this seemingly ordinary notion? Perhaps, to you, a great day involves freedom, adventure, recognition, family, learning, or any number of possibilities.

Or think of a time when you felt frustrated or annoyed. Did you ever consider what personal value was being violated? Perhaps it was respect, integrity, friendship, or honesty.

In business, we express our emotional beliefs and behaviors through the language of our values. When your values are honored, life is good and you are set up to perform well; when your values are stepped on, you will be frustrated and unable to perform at your best. As a leader, you must consciously consider and know your personal values, be able to articulate them, and use them to transparently guide your choices and decisions as well as to self-manage.

Your philosophies, on the other hand, reflect your practical wisdom for how you operate and move through the world based on your experiences and learning. For example, arriving early to a meeting or conference because it provides an opportunity for selecting preferred seating and extra networking time with senior executives might be a philosophy held by an aspiring leader.

> *Having a set of philosophies that frame your actions and behavior in terms of what you want to do and why you want to do it are ingredients for creating your consciously competent leadership practice.*

Being able to articulate your values and philosophies sends a strong message to senior executives that you are thinking not only about learning and applying your knowledge but that you understand how important it is to be able to communicate to others how and why you do what you do.

Using Specific, Targeted Language

Leaders will often avoid important conversations because they don't feel confident that they have the appropriate language to express their wants and needs. Trust, for example, has its own language, as does accountability (see **The Accountability Conversation** in Chapter 3). Using a common language in your organization accelerates mutual understanding and alignment so that you can experience higher levels of performance and productivity because the necessary conversations can and do take place.

I encourage my coaching clients to *name or label the language they use.* An example would be, "Let me put my **visionary leadership** hat on here and remind everyone of where we are going in the future and why I believe we will win in this competitive space as well as how bringing this new business venture to fruition in the marketplace starts to set us apart and offers us additional platforms for growth and momentum."

Alternatively, you could put on your pace-setting hat and say, "Let's be clear that over the next (30), (60), and (90) days, these key milestones dates are going to be critical to achieving our year-end targets."

Yet the language of leadership is more than just words. Frameworks and models create tangible retention of the concepts as well. A picture can provide an anchor for easier recall and can help walk others through an instructional or storytelling approach to the model's intention or application. Don't hesitate to draw the Mindful Leadership Model, the Performance Framework, or the Emotional Intelligence Model on the whiteboard or flip chart as you work through a challenging conversation or problem with your colleagues or team.

We are a population of diversified learners. As mentioned earlier, many of us learn through listening, others through visuals, and still others prefer to learn through the kinesthetic experiences of touch and feel. Whatever your preference, remember that as a leader, you need to convey your messages to a diverse group of individuals, which means you need a multimedia and multifaceted approach.

II. Leadership Presence

"Leadership presence" is an *ambiguous phrase.* Many clients enter coaching engagements with a desire to focus on this concept after receiving feedback that a "lack of presence" is holding them back from their next promotion.

When I ask what specific feedback was used to describe this gap in their leadership performance, they often shake their heads and say, "I really don't know."

Always remember to take a moment to explore in a safe and non-threatening way what "presence" specifically means to your supervisor and, if possible, ask for recent examples of when your presence was not as strong as this individual would have expected.

"Leadership presence" (or "executive presence") is a catchall phrase that can mean almost anything and everything. If you're told you lack it, the one thing it does clearly signal is that how you are showing up and the experience of being with you is creating concern, discomfort, or a general lack of confidence.

Remember, leadership can be learned. This means that your leadership presence can be improved dramatically once you are aware of your specific challenges and have a chance to consciously work on them.

You might be well served to seek potential insights on this by looking first at the MBTI Myers-Briggs style differences between you and your supervisor. You may simply have different style profiles. For example, perhaps you are introverted and your supervisor is extroverted. If so, your reserved nature might be perceived as lacking leadership presence.

Or perhaps you come across in meetings as being too detail oriented, too "in the weeds," a sensor type, while your supervisor is a (30,000)-feet, big-picture, intuitive thinker who believes he or she looks at the business strategically and therefore perceives you as "lacking perspective in this area" when you simply have a different preference for dealing with information.

It is relatively common for style differences to be an issue with respect to leadership presence interpretation. If your style does not naturally support your ability to influence with the impact you desire, seek coaching to learn how to work more effectively with your own hardwiring to leverage and flex your style. This is completely coachable and can make a significant shift in your career trajectory.

Let's now take a look at how the following "from" and "to" sentences frame very different perspectives of leadership presence in the context of our work here in *Leadership Rigor*:

From:

My leadership presence is about the impact and experience I create while interacting and connecting with people.

To:

My leadership presence is about consciously connecting with people to create a positive impact and meaningful experience.

Notice immediately that the "to" statement:

- ☑ Is *consciously owned* and created rather than left to chance
- ☑ Is *"we-based"* rather than "I-based"
- ☑ Is *service oriented*, which means it is about others, not you
- ☑ Aligns your *intention and impact* up front
- ☑ Offers a positive and meaningful takeaway experience for others, with the halo effect back to you of *creating likeability* and increasing your perceived leadership presence!

Let's further break this target definition of leadership presence into pieces to provide context and insights for building your leadership presence with rigor.

First, *the experience you create* can be a conscious or unconscious choice. In **Leadership Rigor,** the goal is to make all of your choices consciously, regardless of what they are, and to highlight the risks of how, if unconsciously left to chance, you may create experiences that have a negative impact because they are not aligned with your intentions, thereby affecting, in this case, your leadership presence.

Reflect for a moment on how you believe you show up in your professional interactions and ask yourself if you appear to be:

- Warm and welcoming *or* reserved and distant

- Comfortable in your own skin *or* awkwardly self-conscious

- Socializing easily *or* forcing yourself to engage

- Open and collaborative *or* closed and directive

- Confidently creating safe space *or* intimidating to others

- Part of the action (inclusionary) *or* standoffish

The experiences you create reflect your confidence and how you feel about yourself (your instrument), so be mindful about how you are bringing your internal perspective into your external interactions with others.

Of course, your emotional intelligence is strongly connected to your leadership presence as well. You need to be aware of your natural tendencies (hardwired preferences) and focus on your leadership mindset so that you can manage how you show up, which is *the first half of the work!*

Self-awareness and self-management approaches contribute to your leadership presence, so be mindful of:

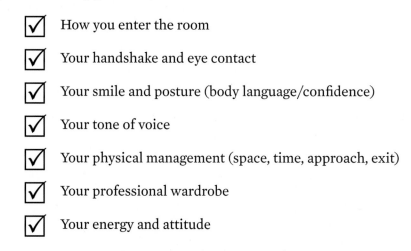

☑ How you enter the room

☑ Your handshake and eye contact

☑ Your smile and posture (body language/confidence)

☑ Your tone of voice

☑ Your physical management (space, time, approach, exit)

☑ Your professional wardrobe

☑ Your energy and attitude

Working a Room with Leadership Presence—Meet and Greet

Walking into a room with your head up and a friendly smile is the fastest way to project self-confidence and make an initial positive impression.

Immediately look around and identify someone you know well. Walk right over with your hand out while you look into their eyes and greet them warmly. Exchange a word or two but stay aware of the room by trying not to get too deeply involved in this first conversation. Quickly look to greet others you know or introduce yourself to those you have not yet met. This may feel awkward, so let eye contact and smiles guide your entry points.

Be brave, walk up to someone new, introduce yourself, and ask a question such as "Where are you from?" while listening carefully to hear the name of the person you are meeting. Your voice tone should be a bit elevated and energetic as you meet and greet others. If you are extroverted, enjoy the moment. If you are introverted, get ready—"It's show time!"

As you become more comfortable in the room, *strive to be a "connector."* Look for opportunities to introduce your colleagues to others they may not yet know. People who can dynamically connect others in social settings are leadership magnets. Remember also to demonstrate your physical management of time and space by appropriately exiting conversations and not lingering too long with one individual or group. Use your time in this social setting for maximum impact by reaching out broadly and stretching yourself to make as many new connections as is reasonable without seeming too superficial.

During my years in corporate America, I could work a huge room during a social event in about an hour, with the goal of "meeting and greeting" to keep relationships building and growing. You can always follow up later with more detailed visits or conversations. For now, rigor it by productively working the room!

The second half of creating your leadership presence is being socially aware of the environmental dynamics and therefore conscious about your interpersonal connections and entry points for capitalizing on—or missing—opportunities for building relationships.

Leadership presence, in part, is about how you hold yourself and your space. We may not all be blessed with great physical attributes, but we can each carry ourselves with confidence and poise regardless of our raw starting material. It all begins with self-awareness about how we stand, enter a room, and move our bodies.

You also project confidence that you derive from your inner sense of self. Please do not underestimate this developmental area of your leadership journey. You must have confidence in order to authentically project confidence! You can "Fake it till you make it" for a while, but doing the real work to build a solid foundation of confidence cannot be ignored.

The concept of leadership really being about everyone else and not about you is explicitly demonstrated in your presence during social situations through your self-management and social awareness.

- ☑ You need to comfortably *ask questions with curiosity* and interest rather than compel an audience with your own engaging stories.

- ☑ You must *be a good listener*, picking up on insights and following up with appropriate but not overly personal questions to authentically connect with others.

- ☑ You need to be able to *enlarge the circle of the discussion* you are in and warmly welcome others into the dialogue. Having social awareness and social grace is an important part of leadership presence. *Always remember that leaders create experiences!*

III. Leading at the Right Altitude

Leadership development is a lifetime journey of consciously creating and mastering your practice with professional skills and applications. Critical to this journey is understanding the playing field you need to get comfortable navigating through as your leadership roles expand and advance. The concept of "altitude" and the level you are expressing your role at coupled with the next model, Do-Manage-Lead, sets the stage for understanding the scope and dynamics of the playing field of leadership. There is a progression here that you need to understand and then be disciplined about practicing if you are going to advance in your career and ultimately be capable of developing teams and organizations.

Altitude, Aircraft, and Leadership

Altitude literally refers to your vertical lift. The altitude you play at is a function of your skills and your role. To use an aircraft analogy, a new pilot learning to fly, a commercial airline pilot, and an astronaut are all operating at different altitudes of flight, and each role encompasses different skills, expectations, and risks.

The same holds true in business. Here, altitude concerns include:

- **Scope:** Are you working in or on your business?

- **Role clarity:** Are you playing your role or the role of others?

- **Talent:** Is your talent bench stretching and growing or stifled?

- **Self-management:** Are you indulgent or disciplined?

Learning to play at the right altitude as a business leader will be an enduring challenge throughout your career! Staying conscious of this and understanding where you are at all times will enhance performance and productivity for you personally as well as for those you lead!

The Do-Manage-Lead Model

One of the most powerful concepts you will be challenged to embrace throughout **Leadership Rigor** is working *"at the right altitude."* The model that formally introduces this approach is called Do-Manage-Lead.

Leaders always need to be conscious about what altitude they are working at and how much time they are investing in different initiatives in an effort to maintain their appropriate "role clarity." The role clarity of the leader sets the stage for how all other roles below and around them are cast.

> *The Do-Manage-Lead Model highlights both the evolution in mindset and the progression in skill set required for creating your leadership practice over time.*

Understanding early in your career the differences between the functions of doing, managing, and leading will ensure that you are focused on acquiring the required skills in advance. Many leaders get caught working almost exclusively at the lowest level of doing because they are not proficient at the higher-level skills of managing and leading.

The implications for understanding and utilizing the Do-Manage-Lead Model are significant for you as a leader and for your organization. If the appropriate altitude is played by each of the participants involved in a project/process, you are set up to maximize your impact. If the appropriate altitude is not played, your resources will be significantly underutilized. This simple concept has significant implications!

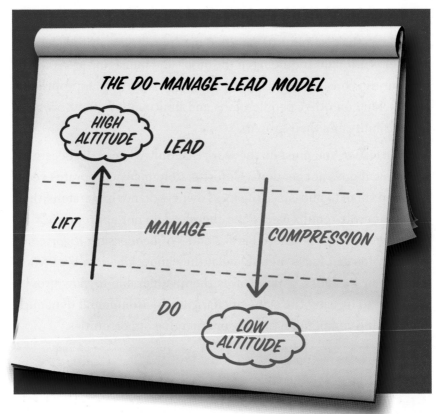

Stretching Performance and Creating Lift

When you as a leader work at the right altitude, you minimize *"compression,"* which occurs when you do the jobs of individuals directly or multiple levels below you. Working at a higher altitude (your actual job level!) as a leader sets up the possibility for creating *"lift"* throughout your organization, with individuals in each level stretching up and preferably beyond their roles to the next level, resulting in higher performance and greater productivity across the organization.

Broad Skill Development

Each of the (3) levels of the Do-Manage-Lead Model has a distinct focus and requires different skill sets. Solidifying technical skills is the focus of the *doing level,* ensuring strong interpersonal skills and getting work done through others is critical for the *managing level,* and prioritizing initiatives as well as allocating resources is the focus of the *leading level.*

Working *on* Rather Than *in* the Business

Having the discipline to maintain the appropriate altitude level as a leader is difficult. Indulging in the doing and managing areas can be fun, but the consequence is that you are likely to be inappropriately encroaching on other people's jobs and limiting both their scope of responsibility and their growth.

As a leader, you must do the work that only you can do, because if you don't, it does not get done. Unfortunately, many corporate executives and small to mid-sized business owners do not understand their leadership role requirements and therefore do not appropriately focus on them. (This is where Parts 2 and 3 of *Leadership Rigor* come in.) They instead focus on only what they know, the details of working in their business, which leaves them vulnerable to slow growth rates due to missing the signs of changing environmental dynamics, encroaching competitive threats, or emerging opportunities.

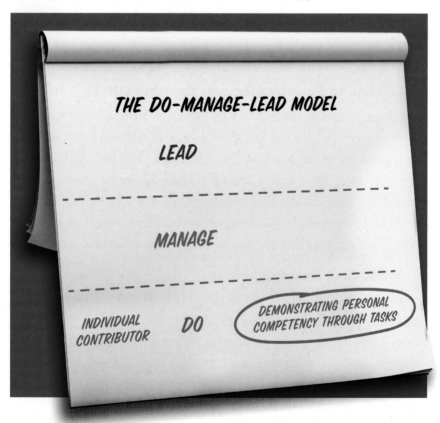

THE DO-MANAGE-LEAD MODEL

LEAD

- - - - - - - - - - - - - - - -

MANAGE

- - - - - - - - - - - - - - - -

INDIVIDUAL DO   DEMONSTRATING PERSONAL
CONTRIBUTOR   COMPETENCY THROUGH TASKS

Doing the Work

In the doing stage, you are mainly a *front-line individual contributor*, participating team member, or subject matter expert. On point for specific tasks and deliverables, you are primarily responsible for *executing a tangible work product*. It is your spreadsheet, financial model, or report. You may involve others for input, but you hold individual accountability for ensuring that the task is completed on time and in alignment with your supervisor's or team's expectations.

Early in your career, you can expect that much of your work will be "doing related" as you build technical skills and capabilities in your chosen profession. Accordingly, you personally grind out the work, becoming increasingly efficient and effective. Your work products have your fingerprints all over them, and you believe they are great. Certainly you are ready to do more and be paid more!

Your supervisor may start to notice and appreciate your good work, and you may become a valuable "go to" person, who "gets things done." Your reputation may build as someone who has a great work ethic and high productivity. You are ready to be promoted, right?

In many instances in the corporate world, yes! There is a propensity to take high-performance individual contributors who are technically strong and promote them into roles where they can share their knowledge and insights in a manager position with direct reports. The rationale is that team productivity will increase under this individual who is herself so productive, right?

More often than not, time and experience reveal that this is not the case. If not prepared for with appropriate training and development for leading others, this move can backfire. It may hold back and set up for failure not only the strong performers who get pummeled with an expanded workload because they don't know how to use the additional resources they are now overseeing, but the team they are surrounded with will stagnate in terms of its learning as well. All too often, team members don't get hands-on structured learning from their newly promoted supervisors because they are too busy "doing all the work" to engage with them!

Managing Interpersonal Relationships

As a young up-and-coming leader, it is important to avoid focusing 100% of your time and effort on the technical tasks of your role. As mentioned earlier, you also need to put time into the process of shifting into the second altitude level, from doing to managing.

At the managing level, your ability to get work done with and through others using your interpersonal skills becomes increasingly important. This level requires you to clearly set expectations, coach for performance while providing space to accomplish the work, and hold accountability for the deliverables. Being disciplined and learning how to increase your bandwidth by getting work done through others creates the "lift process" for your team and organization.

As you advance from individual contributor to task coordinator at the "managing" level, your use of the (2) currencies of leadership, relationships and communication, increases exponentially!

Avoid These Traps When Raising Your Altitude

First, avoid the micromanagement trap that imposes your preferred work style on others. Get the "what" needs to be done clear and then let others have space to implement their own style for the "how."

Second, do not fall into the trap of avoiding the managing approach because you think you can get things done more quickly yourself. *Of course you can get things done more quickly yourself, but that's not the point!* This is the most worrisome trap because it keeps you personally stuck at the lowest altitude of performance while limiting the growth of your colleagues.

The altitude shift from doing to managing is the most challenging for aspiring leaders. Invest in learning to clearly and appropriately set expectations, coach, and allow the successes as well as the mistakes of your direct reports to happen. They must have a chance to "own the work and the outcomes, including the consequences," and you must be clear about "letting go" if real growth is to happen.

To get the longer-term benefits of productivity (momentum), you have to go slower initially (until traction develops).

"No man will make a great leader who wants to do it all himself or to get all the credit for doing it."
— Andrew Carnegie

Prioritizing Initiatives and Allocating Resources

At the leading altitude level, the focus is primarily on the prioritization of initiatives and the allocation of resources.

▶ Prioritizing Initiatives

Being able to appropriately prioritize is a critical leadership skill that must not be overlooked. It relates not only to understanding what is most important but also where, why, and how the various pieces fit together and into the overall sequencing for your project or initiative.

Leading is not often a linear process. It involves complex judgments and ambiguous considerations. Knowing what to act on first and getting the sequencing right can have enormous consequences that can be either positive or negative. Understanding the macro choices and risks are what this leadership level is all about.

An example of a sequencing challenge a leader might face when prioritizing initiatives could be, "Do we get customers on board first and then build the plant to service them, or do we build the plant and then get customers to buy in based on our available capacity?"

Depending on the company, the risk profile, and customer relationships, different sequencing decisions may be made. Understanding how prioritization and sequencing best work for your organization is a leadership level decision.

Another example of how sequencing can affect prioritization might involve a leader's approach to creating the new team action agenda after a recent reorganization. An initial reaction might be to dive right into the metrics and to start creating target performance goals. An alternative approach might consider the sequential impact of first ensuring role clarity with the new changes firmly in place and giving the structure some time to settle in. Taking the time to pause and make some observations before moving into action can be an important first step as a leader.

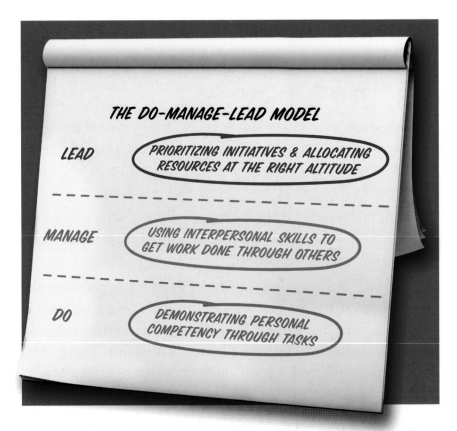

In another take on sequencing, before adding new team members to your relatively new structure, you might first assess whether you have skill gaps that can be trained for or productivity gaps that can be addressed with process-mapping clarification.

> *Being able to see and understand how things fit together sequentially can be a huge advantage for organizations in enhancing both their performance and productivity.*

For this to occur, leaders must play their roles at the right altitude and resist the temptation to just "get things done" because it feels good to them. Remember, leadership is in service to others, which in this case means your team or organization.

▶ Resource Allocation

> *When it comes to resources, there are only (3) that leaders work with: people, time, and money.*

Early in our careers, we usually believe the best solutions to our resource constraints involve adding more people. More people means more boots on the ground and more work getting done as well as potentially more "perceived power" for the individual leader.

While this sounds simple, the "more people" solution is also the most costly and often the most inefficient use of an organization's resources. How can this be the case?

The concept of "throwing bodies" at a problem is not a solution that experienced leaders usually go for initially. They are more interested in ensuring they understand and are solving for the right problem. These leaders ask, *"Do we really need more people, or do we lack the right skills, the right process approach, or the right priorities?"*

Alternatively, a typical pushback from the senior leadership team is that you likely have a "process problem," and if this were fixed, you would not have people, money, or time issues. This may be true, but it could also be senior leaderships' "easy way out," just like throwing bodies at a problem is the employees' easy answer.

The truth is, there are no easy answers! After all, it also takes "additional resources" to fix processes! In all fairness, solving process problems may well be the most effective long-term solution and will likely get at the root causes of many issues. Unfortunately, it can also take you backward a long way before you can even start to move forward, given the required time and energy commitment. This is why you need to carefully consider your potential short-term decreases in productivity against your longer-term gains and plan for the appropriate investment in resources to get this right if you are going to pursue this approach.

> *Sometimes the most pragmatic way to solve a resource or prioritization challenge is to simply be more reasonable with your expectations on timelines.*

Most of us underestimate what is required and how long initiatives will take to complete, so we are overly optimistic and sign up for more than we can handle.

In many cases, supervisors will modify or reset timing expectations if you make a request, though it is better to do so at the beginning of the process as compared to just prior to a project's due date. In the event that a supervisor is not reasonable, you can negotiate for alternative initiatives to take a temporary back seat to the priority in question. As an aspiring leader, you need to consider the multiple options available to you as you seek to solve these challenges at your altitude and presence yourself!

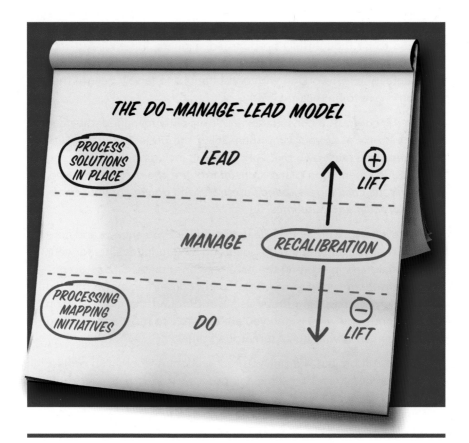

Whatever approach you take, present your point of view and ensure the right issues are surfaced and heard so that the best leadership decisions on prioritization and resource allocation can be made. Don't sit in silence. **Rigor it** with your leadership presence and *veritas* at the right altitude!

Managing a Consulting Project

At times, you may need to bring in outside resources to fill gaps on project needs. If you choose to hire a consultant, make sure you have a strong rationale for this approach or it can look like you are wasting company resources because you and your team can't get things done.

Also, don't underestimate the challenge of managing a consulting project. Consultants are not a panacea to your problems. They need to be thoughtfully on-boarded, aligned, and engaged with throughout the project. Often, leaders have a "delegate and go" mentality when working with consultants and falsely believe they don't have to be that involved.

On the contrary, if consultants aren't properly managed, they can take up more of your time than doing the project yourself. Ultimately, you must own the work product, including the inputs and the implementation plans. *Consultants are there to help frame, facilitate, challenge, expand, integrate, and document your thinking process and outcomes.*

Make sure your project scope is clear before you engage and confirm that you understand the roles and time requirements for your internal participants and the external consultants. *"Scope creep" in consulting projects can be a costly consequence.* Be mindful that larger consulting firms also work around the clock and on weekends and will assume you are available to react and respond to their needs with quick turnaround times.

A well-run project will get you recognition. A poorly run project will also get you recognition, so rigor it with conscious oversight!

Blue Dollars and Green Dollars

In organizations, money comes in two forms: green dollars (cold hard cash) and blue dollars (people resources, or the fully loaded cost of employee time and effort, including blood, sweat, and tears). Because blue dollars involve the seemingly "readily available" colleagues around us and are less likely to be "officially and consciously monetized," they are mistakenly thought of as "free." They are not free. For many companies, in fact, salaries are the most significant cost of doing business. Importantly, working at the leading altitude requires you to have close oversight of both your green- and blue-dollar deployment.

Many leaders get excited about working with the resources available to them in large organizations. Smart leaders, however, quickly understand that being a "resource hog" does not move them up the corporate ladder but rather sidelines them. Managing resources in an efficient, effective, and (most importantly) productive way is critical if you want to advance in your leadership role.

If not allocated to your project, blue dollars (people resources) will be deployed to other initiatives within your enterprise. As a leader, you must always assess where the greatest return is and put your resources there.

Are You Ready for Prime Time in Decision Making?

Every aspiring leader wants to participate in the decision-making process within his or her organizations. These individuals are smart, can add value, and believe they should be given the chance to sit in on senior-level conversations so they can listen, understand, and potentially participate in what is happening as early in their careers as possible.

First, just like compression involves the leader reaching down and doing work that can be done by others, leadership meetings are *not spectator events* in which everyone needs to invest time or participate. Too many organizations have *super high inclusion cultures that work against their productivity* in the other direction.

Second, it is not uncommon for young leaders to be bewildered at the seemingly ridiculous decision making they see their senior leaders engaged in and to think, "Are they kidding? That makes no sense! What exactly is going on in here?"

It's called altitude and landscape.

We tend in our early career roles as "doers" to see only one part of the elephant and not to realize for some time just how big the animal (not to mention the herd) really is. Without a greater perspective on the environmental dynamics, the complexities of the relationships involved, and the effects of the choices on upstream and downstream organizational operations, we look at project decisions in isolation. The leadership altitude level requires looking at decisions within the context of a broader portfolio of choices and potentially *making a relative risk assessment rather than an absolute one.*

Altitude and landscape provide the perspective of framing risk assessments in a greater context over a longer time period. *What we begin to learn as leaders is that there are no good or bad decisions, just different levels of risk that organizations and their leaders are willing to assume at any given time.*

The key takeaway of the Do-Manage-Lead Model is that, as leaders, we operate in all (3) of these areas, but the time allocated to each level changes as we advance in our leadership roles. This is critical for achieving optimal performance and productivity.

Ask yourself this question: if you were to allocate 100% of your time across the Do-Manage-Lead continuum right now, what would the distribution look like?

If you are like most leaders, you will painfully realize that you are spending more time "doing" than you are managing and leading. Do you think your CEO would be impressed with or surprised by your distribution? Would others in your organization who aspire to your role feel the distribution is appropriate? How about inspiring?

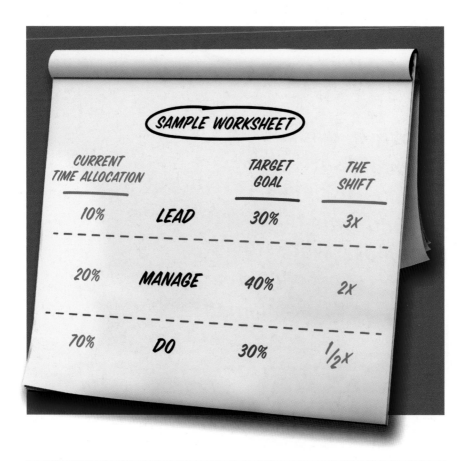

Take the opportunity to recalibrate how you are investing your time and raise your altitude, knowing this will require an ongoing commitment to speaking the language, looking and feeling the part, and then navigating the playing field successfully.

In continuing to build traction and momentum in leading yourself, armed with your leadership mindset and the framework of your leadership practice, you are now ready to learn how to give voice to your leadership. This, in turn, will assist you in facilitating progress on your team and across your organization.

"In a high-IQ job pool, soft skills like discipline, drive and empathy mark those who emerge as outstanding."
- Daniel Goleman

"Leaders think and talk about the solutions. Followers think and talk about the problems."
— Brian Tracy

CHAPTER 3:
Creating Your Leadership Voice

Expressing your point of view with clarity and conviction will be an ongoing area of development throughout your career as you learn to master the communication currency. Aspiring leaders often struggle with being courageous enough to put their thoughts forward, believing they are out of place, are not going to be taken seriously, or won't add significant value to the conversation.

These are natural emotions as you start to develop your leadership voice. Fortunately, with experience comes confidence as well as the understanding that facilitating progress within your team and across your organization requires you to effectively utilize your leadership voice. Eventually, you may even be privileged enough to be a trusted advisor and to sit at different tables, where the expertise you have accumulated over the course of a long, successful career gives you an opportunity to *offer insights to the insiders.*

To Create Your Leadership Voice, You Must Understand:

I.   How to Express Yourself

II. How to Facilitate Progress

III. How to Use **The Accountability Conversation**

IV. How to Become a Trusted Advisor

I. How to Express Yourself

Being clear about your intentions and consciously considering your desired communication impact up front will help you determine the best approach for putting your voice forward.

Here Are a Few Preparation Questions to Rigor:

1. Do You Have Something to Say?

2. What Is Your Motivation for Expression?

3. What Outcome Are You Seeking?

4. How Will You Express Yourself?

5. When Will You Express Yourself?

Do You Have Something to Say?

Recognizing if and when you have something to say is part of the journey of learning to lead yourself. Business happens in real time, so you have to be ready to jump into a conversation and share your point of view, often spontaneously. For extroverts, this can be easy; for introverts, it is more challenging.

How do you know if you have something to say? Let's go back to one of **Leadership Rigor**'s core principles: leadership is emotional. Your feelings are signals, and you want to be both alert and responsive to them. Your emotional intelligence skills can help guide you in identifying potential opportunities for expressing your leadership voice.

For example, an "aha" moment can be born out of your social or self-awareness skills when you have an insight, notice a dynamic in the room, or realize that your gut is talking to you and producing anxious energy. The question now is whether you want to make a conscious choice to communicate. Do you have something meaningful to contribute? Are you willing to courageously give voice to your thoughts?

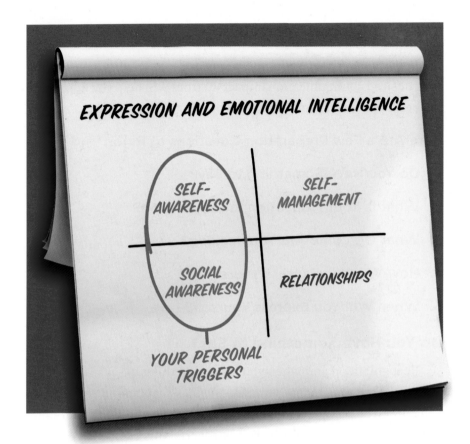

If you don't engage, you will deny the group your input and perhaps even walk away feeling frustrated for having not expressed yourself. You must accept the fact that expressing yourself requires some level of risk taking; what you say may or may not land as you intend or be appreciated by your audience.

Keep in mind that if you do not voice your point of view, others may wrongly assume you don't have one. Perhaps they will even make up a story about whether you are truly a valued player and ready for a leadership role, given your lack of participation. Remember, in the absence of information and experiences, we create stories in our own minds to fill in the gaps.

Often, we do have something to say, but we choose to speak to colleagues outside of the room, in *"the meeting after the meeting."* This is a bad approach to take for many reasons. It limits your personal visibility, slows down trust building, and denies the team the opportunity to enter into productive conflict to address the issues that may be bothering more people than just you. It can also come across as passive aggressive. Weighing in openly on key issues allows everyone to get on board and align with the team direction. Staying quiet holds the process back and can hold you back as an individual leader.

What Is Your Motivation for Expression?

If you are trying to prove yourself, compete for "share of voice" in the room, or grandstand for attention, the likelihood of a negative impact is high, because the way you presence yourself often reveals your true motivations.

However, if you are genuinely concerned or excited about something and believe that you can advance support or appropriately raise concerns that need to be considered, you are coming from an enterprise "we-based" mindset and can be of service to the team by expressing your thoughts.

What Outcome Are You Seeking?

Your motivations need to be linked to your desired outcomes. Are you attempting to influence the room by sharing your insights, are you looking to affiliate with others in the room in a supportive way, or are you looking to advocate a strong position because you fear the team is moving in the wrong direction and you want to change it? Being clear up front ensures greater alignment on the outcome.

When you advocate a strong position, be mindful about demonstrating that you are capable of being emotionally unattached to the ultimate outcomes if they are different from what you were proposing. You always want to ensure that you are a flexible team player and not a sore loser if the outcomes do not go your way.

How Will You Express Yourself?

Use good timing for your entry into conversations and appropriately frame the context of your communication. It can be unsettling to have the floor and know that others are watching you. Be careful to stay focused and confidently put forth your perspective in a declarative voice rather than ending with a fading upward lilt as if you are asking a question (i.e., do not use an inquisitive voice).

If you make this common mistake, you might risk not being recognized as a leader making a point but rather as a participant bringing forward a new question for someone else to answer. In addition to being personally misunderstood and perceived as more passive than assertive, it can be counterproductive to the room if a circular loop ensues to address the question you did not actually mean to ask.

Take the opportunity to *"hold your space"* while presencing yourself by using your hands to gesture and emphasize your words. Speak slowly and purposefully as you confidently express your point while looking around the room to make explicit eye contact with multiple individuals.

Discipline yourself to not just "chirp" into the conversation with feeble, fleeting, or half-expressed comments or thoughts because you are consistently being cut off by others who are filling the space more assertively. Seek your opportunity to enter the conversation, hold the floor, gain the room's attention, and fully express yourself. It will always be better to deliver fewer well-framed messages than to unsuccessfully attempt to deliver multiple messages.

The signature model section that follows this chapter reviews **The Progressive Mindset** model that describes in greater detail how to design and deliver your communication messages with impact.

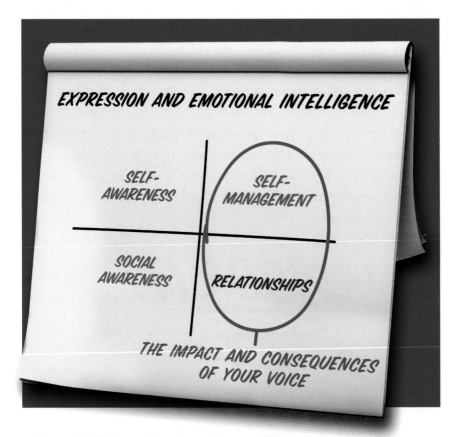

When Will You Express Yourself?

In general, creating your leadership voice will require you to be engaged and expressive in a variety of settings. Preparing for each of your interactions, whether they are one-to-ones or team meetings, will ensure that you are ready to participate and that you come across as "buttoned up."

Again, it is wise to consider this facet of leadership early in your career and to use all your forum exposures to build your presence. Even a town hall meeting can be a smart place to ask a great question that you have genuine curiosity about. In some cases, you might be the bold individual who asks the question that is on many people's minds and, in so doing, provides a service both to colleagues and to senior leaders who need to be aware of the critical issues and concerns of the organizational community.

One practical challenge many of my clients face is literally finding a way to physically enter fast-moving conversations. Raising your hand can seem inappropriate or junior. ***Instead, try moving your body forward and start to motion with your hands that you want to speak.*** This will signal to others that you are in the queue, and an emotionally intelligent colleague with strong social awareness may even verbally acknowledge you and stop the action so that you can more easily enter into the dialogue. If this doesn't happen, you will need to find (and perhaps fight for) your entry point, either politely or by just jumping in!

RIGOR IT!

"The question isn't who is going to let me; it's who is going to stop me."

– Ayn Rand

II. How to Facilitate Progress

The ultimate expression of your leadership voice is facilitating progress in the form of enhanced performance and improved productivity for yourself, your team, and your organization.

> *A facilitator of progress is a leader who is focused on making the right things happen for the organization at all times through a "we-based" enterprise lens and mindset.*

This individual is willing to step in and cover a required or vacated position if necessary, to work at the cross-functional interfaces to ensure smooth transitions on work products, and to bring forward issues from the trenches that need to be surfaced and addressed.

Working at the Cross-Functional Interfaces

Champions of keeping the ball moving forward and of situational problem solving, facilitators of progress break open the logjams and bring together the collective voices required for resolution and alignment.

Facilitators of progress are less concerned about formal role clarity "in the moment" and instead seek to secure relative understandings in real time to get the work product through the hurdles of cross-functional interfaces and transitions. They will, however, take the initiative to come back later and "revisit" the situation to see if they have the potential to identify a system-based solution that, if implemented, can provide an enduring solution to similar challenges that occur with interactions at the interface.

Bringing Issues forward for Discussion

Business is about raising and processing issues in a transparent way so that good decisions can be made, yet what needs to be openly discussed and debated is often ducked and avoided, even by leaders who are attempting to develop their leadership voices.

Why is this? As a leadership coach, I see multiple reasons:

- Fear of personal rejection or offending colleagues

- Discomfort with conflict

- Thinking team leaders should address (i.e., "Not my place")

- Pink elephant or sacred cow fear

- Team leader does not appear to be open to the discussion

- Past experience in discussing this with no resulting changes

- Don't know how to address

While these reasons are disheartening, they are common among senior-level executives as well as young aspiring leaders.

> *All of these issues can be addressed with the learning and insights provided in* **Leadership Rigor** *along with the assistance of individual and team coaching!*

One of the inexcusable sins of leadership is to stop *"forwarding the action and facilitating progress."* Your job as a leader is to be persistent, resilient, and committed to moving your organization forward in spite of the obstacles. If you choose not to play or to stop playing your leadership role, you should also leave your position immediately!

This is a problem in both family and corporate businesses. Leaders sometimes do give up, but more often than not, they stay. Sometimes they stay for a long time, blocking the organization's growth and also the future careers of talented individuals who want to lead but are held back by those in leadership positions who don't play at the altitude their role requires, causing both short-term compression and, in the longer term, a lack of leadership succession.

Senior leaders must hold a high bar for performance and have the courage to remove those who are no longer contributing at an acceptable level.

> *It is not a right to stay in a role because it has somehow been earned with years of service; it is always a privilege that is conditional upon performance.*

How many individuals in your organization are marginally performing and just keeping their heads down and noses clean, hanging on to their roles and hoping to stay long enough to put their kids through college or until they retire?

The unfortunate truth is that their lingering presence blocks up-and-coming executives, causing talent bench development and leadership succession challenges.

To address this, larger corporations are now creating more aggressive talent rotation requirements for advancement and are actively eliminating "talent blockers" in critical roles, thereby creating more opportunities for earlier development. Because this requires assertive and disciplined management of the talent bench, many small companies lack forward progress in this area and remain caught in the trap of having experienced long-term employees, a huge gap, and inexperienced employees not yet ready to take on more responsibility. *This, unfortunately, reflects a lack of organizational leadership.*

Being a facilitator of progress is a daily activity, and it doesn't happen by executing what is known and safe to pursue. It is in raising the issues that are unclear, controversial, and potentially confusing for discussion and resolution that the facilitator of progress has the biggest impact.

Let's also differentiate between a facilitator of progress and a complainer of the status quo who has plenty of ideas but lacks the drive, passion, and commitment to make change happen OTG. Corporations are chock full of the latter; the former is the breed of leader *Leadership Rigor* seeks to develop!

Facilitators of progress use their leadership voices to:

- ☑ *Willingly take on challenges* not only because they are intellectually stimulating and they want exposure in order to facilitate their own learning but also because they see a path that can be created to increase productivity and performance for their team or enterprise ("we" versus "I")

- ☑ *Shape and actively contribute to a project* versus standing on the sidelines criticizing what is wrong or missing to validate their own importance or intelligence

- ☑ *Take time to walk others through their thinking* not only because they value being a coach but because sharing the information provides others with actionable tools they can use to make forward progress for the enterprise

- ☑ *Accept a variable "how" things are done* as long as "what" needs to get done happens; they appreciate the importance of giving space to others to perform using their preferred style choices

- ☑ *Avoid delegating for personal convenience* and instead coach others through the things they actually love doing and need to let go of because they too have new areas to tackle

- ☑ *Challenge the current state* because they are looking to put new thinking and ideas OTG that can provide continuous improvement for their team or organization

Being a facilitator of progress is the precursor for becoming a team leader. By demonstrating your desire to be a "go-to" person who will make things happen for your organization, you are becoming a magnet others will want to work with. Building trust, confidence, and followership is moving you toward your next role.

III. How to Use The Accountability Conversation

Holding accountability is one of the most difficult challenges in the workplace today. In my own experience as a business professional and leadership coach, accountability often feels like a search for the Holy Grail, and many CEOs and leaders I have worked with believe it is equally elusive.

"If we just had accountability, things would be so much easier!" is something I often hear, yet for something we all want so desperately, there appears to be very little time or effort put into securing it!

To lead yourself at a high level of performance and productivity while simultaneously creating your leadership voice, you need a simple and straightforward tool that encompasses both process and role clarity. This tool is **The Accountability Conversation.**

What is most important to realize about The Accountability Conversation is that it is a unique type of dialogue. It is actually an interactive negotiation between two parties that seeks to clarify, confirm, and secure alignment.

Accountability fundamentally has two requirements—something must be given, and something must be taken. Both parts must be consummated in the dialogue or the negotiation is not complete, which means alignment and the progress you are looking for are unlikely to occur.

The Accountability Conversation has (3) parts:

1. Clarify Expectations

2. Confirm Roles and Resources

3. Secure Mutually Understood and Agreed-Upon Deliverables

1. Clarify Expectations

Clarifying expectations means that you take the time to both explore and understand exactly what is being asked of you. There's a difference between being asked to create a report, a presentation, a full analysis, or to provide a simple top-line answer. Be sure you have clarity from the other person regarding what they are looking for and confirm that you fully comprehend their expectations. *Be patient and ask questions!* Don't allow yourself to get anxious, especially if a senior leader is asking you to do something and you feel that you just need to take down the order and go execute!

This is also the time to probe to see if there is flexibility on the scope or timing of the work being requested. There could be a significant difference between what is actually needed compared to what is seemingly wanted. You don't want to take on more than is necessary with a tighter timeline than is feasible. You can also help the individual understand the time and resource requirements that may be associated with the need or want options so they also consciously understand what they are requesting.

2. Confirm Roles and Resources

Confirming your specific role in the request (i.e., as owner or contributor) as well as confirming the availability of the necessary resources for completing your assignment must occur before you accept accountability.

You must confirm that colleagues, for example, have been informed of their participation commitment and actually have the necessary bandwidth to engage with you in the time period required for you to meet your requested deadline.

If your ability to deliver is tied to the resource availability of others, this must be firmly negotiated and confirmed, not just quickly glossed over, so take the time to rigor your role and resources!

3. Secure Mutually Understood and Agreed-upon Deliverables

Securing mutually understood agreements on the deliverables (who does what by when) ensures final *clarity and closure* on the negotiation. With these elements in place, accountability can both be given and received; you now have a locked-in commitment for which accountability can be held.

The Accountability Conversation provides a simple tool and structure for ensuring that your leadership voice is heard, effective, and transparent in terms of either taking or giving accountability. **Rigor it** with negotiated accountability!

"The manager accepts the status quo; the leader challenges it."
— Warren G. Bennis

IV. How to Become a Trusted Advisor

Over the course of your leadership career, you will be involved with innumerable relationships. One important and unique relationship that is directly correlated to the masterful cultivation of both your leadership presence and voice is that of the "trusted advisor."

We all have trusted advisors in our lives. These are unique individuals, often external to our organizations, who know us well, have good judgment about business and people, and are worldly in their views. We listen to these voices, and they have the personal power to influence us.

Becoming a trusted advisor is the end result of building a successful long-term relationship. The cost of entry for consideration of the role often includes credible as well as diversified experiences. You

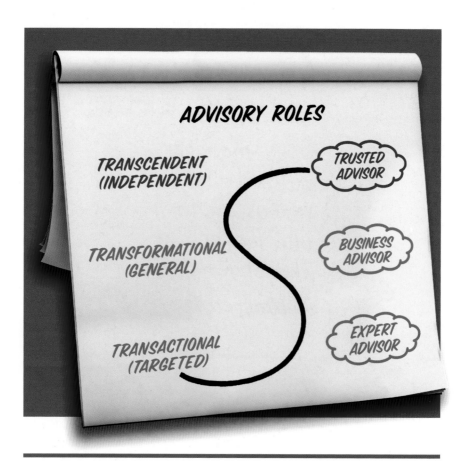

also must have an established independent leadership voice. Finally, your demonstrated ability to manage the dynamics of the relationship must be able to withstand the challenges of business, life, and time.

Being a trusted advisor is *often an "unspoken" role* you cannot apply for but rather are selected for discreetly and without fanfare. You might even act as a trusted advisor unconsciously for a long while before realizing or naming it. Remember, **Leadership Rigor** is about giving you language, frameworks, and structures so you can consciously create your leadership practice.

The role of the trusted advisor is one very few leaders get to play, and if they do, they must consciously honor the rules of engagement that come with it. Let's take a look at some of the important traits of the trusted advisor to gain insight into how to build toward this unique relationship role as a leader.

Credible Experiences That Are Broad and Diversified

Trusted advisors have amassed credible and diversified experiences over a long career trajectory. Thanks to their emotional intelligence, they have learned not to react impulsively or to become easily triggered. They have a grounded approach toward facing life's challenges.

"Credible experiences" implies having had ownership and accountability for delivering performance as opposed to merely being an observer to a process. "Broad and diversified experiences" speaks to the scope of exposure to challenges and opportunities.

If your experiences are long and deep in only one environment, you may be perceived as "siloed" or "something-centric." If you aspire to lead at the organizational level, one of your early challenges is to ensure that you are moving across experiences and diversifying your exposure. If you don't, you are by default potentially selecting or limiting yourself to functional leadership or subject matter expertise roles. Even if your chosen profession is expert focused, such as the law, ensure that you are not stymied by one type of practice or specialty by seeking experiences that broadly widen your lens of exposure.

An Independent Leadership Voice

Trusted advisors have an independent leadership voice and are able to comfortably demonstrate both *gravitas* and *veritas.* They speak with weight and authority, and what they say lands with relevance and resonance. They are viewed as experts, respected voices that express knowledgeable insights from experience, rather than someone politically angling for an advantage. They are not afraid to name "the pink elephant" in the room, go after the sacred cows, or let the emperor know he or she isn't wearing any clothes. They courageously bring forward either the risk or the opportunity side of an equation so that a fair balance exists and a proper assessment can be made.

They have the credibility to influence!

119

The Role of the Devil's Advocate

What's the difference between being a devil's advocate and a trusted advisor speaking with **veritas**?

First, there is a difference between taking a devil's advocate position and being a devil's advocate personality. Those who have a *devil's advocate personality* often mean well but can come across as being self-indulgent and provocative because they constantly challenge others with a contrarian view in order to show how smart they are.

Taking a *devil's advocate position*, on the other hand, means raising a legitimate concern or flagging a potential risk in a world of optimists for the purpose of offering full transparency and fair debate.

Devil's advocates may or may not have the status of trusted advisors. Even if they do, there is still a difference. A trusted advisor speaking with **veritas** integrates the challenges and risks into a broader context and "pressure tests the range of options to consider." There is a credible balance to the approach here, whereas the devil's *"advocate"* by definition takes the extreme position to fully argue against the alternative point or position.

The devil's advocate position, which is always important to hear and consider, is by nature polarizing. It is a risky play for those whose personality is hardwired to always see the negative or the downside of a situation. When these personalities choose to consistently indulge in also playing the role of devil's advocate, their insights are often dismissed. This is unfortunate, because as leaders we need to hear these points of view. It is sometimes better to ask for different participants to randomly represent the devil's advocate position and see where that takes the discussion in terms of appropriately raising the critical issues to ensure they are heard without untoward bias.

Trusted advisors, in addition to being balanced, are not attached to being right or being liked. They offer an objective lens to look through and are a *"safe truth teller" with no personal agenda.* They may speak with emotional overtones to occasionally make a point, but they stay consciously balanced, knowing that the ultimate decision always rests with the other person. Trusted advisors are highly skilled at using their emotional intelligence and personal power.

Because of their independent leadership voice, trusted advisors display quiet confidence and intestinal fortitude. They are not influenced by external accolades that bloat their self-esteem; they simply seek to be there when needed as a resource. Their role may be to listen, ask questions, or tell you what they are hearing. Accordingly, they are relied upon for their acumen (judgment or perspective) and as an aide to the decision-making process.

Trusted advisors are *"outside insiders"* who are able to draw out and if necessary co-create options, although the choices always remain out of their hands and they stay unattached to the outcomes.

What is the difference between a trusted advisor, a coach, a mentor, a sponsor, a friend, or an outside expert advisor?

A trusted advisor is someone you consciously select into your inner circle and rely on to be there when you feel you need to make an important decision or take a position on an issue that can have broad consequences. Perhaps you have a sense of the direction you want to head in and simply want to bounce it around and pressure test it with someone you trust who can speak to you objectively and not just tell you what you want to hear.

Trusted advisors are dispassionately objective. They remain trusted advisors as long as they continue to demonstrate that they can keep self-interest off the table and remain unattached to outcomes.

In short, the difference between those other roles and a trusted advisor is how they play it!

Solid Relationships Withstand Challenges and Time

Like all relationships, the trusted advisor role can have ups and downs. Sometimes you are going to have to deliver an unpopular message, take a difficult stand, perhaps even get passionate about something and then quickly return to your dispassionate objectivity so that an emotionally balanced decision is made.

Nonetheless, the trusted advisor relationship stands the tests and challenges of time. Both good and bad things happen in business and in life. Despite our best efforts, mistakes are made and judgments are sometimes off. What is most important is that the recovery time for a trusted advisor relationship is quick, and whatever needs to be said is put on the table.

The air needs to always be clear with trusted advisors. If it isn't, they cannot do their work. Extreme trust and confidence must always and ultimately prevail in trusted advisor relationships.

Leading yourself is the first step in a continuous journey that is filled with challenges and opportunities for reaching your full potential as a leader. Having the right mindset on what leadership is about today is important to ensure that you are consciously choosing to engage in this journey with your eyes and heart open. Leadership absolutely can be learned. It is also emotional, and it is in service to others!

Move Early and Often to Diversify Your Experiences

As a young high potential in the corporate world, I saw the opportunity in consistently diversifying my experiences, but I was jealous of those who stayed in a role for (3) to (5) years and developed deep expertise. I was tapped early and often to move and round out my experiences, and now I don't regret it. Deep expertise is the right road for some, but clearly assess whether you want to lead at the organizational level and if you desire to later sit on boards or associations where your diversified experiences will be instrumental. Many of the colleagues I was jealous of ended up within a small radius of where they began. I had a whirlwind tour of diversified experiences with large organizations and with smaller divisions all by the time I was (40) years old.

Today, this experience sets my leadership coaching practice apart. I have worked with large and small companies in strategic and operational roles locally, regionally, and globally. Having been an executive team member of a large global business as well as a GM for multiple operational divisions extensively prepared me to be the trusted advisor I am today to CEOs, corporate executives, and business owners.

In developing yourself as a leader, unless you are sure that you want to be a specialized practitioner, take the opportunity to diversify your experiences early and often.

Understanding that leadership is a skilled profession that you need to develop a disciplined practice of confirms your commitment to pursuing your own self-mastery. Putting forth your leadership voice in service of facilitating progress is a start to advancing toward your next leadership role, the team leader.

Before we embrace that challenge, I want to introduce **The Progressive Mindset,** the first signature model in *Leadership Rigor*. Now that the fundamentals are in place for leading yourself, it's time to focus on getting your voice ready to design and deliver messages that can positively impact the forward momentum of your team and organization.

"Once you've found your own voice, the choice to expand your influence, to increase your contribution, is the choice to inspire others to find their voice."
– Stephen Covey

"Simplicity is the ultimate sophistication."
– Leonardo da Vinci

THE *SIGNATURE* MODEL:
The Progressive Mindset

The first signature model presented in *Leadership Rigor* is **The Progressive Mindset**. This simple yet versatile leadership communication tool with its elegant S-curve design can be used for mapping out the framework of a future vision, clarifying the stages of progress on a journey, or outlining phases for a change initiative.

With the fundamentals of leading yourself freshly planted in your mind, you now appreciate the importance of the (2) currencies of leadership—communication and relationships—as well as how vital it is to create your leadership voice. **The Progressive Mindset** model provides you with an approach for developing your messages with conscious discipline and for skillfully delivering them with *veritas* and *gravitas* as you continue to build confidence in your leadership presence.

Each of the (3) signature models in *Leadership Rigor* is an enduring practical use tool that can have relevant applications on the ground (OTG) throughout your leadership journey. Each model is introduced within a contextual framework that explains why, what, when, where, and how the model can be used. This is followed by a deeper dive breakdown of the structural elements of the model and finally several sample applications for practical use.

Let's take a look at how **The Progressive Mindset** model can be used to help you rigor almost anything you need to communicate!

125

Macro Business Challenge

If you seriously want to play a leadership role in today's business world, you must learn to master the leadership currency of communication. This comprehensive set of skills is mandatory for being able to appropriately create and effectively engage in the experiences required of leaders. If you are skilled at communicating, your possibilities in the world of leadership are endless.

The clarity of your expressed communication represents the clarity of your internal thoughts and feelings. Whether you are a natural communicator (unconsciously competent) or a struggling communicator (consciously incompetent), elevating your skills to the level of conscious competency is a critical step on your leadership development journey. The expectations for performance escalate quite dramatically in this currency skill set, as you will see throughout your *Leadership Rigor* journey.

Establishing yourself as a leader requires that you communicate with credibility and conviction. Early in your leadership development, you will mainly need to clearly frame the expression of your technical knowledge or personal point of view. Later, you will need to express a broader and higher level contextual understanding of the issues at hand in an effort to move individuals and teams forward, influencing them with your personal power.

> *You have already learned that your impact is all that matters as a leader, regardless of your intentions. Therefore, it is critical that your communication is delivered and received in a way that inspires confidence and builds trust. So how do you communicate like a leader?*

Communication has two parts, what you say and how you say it. **The Progressive Mindset** model will help in both areas. First, it will guide you through appropriately preparing to *frame the context* of what you want to express. Second, it will remind you to deliver your messages with directional momentum so the impact you create always has an inspiring *"go forward energy"* as you articulate your expectations, tell a story, or create an ongoing narrative.

Calibrate Your Leadership Altitude and Attitude

Communicating at the right altitude means striking the right balance between being too far removed from the issues or being too low into the weeds and sounding too technical.

You also need to have the right attitude or mindset before communicating. Your behavior comes from your beliefs, and your beliefs come across in your attitude. If you believe it is important to communicate like a leader, this will be demonstrated in how you frame and deliver information. If you don't believe it matters, this too will be made visible to others in how you handle and present yourself as a communicator.

How you show up (your behavior) and *what it is like to be with you (the experience you create)* reflects both your attitudes and your beliefs. You cannot hide this, but you can work to consciously understand and change your attitude if you believe it's limiting your ability to successfully communicate and build relationships.

A Disciplined Approach to Preparation

Take a moment to honestly reflect on your own behavior with the following question: before you enter a meeting, do you give conscious thought to the potential dynamics, the participating players, and the point of view you want to express on the topic being discussed, or do you casually enter the meeting and observe how things unfold, leaving to chance if or how you will engage?

Unfortunately, more often than not, the latter is how most leaders operate. They typically believe they can extemporaneously participate as necessary and seldom prepare beyond reading the obligatory pre-work material that may or may not be sent out in advance. It is important to acknowledge that if you enter a meeting with an unconscious mindset, you are not fully prepared to actively influence the room as a consciously competent leader.

A consciously disciplined approach to your communication preparation includes considering the audience you are engaging with (both their emotional and technical orientation) and the subject you are engaging on (your personal point of view regarding whether you are an active supporter, a reluctant supporter, opposed, or neutral) as well as thoughtful contemplation of the following questions:

- *Where were you* on this issue the last time it was discussed (why is it important now and what has recently changed)?

- *Where are you now* with the choices at hand (which do you favor or have concerns about and why)?

- *Where do you suggest "considering" going next* (keeping in mind the current conditions, risks, and opportunities)?

The crux of using **The Progressive Mindset** model for disciplined preparation is asking a series of questions framed around where you were, where you are now, and where you are going. Answering these questions provides you with the up-front context to engage in a productive discussion with a clear initial point of view as well as potential action steps to consider. Just keep in mind that the interactive dialogue may also cause you to shift your ultimate perspective and decision, which is always a reasonable in-going expectation as you enter a meeting. ***Rigor it with preparation and be ready to engage!***

YOUR PREPARATION

CHOICE OR CHANCE?

Message Clarity with Forward Momentum

Drafting out your perspective ahead of time using the S-curve framework allows you to be clear on the points you want to make during the discussion as well as where you may see the initiative going next based on your preliminary assessment.

You can also use the model to easily *make relevant notes and comments* of agreement or disagreement in the areas you have outlined as the conversation takes an iterative and circuitous course toward alignment and resolution.

Always remember that if you are going to influence others through the use your personal power, you must also be open to being influenced by them. Regardless of the outcome, what is most important is that through the dialogue you create alignment, clarity, and closure on where you are collectively going from here as you continue to create forward momentum on the topic.

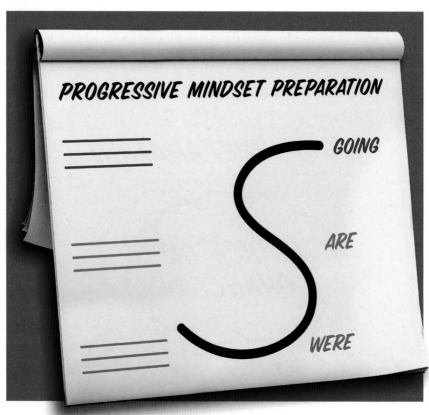

A Storytelling Context for Influencing and Inspiring

How you communicate using the framework of **The Progressive Mindset** model can be the difference between simply listing your message points or delivering an inspiring and integrated message that resonates with your audience. In going for the latter choice, consider delivering your messages in a storytelling format as illustrated below:

As I reflected in preparation for today's meeting, I was reminded that it was only (6) months ago that we decided to change our technology platform. We knew it could no longer take us where we needed to go with our customers and our internal needs, so we did the right thing in getting proposals on the table for change [where we were].

We are now facing the hard choices. We are looking at an expensive project and a significant investment of our resources (people, time, and money), and we are all concerned about whether we can pull it off successfully. I too am worried that I won't have the personal bandwidth to complete all the projects we are currently committed to if we go forward with this initiative [where we are now].

We can either move ahead or we can delay this project short term, knowing that at some point the pain cannot be avoided and we will need to make a change. Whether that is today or (3) to (6) months from now, we can debate. That being said, I am committed to doing what it takes to make this work and will offer whatever resources I can to assist. I feel the risk of stopping now will be more of an emotional setback than the challenge of managing our concerns and frustrations for getting over the work-flow hurdles. One suggestion I have is revisiting our priorities and restaging them so that we can create time and space for getting the technology up and running if we go forward [where we are going].

How The Progressive Mindset Model Provides Clarity

By breaking big issues into discreet pieces, **The Progressive Mindset** model can provide greater clarity. When one of my CEO clients was uncertain about a candidate's broader leadership capabilities beyond his project-based technical expertise and wanted to further assess this individual's qualifications, I coached him to engage the potential employee in an exercise and mapped out **The Progressive Mindset** model using projects, processes, and people.

The challenge was to see if the candidate could identify the priority projects and required process changes as well as preliminary thoughts on the critical people initiatives he would

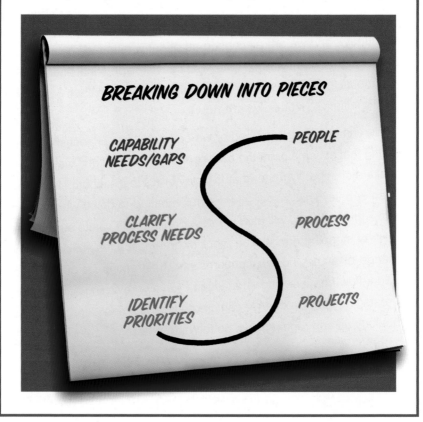

need to address to build bench strength and capabilities in a broader functional leadership role. His response would reveal his perspective and philosophy toward prioritization and resource allocation (people, time, and money), and therefore what altitude he would perceive himself working at in this expanded role.

If the candidate came back with a thoughtful approach, the CEO could have confidence in his broader leadership capabilities. If he lacked a clear and thoughtful response, the exercise could serve as an opportunity for further dialogue, coaching, or as a confirmed reason to pass on hiring him.

The Progressive Mindset model offers leaders a framework on how to ask better contextually staged questions so they can gain greater clarity on how people think issues through and communicate their approach.

"Of all of our inventions for mass communication, pictures still speak the most universally understood language."
— Walt Disney

Why The Progressive Mindset Model Was Created

I have personally been using **The Progressive Mindset** model instinctively ever since I can remember and certainly for my (25) years in business. Becoming consciously competent at using this tool for leadership communication, however, started in Canada for me.

When I was (35)-years old, I was asked to lead the turnaround of Bayer Healthcare's consumer care division in Toronto. This was my first general management assignment, complete with full P&L accountability and responsibility for all functional areas.

The division's performance had been disappointing, as it had missed its budget targets for each of the last (5) years. A history of overpromising and under delivering prevailed, mostly due to a lack of understanding the dynamics of a consumer packaged goods business. In addition, the country itself was complex, with multiple provinces, each having unique governing authorities, (2) mandatory languages, a hybrid regulatory environment (a cross between North America and Europe), and an authoritative versus collaborative customer base, all of which made business agility challenging and mistakes difficult to recover from.

> *The division needed to understand where it had gone wrong, where it was now, and what it was going to take to turn things around for the long run. It needed to create a new story for success.*

As the new GM and *"communicator in chief,"* I knew it was my role to create the story for our future. A marketer at heart, it occurred to me that *branding our adventure* would be a way to create some excitement around it, so I named the first year of our business challenge together *"Turnaround 2000."* I took every opportunity I had to *show and tell* the story of Turnaround 2000 in terms of where we had been, where we were now, and where we were going. **The Progressive Mindset** model was consciously born!

The approach was successful in getting everyone aligned and focused on the sequential stages required for our turnaround in performance. It was both pragmatic and inspiring because it framed our journey together with a grounded understanding of our current state, the next stages we needed to address, and where we ultimately wanted to land together. We used the language consistently, and we always knew where we were and where we were going on our journey.

We achieved Turnaround 2000, and in each of the (4) years that followed, I continued to use **The Progressive Mindset** model to set the stage for performance and productivity. I also continued to name subsequent years with emotional themes such as Stretch 2001, Momentum 2002, and so on.

Each year, we tackled new challenges and growth targets *managed to the cadence and rhythm* of where we had been, where we were now, and where we were going next. The division completed a full turnaround, and together we enjoyed (5) years of success in consistently achieving our budgets, establishing operational excellence throughout the organization, and building a bench of competent and confident executives to take the division to its next levels of growth in the Canadian marketplace.

Why You Need The Progressive Mindset Model

As an aspiring leader, you are becoming an agent of change within your organization. **The Progressive Mindset** model serves as a *conscious road map* for creating your communication messages and staging the journey you are about to begin. It also provides a powerful framework for developing the story or narrative of how progress will unfold around your collective experience.

Each stage of **The Progressive Mindset** model has an emotional energy associated with it. Things will look, sound, and feel different as you move through the change or staging process. Some things you will be able to anticipate, name, and prepare for as a leader, while others will need to be dealt with in real time as they unfold.

Remember that leadership is emotional. Using **The Progressive Mindset** model to highlight the emotional cycles (both positive and

Framing the Stages of the Leadership Team Journey

In my coaching practice, when setting the stage for an intact team leadership journey, I use **The Progressive Mindset** model to illustrate that teams come together initially as independent individuals who grow and develop by learning how to collaborate and work interdependently. The ultimate target for a high-performance team, of course, is to work together on initiatives with an integrated "we-based" approach at the appropriate altitude.

As shown below, by *simply selecting (3) words* that describe the forward momentum being targeted, you can set the stage for the development process and the story of the journey.

negative) your team members will collectively experience as changes take place will help people accept them more readily because they were anticipated and expected.

The Benefits of Using The Progressive Mindset Model

The most significant benefit of **The Progressive Mindset** model is that it offers a structural reminder to simplify and clarify your communication objectives.

> *Scientific research reveals that the brain has an ability to remember (3) things. Accordingly, the model utilizes a (3)-step approach in an effort to be both impactful and memorable.*

Using the model's S-curve visual can serve as a continuous reference point as your project or journey unfolds. Reminding everyone "where we are" in each of the stages can provide credibility to the leader and comfort for the travelers on the journey. It provides the mental road map for where you are going together.

Aligning Expectations and Experiences

As a leader, you need to set the expectations for the experiences you will create with your team or colleagues. This can be as simple as explaining the type of meeting you will conduct in the next hour or as visionary as introducing the type of journey you will embark on over the next year. When you set expectations, you set intentions for the experiences that will now unfold. When the experiences match or exceed the expectations, people feel good. When they don't, people feel frustrated or disappointed. As a leader, you always want to align the expectations with the experiences (intention and impact). When you don't specifically articulate expectations, they are in fact still set, just not consciously or by you. Individuals will create their own expectations, and you as a leader will either randomly hit or miss them.

Choose to be consciously competent, set expectations, and deliver on the experiences. **Rigor it!**

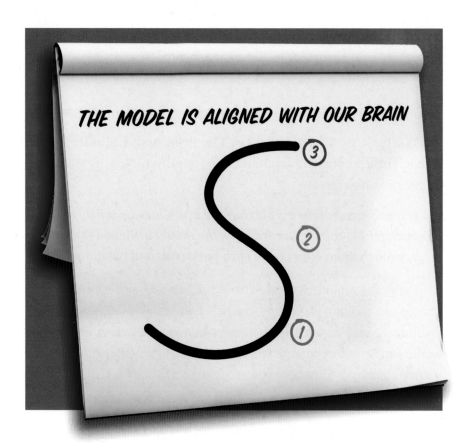

Using **The Progressive Mindset** model is also a way to stay present in where you last left each other with the various conversations you are having and where you are now. As a leader, remember to avoid lunging into the middle of a conversation with specific content without setting the context first. The consequence of doing this is that you leave an impression of not being strong in the critical leadership currency of communication. Using **The Progressive Mindset** model to ground, structure, and guide your communication will give you the altitude you need and will be appreciated by your audience, especially if they are senior leaders.

What Type of Tool Is The Progressive Mindset Model?

The Progressive Mindset Model is both a mental compass and a literal road map leaders can use to lay out a communication plan for a journey or way forward.

For example, when teams are running efficient (1)-hour meetings yet feel they are stuck at a low altitude because they are only information sharing in an effort to keep the team leader up to date, **The Progressive Mindset** model can be mapped out as a reminder for getting to productivity, which is a higher level meeting experience.

While *being efficient* feels good to the time-sensitive leader, an exclusive focus on the clock without full attention to the quality of the issues being discussed will have you quickly getting nothing done or, worse, getting the wrong things done. *Being effective* means selecting appropriate topics and being appropriately generous about the time required to discuss them to secure insights. *Being productive* involves investing appropriate amounts of time with the right people on the right issues while confirming meaningful progress with clarity and closure on go-forward agreements and outcomes.

What Skills Does the Model Develop?

Multiple leadership skills can be practiced and further developed through the use of **The Progressive Mindset** model. One application involves using it to demonstrate the diversity of your leadership styles, as several naturally lend themselves to the forward-moving and staging applications of the model.

The model also serves as an effective tool for calibrating your altitude on an issue by anchoring you in the required details or taking you up a level into the bigger-picture implications.

Leadership Style Applications

The Progressive Mindset model can be used with all the leadership styles that were briefly covered in Part 1 (and are further developed in Part 2). Here are a few examples.

When you sit down with a supervisor or colleague to discuss how you want to engage on a project together, you can use **The Progressive Mindset** Model to clarify your choice and approach. For example, if you are *directing* an individual on a task, you can map it out in (3)phases to make it easier to understand the learning required at each step in the process.

If you are *coaching* an individual, you may suggest that you check in with each other at (3) different milestone points along the project's continuum where you can align on whether there are information gaps or questions that need addressing so you as the supervisor can feel comfortable that both the individual and the project are on track.

If you are *empowering* a direct report, you may use the model to map out the expectations, define the ultimate accountability for the project outcome, and agree on how you will touch base during the performance phase of the project. Your direct report is best positioned to drive this process, given that the empowerment style of leadership is intended to give more room to the individual for independent ownership.

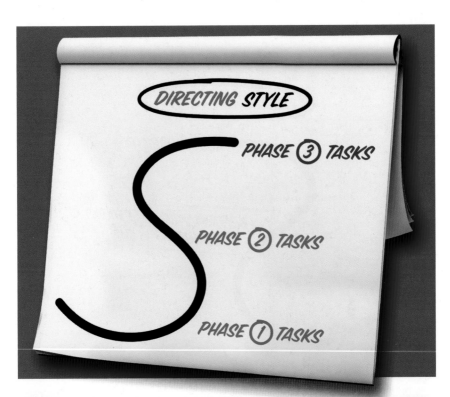

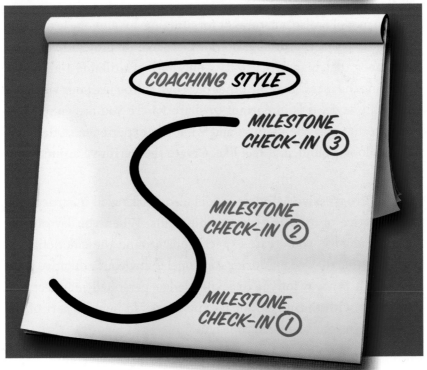

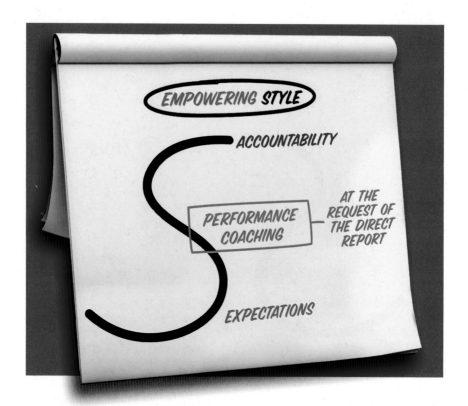

The model is also a natural fit for utilizing a *visionary* leadership style to map out the progression of a change or project over time. Remember that mapping it out is one part of utilizing the model; delivering the message is the other part. When you use your visionary leadership style, it is important to share where you are going; how everyone fits into the picture; and what the experience of the journey will look, sound, and feel like. Create the narrative around your vision!

The Progressive Mindset model also works well in structuring your practice of *affiliative* leadership skills. When you lay out the stages of change, you create expectations around the emotional experiences that may occur during each one. Using your affiliative leadership style is a way for you to acknowledge, personally connect, and empathize with those emotional experiences in being a part of the process with your team and colleagues.

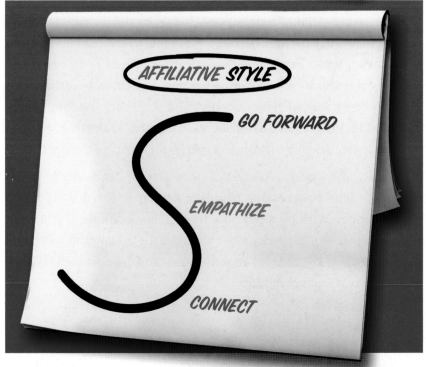

The nature of **The Progressive Mindset** model is that it is always moving forward. This allows you to avoid one of the common pitfalls of affiliative leadership I mentioned earlier, which is an emotional downward spiral in which you get trapped in the "collective complaining, negativity, or heavy energy" and stay stuck too long where you are. **The Progressive Mindset** and affiliative leadership style can be used synergistically to *"connect and go forward"* to the next stage.

Finally, the leadership style of *pace-setting* can easily be practiced with **The Progressive Mindset** model, as it naturally sets a plan in motion with targeted time frames. For example, if you want to embrace a change management initiative in (18) months, you could highlight (6)-, (12)-, and (18)-month targets and expectations for each phase on your S-curve model.

Altitude Calibration Applications for Your Hardwiring

The Progressive Mindset model is an effective tool for calibrating your altitude and appropriately framing your communication based on your hardwiring. As an MBTI intuitive (N) big-picture thinker, it is easy for me to map out patterns at (30,000) feet and create a vision of where I see things going. **The Progressive Mindset** model helps frame my macro-conceptual thinking. I can then take each of the (3) big-picture macro areas and *break them down* into (3) smaller pieces that get closer to the ground with more details, satisfying the information needs of MBTI sensors (S) who want more of the practical specifics on what all of this means.

Of course, the reverse application can be used for the MBTI sensors (S) who have specific details to integrate within their communications. These individuals can use the model to assist them in *aggregating* their detailed information into bigger picture goals within a collective "bucket" that the intuitives (N) can get comfortable with.

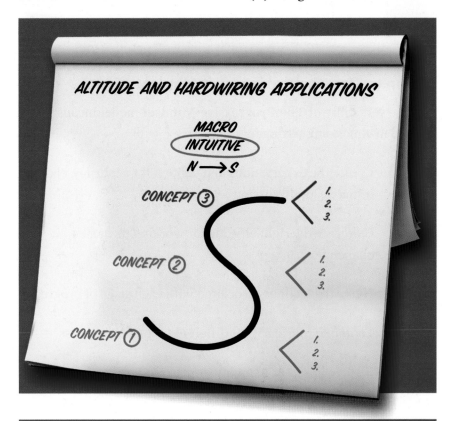

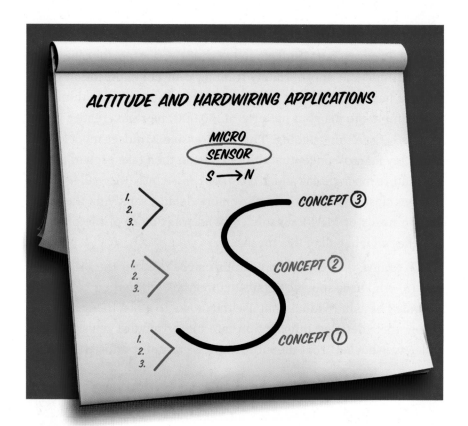

When to Use The Progressive Mindset Model

The versatility of **The Progressive Mindset** model means it can be used in almost any setting to:

- ☑ *Create* the expectations and context for a journey, change initiative, or discussion

- ☑ *Calibrate* the right altitude for working through a challenge

- ☑ *Name* the feelings associated with each stage of progress

- ☑ *Establish* role clarity at different points in a process

- ☑ *Engage* in career planning or progression discussions

> *Consider using this signature model whenever you want to ensure that you have a communication road map for conversations on how something will unfold, progress, or change over time.*

Where to Use The Progressive Mindset Model

The Progressive Mindset model can be used in multiple forums, including one-to-ones, team meetings, workshops, and town hall gatherings. Whether a pre-formed road map or a spontaneous application in real time, the model can be used to simplify, clarify, or codify a message or a path forward.

In my coaching practice, I use the model as I listen to the challenges and initiatives my clients face and play back what I hear, capturing it in an easy-to-understand **Progressive Mindset** framework. My clients are often amazed at how I quickly structure and frame communication, but there is no magic, just a consciously disciplined use of the model so that it appears effortless. Create your own communication magic and rigor it with **The Progressive Mindset**!

"You don't lead by pointing and telling people some place to go. You lead by going to that place and making a case."

— Ken Kesey

Using The Progressive Mindset Model: A Deeper Dive

Now that you have an understanding of the (3) phases that underpin the model (where you were, where you are now, and where you are going), let's dive into the **practical considerations** associated with the model and the **emotional feelings** at each stage.

Level 1: The Struggle—The Bevel

Imagine being told that you are a strong performer in your technical area of expertise but that you have not yet demonstrated the leadership skills for advancing to the next level in your career.

If you choose to embrace this feedback, you are at the start of the conscious change process. You recognize that there is learning and development that needs to take place for you to get to where you want to be in the next phase of your career. You might intellectually and emotionally understand that this will be challenging, yet depending on your personal hardwiring, you might either have initial optimism or anxiety and fear about what lies ahead.

As you learn more about your particular challenge and clarify the magnitude of the change you are undertaking, you start to see that this process is going to be harder than you thought. Your exposure to the leadership concepts suggests this is a whole different language and will require significant work. What you thought would take a few days will in fact require a great deal of time, energy, and effort. What will you do? Slowly struggle to move forward or simply give up?

If you give up, you are likely pigeonholing your career into an individual contributor role. If this is the right fit for you, full speed ahead. Just be aware that this is a game- and career-changing decision.

Or perhaps the struggle is worth a try; maybe you can power through in a shorter time period with focus and determination. After all, your technical skills are great, so with effort here on the leadership front, it might just be enough to get you through the next level!

Not surprisingly, you begin to look for quick, high-visibility wins as well as efficient shortcuts to demonstrate that change has occurred and you have magically already grown into a leader.

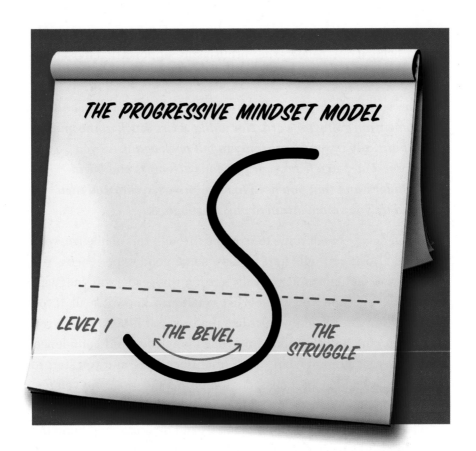

THE PROGRESSIVE MINDSET MODEL

LEVEL 1

THE BEVEL

THE STRUGGLE

> *Unfortunately, these attempts are often short-lived staged events rather than longer-term solutions that address the root causes and fundamental skill building and behavioral changes that need to take place. And those who are coaching you and overseeing your development actually know this!*

As your efforts fail to provide you with the fast results and recognition you seek, you take an emotional dip down further from where you initially started. *The bevel has hit!* The painful fact is that true change and growth do not happen until you are at the bottom. The bevel represents that bottom curve you rock back and forth along as you work through fully accepting the challenge of what moving ahead requires, rather than the delusional surface approach or shortcuts.

You soon learn that giving this lip service along the lines of "Yeah, let's go; bring it on!" reflects the enthusiastic euphoria that most leaders face before reality sets in.

> *The reality, the bevel, is the struggle to achieve traction and momentum going forward. Not unlike a tire stuck in the mud, you initially try and push, only to fall back again. As you engage, you learn from your previous attempts and begin to understand that you need to rock into a rhythm and then build up your momentum to push through.*

If you decide to continue to struggle through this challenge, with time and effort, you will start to have some good experiences. You will begin to feel like you are really getting this leadership language down and then, *bam!*, you will feel like you hardly know it at all. If you do "know it," you certainly don't feel ready to put it OTG yet, so you play it safe and and keep building your knowledge and confidence. A few low-risk attempts with some small successes, and you start to feel better. A bad day or a missed attempt in a meeting, and you feel deflated and believe this leadership work is going nowhere.

The bevel is a place of emotional ups and downs as you build the critical mass of knowledge and readiness to break through consistently to another level. Sheer willpower can propel you to a degree, but you will continue to make only limited progress and have recurring dips until you start to change the way you are doing things and how you are fundamentally showing up and being perceived as a leader. It is time to accept the fact that you can't just act your way through this leadership challenge. Remember, leadership is a skilled profession and a being state!

Getting out of the bevel is hard. You have to stop resisting and acknowledge that this is a process you will need to embrace and work at over time. Once you emotionally accept who and where you are, you can consciously choose to move forward with sincere effort to start achieving traction and momentum.

Nonetheless, depending on your *resistance levels*, you may go through multiple dip cycles. When your desire to really power through is greater than your frustration at your setbacks, you are ready to start taking the hill. Remember that where you were was not where you wanted to be. With *conscious discipline* and *practice* of your self-awareness and self-management, you can now start to really move forward.

Emotional Challenge—Rallying Together!

The S-curve emotional challenge is extremely prevalent in the leadership team journeys I create. The bevel of working through forming/storming together is a frustrating time for teams before traction occurs. Learning to work together and trust each other forms the basis of the traction/momentum phases. The ability to engage in productive conflict without fear of hurting each other's feelings, grudges forming, or potential mean-spirited retribution is all part of working through the bevel and the dips. When the team members finally realize their old reality will not change without significant effort, they rally together and pull in the same direction toward norming/performing because they want to get to a new place and reestablish comfort and confidence. At this point, they take the hill together!

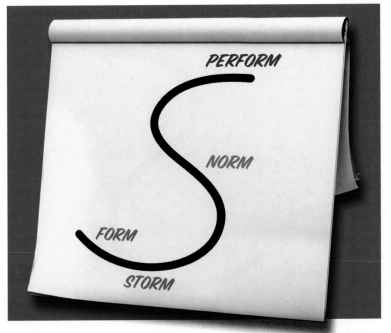

Level 2: Taking the Hill—The Inflection

The second stage is where you have truly made the commitment to change and are working to take the hill and *climb through the discomfort* to make tangible adjustments and visible progress. You now fully understand the challenge and know it will be *frustrating and hard,* but you also know that the only way out is through it!

> *You also have come to realize that the change you must make is more than superficial. Fundamental shifts in how you show up, engage, move, and work through this phase of the change process must occur.*

Emotionally, you are turned around, out of balance, out of your comfort zone, and feeling vulnerable because you are not yet confident in what you are doing and how you are doing it. *It feels like ev-*

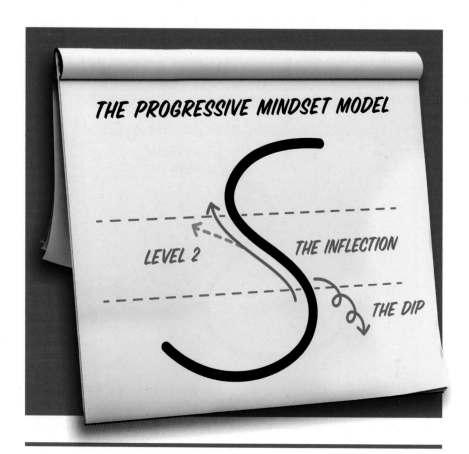

THE PROGRESSIVE MINDSET MODEL

LEVEL 2

THE INFLECTION

THE DIP

erything is a challenge; it's all too slow and too hard. It takes both mental and physical strength to accept that you are consciously incompetent as you work on your growth opportunities at this stage of the journey. Some days, you just want to give up!

When another dip sets in, your old patterns emerge and you go back to being unconsciously incompetent. At first, you don't care, but when additional feedback from your supervisor reminds you that you have slipped back into your old behaviors, frustration consumes you. You need to start all over again, and you feel like you have been belly punched!

The good news is that you don't actually have to start all over again because the process is circulinear. You are still progressing; you are just experiencing another frustrating dip along the continuum forward!

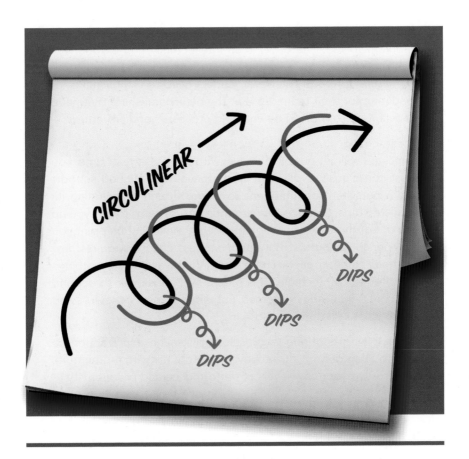

The inflection is a *subtle but significant change in the curve.* It is not more of the same, it symbolizes a new and different approach as the way forward. A genuine shift, a "breakthrough" in perspectives, philosophies, and interactions, is what allows the inflection to occur. With this new understanding and flow, you find that putting your new skills OTG and into action is like finally mastering the breathing, the kick, and the turn of the butterfly stroke. In short, it feels great!

Stuck in the Bevel—Organizational Change Initiatives

Organizational change initiatives, whether they are structural or process oriented, will be challenged to get out of the bevel if they do not have clearly defined goals with disciplined leadership and role clarity to drive them forward. Change is hard, and it happens in systems. This means that changes have upstream and downstream effects as well as emotional impacts on the people involved. The bevel is an intellectually and emotionally challenging place to be under any circumstances. To overcome the natural forces of the bevel, leaders need to establish a clear road map for their teams so that the behavioral shifts that need to occur are supported by enabling processes and structures.

These changes will not happen easily or passively. Don't assume you will get out of the bevel with the passage of time; you must consciously evolve out of the bevel with aligned support and a persistent commitment to work through it, including its expected dips. Creating forward momentum helps to get you up and out of the bevel, but remember that the inflection point you experience during a structural or process change requires new methods to be applied. These alternative ways of doing things are often uncomfortable. This means you are slower to act and less confident in the outcomes, but, after all, new behaviors and approaches take time to settle in.

Rigor it with continuous conscious discipline and traction so that you can get out of the bevel, take the hill with momentum, and crest to your new levels of performance and productivity.

Unfortunately, not everyone will make it out of the bevel and through the inflection as leaders. Those who are able to realize their potential will pursue and find the shifts they need to make in themselves and learn to practice them to gain proficiency, but others will plateau and never get there.

On an individual basis, this may mean taking your career only so far and not being able to advance into larger leadership roles.

In a team setting, you may have players who will potentially hold the team back and who will either need to self-select out or be asked to leave if they cannot work through the inflection changes with the team to ultimately reach the next stage, the crest.

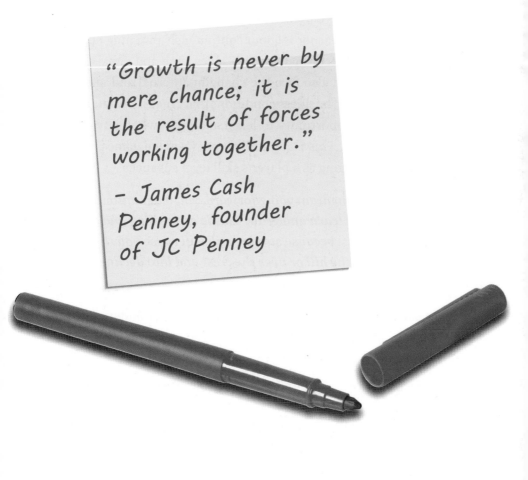

"Growth is never by mere chance; it is the result of forces working together."

– James Cash Penney, founder of JC Penney

Level 3: The Next Level Entry Point—The Crest

Having consciously navigated through the inflection, you are energized and motivated to reach that feeling of control again, that place where your confidence in your own capabilities is strong. You can see and almost touch the crest!

As you use your leadership skills in real time and continue to get exposure to others who are more advanced, you start to appreciate that there is still so much more to learn. While you thought you had it pretty well down, there are parts you did not anticipate and obstacles you did not initially see. Slowly but surely, you realize this is never going to end! Yes, that is true! Learning and growth are continual; there will always be another level to take on and embrace.

In the leadership development area, whether as an individual or a team, being a lifetime learner is about continuously pursuing personal mastery and high performance. This takes time and consistently applied effort. You will also face the changing internal and external dynamics of people and business conditions that create new challenges. There is always opportunity to learn and grow when advancing your leadership skills. This is not unlike today's video games, which become more challenging as a player's skill level advances.

> *To keep your momentum going forward, you must anticipate "cresting" as you learn and grow. This is an ongoing and necessary process, because staying still will cause you to fall backward down the hill or over the crest and into decline.*

Stay alert as you approach the crest and seek to understand the changes needed to progress to the next level. As you complete several cycles on your journey, you will find your speed increasing, your dips shorter, and your anticipation for the next cycle quicker.

Embrace the crest as the next entry point to increased levels of performance and productivity on your leadership journey as you take a leap of faith to advance to your next level of mastery. **Rigor it** with cresting!

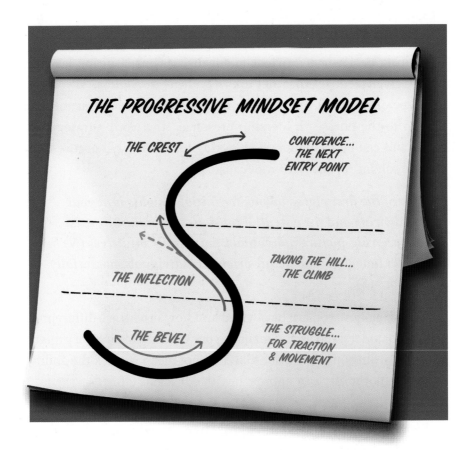

Targeted Applications of The Progressive Mindset

New and emerging leaders face a number of challenges in building their leadership practices, many of which can be addressed with the tools and insights provided in *Leadership Rigor.*

Let's take a look at some of the challenges **The Progressive Mindset** model can specifically assist with. These include:

- Being More Strategic

- Becoming an Inspiring Leader with a Clear Vision

- Developing Presence with Empathy and Compassion

- Creating the All-Important Narrative

Being More Strategic

During performance management discussions, aspiring leaders may be given feedback that they are *"not strategic enough."* If you get this type of feedback, ask for specific examples of what this means. Similar to the phrase "leadership presence," the word "strategy" is vague and can be misunderstood; asking for clarity will ensure that you are solving for the right root cause.

> *One of the first places to look for initial insights is at your hardwiring and the potential tensions that naturally exist between big-picture individuals, potentially intuitives (N) in MBTI language, and detail-oriented individuals, potentially sensors (S).*

Knowing how you are hardwired and how others are different is critical to understand as you manage your career. We all have preferences regarding our styles, but that does not mean we lack the ability to flex to another style or approach with conscious effort.

Many executives, in fact, fail to fully appreciate the needs of their audience when framing information. They wrongly think, for example, that everyone is as interested in the details as they are. Some individuals probably are interested, but many senior-level audiences prefer the big-picture framework and only want to dive down with specific, detailed questions on an as-needed basis.

Understanding this dynamic allows you to use **The Progressive Mindset** model to frame your information into (3) macro areas first while being prepared to get into the details as requested. This macro framing, or synthesizing complex information into conceptual groupings that senior leaders can quickly get their heads around, communicates in headlines and creates a flow or pattern to what you are talking about while giving the impression that you are in command of your material.

Because of its higher altitude versus being in the weeds, this approach gives others the impression that you are operating at a more strategic level. Be mindful, however, that depending on your audience, you may need to have the flexibility to dive deep and fast into specifics in a room full of sensors. Demonstrate that you can flex to both sides of the range as necessary.

Part of projecting that you are a strategic thinker is using the language of strategy. Strategy is about creating competitive advantage, deciding where to play, and confirming how you will win over the competition in the marketplace. **The Progressive Mindset** model can help you frame your strategic considerations along a risk continuum for a particular project, as some decisions will be lower risk with lower rewards compared to higher risk with higher rewards. Understanding the risk, change, and growth aspects of projects and decisions is working at the strategic level.

Speaking to the dynamics of innovation is also the language of strategy. You might use **The Progressive Mindset** model to frame the strategic challenges for the pros and cons of being a *first mover* in the market, a *fast follower*, or a *reactive laggard* as you frame the innovation challenges you face. Mapping it out conceptually allows you to do more detailed work around the implications of each as needed.

In terms of assessing the environmental conditions for your strategic work and identifying your current state of competitiveness, you might use the model to frame what *surviving* in this market looks like versus *driving* for market share or *thriving* in a leadership position.

The Progressive Mindset model provides a way to think through and frame your challenges and opportunities with simplicity, clarity, context, and at an altitude that will create an increased comfort around your abilities to be seen as a higher altitude, strategic thinker.

Becoming an Inspiring Leader with a Clear Vision

As your communication currency builds from merely expressing your technical point of view to passionately advocating for ideas and people, you will increasingly be looked at as a confident leader.

Advancing into expanded leadership roles comes with the expectation that you have a vision, a plan for how to get there, and the competency to deliver. You can use **The Progressive Mindset** model to develop and deliver all (3) of these messages in ways that create clarity and comfort about the future and how everyone will fit into it.

Demonstrating transparency in your thinking, outlining the steps that are involved, and explaining what the outcome will look, sound, and feel like when you accomplish it together help create the conditions of inspiration that will motivate your colleagues to take on the challenges inherent in realizing your vision.

The Progressive Mindset model can assist you in positioning your thoughts and ideas in ways that naturally lend them to being viewed as visionary. Once again, the most simple example is the where you were, where you are, and where you are going approach. This shows a target and forward momentum to get there, which is what you want most in a vision.

You might even choose to use a framework such as, "Yesterday, our focus was here, today we have advanced to this approach, and our longer-term vision is that tomorrow we will be using this new and different approach."

Another example is to describe your organization or department in terms of its phase of operation and how you see it advancing. For example, depending on a variety of factors and goals, perhaps your description of your organization changes from *"service provider"* to *"service advisor"* and ultimately to *"service partner."*

> *Being an inspiring leader requires a message with context, content, and credible delivery.*

You are setting the framework and conditions in which expectations are clear and the emotional evolution of the experiences being created together are outlined. **The Progressive Mindset** model can anchor and guide you so that your messages are delivered and heard!

Developing Presence with Empathy and Compassion

Another example of feedback that emerging leaders often receive is that they need to work on their *"executive presence."* Again, it's a good idea to ask for specific examples first to ensure you are addressing the right concerns.

> *Typically, this feedback is a combination of not expressing self-confidence, not voicing veritas, or not proactively and visibly demonstrating comfort around your use of personal power so that you connect and engage with others.*

You will need to address all these areas as you learn to lead yourself and work to create your leadership mindset, practice, and voice.

Once again, **The Progressive Mindset** model can be used as a structural anchor to ensure that your technical and emotional message preparation on both a macro and micro basis is solid so that you can focus more on your delivery. With increased comfort in the material, *including how others will feel and potentially experience it,* you will project more empathy and compassion, opening yourself up to create greater connectivity with your audience. This positive experience will start to create executive presence because it draws others to you and therefore will naturally increase your self-confidence.

Once established, your confidence will allow you to be more present in the room and to exert more social awareness as you read and adjust to the dynamics. If, for example, you begin to see looks of concern or confusion, you might stop speaking and pause to see if there are questions. This type of command of the room powerfully communicates a sense of your executive presence.

> *Don't dismiss or be intimidated by questions from your audience; invite, acknowledge, and embrace them as entry-point opportunities to meaningfully engage rather than assuming they are a personal assault on your credibility. This common mistake by aspiring leaders ultimately detracts from their leadership presence.*

You will be well served to ensure that **The Progressive Mindset** framework you have mapped out contains both technical and emotional points you want to make about a project's challenges. This will also further connect you with the room (remember, leadership is emotional) and will demonstrate your empathy and compassion associated with the choices and decisions that will be made and how they will affect other people in the organization.

The **Progressive Mindset** model, while not the direct answer to executive presence, is a framework for considering your questions and answers upfront so that your context, content, and delivery of your messages creates the impact you want to have.

Creating the All-Important Narrative

Finally, **The Progressive Mindset** model can be used when creating a narrative. A narrative is more than just a story to express a learning or insight; it has a forward momentum that evolves and changes as it progresses. Like the narrative I created around my Canadian GM experience with Turnaround 2000, this ongoing story of development with an overarching theme has fluid dynamics and shifts throughout the process, which includes bevels, dips, inflections, and crests that lead to new and next levels.

A narrative, which is easy to map out using **The Progressive Mindset** model, keeps the journey you are on front and center. It keeps you focused on delivering consistent messages with the same language and reinforces both the technical and emotional aspects of the process. It also ensures a continuous forward momentum.

Like a story, the narrative has a flow that mirrors a beginning, middle, and end, but it is different in that it is ongoing and continuous, whereas a story often has a clear and defined ending. **The Progressive Mindset** model can help you map this out with the headline words and phrases that will capture your journey throughout the iterative process of its evolution. As you take the hill and crest in one phase of your narrative, as a leader, you must take that next leap of faith and create the next cycle of the ongoing narrative.

By articulating your messages using **The Progressive Mindset** model, you demonstrate clarity in direction and a determination to work at the right altitude. You are not just randomly moving forward. Understanding the dynamics of the bevel, the inflection, and the crest will demonstrate that you are becoming a consciously competent leader.

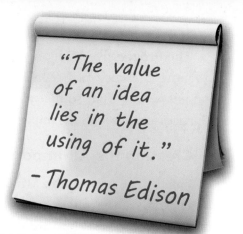

"The value of an idea lies in the using of it."

— Thomas Edison

THE *TENSION* TO RESOLVE:
Crossing the Knowing-Doing Gap

Part 1 of *Leadership Rigor* explored what it takes to have a leadership mindset, create your leadership practice, and develop your leadership voice. The claim was made that if you can't lead yourself, you simply will not be able to lead others. After all, you cannot authentically give what you do not have, and if you are not a credible leader, others will simply not follow you.

Part 1 also focused on the (2) currencies through which leadership operates, the factors that contribute to performance, how mindfully seeking conscious competency is the target goal for leaders, and why personal power trumps all other types of power. A closer look at emotional intelligence revealed insights into how to build relationships, while a quick glance at MBTI personality types offered a baseline perspective on personal hardwiring.

The *signature model* presented in Part 1 was **The Progressive Mindset** model, a versatile communication tool for framing messages, staging a journey, or explaining the phases of a challenge.

You Have Now Arrived at the First Tension ...

Assuming that this material resonates with you and you are genuinely inspired to continue to rigor it forward, you have reached the first tension to resolve on your leadership development journey.

Before proceeding to fill your mind with additional learning, you have a choice to make. To advance into being viewed as a potential leader by others and a candidate for leading a team, you need to explicitly cross the gap between knowing and doing. You are now armed with new tools, ideas, language, and concepts to use on the ground.

Your Choice Is...

▌ *Will you take action?*

This may at first seem like a ridiculous choice or question, yet many aspiring leaders never do take action and cross over from the "Yes, I know what to do" to the "Let me show you that I know how" stage by applying their knowledge *on the ground (OTG) in real time.*

Seeking to gain knowledge is something many of us love to do. We want to gather facts, insights, and new ways of doing things. We take notes, write things down, and thoroughly enjoy the learning process. After all, most aspiring leaders are lifetime learners! Yet how often do we seek to apply what we have learned by creating an action plan and putting it into practice?

The truth, for many leaders, is never. ***They are "reluctant" leaders who prefer to acquire knowledge rather than apply it.*** Not surprisingly, many reluctant leaders can respond intelligently to both conceptual and theoretical principles when asked a question. They can likely talk about leadership concepts with great insight but also with misplaced confidence, given their lack of tangible on-the-ground experience.

Typically, their lack of action can be attributed to one of three things: there's been "no opportunity" in their view for true application, they haven't gotten around to it yet, or they lack the passionate desire to step up and lead, preferring instead to just continue to take notes and think about things.

As a leader, you must recognize that nothing happens unless you perform. ***Performance means putting your knowledge OTG and in motion!*** Without action, there is no progress. Without progress, there is no growth. ***If you don't cross the knowing-doing gap, you are a perpetual student of leadership rather than a leader.***

Obstacles to Overcome

Let me be clear, crossing the knowing-doing gap isn't easy. It requires you to rigor through some challenging obstacles that leaders must have the courage to face head on.

▶ Overcoming Resistance

You must overcome the resistance of your own inertia or even perhaps your own intellectual arrogance. Sometimes people continue to stay stuck because they convince themselves that knowing is the most important thing and that it is almost the same as doing (it's not), or they tell themselves that it's okay to stay there a little longer while they strive for reaching a greater level of competency first (again, it's not okay). Or worst of all, when you challenge them on this, they shake their heads and proclaim, ***"I know, I know,"*** which metaphorically says it all!

▶ Taking a Risk

You must take a risk and start to visibly apply yourself to things you are not expert at or even comfortable with yet. Leadership is about consciously demonstrating behaviors, in real time, through disciplined practice. When you "do this," you will be creating experiences from which you can learn and grow.

▶ Being Vulnerable

You must be vulnerable as an aspiring leader by showing others that you acknowledge being consciously incompetent in certain areas and that you are willingly struggling through the necessary learning curve to reach conscious competency. This is a strong signal that you are working to realize your leadership potential. You will also need to get used to this struggle, as it will be an ongoing part of your leadership development process.

Of course, *it takes courage* to overcome these obstacles and inhibitions. When fear stalls the transition from knowing to doing and you *get stuck in the "getting-ready-to-do-it" zone,* self-coaching can help facilitate a breakthrough.

Resolving the Tension

Ask yourself the following questions and determine whether you can get over these hurdles and resolve the tension inherent in crossing the gap between knowing and doing:

1. What do you need that you are waiting for?

- "More time; I'm too busy; this isn't that important."

- "A low-risk environment to try material out; still too new."

- "I don't know."

If you want to develop into a leader of others, you need to realize that all (3) of these reasons sound *terribly uninspiring.* In fact, I doubt you would feel comfortable saying them out loud to a group of people who report to you or look up to you.

2. What fear is holding you back?

- "I'm not afraid; I'm just not ready yet. There is a difference!"

- "I don't know material well enough to explain it to others."

- "I might get stuck and embarrass myself."

Welcome to the world of learning and leadership! Remember that your leadership development is a *"practice."* This means you are continuing to build your expertise and still have more to learn. You will need to try out new things on a regular basis as you advance into expanded leadership roles, *so stop reading the "how to" manual already!* Instead, start taking some swings at the ball with your club!

3. What environmental conditions do you want to create so that you can get into action?

- "A friendly, low-risk meeting environment."

- "An easy problem to try these techniques out on."

- "A challenging problem worth taking a risk on."

Seriously, any situation is a good place to start because the idea is that you will begin using these leadership skills and concepts *everywhere.* Consistency of use will increase your comfort. In fact, once you experience firsthand the benefits of performance and productivity these leadership tools bring, you will become energized and will later reflect that you should have begun using them sooner, so start to rigor it now!

The Service You Provide

The service you provide by crossing the knowing-doing gap is that you will become a credible on-the-ground leader who *"does things and gets things done"!* As a result, you will authentically be role modeling what active engagement and full participation look, sound, and feel like. Instead of quietly observing from the sidelines, you will start to visibly and credibly build your leadership practice, create a legitimate presence for yourself through taking action, and share the outcomes and experiences in discussions with your team/colleagues to facilitate the learning and growth of others.

Your on-the-ground experience will build your confidence so that you will ask more questions, express direct challenges, offer emotional support, and attempt to hold your peers accountable to agreements as you become more comfortable using your personal power to influence and connect with others on your team.

The new perspective you take on is that of a confident individual contributor and valuable team member who is actively engaged. You now provide not only technical expertise but are also beginning to demonstrate your leadership skills through the currencies of communication and relationship building.

More than anything else, crossing the knowing-doing gap requires that you learn to trust and believe in yourself. I assure you, the professional community you are part of will appreciate and actively support you in your efforts to stretch, learn, and grow as a leader. Take the first steps; you will be met with encouragement!

Practical Considerations in Crossing the Knowing-Doing Gap

Courageously crossing your knowing-doing gap can be easier if you embrace the following practical considerations.

Learn to Trust Yourself and Understand Your Self-Talk

While crossing the knowing-doing gap can create feelings of trepidation, fear, and the embarrassing consequences of perceived failure, remember that these are mainly *self-imposed barriers* based on your own negative self-talk. The rest of us are not playing that same tape in our heads as we engage with you! Trusting yourself, as mentioned previously, is critical. We all have saboteur voices playing in our heads that are trying to keep us safe by not letting us take risks.

Acknowledge this voice, appreciate it, and then consciously decide to move forward anyway! Recognizing that only with risk will change and growth happen is a fundamental insight you will need to embrace as you cross your knowing-doing gap. It is also important to trust the environment that has been set up by your leaders and through the support of your colleagues.

Hardwiring May Affect Crossing the Knowing-Doing Gap

Our individual preferences for how we process information, make decisions, organize our lives, and use our energy may affect how we choose to cross the knowing-doing gap.

For example, using the Myers-Briggs language, an extravert (E) may engage in active meeting dialogue or productive conflict with peers more readily than introverts (I).

An individual with an MBTI intuitive (N) preference may be attracted to the *Leadership Rigor* concepts and visuals, quickly embracing their immediate utilization, whereas an individual with a sensor (S) preference may need to understand the value and practical utility of the information through his or her personal experiences, needing some time to increase his or her confidence before taking public action.

An individual with a judger (J) preference might make a specific plan of action for how and when to try this new learning, whereas an individual with a perceiver (P) preference might be more spontaneous and less structured around when to use it.

An individual with a feeler (F) preference might be personally guarded about taking a risk and trying out new techniques for fear of being criticized or embarrassed, whereas an individual with a thinker (T) preference might just courageously try them out and be pretty objective about whether or not they work.

Regardless of your natural hardwiring, you need to be able to flex your style and lean into your discomfort so that you can use your learning and knowledge to make an impact and create value.

In terms of individual learning styles, since those who are kinesthetic in their preferences learn by doing and experiencing, opportunities to role play or participate in learning exercises through workshops will facilitate comfort with this type of material.

Individuals whose preferred learning style is listening will appreciate reading the material in this book. Those who are visual learners will gravitate to the pictures of the models.

Hopefully, all learners and personality types will get what they need from *Leadership Rigor*!

That said, the feelings you are having right now are important for (2) reasons. First, they offer you an opportunity to acknowledge, work through, and appropriately choose how to manage them so they don't overwhelm you or limit your ability to connect with others. Second, they will sensitize you to the journey of others you will soon be shepherding as you advance in your leadership roles. Your empathy and your compassion plays a role in building confidence, both in yourself and in others.

Be Patient and Let Things Unfold

As you attempt to cross the knowing-doing gap, be aware of the anxiousness you may feel and exercise self-management (breathe deeply and perhaps repeat an empowering positive statement in your self-talk) in being patient with yourself as well as with the process. Others will be involved with you in co-creating the outcomes, so don't let the fear of not seeing exactly how things will unfold prevent you from stepping out and starting the process.

You may also feel self-imposed pressure to rush through the process if you are facilitating a discussion. Don't do it! Again, *resist the trigger* of impatience. **Slow down and continue to trust the process, engage the collective input of others so you are not the sole center of attention, and allow things to naturally unfold without forcing or overengineering the dynamics.** Creating value and revealing insights comes from engaging in discussions, so ensuring an appropriate amount of time here is critical to getting better outcomes.

Crossing the knowing-doing gap requires taking a leap of faith and believing in yourself! I cross it every day as a coach and facilitator. While I may have an idea of where we need to go, how we get there is always a unique and often spontaneous journey. What I have learned through experience is that whatever needs to unfold will, and what needs to show up or happen does, as long as I "let go" and trust the people involved as well as the process to reveal its natural course and reach its innate conclusions.

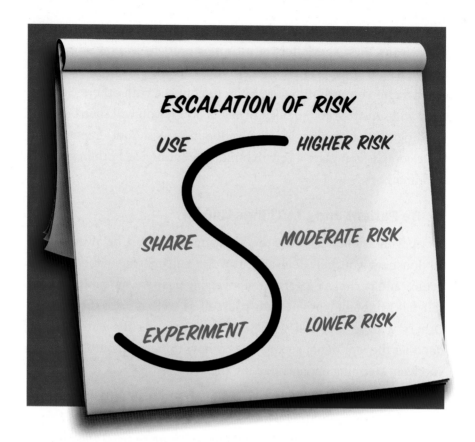

Take an Escalation-of-Risk Approach

Applying the concepts, frameworks, and models presented in **Leadership Rigor** is an example of crossing the knowing-doing gap. You may appreciate a specific model and see its intellectual value yet hesitate to share it because you lack the confidence to competently explain it to others.

This is something you need to get over. Pick a one-to-one conversation or small group setting and simply begin to explain the potential value you see in the model or framework. Consider trying it in a meeting as an experiment to see how it works. Presented in this way, you are taking a *low-risk* approach to putting it into action.

A more *moderate-risk* approach would be to take a stronger leadership position and say to a group of associates, "Hey, here is a model

I have been learning about that I would like to share with you because it may have direct applications to what we are doing here. Let me walk through it and let's talk about its potential use. I will try my best to answer any questions, and together we can figure out how we can integrate this into our work if it makes sense to do so."

The *highest risk* approach would be to say, "I have a model I would like us to use here. Let me walk through it and then share with you how I think it can be applied to our work to improve our performance and productivity."

Crossing the knowing-doing gap and getting into action confirms that you have made a conscious choice to lead yourself, courageously engage in real-time business dynamics, and put your learning on the ground in a visible way. With a continued commitment to practice honing your skills and expand your leadership toolbox plus a genuine desire to lead others in their journey forward, you are now ready to explore the leadership challenges of leading teams.

"You can't build a reputation on what you are going to do."
– Henry Ford

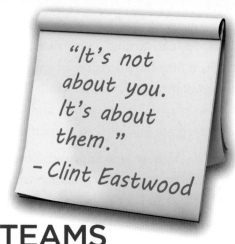

"It's not about you. It's about them."

— Clint Eastwood

PART 2:
LEADING TEAMS

Congratulations! You are interested in learning more about the rigor it will take to become a performance-based team leader. Whether you are a newly named team leader or an experienced professional looking to raise the bar on your current performance, investing time in understanding what it takes to successfully serve in the team leader role is an important step in your leadership journey.

Imagine for a moment that you have just been named to a new team leader role and the written announcement has just been issued to your organization. On your mark, get set, launch into action, right?

Not exactly. Your first step is to exercise emotional intelligence through self-management by pausing and doing nothing.

That's right, pause and *do nothing!*

While the announcement of your new role is the visible moment of change, managing the transition into your role is critical, because this can distinguish a successful start from a series of false starts.

The insights and learning on leading yourself that you have begun to put into practice from Part 1 of *Leadership Rigor* will carry over into Part 2, but the team leader lens you will now be looking through will continue to challenge and change your perspective, requiring both significant and subtle shifts in your behavior.

Part 2 examines the *fundamental building processes* associated with leading teams. The focus is on building healthy and cohesive team dynamics, building an integrated work product, and building alignment across the enterprise.

The signature model introduced in this section is **Analytical Rigor,** a sequential and integrated framework for engaging and aligning the diversity of a team's thinking to accelerate performance and productivity in decision making as well as in discussing challenging business issues.

The tension you will need to resolve is to *become both a practitioner and a philosopher* of these leadership concepts so that you can be an active role model for the technical skill development of your team members as well as a champion for their leadership growth.

Leading with rigor at the team level will require you to stretch and cover the full spectrum of doing, managing, and leading. So fasten your seat belts: your altitude is about to dramatically change!

The Fundamentals of Leading Teams:

CHAPTER 1:
Building Healthy Team Dynamics

CHAPTER 2:
Building the Work Together

CHAPTER 3:
Building Alignment across the Enterprise

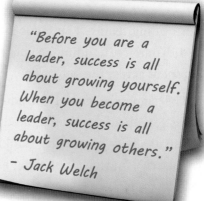

"Before you are a leader, success is all about growing yourself. When you become a leader, success is all about growing others."

– Jack Welch

CHAPTER 1:
Building Healthy Team Dynamics

Team dynamics are always complex. Beyond needing to establish a strong relationship with each team member, the diverse nature of the collective personalities coming together to interact will provide challenges for you to rigor through as a team leader. For individuals to grow into becoming a team and to play at a high level of performance and productivity together will require healthy communication and relationship dynamics.

Healthy team dynamics do not develop passively, easily, or quickly. They require the rigor of *team leadership,* a combination of your personal engagement, commitment, and resilience in addition to your ability to nurture and build a team of leaders around you.

The Fundamentals You Will Need to Understand Include:

I.   Your Role as Team Leader

II. The Tools in the Team Leader Toolbox

III. Facilitating Communication across the Interfaces

IV. How to Champion the Team's Journey

I. Your Role as Team Leader

Leadership is both a service to others and a performance-based role that requires the application of skills and capabilities with conscious discipline. Earlier, **Leadership Rigor** established that performance is measured by getting both the results and behaviors you are looking for on the ground. As a team leader, you now have to get that performance on the ground *through others.*

As you navigate your way through this challenge, be aware of the following environmental dynamics:

- You now have position power as a team leader. **Be mindful to minimize your utilization of it.**

- You may now have a new peer group. People will be curiously watching and noticing how you interact both verbally and non-verbally through your body language. **Be mindful of the fishbowl effect.**

- You are not the only one experiencing changes and transitions. Your team will want to know what your vision is and what your expectations are for them. **Be mindful of the expectations of your direct reports.**

- Your supervisor will want you to get up to speed as soon as possible and may have a mandate for you to accomplish in this new role. **Be mindful of the expectations of your supervisor.**

As a new team leader, it is natural to feel an anxious desire to quickly get to work and put your action agenda into place so you can prove to yourself and everyone else that you are the right choice for this new role.

Breathe, stop any negative self-talk (or perhaps the overinflated sense of self-confidence in your head), and focus on self-management.

Resist the temptation to move into action and instead consciously go slowly at first; you will move forward with greater speed and purpose later.

Remember that how you handle your transition into this role will say a lot about how you will *be* in this role. Stay alert to the fact that leadership is a being state, not a doing state.

The good news is that time is initially on your side, despite the pressure you feel, the urgency others may attempt to impose upon you, or the messages running through your head. Remind yourself that this is a new start and that you want to mindfully take advantage of the opportunity to create your new story.

Composure and emotional intelligence are needed here, not your expertise in quickly solving low-altitude problems, so lead with your personal power. Listen more than you speak, ask questions, and lean into your curiosity as you learn about your new role, team, supervisor, and peer group. Your ***relationship currency*** is what you want to consciously rigor now!

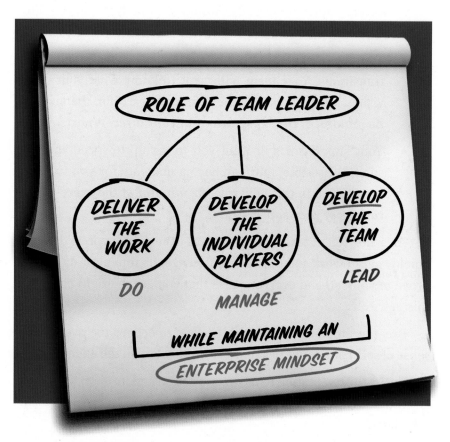

As a Team Leader, Your Role Has (3) Parts:

- Delivering the Work of the Team

- Developing the Individual Players

- Developing the Team as an Entity

All (3) areas are important, but the (2) developmental areas are critical because they ensure the sustainability and scalability of the organization for the mid to long term, which is leadership work.

The developmental areas will also require significant investments of your time and energy because they will involve behavioral changes from both you and your direct reports. You will be working to raise your altitude by applying your managing and leading skills with conscious competency, and they will be attempting to learn fundamental individual as well as team behavioral skills, perhaps for the first time.

Delivering the Work of the Team

As an individual contributor, you previously only needed to deliver your own work and develop your own skills, *so the scope of your responsibility now expands exponentially.*

As a team leader, you will now have collective goals to both establish and deliver. While your team members will be the primary doers of the work, your focus will be ensuring that they have the confidence, skills, and resources to deliver it. In other words, your efforts will be focused on getting work done through others, which is an adjustment for you as you learn to let go of your own doing preferences and raise your altitude into the managing and leading areas.

To be fair, many team leaders initially are both players and coaches. It is not unusual to have a personal book of work that you do in addition to shouldering team leader responsibilities.

The message here is to recognize this shifting dynamic and to consciously balance your new altitude and approach even as you address the challenges of delivering the work of the team.

These challenges require you to:

- *Avoid* micromanagement
- *Avoid* "delegate and go"
- *Avoid* becoming a member of the team

▶ Challenge 1: Avoid **Micromanagement**

As a team leader, you have already demonstrated a degree of functional excellence with your technical skills and have started to amass expertise power. You are likely to be an efficient and effective problem solver who easily navigates through your organization's processes with preferred ways of doing things.

Stay alert here! Don't fall into the trap of micromanagement, in which you impose your ways of doing things on your new team. Your approach works for you, but others will need to find their own way forward rather than simply adopting your approach.

Your role is to be clear about *what* needs to be done, by whom, and when. The *how* it gets done is now up to your team members. Give them some freedom to operate and encourage them to learn by doing, asking questions, and asking for help; this is important for their development as well as yours.

▶ Challenge 2: Avoid "Delegate and Go"

In this extreme, you delegate everything, with little to no oversight, under the assumption that your direct reports have the skills to deliver. When the work product does not meet your expectations, you react impatiently with a heavy-handed "directing" or "do it yourself" approach that undermines their confidence.

In the long run, actively engaging with your team members throughout the work process and developing their skills will be far more beneficial to both you and the organization than just making sure the work gets done. Take the time to coach and develop your team members through their initial performance challenges.

▶ Challenge 3: Avoid Becoming a Member of the Team

Many leaders struggle with the desire to be liked. They want to be friends with the members of their team, and they believe it is their role to look after, promote, and protect them. Unfortunately, these leaders fail to realize the risks associated with becoming viewed as a member of the team and how it can compromise their leadership role.

As a team leader, you play an interface role between the organization, your team, and your direct reports. Your focus and loyalty is always to the enterprise first, and you demonstrate this by developing your talent bench while delivering the work.

> *It is not your role to protect your team and its members; it is your role to stretch them, challenge them, and develop them to be high performers, including giving them the space to make mistakes and occasionally fail!*

Being respected is mandatory; being liked is an optional extra. Establish your principles, stand behind them, and be consistent. Being too friendly and informal early on with your team may cause you to be reluctant to make the tough decisions later that can affect the roles and careers of your team members as well as the strength of your organization.

You might also undermine the development of your own career if your supervisor or peers view you as having misplaced loyalty, a lack of objectivity, or bad judgment when it comes to assessing talent. Leaders who are highly personable and overly focused on the relationship side of the continuum can get stuck here, often with surprisingly negative repercussions to them, their team members, and the organization as a whole.

Developing the Individual Players

As team leader, you must coach and develop the performance of your team's individual members. The (2) areas you need to focus on are their technical skills related to the work product and their behavioral skills related to how they get the work done. Both areas require equal emphasis.

> *Investing development time with your direct reports is your job; it is not what you do after your day job is done!*

Having both the desire and capability to develop others should be why you were given the team leader role, but in many organizations, this is simply not the case. Often, individuals are promoted or moved into roles without sufficient consideration given to their existing leadership skills and their willingness to lead. This is also why most organizations claim among their most critical business challenges *a lack of "ready now"* leaders and a weak talent bench.

Let me be brutally clear: if you are not passionate about developing others, please don't pursue a team or organizational leadership role just to satisfy your ego or power needs, because you will negatively affect the growth of your enterprise as well as those you are supervising. Consider instead the thought leadership role discussed in Part 1 of **Leadership Rigor.**

Assuming that developing others is something you want to passionately invest your time in, the team leader role gives you the opportunity to coach performance, shape careers, provide developmental feedback, and help build the leadership capabilities of your direct reports, which in turn will build your capabilities as a leader.

Developing the Team as an Entity

When performing at a high level, a team can have a transformative energy that catalyzes its members, other functional teams, and the broader organization. Your role is to develop your team as a high-performing entity.

To reach this performance level, the team must develop trust and be willing to address important issues with productive conflict, including calling out unproductive behaviors that may be holding the team back. Only with this dynamic interaction in place will you as a leader be able to secure commitment and alignment to working through the challenges of your business goals.

Even with this commitment, teams and their leaders must address another critical challenge: the challenge of accountability.

> *Many teams and organizations claim that a lack of accountability is their single biggest challenge.*

In Part 1 of *Leadership Rigor,* **The Accountability Conversation** was introduced as a tool for leaders to negotiate clear expectations, ensure appropriate resources are in place to successfully complete the work, and align on mutually agreed-upon deliverables.

Now let's look at accountability through the team leader lens, remembering that **Leadership Rigor** is focused on performance and productivity.

With this in mind, consider the (3) disciplines a team leader must consciously use in building an accountability-based team:

- The *discipline* of setting expectations
- The *discipline* of coaching for performance
- The *discipline* of holding accountability

▶ The Discipline of Setting Expectations

Accountability starts with confirming mutual clarity on what is being requested. Most leaders set vague expectations and just assume their direct reports "get it" and will deliver exactly what they want. Unfortunately, this is seldom true, and team leaders often receive work products that are out of alignment with their expectations. As previously mentioned, out of frustration or concern about the lost time, many team leaders react impulsively by lunging into microman-agement or "do it myself" mode to fix the work product.

Instead of going this low-altitude route, exercise discipline by taking the time to be clear about your expectations up front. Ensure that these expectations are both heard and understood by asking your direct reports to explain to you what they are going to do based on your request. Discuss how your request will be delivered (by report, email, or presentation) and when it is expected (on what day and by what time) so they can plan and appropriately sequence the flow of their work.

You must also confirm that these individuals have the bandwidth to accomplish their work. For example, they may need assistance in reprioritizing other initiatives or in securing resources from other departments that require your outreach to a peer to ensure availability.

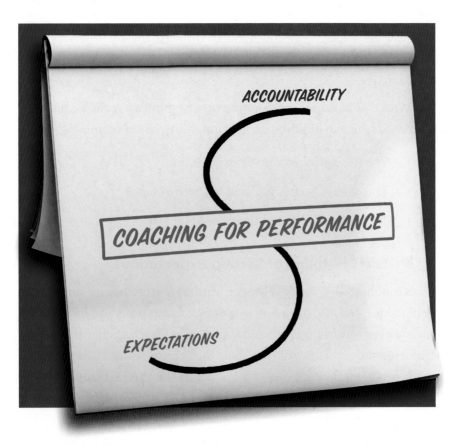

▶ The Discipline of Coaching for Performance

Once expectations are established, most leaders believe their work is done and that they merely need to wait for the deliverable to be handed to them.

In fact, only after the expectations are clearly established does the real work of the team leader begin!

Being in communication and relationship with your team members so that you can coach them for performance is now what you must take on and rigor as the team leader!

Coaching for performance requires you to be actively engaged and to make conscious choices about how to best assist your team members on both the technical skill building and the behavioral fronts. For example, you might need to map out the process with them for a project, you might need to be a sounding board for potential solutions, or you might even need to practice role playing challenging conversations they need to have with others so they feel more confident.

Your role as team leader requires you to be engaged with your team members as you coach the development of their skills and capabilities to help them deliver the work.

▶ The Discipline of Holding Accountability

What exactly does holding accountability mean, and what does it look, sound, and feel like in business?

Holding accountability can be a relatively straightforward discipline if you have set clear expectations and coached for performance along the way. In essence, through this process, you appropriately ask others to "be accountable and take accountability," which diminishes the pressure on you having to "hold accountability" as a team leader.

There are (4) levels of accountability:

1. **Holding yourself accountable** means that you consciously make a commitment, own it, and deliver against it. In the event that you cannot deliver, you proactively renegotiate on a deliverable or realign the expectations to minimize the disruption that will result if no advance warning is provided. This should also be accompanied by an apology and an assessment of your learning so that you can better manage your commitments and deliverables in the future.

2. **Being accountable to your team** means that you challenge your peers on their performance (results and behaviors) and hold a high bar for delivery against expectations, both yours and theirs.

3. **Being accountable to your team leader** means courageously engaging in productive conflict and demonstrating *veritas* on issues you believe in strongly. It may also mean giving your team leaders feedback to reveal blind spots that help them understand their impact (positive and negative) on the team.

4. **Being accountable to your organization** means that you live the values and role model the behaviors of your culture. You also use your personal power to call forth or challenge others who may not be demonstrating these shared values.

As team leader, you hold ***ultimate ownership*** for the team's collective accountabilities. If expectations are not met and accountability is not held, *consequences are appropriate and even necessary*. As students, if we did not complete our papers on time, we received a lower grade. As athletes, if we did not put our full effort into practice, we didn't get as much playing time. The world of business is no different. If your goal is to be a performance-based organization, consequences are required when expectations are not met.

4 LEVELS OF ACCOUNTABILITY:
- **YOURSELF**
- **YOUR TEAM**
- **YOUR TEAM LEADER**
- **YOUR ORGANIZATION**

> *The consequences (both positive and negative) regarding accountability for performance impact the development of your reputation and therefore the quality of your relationships.*

Part 3 of **Leadership Rigor** will discuss *"consequential leadership"* in greater detail. For now, just know that consequential leadership means putting both *positive* (feedback, recognition, and rewards) and *negative* (corrective feedback and minimized bonus potential, salary increases, and promotional opportunities) actions into place regarding performance. These actions, consistently applied, create the foundation for the performance-based culture that is at the heart of **Leadership Rigor**.

II. The Tools in the Team Leader Toolbox

Part of what defines being a team leader is that you have consciously crossed the knowing-doing gap and are putting into practice the leadership concepts you have learned. Because you are now serving others in their development, your toolbox needs to be full of resources to help you further advance your own leadership practice. Later in the tension section, we will discuss how you will need to be both a versatile practitioner on the ground and a philosopher who can create context and meaning for others.

The fundamental practices and philosophies in the team leader toolbox include:

- (3) philosophical (ors)
- (3) practical ands
- (3) philosophical choices
- (3) practical stages

(3) Philosophical (ors)

The (3) philosophical "ors" require you to make conscious decisions on how you will set the framework for engagement with your team. These decisions will also determine the type of relationships you will build as a leader.

1. As a leader, will you give trust (or) require that trust be earned?

Ask a roomful of leaders whether they are givers of trust or earners of trust, and you will likely get a split right down the middle. Many believe that trust builds slowly and is earned over time. Others give trust generously up front, fully aware that they will at some point be disappointed, yet willing to take the risk.

Which leader would *you* prefer to work for?

For me, the answer is simple: I want to work for the givers of trust, and I will reward their confidence in me with incredible determination to exceed their expectations in order to show that their trust is well placed and appreciated.

Research shows the most admired leaders are givers of trust.

If you choose to give your trust to your team, make sure you clearly communicate that you are doing so up front. *Let your team know that you are willing to take this leap of faith because you believe in them.* In so doing, you are creating a safe space for your direct reports to act with independence and confidence. You will also be making the choice to trust yourself by playing at the altitude of managing and leading, thereby creating the conditions for potential lift on your team.

Just be prepared, because certainly at some point you will be disappointed! The most admired leaders express their disappointment in the form of direct feedback and then give their trust again. This reinforces confidence and independence with a heightened sense of responsibility. Mistakes happen, and we must be accepting of them as worthwhile investments in the learning and growth process, but we also need to ensure that the same mistakes are not repeated. If they are, our trust is inappropriately placed.

2. As a leader, will you address (or) avoid the issues?

Remember, you create and influence the environmental conditions in which the dynamics of your team develop. Your team will quickly assess whether you are going to be open and direct in tackling the real issues or whether you are going to duck and avoid them.

You get what you tolerate, and initially *all eyes will be on you* to see if you have the courage to call out unproductive behaviors that may be present on the team. If you laugh at or ignore the behaviors, you will be sending a message of tolerance and low performance. If you address them immediately, with respect and specific requests for change based on their potential negative impact, you will be creating clear expectations for high performance.

Personally engaging in productive conflict and role modeling carefrontational feedback will set your team up to do so as well. Your on-the-ground leadership choices shape the performance of your team. The leader must always go first by setting the right example!

3. As a leader, will you provide questions (or) answers?

You may think you can develop team members more quickly by providing answers, convincing yourself that you are "training" or "teaching" them, but in reality this actually shuts down the learning process, which is interactive and iterative. Instead, *patiently engage your team members by encouraging their natural curiosity through the use of open-ended questions.* This will provide more possibilities and opportunities for them to learn to solve problems on their own and become more self-sufficient in a shorter time period.

For a moment, reflect back on the Power Model presented in Part 1 of *Leadership Rigor.* Remember how questions and active listening drive your connectivity to others? Simply providing answers utilizes your expertise power. While this may be efficient for you, it deprives your team members of the struggle to learn and find their own answers.

Helping others become more capable is sometimes more important than just getting the work done. At times, you will certainly need to teach and advise. Just be aware of when you are doing so because it is convenient for you as opposed to when it is in genuine service of the learning and growth of your team. In other words, lean toward investing time in teaching your team to fish and manage your impulsivity to just throw fish at them.

It is also important to remember the new dynamic at play in your team leader role, position power. There is tremendous gravity associated with your position power such that a seemingly simple comment, one with a harmless intention in your view, can land as heavy as a rock on team members' heads. Ensure that your communication is well framed and not overly dictatorial or dogmatic. You always need to own your impact and be mindful about creating safe space for others, especially during the learning process!

Ironically, we rarely have to assert our position power as leaders. Others typically over emphasize it in how they act toward us, taking what we say as an edict or non-negotiable request.

To consciously address this, take the time to help your team understand that you always want the best ideas and thinking put forward. While you will occasionally offer your own ideas, encourage team members to challenge you on why a specific idea might not be a good approach or, better yet, invite them to offer alternative options they believe are better solutions.

Don't assume your team will naturally "get" this. State it and make it clear with both your words and demonstrated behaviors, including publicly recognizing with positive reinforcement those who courageously challenge you!

(3) Practical *ands*

The (3) practical "ands" are a reminder of the dualities you must differentiate between, balance, and utilize as you work with your team.

1. You must differentiate between motivation *and* inspiration.

The words "motivation" and "inspiration," which are often used interchangeably and incorrectly, are leadership concepts that team leaders need to clearly understand and appropriately utilize.

Our *motivations* are our personal, individual, and intrinsic reasons for taking action. For example, certain team members will be motivated by achievement, others by recognition, and still others by money, learning, or status. As a leader, you need to understand what the intrinsic motivations are for each member of your team by getting to know them, asking questions, and watching them perform. This is important for a simple reason:

> **You cannot motivate people. People must motivate themselves.**

Inspiration, on the other hand, involves setting up the external conditions through which team members can express their personal motivations, and this is where you play your role as a leader. An example would be giving a team member who is motivated by achievement a challenging project that has never been done before or giving a team member who is financially motivated an open-ended bonus for successfully launching a new product.

LEADERSHIP CHOICES FOR TASKS

EMPOWER	COACH
DELEGATE	DIRECT

2 QUESTIONS: 1. CONFIDENCE
2. COMPETENCE

their direct reports, who don't receive sufficient space to try, fail, and learn on their own.

These *"micromanagers"* frustrate strong talent and slow down the development of their talent bench by causing compression (this occurs when team leaders play at a low altitude) rather than lift. Ultimately, this has a negative effect on the performance and productivity of the entire enterprise.

The delegating approach, or the "Here you go; take this off my plate and you handle it" approach, is also a favorite style of many team leaders. This choice is wise if individual team members have previous experience as well as the confidence to successfully deliver with complete independence, but this style is often inappropriately used by team leaders who do not properly assess the level of engagement needed by employees and who are just looking to get things off their plate. When the task is not completed the way they expected, they are disappointed and frustrated. As noted previously, disappointed leaders tend to respond with a *"reactive directive"* style in which they tell their employees exactly what to do. Sometimes they even completely lower their altitude and complete the task themselves.

Delegation is best used as a leadership style when employees have had successful experiences on similar or related tasks and your goal is stretching the bandwidth of your more senior direct reports as well as exercising increased discipline with your own leadership altitude.

Let me be clear that while the directing and delegating approaches can be useful in certain situations, they are the easiest style choices for team leaders to make. In the long run, they are often a mistake for leaders because they fail to consider the real learning and development needs of direct reports. For this reason, I call these (2) styles "playing below the line."

The coaching approach is often a better choice for new leaders, though it requires more discipline, time, and engagement. Here, *questions are your most important tool,* and both you and your direct report should ask them.

You will also need to exercise self-management and patience while the learning process unfolds. You may feel like you want to move quickly to answer questions, but *silence is your second most important tool in coaching* because it creates the space for your direct report to think in a safe environment and to work with you to figure things out in real time. Your oversight and involvement, which occur during regular check-in points or at specific milestones for a project, ensure that the task is completed, and your direct report's confidence *and* competence increase due to your investment of learning time.

Unfortunately, many leaders avoid the coaching approach because they do not believe they have the time or skills to coach properly. The time excuse is not acceptable. After all, this is your job!

Competency may be a legitimate limitation, and if so, it needs to

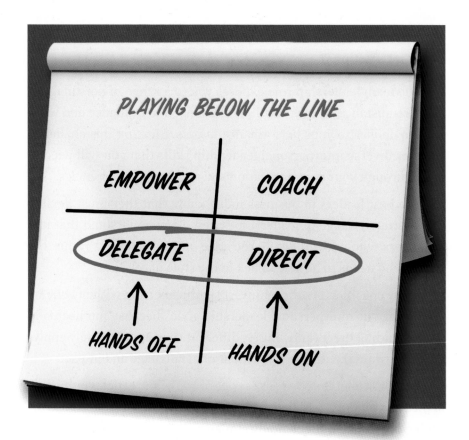

PLAYING BELOW THE LINE

EMPOWER	COACH
DELEGATE	DIRECT
↑ HANDS OFF	↑ HANDS ON

be immediately addressed. Coaching skills are absolutely critical for a team leader, so be proactive in securing them. Ideally, you have had exposure to excellent supervisors who have role modeled coaching for you, but if you haven't, you might need to seek training or even hire a coach for yourself so that you can personally experience the process of coaching for development. This is a skill you must have, so make sure you **Rigor it!**

The empowerment approach acknowledges that there is still a need for checking in and connecting during the life cycle of the project, but this occurs more at the discretion of the direct report who has both the confidence and competency to complete the task at hand. As team leader, when you use this style, remember to self-manage your desires for engaging based on your own information needs and consciously *provide as much space as possible for ownership and growth* to your direct report.

2. What are your leadership style (choices) for interpersonal interactions?

The team leadership role exposes you to a range of personalities and circumstances that you will be challenged to influence and work with to deliver to your performance targets. Meeting this challenge requires diverse interpersonal leadership skills that you will need to apply through your communication and relationship currencies.

The best leaders in business today know that they must flexibly demonstrate a range of leadership styles. They understand that it is not others who need to flex to the style of the leader but rather the leader who needs to be able to flex to the style of others.

In my coaching practice, I invest significant time with my clients on the various interpersonal leadership styles because intellectually understanding them (knowing) is different than appropriately applying them (doing) with the right situational language and impact.

Author Daniel Goleman, in a series of books and articles published in the *Harvard Business Review* and by the Harvard Press, outlines (6) leadership styles fundamentally at play in terms of our interpersonal interactions.

Using his work as a stepping-stone,* let's explore the following (6) leadership styles:

- *Directing*
- *Coaching*
- *Visionary*
- *Pace setting*
- *Affiliative*
- *Participative/Facilitative*

Goleman uses "Coercive" instead of "Directing" and "Democratic" instead of "Participative/Facilitative."

The *directing* **leadership style** can feel heavy-handed and prescriptive, so its use needs to be selectively applied to situations where "telling and imposing" is appropriate. This style is not highly inclusive and engaging of others so it is not typically a "relationship building" style. Instead, it is mainly focused on the leader solving the problem or situation at hand with little involvement in debate or discussion. This style is important when a decision must be made quickly, communication must be unambiguous, or skills for this type of problem solving may not be in place with the team. Positional leadership or expertise power is often used here.

The *coaching* **leadership style** uses questions, silence, and space as its primary tools to extract answers and insights from the team members as opposed to the leader simply sharing knowledge. Utilizing a coaching style provides an opportunity for direct reports to pause and reflect on how what they say or do impacts other people. It provides the opportunity for leaders to ask direct reports to consider how it feels to hear a certain message, which can sensitize them to how their delivery comes across. Role playing, exploration, and self-discovery (creating awareness of a blind spot) are the hallmarks of this approach.

The *visionary* **leadership style** has (2) important components. The first is creating a compelling picture for the future. The second is meaningfully connecting that future to the audience. Specifically, team members need to see themselves playing a critical role in this future vision. The role of the team leader is to put them there by creating the stories and mental pictures of how things will look and feel to them, what will be new, what will be different, and why you as leader need their commitment and engagement to make this vision a reality. By connecting the audience to the vision, it becomes shared, and a shared vision is one that is going to be realized.

The *pace-setting* **leadership style** has similarities to the directing style but is typically targeted to a larger "team or group audience level" with specific target dates for collective deliverables. This style is best utilized for short time periods and specific challenges because it carries intense energy. It is appropriate to use when there is a short-term sales goal for an organization, a final push for a new product launch, or a burning platform for change in which target date milestone achievements are critical to success and you are looking to inspire collective breakthrough performances. As with directing, this is not a go-to style you want to overly utilize, as its consistent use will result in personal frustrations and strained relationships.

The *affiliative* **leadership style** is highly focused on relationship building, and it also has (2) components when utilized appropriately. As the word "affiliative" suggests, the first part of this style is about creating an emotional connection by authentically expressing compassion and empathy, most likely for a setback or disappointment.

Pace-Setting Challenges

Be aware that the pace-setting style can cause frustration if the goal is too big or is perceived to be unrealistic. Take the concept of the BHAG in Jim Collins' book *Good to Great*. A BHAG (Big Hairy Audacious Goal) is a far-reaching goal intended by design to be unachievable.

According to Collins' philosophy, though you will likely fail to achieve this goal, you will still attain great success because you are simultaneously setting an RBR (Reach But Reasonable) goal that you are also measured against.

Leaders who choose this approach need to consider the emotional implications on highly motivated, goal-oriented team members who will feel disappointed because they achieved amazing results but failed in their own minds because they fell short of an unrealistic goal or BHAG.

If this is a style you use, be careful not to lead by sequential pace-setting goals. You will exhaust your team, lose their long-term commitment, and diminish your leadership effectiveness because behind each goal they realize is just another pace-setting goal. Limit your use of pace setting and expand your toolbox with other styles.

This might occur, for example, during an organizational restructuring initiative, when a leader reveals personal anxiety and sadness and in so doing creates loyal bonds with his or her team.

The affiliative leadership style does not stop here, however. It has (2) parts that I personally refer to as *"connect and go."* This means that once you connect interpersonally, you must go forward as a leader and take people somewhere. This is the most critical part of appropriately using the affiliative leadership style. Many leaders affiliate only to find themselves stuck in a downward spiral of shared negative emotion. True affiliative leadership first connects and then inspires a go-forward message such as this:

We were all heartbroken over the recent downsizing initiative, which has required us to say good-bye to so many of our talented colleagues, all of whom I personally admire and have worked with for much of my career. While it has been emotionally draining, let's not lose sight of the fact that we do have an opportunity to re-create our company for the future. Our colleagues who are leaving us will always be remembered for being a part of the accomplishments that have established this solid foundation. Our challenge now is to honor their spirit and contributions as we keep our momentum going and create the next generation of this great company.

The *participative* **(or facilitative) leadership style** uses the collective wisdom of the team to bring forward issue identification or resolution. Leaders using this style actively listen and facilitate the dialogue with questions but do not typically add their opinions or points of view to the mix until the team fully socializes its perspective. This requires confidence in the team and strong self-management by the leader. The benefit of this style is true "team ownership" of the possibilities and outcomes.

3. What "old story" and "new story" (choices) are on your team?

Being a team leader requires you to be a facilitator of change. Not surprisingly, some leaders are emotionally challenged by team members who are either slow to adapt or are complainers of the status quo. While some individuals don't like change and actively resist it, others simply need more time and detailed information to accept the change process. Still others choose to be sideline commentators as opposed to getting involved in the process. These individuals cause the most damage to team progress and offer yet another reason why team dynamics are so complex!

As a team leader, you need to realize that *change happens in systems.* To get to a high level of performance, you need to get the entire team on the same page at the same time, which can be a long and messy process. Even those who willingly make a personal change and readily adopt a new approach affect others by changing the team dynamics with their new perspective. In this instance, tension or resentment may grow in those who do not choose to adopt these changes as quickly or who are frustrated by where the new discussions are now going without them on board.

In building healthy team dynamics, you might find yourself needing to facilitate the transition of your members from the "old story" of who they were and what they previously believed to a "new story."

For example, an individual on your team may be consciously trying to evolve his or her leadership profile by becoming less controlling and more collaborative but may occasionally oscillate between the old and new stories while working through the behavioral change process.

A natural tendency some of your team members may have is to expect the same traditional behavior of this colleague in spite of his or her real efforts to change and grow. Here especially, as the team leader, you must provide space and encouragement for the seeds of

STORY DYNAMICS

NEW STORY-CHANGE IS HARD

1. STOP THE DOWNSLIDE
2. ACKNOWLEDGE A SLIP
3. CHOOSE TO CHANGE

OLD STORY

this individual's new story to develop. For example, you may have to call out in a team meeting that comments being made about this team member are "old story" comments that do not reflect what is showing up here and now in the room.

Changing an old story is hard work, and almost everyone lapses into previous habits on occasion. The key is to self-manage and get back on track quickly.

Here are (3) steps to coach the process with your team:

1. *Stop* the action that is off track as quickly as possible.

2. *Acknowledge* lapsing into the old story.

3. *Choose* to consciously demonstrate the new story behavior.

Be on the lookout for the old stories that are holding your team or individual direct reports back from reaching their full potential and work with them to create the new empowering stories and behaviors that will result in healthy change and growth.

(3) Practical $\boxed{stages}$

Finally, team leaders can use (3) practical staging tools during different phases of their leadership role to evolve the team dynamics and raise the bar on performance.

1. Use the stop-start-continue $\boxed{stages}$ early in your tenure.

A simple yet impactful way to get started with your new team or to establish a fresh page with an existing team is to use the stop-start-continue staging process.

Teams get overloaded with processes, reports, and meetings that may have originally served a meaningful purpose but are now an extra burden with limited value. To create fresh energy, discuss what the team needs to *stop doing* because it has no current value, *start doing* because there is a value-added need gap, and *continue doing* because it is working well.

This approach also gives your direct reports a say in creating the new team action agenda and having their voices heard, which can be energizing.

2. Use the push-pull-pause $\boxed{stages}$ later in your tenure.

Periodically, you will want to recalibrate your leadership action agenda in the context of competing organizational priorities and the emotional dynamics of your team.

Consider classifying key initiatives as things you want to *push actively,* consciously encourage your team to *pull forward* more deliberately toward, or temporarily *take a pause* from.

This approach is different from stop-start-continue because it is more about working to establish your internal leadership focus as opposed to facilitating an external team-based exercise.

For example, you might be *pushing your team* to proactively reach out to another department with whom you have made a commitment to improve the current working relationship. Every opportunity you have, you request that this particular department be included in the dialogue and decision-making process with your team. You are pushing your team to be more conscious in this area.

On the pull side, you may be looking to raise the bar on accountability within your team. You may ask if a particular member has ensured alignment on mutual expectations and a deliverable for a particular initiative. Hopefully, this serves as a cue to confirm that they have had **The Accountability Conversation**. If the answer is no, you might ask this individual to specifically do so, with your goal being to pull this behavior consistently forward.

The perspective of a pause, or a break in the action, is when you sense that the team's plate is full and you want to stage an initiative for a later time when it can be well received and executed with excellence versus mediocrity or resentment. Suggesting the pause to your team signals your social awareness of their full plate and demonstrates your affiliative leadership style.

Be sure to offer a time frame expectation for the pause, such as, "We will revisit this again in the third quarter," and be careful not to let a pause simply become a dropped initiative; pauses are not intended to be a final step but rather an interim one. Remember, the goal of *Leadership Rigor* is consciously competent performance, which includes tracking projects through to full completion or closure.

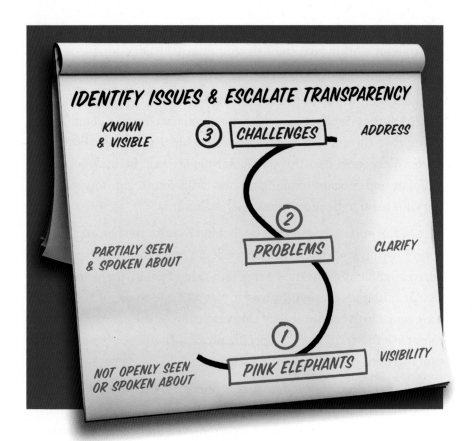

IDENTIFY ISSUES & ESCALATE TRANSPARENCY

KNOWN & VISIBLE — ③ CHALLENGES — ADDRESS

② PROBLEMS — CLARIFY

PARTIALY SEEN & SPOKEN ABOUT

NOT OPENLY SEEN OR SPOKEN ABOUT — ① PINK ELEPHANTS — VISIBILITY

3. | *Stage* | **a continual hunt for pink elephants!**

As a team leader, you need to stay socially alert to a concept called the ***pink elephant***. A pink elephant is an issue or concern that palpably blocks progress and open dialogue. It can negatively affect team dynamics by holding back trust building due to the fear and risk associated with surfacing the concern, so it often goes unaddressed. Even more challenging, it may not be visible to most team members.

If you don't clearly see it but you do sense an obstruction, introduce the concept of the pink elephant to your team so that individual members are more prepared to courageously deal with it. ***Pink elephants must be named so they can be made visible.*** Only then can they be transformed into problems and/or challenges to be addressed and resolved.

You Are Going to Be Fired!

Pink elephants can occur in one-to-one conversations just as easily as in group settings. One of my clients was an underperforming CEO in over his head working for a company headquartered in Asia. While we openly talked about his performance and the urgent need for changes, this did not happen fast enough to prevent the inevitable. He called me one day and told me he had been called to New York City for a meeting at a specific time but had not been given a subject. I told him, "Okay, let's just name this pink elephant right now...You are going to be fired, and it will all be okay." Saying it out loud and talking through it up front prepared him for the experience. On his way home the next day, he called me to confirm that he had in fact been terminated and that, yes, "It was okay."

Using **The Progressive Mindset** signature model from Part 1, there are *(3) phases of escalating transparency* in communication associated with critical issues. The most challenging level of communication occurs on the level of the *pink elephant,* when a concern is *not visible* to all or is not openly talked about in the room.

The issue is often either about naming the unproductive behavior of an individual who is feared to be emotionally imbalanced in their response to potential feedback or challenging an approach when you believe someone (often the leader) is making a mistake but is emotionally attached to it and seemingly unwilling to hear alternative views. The result is that the team is stuck and avoids the debates and courageous conversations it needs to have. Only if publicly named and given visibility can this pink elephant be appropriately dealt with.

A *problem* is the next phase of communication transparency. Here, some of the members may be open about discussing a topic but the team as a whole has not had collective conversations on the subject. The key here is to *clarify* a partially seen and partially spoken about concern so that the team has a full line of sight to the problem.

A *challenge* is a known and visible problem that everyone on the team sees and acknowledges. The next step here is to appropriately prioritize the challenge and move into action to **address** it.

I have often led team exercises in which we name a team's pink elephants, problems, and challenges and start prioritizing their action plans. Not only does this relieve hidden stress but it also takes teams to a new level of confidence and trust with one another. Teams need to act with complete transparency to be high performing.

Caution: it is sometimes better to have a trained facilitator in the room when pink elephants are discussed so that the team leader can actively participate in the discussion. If the discussion becomes emotional, it can be appropriately worked through rather than shut down, which might create new pink elephants and additional problems for the team to address.

RIGOR IT!

"A real leader faces the music even when he doesn't like the tune."

– Steve Jobs

III. Facilitating Communication across the Interfaces

Because communication is one of the (2) currencies of leadership, we will continue to spend time developing this essential skill throughout *Leadership Rigor.*

Team leaders can integrate into their leadership practices communication approaches to build stronger emotional bonds with their team members and colleagues.

(3) Techniques to Rigor Include:

- **Using Your Personal Power to Be Charismatic**

- **Creating Moments and Memories**

- **Cascading Communication Effectively**

Using Your Personal Power to Be Charismatic

We have all been asked to ponder the question of whether we believe leaders are born or made. Earlier in *Leadership Rigor,* I emphasized that leadership most definitely can be learned and that reaching conscious competency is the target for high-performance leaders.

Even so, many leaders have natural gifts and talents that facilitate the trajectory of their leadership careers, especially if they learn to consciously use and share them with others. The concept of "charisma" is related to the "leaders are born" story in which some leaders, for example, have a personal magnetism that naturally attracts others to them.

If you strip away the external attractiveness these individuals often have (i.e., they might be tall, nice looking, well dressed, confident, have a great smile, and so on), they also have a way of intimately connecting with you in terms of how they communicate. In other words, they are charismatic. This connection power is what truly sets them apart and pulls you toward them, and the result is that they influence you! You believe what they say because you believe they understand you. Consequently, you want to follow them.

While charisma is often an unconscious competency for some lucky individuals, everyone has the ability to be intentional about *"creating the essence of charisma."* How do you go about this?

> *You can create your own charisma by consciously expressing your personal power through an engaged and authentic connection with others. Personal power is about connecting to and believing in others in a way that inspires and influences them!*

Your fervent focus on them *creates an attraction towards you.* The difference is that personal power is truly in service of others, while charisma may or may not have the same consciously altruistic target!

Creating Moments and Memories

In addition to leadership being emotional, it is also *experiential.* Great leaders understand that setting the emotional context for a story or an experience significantly enhances the intensity of the connection others feel to it. These connections are so powerful that a phrase, word, or song can trigger the entire emotional experience all over again.

An example of this is hearing a favorite song. Perhaps this was the song that was playing when you had your first date with your significant other, or perhaps it was the theme song to a successful new product launch. Hearing that song triggers the feeling that brings up the experience, and as if by magic, you are emotionally transported there again!

Creating moments and memories is a powerful communication tool for leaders to understand and utilize, but it's not just about songs. Themes, mantras, and phrases you use in business settings can make moments and memories, too.

> *As a leader, you need to be looking for entry point moments that allow you to make an impact with your team and to create positive, inspiring memories that will live on in your organization's culture and history.*

Years ago, when I was asked to take on an expatriate assignment in Canada, without having met or spoken with a single employee, I found myself on a plane flying to Toronto and my first day on the job.

Looking back on it now, I was unconsciously competent at utilizing a visionary and affiliative leadership style in my initial divisional communication meeting as I explained where we were going and what we were going to change and achieve together as well as how it was going to feel. I was direct in stating that some team members were going to be inspired and motivated while others were going to conclude that this was not what they had signed up for and would self-select out or be asked to leave. Naturally, I also expressed a genuine interest in learning about hockey and becoming a Maple Leafs fan. I took advantage of stepping into an entry point moment to deliver a communication message that began to establish my relationship with the division as its new leader.

To frame the experience we were going to have together, I created a theme called **Turnaround 2000.** Everything we did that first year was in support of fundamentally turning around our business and delivering to our performance expectations.

At the end of the year, when we hit our goals, we celebrated with beautiful jackets embroidered with "Turnaround 2000," a division picture of all of us wearing them, a desktop glass paperweight inscribed with "Turnaround 2000," and a national sales meeting in Jamaica. Now that's what I call creating both an experience and a memory!

As I continue to occasionally check in with my colleagues from Canada, I am always touched when they mention how impactful Turnaround 2000 was for them and how it created some of their greatest learning insights that they continue to apply today. As a leader, it was clearly one of the most exciting moments and meaningful memories of my professional career.

Cascading Communication Effectively

Depending on your team structure, you may have direct reports supervising others who will need to share messages further downstream in the organization. This is why it's important for team leaders to understand how to cascade communication effectively.

Unfortunately, as previously mentioned, communication is often an illusion. People who think they are communicating with each other are instead often speaking at each other without truly understanding or interpreting the messages the same way.

Minimize the potential for miscommunication and misalignment by working with your team to develop and deliver clear and concise communication messages.

For example, your team will occasionally hold off-site meetings to discuss important business issues. Being out of the office does not go unnoticed. Since people are storytellers at heart, if you don't tell your colleagues what you are doing, they will make up a story about what they think is going on. You may not like their particular creative outcome, not to mention the time and energy they waste as they try to guess or imagine what did or did not happen.

To develop an impactful cascading communication message that eliminates this problem, use the following steps:

1. *Purpose:* **We met to discuss... (state the topic)**

2. *Productivity:* **We accomplished... (assess the progress)**

3. *Aspirational close:* **The outcome is... (benefit)**

That's it. The cascading communication message consists of (3) simple, short sentences developed at the close of your meeting and delivered consistently by each team member. The less embellishment, the better, as extraneous details only dilute the core message.

In delivering this message, you ensure that your team is aligned and focused in driving the business forward and understands how the outcomes you discussed relate directly to the people you are leading.

IV. How to Champion the Team's Journey

One of your (3) deliverables as a performance-based leader is to develop your team as an entity. You can do this by taking your team on a leadership development journey.

Within days of assuming my new role in Canada, I boldly declared to my leadership team, "We are all going to general management school together." What followed was an amazing (5)-year growth and development journey for all of us. Since then, each of those individuals has gone on to excel in their professional careers and to reach new levels of leadership performance.

Determine the Type of Leadership Journey to take:

- **Where Is Your Team in Its Life Cycle?**
- **What Is the Culture of Your Organization?**
- **Is Your Team Open or Resistant to the Journey?**

What Is Alignment?

I am often asked what "alignment" means. Very simply, while your team members may enter a room with different points of view, you all leave with one unified position that you collectively support and stand behind. It also means that you don't throw your colleagues under the bus after a decision is made with language like, "Yeah, I told them that was the wrong approach, but they decided to go forward anyway." Such comments are unprofessional and inappropriate.

Even when a decision is made that you do not initially support, the language you use needs to reflect team alignment. For example, you might say, "We thoughtfully considered several recommendations and debated their merits, but after considering all the possibilities, we chose the following approach. Here is why I fully support it and ask that you do as well."

Where Is Your Team in Its Life cycle?

The life cycle of a team can be assessed in terms of the tenure of the members (i.e., are they new or seasoned team members) and/or the life cycle of the work (i.e., are you undertaking a new or well established challenge).

You might expect these different scenarios to call for different approaches, but my leadership coaching experience suggests that regardless of the experience level of a team or the challenges it faces, a review of leadership and team-building basics is always a great way to start. This provides an opportunity to learn and use a common language as well as to create a unique experience together that builds cohesion.

While many of your members may have had training and team-building experiences before in their careers, they have not had them together as an intact team with you or with each other, which now creates a completely different dynamic and experience.

What Is the Culture of Your Organization?

Your organization likely has written values that describe the behavioral expectations for its employee community and that help to define its culture, which is "How we do things around here." You will want to rely on and reinforce these in whatever journey you create.

For example, if one of your values is creating a learning environment, you as team leader will want to shape your journey with this value in mind by creating a safe learning environment for your team members as they experience this process.

Alternatively, if one of your values is transparency, here too you will want your team-based work to support this value. You may include up-front conversations around the expectations and outcomes expected of your team journey so there are no hidden agendas or unforeseen consequences.

Is Your Team Open to or Resistant to the Journey?

Experiencing initial hesitation and even resistance from team members who question the time, costs, or benefits associated with team-building and leadership development initiatives is common.

Unfortunately, many employees view their technical work as their "real and only" job and believe that investments in leadership development and teamwork are an unnecessary or costly distraction. Sometimes this belief is based on a lack of knowledge and maturity within the team. Other times it has been shaped by previous ineffective team-building experiences. Clearly, a two-day workshop billed as a way to transform your team into a high-performance machine is not something you buy into twice, and rightfully so. The leadership journey needs to be appropriately framed for your team, clearly understood, and based on targeted realistic expectations.

Spend some time exploring where your team members are on this subject and ask questions to find out what has shaped their perspective. Your subsequent approach should reflect an understanding of where they are starting from and a proposal for how and why moving in a given direction will add real value and enhance on-the-ground performance.

In the end, what makes a journey successful or limits its impact is one thing: *the commitment and persistence of the leader.* In the face of resistance, complaints about the time it will take to implement, assertions that this is nonsense, or even gratuitous affirmations about how great this is, you must remain steadfast, committed, and persistent or real growth and change will not happen.

Remember, this is a journey about developing a set of behaviors that will guide working together as a team. *It requires patience, reinforcement, and time.* Championing this journey is a choice that requires discipline and vision. Along the way, you will need to challenge your team members to ask themselves if they really want to lead as they realize just what leadership is and what it takes to learn and apply the requisite skills with conscious discipline and practice.

▶ Creating the Framework of the Journey

As a leadership performance coach, I specialize in facilitating customized team leadership journeys. Perhaps surprisingly, every team has similar obstacles it must overcome and experiences it must have together in order to become high performing. What is unique is how each team member emotionally and intellectually navigates through learning about themselves and their colleagues. The individual barriers and relationship baggage that each team must work through present the biggest challenge, but on the other side of the experience await great breakthroughs for both the individuals and the team as an entity.

A group of individuals reporting to the same person does not necessarily constitute a team. A team has a palpable energy or spirit and an integrated approach to how it operates. What matters is on-the-ground performance, and teams know it!

What behaviors and actions would you expect to see from a team, and what are you trying to build in the team journey process?

> *You are looking for open-minded individuals who are willing to learn, not afraid to be vulnerable or to challenge each other on their technical and behavioral performances, and who are passionately committed and accountable to themselves, their team, their team leader, and their organization in their pursuit of collective performance goals.*

It is amazing to me how many leaders, especially those in small to mid-sized companies, confidently claim, "Yes, my team does all of that; we are pretty good in all those areas."

With experience, I have learned to just smile and start asking questions. As I do, I continue to appreciate just how challenging it is to be a consciously competent leader. Team leaders often have so many blind spots at the beginning of the process that they don't know what they don't know. If they are not challenged or questioned, they continue to believe they are already running high-performance teams.

This is because many leaders lack meaningful hands-on experiences outside of their own companies and don't know what high-performance teams look like. Others myopically focus on the tasks of their role and don't value the impact of teamwork. In the final analysis, many companies struggle with leadership performance, accepting and tolerating what is, because they lack the knowledge or do not have an expectation about what can be better!

By contrast, an aspiring performance-based team leader interested in providing rigor to his or her team's development would express *pragmatic humility* and admit, "We may be good in some of these areas, but we sure can improve in many if not most others."

With this open-minded team leader approach, your real journey of growth can begin!

▶ Creating the Experience of the Journey

While your journey can take many forms, having a team coach create a customized approach and facilitate your sessions will accelerate your progress and maximize your learning, experience, and opportunity to develop yourself as a leader as well as that of your team. Let me explain why.

Team building and leadership development are best accomplished through *structured experiential learning.* Adult learners in particular need to speak, share, engage, and most importantly challenge the material to fully wrap their heads and hearts around it. Heads come first and hearts follow more slowly, in my professional experience.

For this reason, it's important to structure the experience and utilize the skills of a facilitator or team coach to manage the challenging and often unpredictable dynamics in real time. When the conditions are set up properly, the outcomes can be breakthrough and magical. If conditions are not set up properly, the outcomes can be frustrating, disappointing, and potentially destructive.

If you make the decision to work with a team coach, the next challenge is working together to create an approach that is right for your team. Team journeys can occasionally be designed as short-term initiatives to jump-start a team into action, but more often they are longer-term commitments to thoroughly ground a team in behavioral changes that establish a disciplined focus on performance and productivity. Occasionally, the team leader commitment is so strong and the vision for change so aspirational that a leader will commit to a multi-year journey that helps to shape the team's organizational culture and leadership philosophy to a level of excellence. This breakthrough level of leadership is fully developed in Part 3.

In addition, while custom-designed exercises and experiences are critical, your team coach will likely suggest some tools and approaches to be used that have a track record of successfully moving teams forward.

One of the tools I use at the start of many of my team-building initiatives is Patrick Lencioni's book *The Five Dysfunctions of a Team*. This short, easy-to-read fable captures the essence of most team challenges with characters we can all recognize. In addition, it includes an easy-to-use online survey that can help you assess your team against the criteria discussed in the book. Armed with this material and assisted by an experienced team coach or facilitator, the provocative dialogue and learning begins.

In addition to team-building tools, I also use diagnostics that assist teams in understanding more about how they are individually hardwired and how their teammates are similar or different. While multiple diagnostic options are available, as mentioned elsewhere in **Leadership Rigor,** I frequently use the Myers-Briggs Personality Type Assessment (MBTI).

Based on Jungian psychology, the MBTI diagnostic is the most widely used personality assessment instrument in the world. I have used it hundreds of times and find it incredibly insightful. Because my work with teams and organizations occurs over a period of time, the language and concepts of the MBTI diagnostic become established with traction and create tangible momentum in the form of accelerated decision making, change management, and conflict resolution.

In addition to these tools, my work as a leadership coach has provided me with the challenge and creativity to develop hundreds of customized exercises that bring out the real issues teams face so that individual team members can learn to fully appreciate what being a high-performance team looks like, sounds like, and feels like in their specific organizations.

Unfortunately, reading books or attending a general classroom training session is not the same as creating an engaging, customized, real-time leadership journey with your intact team and its unique personalities and issues. I have had, and I am sure I'll continue to have, clients who naively attempt to facilitate these initiatives on their own. Typically, these efforts are short lived, and they shortchange the real value that can be created with objective professional facilitation to guide the journey and extract insights and breakthroughs. If you could really do this work on your own, your teams would already be high performing.

That's why you need to get real and Rigor it with a team coach!

Regardless of your ultimate approach, as team leader, you must take ownership for creating the healthy team dynamics that will allow the talent on your team to fully present itself and contribute to building the work together.

RIGOR IT!

"If the blind lead the blind, both shall fall into the ditch."
— The Bible

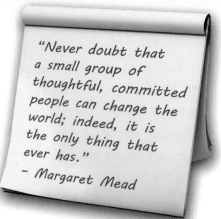

"Never doubt that a small group of thoughtful, committed people can change the world; indeed, it is the only thing that ever has."

— Margaret Mead

CHAPTER 2:
Building the Work Together

Now that you have started to build healthy team dynamics, it's time to get to work on the next part of your role as team leader!

What you do and how you do it as a team needs to be designed so that roles are clear, the fundamental expectations of the team are in place, and you are working with a vision of operational excellence to build the work product together.

The Fundamentals You Will Need to Work Include:

I. Confirming Your Rules of Engagement

II. Establishing Role Clarity

III. Running the Basic Operations of a Team

IV. Creating Operational Excellence

I. Confirming Your Rules of Engagement

High-performance teams take the time to establish their "rules of engagement," or ROE. Developed as early as possible in the team's life cycle, this common set of behavioral expectations outlines how a team will operate and interact together, providing criteria that team members can calibrate their performance against.

Creating this visibility makes it less likely that unproductive behaviors will be tolerated and more likely that sought-after behaviors will be displayed. It also gives the team collective ownership for its performance so it is less reliant on only the team leader for coaching and feedback.

Rigor These (5) Areas to Customize Your Team's ROE:

- Expectations
- Performance
- Accountability
- Transparency
- Decision rights

Expectations

Establish clear expectations with (3) considerations:

▶ **The leader's expectations for the team**

▶ **The team's expectations for the leader**

▶ **The team's expectations for each other**

Armed with a set of clearly articulated and documented expectations that serve as a reference and reminder, the work of a high-performance team can begin.

Performance

In *Leadership Rigor,* remember that performance is an equal function of both results and behaviors. Results refers to *what* you will collectively deliver as a team in terms of the work product while behaviors refer to *how* you interact with each other as you work.

These behaviors need to include the values your organization has developed, and you may want to enhance these with additional requirements to meet the needs of your team based on its membership and the specific challenges it faces. For example, perhaps your team is attempting to accelerate innovation at this stage in its life cycle, yet several members who have significant tenure on the team tend to quickly dismiss many of the ideas brought forth by newer members. One of the behaviors you may want to encourage as a team is "embracing creativity." This calls forth the expectation that potential pathways to overcome initial obstacles will be identified and discussed among the team members with the intent of collectively driving more new ideas into your pipeline.

Accountability

As mentioned in the previous chapter, there are actually (4) levels of accountability you will want your team to embrace:

▶ **Self-accountability** is a commitment that you will hold yourself to your words because your words have meaning.

▶ **Team accountability** (peer-to-peer) means that you will hold each other to perform to your stated expectations of delivering results and behaviors consistently.

▶ **Accountability to your team leader** recognizes that this individual holds the ultimate ownership for the team's collective performance along with the consequences, if negative, which means the leader too needs feedback if his or her behaviors or results are not in alignment with expectations.

▶ **Organizational accountability** means that you understand how your team's contributions fit into the work of your larger organization and that you serve in your team role with an enterprise mindset.

Team accountability, or peer-to-peer accountability, is often the most challenging. Regardless of the discomfort, you are well served to establish your ROE to include an expectation for holding team members accountable and for allowing them to do the same for you as their team leader. Only teams that learn how to do this in a productive and carefrontational manner achieve high levels of performance.

Encouraging the use of **The Accountability Conversation** in your ROE for both internal team use and externally with cross-functional partners can help to ensure that you are disciplined as a team in only signing up for what you can deliver. It can also provide you with some assurance that others both upstream and downstream from you will not drop any balls, causing you or your team to miss a deliverable.

Transparency

High-performance teams work with full transparency and look to eliminate sidebar conversations or "the meetings after the meeting" that undermine trust, the glue that holds a team together.

Your team's ROE should include a commitment to hunt for pink elephants and make them visible, turning them into problems to solve or challenges for prioritized resolution, on a regular basis.

Decision Rights

In the business world, we all tend to believe we are experts in decision making, but what happens in a team setting when everyone wants to be the decision maker or the team leader chooses to make all the decisions? How will your ROE address this?

The answer lies in establishing what are called decision rights. This is language, criteria, and expectations that define who will own which decisions and that explain how others will be involved in the process.

There are no hard and fast rules for establishing decision rights; many teams just consciously rigor it with a discussion to establish who the decision maker will be for a particular initiative.

The key is to declare the decision maker up front, before the dialogue and debate unfold and emotional dynamics come into play.

As a new team leader, you may want to initially establish decision rights more formally. One simple way to do this is by **using the RACI framework.** Here, you give one individual *the "A," or the accountability* for owning and delivering an initiative, including making the decisions that concern the progress and outcomes of that initiative. As the decision owner, this individual determines how and by whom the decision will be made (i.e., by group vote, by the individual holding the "A," or by another decision maker).

Other individuals on the team may be given (R) responsibility for tasks associated with the decision, may need to be (C) consulted

Eliminate RACI Take-Backs

When using the RACI framework, make sure you carefully consider when and to whom you give the "A" (accountability). This is a tool that involves both role clarity (i.e., ownership and participation) and decision-making authority. If you give away the "A" and then decide to take it back, choosing instead to make the decision yourself (this commonly happens with new leaders), you will undermine confidence, confuse role clarity, and cause compression in your team as you lower your altitude by taking on a challenge that someone else could have handled. Take the time to consciously decide how to appropriately use the RACI tool!

before the decision is made because their insights may influence the choices under consideration, or may be designated as someone who is (I) informed, meaning that before the decision is made public, they are given a head's up by the decision maker so they are prepared to answer questions and provide perspective as necessary.

Notice the link to the Do-Manage-Lead Model here as well!

Any structured approach to decision rights can work. Just agree on an approach and commit to using the appropriate language with discipline and consistency. In other words...

II. Establishing Role Clarity

When individuals are *not clear on their roles* or the roles of others, effectiveness and efficiency evaporate, which *minimizes productivity and compromises performance,* the two critical focus areas for the team leader. Clearly, the stakes are high with respect to role clarity, and while this can be a significant undertaking, both formal and informal approaches exist to secure it.

The formal approach for role clarity is a written job description that outlines the performance expectations (behaviors and deliverables) for each position including areas of ownership, participation, and contribution as well as critical stakeholder relationships relative to successfully fulfilling the job requirements. If you are working for a progressive organization, you might also have a job profile outlining the targeted technical and behavioral competency expectations for each level within the organization.

With these two documents, executives will have a clear understanding of the performance requirements they are expected to demonstrate in a given role.

The informal approach (either used alone or in combination with the formal approach) is a practical reinforcement or confirmation of role clarity through conscious discipline and practice, and here the tools in *Leadership Rigor* can be instrumental in providing additional support to your efforts. Specifically, you can establish and reinforce role clarity by:

- Using **The Accountability Conversation** to ensure that expectations, resources, and deliverables are clear

- Overcommunicating at the project interfaces with key stakeholders so there is limited duplication and problems can be solved in real time

- Seeking role clarity solutions that target the people and process levels rather than problem levels so that sustainable, system-based versus situational-based approaches can be developed

When you utilize this **Leadership Rigor** approach and invest in defining role clarity up front, you will uncover a worthwhile percentage of resources that have been previously wasted and that can now be applied more productively moving forward!

III. Running the Basic Operations of a Team

Running the operations of a team can be a challenge for both new and veteran team leaders. Here, your ability to manage time and meetings critically comes into play. What's at stake is whether you have the skill and discipline to realize the value of the potential talent on your team in successfully growing your business.

Your role as team leader is to establish the *internal conditions for success.* Success means delivering a high-quality work product, developing the team as a high-performance entity, and developing the individuals on your team.

Rigor the Operations of Your Team with (3) Disciplines:

- **Administrative Discipline**

- **Engagement Discipline**

- **Productivity Discipline**

Administrative Discipline

The leader is the architect for setting up the administrative structure of the team, which includes meetings, one-to-ones, and reporting requirements.

Whether it is a personal strength or something you struggle with, setting up the administrative structure for the team is a vital part of your job, and you must own it! You can choose to engage in it personally or you can work in partnership with a strong administrative executive to get it done. Either way, addressing the following questions will help you proactively *set up the logistics* for how your team will operate by establishing your administrative expectations and rhythm.

▶ How Often Will the Team Meetings Occur?

The rhythm and frequency of structured meetings should reflect the life cycle stage of the team. New teams should meet with greater frequency, while established teams can meet with less frequency, but all teams are well served by meeting at least once per month.

If critical projects need to be discussed with deeper dives, they may need to be supplemental to these forums. There is always a balance to strike. You do not want to overburden your team with too many meetings, and for this reason, they should be limited to discussions that require interactive debate, input, feedback, problem solving, and securing alignment.

Note: The next chapter of **Leadership Rigor** covers how to maximize meeting time through the discipline of selecting appropriate meeting formats.

▶ How Often Will You Hold One-to-Ones?

This answer depends on the development stage of the employee. Minimally, you need to meet with each direct report at least once per month for at least an hour, but you should meet with less experienced executives more frequently to accelerate their learning curves.

Do not cancel these meetings, regardless of how extremely busy and occasionally overwhelmed you are by your own commitments. Maintaining the rhythm of the one-to-ones is critical for building capability and confidence in your direct reports. If you do need to occasionally reschedule, be respectful of this important interaction by immediately offering an alternative date and time to connect, but do not make a habit of it!

One-to-one meetings should be owned and driven by your direct reports. This is their opportunity to ask questions and get coaching on the challenges they face as well as to talk about their professional development. It is also valuable to embrace this forum as a safe place where your direct reports can give you feedback so you can learn, grow, and better serve them and the team.

Your role is to ensure that your team members are progressing in building both their technical and behavioral skills and that you are stretching them to grow. Using one-to-ones to get project updates so you feel informed shortchanges your direct reports, so consciously look for other ways to get this basic information.

▶ Where Will You Meet and for How Long?

Do not be passive regarding the space selections for your meetings. The venue is critically important to mood and energy dynamics. A few tips:

- ☑ Pick a location with natural light, if possible, and make sure it is big enough to comfortably sit and move around in so team members can occasionally stand or stretch their legs. People who are uncomfortable will not be as fully engaged, so set the right conditions.

- ☑ Team meetings will vary in length, but connecting for at least (2) to (3) hours once a month is a minimum target. This allows for several subjects to be fully discussed, time for questions, and the ability to add late-breaking important issues to the agenda as necessary. If you find yourself rushing through your agenda and team members mainly report information without much dialogue, you are not really conducting a productive team meeting. You may want to consider issuing an update report that can be read instead.

☑ Team meeting times should take advantage of the diversity of ideas, insights, and opinions in the room. This is where issues should be debated, ideas flushed out, risks discussed, and options considered in the decision-making process. This time should be marked by high energy and high engagement, and therefore relevant for all involved.

☑ One mistake I commonly see is team leaders trying to conduct one-to-ones with each member in the team setting and getting into specific updates that are not relevant for the broader team. Avoid this trap. Make sure your agenda items are appropriate topics for the entire team and that your altitude is at the right level.

☑ If appropriate, have water and coffee in the room and take regular breaks to ensure energy levels remain high. The rule of thumb is a (10)–(15) minute break for every (90)–(120) minutes scheduled.

☑ Confirm in advance that the supplies you need (i.e., flip chart, markers, LCD, copies, Internet access codes, etc.) are in the room so the meeting is not delayed with set-up disruptions.

☑ Start and end your meetings on time. Be clear about respecting each other's time and role model this with your own behavior. If this is a challenge for your team, incorporate specific expectations in your rules of engagement.

▶ How Far in Advance to Schedule the Calendar?

If your meetings occur once a month, set them for the entire year up front and proactively work around standing company events, major conferences, and your own senior leadership team meetings so you don't have to reschedule later. If meetings are held more frequently, schedule them quarterly or semi-annually. Calendars fill quickly, and staking out your ground early will save administrative time and re-work later.

Publish the list of potential meeting dates before solidly booking, and give your team a chance to weigh in on personal/professional conflicts they may have that can be accommodated with early planning. Consider a consistent week and day of the month, such as the third Thursday or the first Friday, so that team members know this is a standing meeting date they need to hold.

Once agreed to, these dates should be locked in with the expectation of 100% attendance, barring emergencies or unforeseen issues.

Keep Your Commitments!

External customer meetings do not automatically trump internal team meetings! Your customers are critical to your success, but don't create an expectation that if a customer wants to meet, you will drop everything, including any internal commitments you may have. Just like with any other relationship, customers are partners with whom you need to negotiate. You do not want to be in the habit of surrendering to their perceived power position and labeling yourself a "vendor" who jumps when they call, justifying it as "outstanding customer service."

The expectation should be that your team meetings are locked in. If a customer meeting is requested, either negotiate an alternative date and time that works for both of you or send another representative to cover the customer meeting. If you feel that no one except you is qualified to handle the meeting, ask yourself if you are appropriately leading and developing the talent around you.

Now, if you are not running productive meetings and they are a waste of time that you would prefer to get out of, you have other challenges to work on. **Rigor it** with respect, both internally and externally!

You are going for discipline and consistency here, since this is what rhythm is all about.

> *Up front logistical planning can eliminate the frustrations of partial attendance that can affect productivity and undermine team performance.*

▶ How To Set the Agenda for Meetings

To ensure that you have a high-performance interaction, issue a written agenda for meetings at least (2) to (3) days in advance to allow for appropriate preparation. *The purpose of the agenda is to set the direction for how your time will be invested together* and should include at least (5) pieces of information for each topic covered:

1. *Topic* name and owner

2. *Purpose* (input, discussion, or decision)

3. *Time required* (both presentation and Q&A)

4. *Pre-work* reading required (attachments)

5. *Action steps* agreed to at last meeting

Action steps and agreements should be published within (24)–(48) hours post meeting, with each issue owner providing the language to the designated individual who will issue the follow-up notes. Projects should be tracked through to completion and then taken off the list.

One-to-one agendas need be developed by your direct reports. You can request that items be added to their agendas as long as their priorities are addressed first. You might choose to develop a *standing agenda* format with specific topics (i.e., project challenges, stakeholder relationship issues/opportunities, learning and development needs, areas for coaching, etc.) that are covered each time in order to maintain rhythm and consistency.

Engagement Discipline

Being present is not the same as being engaged. To run the operations of your team with a high level of performance, you and your members need to be game-ready for engaging in your meetings, which includes *preparation, presence, and active participation.*

Engagement discipline is required to both drive the business forward and to grow the team together through experiences. As the team leader, you must role model passionate engagement and facilitate meetings for this discipline, keeping in mind the following criteria:

- **What Engagement Looks, Sounds, and Feels Like**

- **Creating Shared Ownership for Team Meetings**

- **Coaching Engagement during Team Meetings**

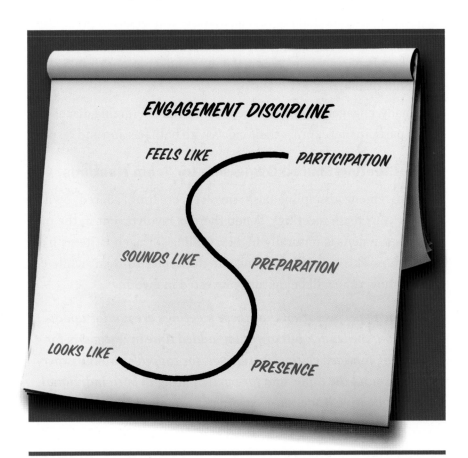

▶ What Engagement Looks, Sounds, and Feels Like

Engagement discipline *looks like* arriving on time to meetings and being ready to go to work. Team members who are engaged display positive, open body language, pay attention (i.e., they are not distracted by electronic devices, etc.), and actively listen. They are disciplined about taking notes and watching their colleagues around the room for social awareness cues.

Engagement discipline *sounds like* insightful, curious questions that reflect preparation and an understanding of the issues. Team members purposefully put forward their points of view while acknowledging how the interactive dialogue may be impacting, changing, or influencing their perspective. Challenges are expressed in a carefrontational way, team members attempt to process new information in real time, and they confidently make suggestions on new patterns or insights that are revealed as the conversation progresses. Members also call on the introverts in the room to weigh in if they haven't spoken in a while. Personal power and emotional intelligence are on full display!

Finally, engagement discipline *feels like* an energizing discussion where participants express their views with both passion and respect.

▶ Creating Shared Ownership for Team Meetings

Engagement discipline also involves creating shared ownership for your team meetings. When there is involvement in the process, engagement is naturally higher. Calling for agenda items from the team reveals relevant and meaningful topics to them while co-creating how time will be mutually invested in meetings.

> *Frame the expectation that these meetings are not for updating you, the leader, but are value-added time investments for moving forward critical initiatives, for tapping into the expertise around the table, and for participating in both individual and collective leadership learning.*

As team leader, you can get everyone grounded and involved early in the meeting process by facilitating a quick two-minute roundtable update (a lightning round) on priority initiatives or by asking a provocative opening question.

You may also request that your team members assist in running a meeting. For example, someone may be asked to serve as the timekeeper to ensure the agenda is honored. Another member may be asked to facilitate a brainstorming session. You may challenge one individual to summarize the session to ensure clarity and closure has been secured. Actively involving team members builds your bench strength by providing structured opportunities for crossing the knowing-doing gap.

▶ Coaching Engagement during Team Meetings

You can also look for entry points to coach for additional engagement. For example, if team members are engaging in healthy productive conflict and this is not a common practice, take a moment to acknowledge, recognize, and openly encourage more of this behavior. By making it consciously visible, others will understand what productive conflict looks like and will have less fear about engaging in it.

On the other hand, if the team appears to be stuck and is going in circles, ask team members if they are working at the right altitude. Should they go up a level in perspective? Is there a question they need to be asking themselves or a pink elephant they need to name right now that would break through their logjam?

Make sure that your team members do not rescue each other! If someone is on the hot seat, do not let another team member come in and make excuses or speak for this individual or, worse yet, make a humorous or sarcastic comment to relieve the tension in the room. Let the team member fully experience the challenge, discomfort, and perhaps even the disappointment of this particular moment. See if the individual will step up to own the situation as opposed to sitting there speechless or making an excuse.

Rescuing a team member takes away a real learning opportunity while selfishly serving the rescuer who is most certainly uncomfortable with the situation. Don't rescue. Instead, rigor the situation with self-management and social awareness!

Productivity **Discipline**

Running the operations of a team with productivity discipline requires an integrated utilization of all that *Leadership Rigor* has covered so far while encompassing a few new challenges. These include:

- **Leader's Role in Opening and Closing Meetings**

- **The Leader's Role as Facilitator**

- **Use Discussion Formats to Drive Productivity**

- **Use Decision Rights to Drive Productivity**

- **The Accountability Conversation Drives Productivity**

▶ Leader's Role in Opening and Closing Meetings

I have run thousands of meetings, and I continue to learn in each and every one that the first (2) to (3) minutes are critical in determining the mood and outcomes. Be mindful and create the opening impact you want to have.

The team leader should *frame the context* of how time is going to be invested up front. You might do this by stating the purpose, the expected outcomes, or the level of engagement you want to see in the meeting.

As previously mentioned, it is important to use conscious discipline to close each segment that is discussed. You will want to make sure there is *clarity on agreements* and decisions as well as an understanding of *who will do what by when.*

At the close of the overall meeting, try not to finish in a rush that concludes with the team urgently flying out the door. Even worse is to end the meeting late and have people slowly exiting one at a time because of other commitments. Make sure your overall agenda includes a small amount of time dedicated at the end for ***appropriately wrapping up and summarizing the meeting.***

As the leader, this is when you will want to make *positive acknowledgements* of the work the team has done together and point out any behaviors that support the leadership development process (i.e., good productive conflict, use of self-management and social awareness, or peer-to-peer accountability). You will also want to develop a few cascading messages that the team can share with direct reports or key stakeholders, if appropriate.

Finally, consider using a closing plus/delta exercise to conclude the meeting. This is a quick way for the team to provide feedback on what went well (plus) that it can continue to do and what did not go well (delta) that it wants to change in order to increase performance and productivity together during the next team meeting.

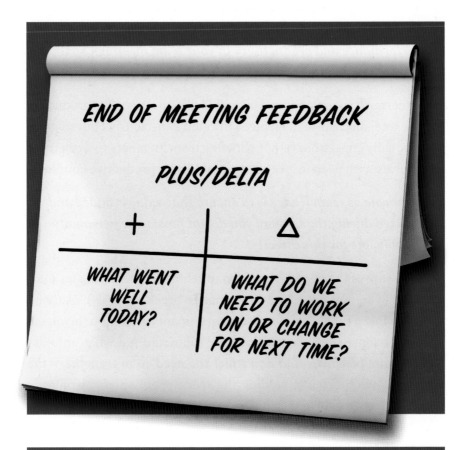

▶ The Leader's Role as Facilitator

Facilitating your team meetings will require that you flexibly utilize several of the interpersonal leadership styles previously discussed in Chapter 1 of this section. For example, when you open the meeting, you might choose to use a *visionary style* to set the context for why a particular topic is on your agenda today, or you may open with an affiliative style that empathizes with a current challenge the team is facing and then takes the team forward to demonstrate how today can be the start of overcoming and addressing this challenge.

During the course of a discussion being led by another member, you might use your *coaching leadership style* to engage in a teachable moment for team learning. If the team gets stuck, jump in and direct, ask a participative question, or pace set the conversation forward.

> *Your agility in appropriately applying these various leadership styles will directly impact your ability to drive performance and productivity in your team meetings, so it is worth taking the time to Rigor it!*

In certain circumstances, you will facilitate the team's productivity by exercising self-management through consciously choosing not to personally engage but rather allowing team members to work it out themselves with peer-to-peer accountability or productive conflict.

> *Your role as team leader is to ensure that value is added and created during the session; you do not have to be personally responsible for this directly!*

Be aware of the energy level of your team members and stay alert to social awareness cues. Is it time to take a break, move to closure on a topic, name a pink elephant, ask a participant to get more involved, or just let some silence come into the room and see what unfolds? *Follow your instincts, and don't feel the need to overengineer the meeting.* Sometimes just holding the space open while trusting the process allows magic to take place, and what needs to happen, does!

▶ Use Discussion Formats to Drive Productivity

As a leadership performance coach, I consistently find that most teams operate at a low level of productivity in their meetings. Most of the meetings are either general information sharing or a group one-to-one in which each individual addresses the leader with the remainder of the team more or less in observation mode.

To overcome this tendency, consider consciously utilizing one of the following (4) basic formats for conducting team discussions:

- **Information sharing**

- **Coordination orientation**

- **Operational focus**

- **Strategic planning**

Information sharing formats are *best used sparingly, if at all,* since collective meeting time should be reserved for interactive discussions. Reporting information can be done in a passive format such as an email or a report that can be read ahead of time. Be disciplined and ensure that information sharing in a team meeting is strictly limited to high-energy (1) or (2)-minute roundtable updates on critical issues that are relevant to the whole team.

Coordination orientation formats are best used for integrated activities that need to be completed on common timelines or that have interactive, sequential, and cascading impacts on other parts of the organization.

An example would be your annual/mid-year performance reviews or talent management processes. Certain documents, coaching conversations, cross-functional calibration meetings, and bonus allocation decisions all have to be completed by certain time frames driven by your overall organizational calendar.

Another example requiring coordination might be your annual budget planning process. Your division might roll up its numbers to a board or senior leadership team, requiring that each team provide input into the process several weeks prior to a specific organizational roll-up approval meeting. Each team will need to coordinate its own internal efforts to achieve this integrated input with time for debate, changes, and functional team alignment on agreements prior to the broader submission.

Operational focus formats are used to discuss alternative options, debate trade-offs and make collective decisions on how best to move forward with resources a particular challenge. An example of this may be that your organization is not hitting its overall financial targets and needs to cut discretionary spending budgets by 10%. Accordingly, your team needs to come up with its contribution. As team leader, you can choose to just cut 10% equally across the board, or you can have your team discuss and debate how best to get to the 10% while preserving the most important initiatives you are collectively working on.

In an operational focus approach, several members of the team may need to take a significant cut in resources in order to help another member preserve an important investment in a tight budget environment. These trade-offs are the essence of performance and productivity at the operational level.

Strategic planning formats are where most teams want to spend their time because business leaders are overwhelmingly attracted to the word "strategic," yet this word is often misunderstood. Strategic decision making is about the choices you make to create competitive advantage and win in the marketplace, with the operative words being "competitive advantage." If you are not externally focused on creating competitive advantage, you are more likely discussing an issue related to delivering on the internal operational plan.

Most functional team discussions are not strategic. However, they need to be predominantly operational as compared to coordination or information sharing. Below the executive leadership team of an organization, teams either do not have the decision rights for choosing among the strategic options or the altitude they are working at is pri-

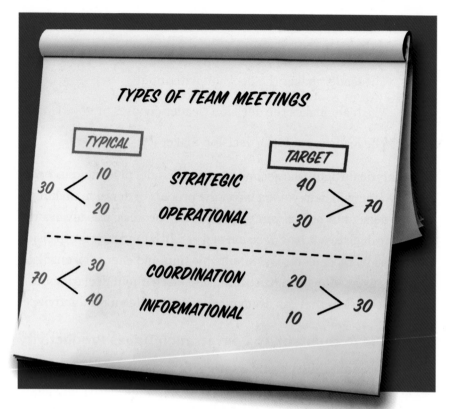

TYPES OF TEAM MEETINGS

TYPICAL			TARGET	
30 <	10	STRATEGIC	40	> 70
	20	OPERATIONAL	30	
70 <	30	COORDINATION	20	> 30
	40	INFORMATIONAL	10	

marily the operational level, which by the way, in running an entire business or a piece of the business, is incredibly important!

Clarifying expectations up front about the meeting approach that is going to be used in a given circumstance (i.e., operational versus strategic) provides the team leader with an opportunity to deliver an experience that is more engaging and rewarding. When the approach is not clarified, everyone has a different set of expectations, and some participants will be frustrated when the meeting does not go as they expected. **Rigor it** with alignment on expectations and an experience to match!

▶ Use Decision Rights to Drive Productivity

Team leaders play an essential role in the decision-making process. Specifically, the team leader needs to determine who the decision maker will be and then allow that individual to decide how the decision will be made.

There are several options to consider as you rigor it forward:

- The leader is the decision maker

- The leader makes the decision with input

- The team makes the decision (leader chooses method)

- The leader appoints a decision maker

Analytical Rigor, the second signature model presented in ***Leadership Rigor,*** will help you focus on the process of decision making in greater detail, but before you move into any process, it is always important to declare who the decision maker will be and how the decision will be made. Most teams waste valuable time and energy by engaging in long conversations and frustrating debates without declaring these (2) simple choices that can dramatically improve team productivity!

▶ The Accountability Conversation Drives Productivity

The Accountability Conversation, first mentioned in Chapter 3 of Part 1, provides a common language for securing clarity and alignment on expectations and deliverables. By negotiating up front what is needed, in what format, and by when, team members can be disciplined in planning their work and more productively utilizing their limited resources.

IV. Creating Operational Excellence

As a general manager in my first full divisional P&L (profit and loss) role, I coined a phrase with my leadership team that became the framework for delivering our work product. ***The phrase was "operational excellence," and the work product was the*** *integrated delivery of the division's performance* from a sales, marketing, and financial perspective. The approach was comprehensive and included revenue, cost of goods, discounts, forecasting, inventory, receivables, cash management, customer/account focus, market share, advertising, promotional investments, overhead cost management, and bottom-line profitability.

Take a moment to consider the elements that determine the optimal framework for your unique operational excellence philosophy.

Rigor and Understand the Following:

- Know What You Are Driven By

- Determine Your Scoreboard

- Differentiate between Blue and Green Dollars

- Use a Portfolio Management Approach

- Be Ready to Make Tough Choices

Know What You Are Driven By

Teams can proudly tell you whether they are sales driven, marketing driven, customer driven, profit driven, and so on. In fact, what a team is driven by sets the stage for most of its decisions because it becomes a "driving" part of the culture, defining "How we do things around here."

On the surface, this seems positive, but what I have learned through my business and leadership performance coaching experience is this:

> *If you are leading a team, functional area, or organization in which integrated performance is your ultimate goal, being driven by anything that does not represent an integrated approach is limiting and distracting if not downright counterproductive and dangerous!*

Let me provide an example. If you are a sales-driven organization, chances are you are extremely focused on giving customers what they want and you likely subscribe to the age-old philosophy that the number one rule is that the customer is always right, and if you don't get it, check out rules two and three, which reconfirm rule number one, which is that the customer is always right.

Consequently, your organization jumps through hoops and does all it can to satisfy the customer. This may include special packaging, shipping requirements, service requests or discounts, most of which are not profitable for your organization to deliver.

Once in this *sales-driven cycle*, when you finally realize the financial impact of what you have been doing over time and find you have to push back on a customer, your sales people will claim you are taking a monumental risk. Further, they believe they now have to be heroes to secure this business. This cycle, if continued for a long time and left unchecked, can erode profitability and performance by shifting your organizational resources to places that do not serve your long-term business health or growth interests.

This was the case when I arrived in Canada. We were a sales-driven division *"pushing the business"* into our customers, causing overblown inventory levels both in our own and in our customers' warehouses. We were paying with deep discounts to push our products in and then paying even more money to run promotional programs with our customers to pull product out. *We were caught in an endless trap!* All of these efforts stagnated our sales growth, eroded our margins, decreased our overall profitability, and increased our dependence on any and all customer requests, regardless of their business merits.

Our biggest problem was that as a packaged-goods healthcare company selling branded products to consumers such as Bayer Aspirin and Flintstones vitamins, the fundamentals of our business model were to drive market share by consumers *preferentially choosing or "pulling"* our brands off of store shelves because of our superior quality and perceived benefits, yet we were taking the exact opposite approach and managing our business by discounting our way to sales.

Of course, in some ways, you could call this a consumer-driven marketing approach, and you would be right. The point is, sales driven, marketing driven, or financially driven, any singular approach is potentially disastrous!

> **The only way to run an integrated team or organization is to be business and operationally driven.**

Operational excellence begins with integrating your overall approach to the business and eliminating the trap of skewing your organization's view of your performance by being functionally driven.

When my Canadian team became operationally driven, we immediately changed our altitude as well as the quality of our discussions and decisions. We debated the trade-offs on the right issues and challenged ourselves to *make the opportunities we had work on an integrated basis or to pass on them.*

This philosophy of operational excellence turned our organization into an entirely different place. Yes, we experienced pain, resistance, and the challenge of losing business throughout this transition because we were in a turnaround situation, but we ultimately persisted and prevailed. We ended up exceeding our budget for each of the next (5) years that I served as GM, and we progressed to be in the top (10) countries based on organic growth rates. **Rigor it** with an integrated approach and watch your operations soar!

Determine Your Scoreboard

Once you decide on your approach to operational excellence, identify the critical metrics to track your progress as well as your leading and lagging indicators so that you know how you are progressing and whether changes are needed. For example, you might be tracking:

- ☑ **Market share**
- ☑ **Conversion rates**
- ☑ **Activities that drive leads (e.g., sales calls)**
- ☑ **Macro-economic trends**
- ☑ **Inventory turns**
- ☑ **Sales velocity**
- ☑ **Distribution and penetration levels**

One difference I often see between large organizations and smaller private companies is that leaders in large organizations know how they are performing at all times relative to the marketplace, their competitors as well as what the relevant and critical trends are (both qualitative and quantitative) in their external environment.

Many private business owners know whether they are growing year to year (or not), but they can't give a relative perspective on where their competition is or whether they are doing something unique that is allowing them to grow disproportionately. They will try to give explanations, but they often lack the data to support them.

Wherever possible, try to have an anchor with which to *gauge and benchmark your relative performance in a quantifiable and measurable way.* In other words, rigor it with an investment in the metrics!

Differentiate between Blue and Green Dollars

Nothing in business (or life) is free. There are costs associated with everything. The question is whether they are visible to you.

One of the best examples of this is the difference between blue dollars (the fully loaded cost of employees, including benefits) and green dollars (the money spent when you write checks).

Additional resources are occasionally needed on a particular project, and leaders will often shift people here or there as needed to cover workload. If a shift is short term, important, and offers a learning opportunity, it might be a smart move. Even so, as a team leader, you need to watch for appropriate and inappropriate resource (re)allocation; this is your altitude responsibility. You manage the resources of people, time, and money, so you need to be mindful of how your blue-dollar people resources are being moved, shifted, and utilized.

There is always a cost/benefit assessment that team leaders need to consider regarding where their people resources do and do not focus their time. Having conscious discipline in making these trade-off decisions on both blue and green dollars is critical to maximizing operational performance and productivity.

Use a Portfolio Management Approach

As a team leader, you may be responsible for multiple products or investments. One of the critical elements of operational excellence is having a transparent portfolio management approach. You need to know how your assets fit together and establish up front how to make investment trade-offs to deliver against performance expectations.

In Canada, I created (4) categories for our business portfolio of consumer healthcare brands. They were:

- Invest for *growth*

- High *maintenance*

- Low *maintenance*

- Manage for *profit*

Each quadrant had defined criteria for performance expectations (growth, market share, margin, and profitability targets) aligned with resource allocation targets.

> *Investing equally across a portfolio is never a smart or sustainable approach; you always need to make choices on where to place your bets for growth. The question is, how do you make these choices?*

In our case, these choices were made by our brand managers pitching for resources according to one of the portfolio quadrants they believed best matched the life cycle potential for the brand as well as what they could deliver. The leadership team listened to the pitch, challenged with questions, and then either approved the plan based on the risk profile and our confidence in the brand manager or did not, suggesting instead an alternative approach. Our investment choices were funded by other brands scaling back or not receiving

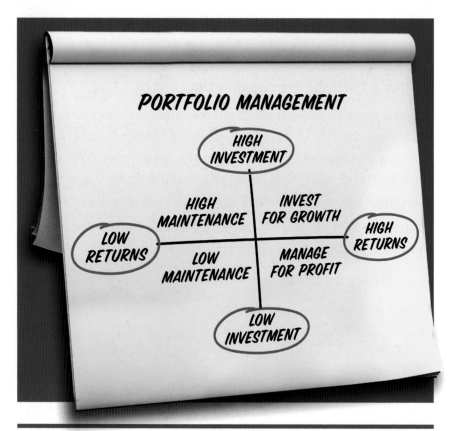

support. We aligned our inventory levels and production schedules with our portfolio strategy, and we tracked and measured performance weekly and monthly to ensure that our choices were working in the marketplace. If they were not, we either took the risk to double down for a defined period with an adjusted performance target or we changed the choice selection and realigned the portfolio.

This was a productive way to dynamically manage the operations of the business, and because it was visible and well communicated, our entire organization was engaged in the delivery of the work.

Rigor your investment portfolio and make your choices transparent so that your team is fully aligned!

Be Ready to Make Tough Choices

One of the positive consequences of being operationally driven is that your objective and integrated approach gives you the clarity and the freedom to make tough decisions.

For example, it will at times be clear to you that you need to fire a customer or stop doing a piece of business with a client because it no longer makes sense for your organization. Perhaps this client consistently requests adjustments to specs and is too resource intensive with your organization's time (i.e., consumes significant blue dollars), the relationship is no longer profitable, or the client is simply too difficult to work with.

Don't be afraid to make the unpopular decisions.

You must be able to model to your team that you will maintain the integrity of the operational excellence approach. If you can renegotiate a more favorable partnership, adjust expectations, or work out your business challenges, do so. If you can't, walk away. If you don't, the emotional drain on your organization will be more costly than the loss of the business!

Building the work together as a team requires disciplined logistics with an operational focus. Your team's setup, the rhythm and format for meetings, and how you manage the work product all contribute to your performance and productivity.

"Individual commitment to a group effort— that is what makes a team work, a company work, a society work, a civilization work."

− Vince Lombardi

CHAPTER 3:
Building Alignment across the Enterprise

Team leaders play an important role at the interfaces of their organizations. This is the point of complexity where work products change hands as they progress forward and where different stakeholders get involved in the prioritization, resource allocation or decision-making process.

From cross-functional alignment with peers to working between the interfaces of senior management and their direct reports, the team leader must focus on building alignment across the organization. Relying on the utilization of the leadership currencies of communication and relationships, the team leader needs to ensure that everyone is on the same page and pulling in the same direction while working out concerns and conflicts.

The Fundamentals You Need to Rigor Include:

I.   Being an Advocate for Integrated Operations

II. Managing Your Stakeholder Relationships

III. Developing Your Internal and External Networks

Team leaders who demonstrate strong skills in these areas set themselves apart in performance and start to become viewed as potential candidates for advancing into organizational leadership roles.

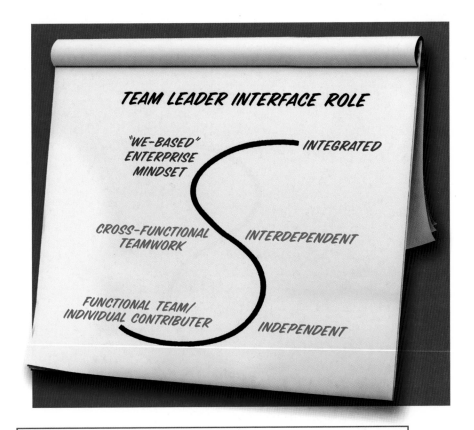

TEAM LEADER INTERFACE ROLE

"WE-BASED" ENTERPRISE MINDSET — INTEGRATED

CROSS-FUNCTIONAL TEAMWORK — INTERDEPENDENT

FUNCTIONAL TEAM/ INDIVIDUAL CONTRIBUTER — INDEPENDENT

I. Being an Advocate for Integrated Operations

The role of a team leader is itself an interface between the work of the team and the broader work of the organization. Using **The Progressive Mindset** signature model from Part 1 to frame this, the team leader has evolved from being an independent individual contributor into being interdependent and working across the organization.

The challenge for the team leader is to use this new altitude and perspective to become an advocate for the integrated operations of the company while focusing on getting his or her team members to move to the next level of collaborative interdependence from their current independent (individual contributor) roles.

Being an advocate for integrated operations requires a team leader to be inclusive, collaborative, and to have the ability to provide ideas and negotiate *in service of an enterprise "we-based" agenda.*

254

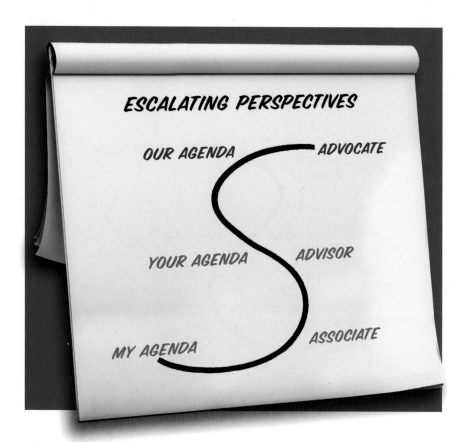

This approach is distinct from either being merely an associate or advisor and is the target for this level of leadership.

An associate will come at interfaces from the mindset of "my agenda/my work" and look to satisfy personal needs. An advisor looking at the interface will likely try to take on the perspective of "your agenda/your work" and help you accomplish your tasks for the good of the team. The advocate with an overall enterprise perspective attempts to provide guidance and counsel that serves the organization as a whole. This may include going back and making changes within his or her part of the organization or asking that colleagues be requested to makes changes in their respective areas of responsibility if that is what is needed to serve an "our agenda/our enterprise" approach.

Being an advocate for integrated operations also means that you value open access to talent and resources for enhancing communi-

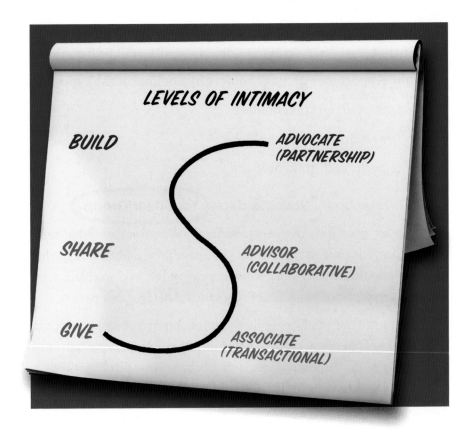

cation and accelerating workflow across the enterprise. *You do not operate with a silo mentality that places people in boxes and asserts position power over access to resources.* The overall goal is always productively creating value and return for the enterprise through the allocation and prioritization of limited resources.

II. Managing Your Stakeholder Relationships

In building alignment across the organization, team leaders must to be able to develop, leverage, and ensure healthy relationships with their stakeholders.

What Is a Stakeholder?

A stakeholder can be an internal or external individual or company with a vested interest in the success of your work. That vested interest can mean an investment of time, money, or personal engagement. Stakeholders have "skin in the game" and want good things to happen because there is a direct or indirect impact on them.

Rigor the Importance of Stakeholders by Looking at (3) Types:

- *Interactional* **stakeholders**

- *Observational* **stakeholders**

- *Reputational* **stakeholders**

▶ **Interactional Stakeholders:** (Your Peer Group)

Without question, the most underestimated stakeholder relationship in your professional life is your peer group. Shocking, right? Surely it should be your boss, your executive leadership team, your board of directors, or your direct report team before your peers!

Sorry, but your peer group is the most important stakeholder in your professional life because your ability to get work done, advance personally in your organization, and advance your direct reports is directly related to your ability to build solid relationships with your peer group.

With peer-calibrated performance reviews and peer-group succession planning becoming the standard of best practices in corporate settings, working side by side with your peers on organizational business has never been more prevalent.

Now don't rush out and start "making nice" with your peers just for the self-serving reason of being in good standing with them; these relationships need to be authentic!

You can assess the quality of your professional business relationships with your peers based on criteria such as whether you:

☑ **Advocate with an enterprise mindset**

☑ **Take a leadership approach "in service of others"**

☑ **Are open to learning and growth (yours and others)**

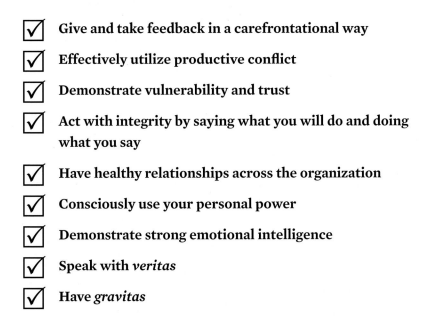

- ☑ Give and take feedback in a carefrontational way
- ☑ Effectively utilize productive conflict
- ☑ Demonstrate vulnerability and trust
- ☑ Act with integrity by saying what you will do and doing what you say
- ☑ Have healthy relationships across the organization
- ☑ Consciously use your personal power
- ☑ Demonstrate strong emotional intelligence
- ☑ Speak with *veritas*
- ☑ Have *gravitas*

Be mindful that before a promotion happens for you, it is likely that many of your peers will weigh in either informally or formally through speaking to their supervisors (or yours) about their relationship with you and about your reputation. Relationship building is a leadership currency, so it is always a highly visible topic and consideration when contemplating potential roles an individual may be asked to play. The risk of a high-performing individual leaving or several members of the team not supporting your promotion may be taken into account in the decision-making process.

Depending on the circumstances, risks, and alternatives, strong technical candidates may be passed over for candidates who pose less risk on the relationship front, even if their technical competencies aren't as strong. Remember, at the team and organizational levels of leadership, your skills in communication and relationship building will start to trump your technical capabilities. Leaders are promoted in performance-based enterprises based on their interpersonal skills and their desire to grow and develop others. How you handle your peer relationships is a strong indicator of how you build relationships with others in general.

Remember that as a team leader, you are now in "the fishbowl" and will be openly watched for how you move through the organization and build your relationships.

In large organizations, the spotlight shines especially brightly on anyone just promoted. Everyone wants to see in action the individual who has just been recognized as "an up and comer." You will need to be consciously competent about how you appear on this stage. Are you energetic, walking through the hallways with your head up and a smile while greeting others, or do you walk with your head down, seemingly oblivious and in your own world?

The fact is, as others observe you, they do a natural thing: they start to create a story about you. Based on their initial impressions, they accumulate additional observations that support their experience. This happens both in your organization and externally among your industry colleagues or personal associations as well.

The story they come up with might be negative: "Hey, she doesn't seem that interested in meeting me; I wanted to congratulate her, but I guess she's too busy."

Or perhaps the story is more positive: "I really like how he finds the time to meet with everyone. He really seems approachable."

Whatever the story, it will be true in the observer's mind. As a leader, you need to be conscious about how you are showing up in the fishbowl and avoid creating a series of negative impressions unconsciously when you have the opportunity to create positive ones in a consciously competent way.

In addition, because we humans like community and communication, it's only natural that we share our observations with others. This can play to your advantage if a strong supporter can positively vouch for you to an observational stakeholder who may not have seen you at your best, thereby assisting in building or preserving your reputation. It can also play out negatively and cause cascading damage to your reputation if someone you have a poor relationship with gives an observational stakeholder who initially had a positive experience with you reason to pause.

▶ **Reputational Stakeholders: Your Global Community**

Reputational stakeholders are people who have not had personal interactive experiences with you but may have heard about you through others, either directly or indirectly. Comments that might come from a reputational stakeholder include the following:

- "I hear he's hard to work with."

- "I hear she doesn't let anything get in her way."

- "I hear he's really fair."

- "I hear everyone loves to work for her."

- "I heard he threw a fit in the conference room."

- "I hear she mistrusts other women."

What other people hear about you can be as important as their own firsthand experiences. In today's world of social media, your reputation can be built or destroyed with just a few tweets.

> *Leadership works through communication and relationships, and the consequence of your current level of mastery of these (2) currencies is your reputation.*

Having a good reputation is important for everyone, but if you are a team leader aspiring to advance within your organization, it is your most valuable personal asset, so you will want to protect and add value to it in all that you do.

Because your reputation with your stakeholders can affect whether people want to work with you, it can affect your ability to attract talent and, depending on what it is like to work with you, to retain talent. In turn, because it will influence the perceptions of the people who may hire you, it can affect your professional opportunities. Your reputation is your story, and in the minds of some, it might actually be an old story. If you want to change it, you must be vigilant and disciplined with every new interaction you have.

Being consciously competent about managing your interactions and consequently your reputation is vital as you look to build stakeholder confidence, so rigor your reputation early and consistently!

What Are Stakeholders Interested In?

The answer to this will vary based on the individual and the circumstances, but a few things are clear with respect to what stakeholders are interested in:

- The health and prosperity of the enterprise

- Their unique interests (a project or investment)

- You as a champion of their interests

- Truth, trust, and transparency

Managing or balancing these interests is something you want to be mindful of as you communicate, interact, and work with your team across stakeholder interfaces.

III. Developing Your Internal and External Networks

Networking is often a vague and misunderstood concept. It is also like leadership in that it, too, is *surprisingly all about service.*

If you need immediate help with something and start to feverishly work to build a network from ground zero for assistance, good luck. The concept of networking is really all about giving to and helping others, learning about their challenges and opportunities, and most importantly, building relationships for the future. These *proactive deposits of goodwill, nurtured over time,* will provide you with the opportunity to reach out and seek assistance later when you may need it.

In today's high-tech world, networking is also about building interactive virtual communities with like-minded individuals who share mutual interests. Networking is far from just being social; it is *professional, educational, and influential,* so it is in your best interests to learn the critical skills that will facilitate the development of your internal network within your own company, your external network across your industry, and the personal charities or associations with which you are engaged.

Many leaders choose to work in larger organizations because they are attracted to the brands, services, and access to resources that a big corporation provides. To fully realize your potential and take advantage of these opportunities, you must learn to network and build your reputation. Here's why:

- Visibility plays a critical role in being perceived as a leader, and in large global corporations and industries, this can be a challenge to establish.

- Your network facilitates access to information and getting things done quickly. Knowing how to navigate the complexity of a large organization takes a lot of communication and relationship building as well as a significant investment of time and energy to set up, maintain, and leverage. Many leaders miss this point and tend to keep their circles small, which means they have to rely on their supervisors to open most of their doors for them.

- Your skills at networking and relationship building will spread through the voices of others. How well you are known is a measure of your visibility and networking impact. In fact, some large corporations appreciate the value of networking so much that they measure their executives on how well they are known and visible across their organizations.

- Talent is an enterprise asset, and you want to be well networked in the internal workings of your organization so that when jobs open up or succession planning is being discussed, you are on the radar screen and spoken of in a positive light with a number of diverse and active supporters in your corner.

- Effective networking requires utilizing your personal power. People remember how you make them feel, so if you impose your position power on them or spend a great deal of time talking about yourself and your own expertise, you may make them feel put off or annoyed. If you engage them with curious questions about themselves and their needs as well as support or acknowledge some of their work and accomplishments, you likely make them feel seen and heard. You therefore leave them with a positive impression about the exchange and, importantly, about you!

- External networking helps to build your personal brand and your organization's credentials, both of which are important to reputation building.

- The impact of productive networking can have a long cycle time. You may connect with someone who, years later, reaches back out to you. The challenge but also the power of networking is to do it daily, integrating it into your natural state of being. It is a continuous investment in your future!

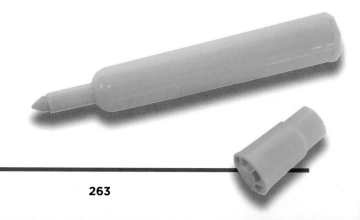

Building Powerful Internal and External Networks

To build powerful internal and external networks, you must rigor:

- Intimacy with others

- A service-based networking orientation

▶ Creating Intimacy

One important skill to learn in networking is how to create an appropriate level of intimacy with your contacts. In fact, networking is for your relationships what exercise is for your body. It is not a one-time event or something you do every few months. Networking is a way of staying in touch with your current relationships to keep them healthy and up to date as well as a way of building new ones. It takes daily initiative and investments of time as well as energy!

Creating intimacy can be a challenge for many. Initially, it was extremely difficult for me. As an MBTI "extraverted thinker" who is focused on tasks and communicating with objectivity, the ease and grace of relationship building did not come naturally, though watching me today, you might observe that I do a pretty good job at it. Networking and leadership skills can be learned, practiced, and applied more comfortably if you are willing to rigor it to get there.

One of the ways I encourage my clients to create intimacy is by *learning and respecting other people's communication preferences.* We each have preferences for how we like to connect. Some people prefer face-to-face communications, others are quick to pick up the phone, and many rely on emails, texts, or tweets. Being observant of people's preferences allows us to connect with them using their preferred methods. This in turn results in a higher likelihood of responsiveness and, eventually, of relationship intimacy.

For example, spontaneous phone calls seldom work well for me. Because my coaching schedule includes many face-to-face meetings and phone calls that are booked back to back, it is hard to catch me. Meanwhile, I get frustrated with the game of phone tag.

I am disciplined in terms of scheduling my phone connections so that I can be prepared and focused on the relationship on the other side. Most individuals in my close network know this about me. My network also knows that I am in my office very early each day and tend to be incredibly quick and responsive to emails and texts, assuming I am available and not booked with an appointment. Thus, if you want to build a relationship with me, your best shot is to use these methods because frequency of contact is a driving force for building intimacy and connectivity.

One of the measures I also look at within my own network is *"response time."* Those who are closest to me in my network and are therefore most intimate with me tend to have fast response times when I reach out to them. Those who are less responsive, I assume, are letting me know that our relationship is not as critical to them (or that they are not administratively proficient, which is critical to me). This is important information because networking is about building relationships at different levels of intimacy. Being in "association" with someone is different from being in "relationship" or "partnership" with them; each has a different feeling associated with it and very likely a different intensity and level of commitment.

Intimate Connections

Intimacy does not require physical contact in today's technological world. Many people have highly intimate relationships via email and texting! Others are in constant physical proximity with daily interactions with each other and have no intimacy; their relationship is purely transactional. Creating intimacy is about "connecting and interacting" with each other in a meaningful and impactful way.

▶ Developing a Service-Based Networking Orientation

Earlier, I noted that networking is about service. This service includes education as well as helping other people make connections. If you help someone in need connect to an individual in your network, you likely get one of your personal advocates to share some personal thoughts about you. This helps build your reputation and creates a win/win/win situation: your credentials get talked about by the advocate in your network, the individual in your network gets a potentially warm referral or new relationship, and a new associate in need gets hooked up with an expert he or she is looking for!

Overall, working horizontally to build alignment across the organization solidifies your understanding of how your enterprise operates and provides you with the opportunity to interface and build relationships with your peer group. This helps you to network internally and to develop your reputational equity with stakeholders.

In the signature model section that follows next, you will learn how to facilitate decision making and guide the discussion of critical issues for resolution with *Analytical Rigor*. This signature model will integrate many of the leadership skills you have been exposed to thus far in *Leadership Rigor.*

"The way a team plays as a whole determines its success. You may have the greatest bunch of individual stars in the world, but if they don't play together, the club won't be worth a dime."
– Babe Ruth

"In any moment of decision, the best thing you can do is the right thing. The worst thing you can do is nothing."

– Theodore Roosevelt

▌*SIGNATURE* MODEL:
Analytical Rigor

Analytical Rigor is the second signature model presented in **Leadership Rigor.** A sequential and iterative discussion road map, it represents the most versatile and comprehensive leadership tool in this body of work, providing a disciplined approach for facilitating problem solving and decision making. If you are not already saying it, you will be soon, so let's **Rigor it!**

As in Part 1, the case will be made for why, what, when, where, and how this model can be utilized on the ground in your leadership practice to enhance performance and productivity.

Macro Business Challenge

Business is about *managing risk and change in the pursuit of growth.* You want your organization to advance successfully, but not at all costs. Yet many business leaders act impulsively by making surface assumptions and basing large or important decisions on them.

The choice of "here now for the taking" often wins out over "thoughtful and appropriate deliberation" because leaders can fear overthinking, being accused of analysis paralysis, and missing "the big opportunity." As a result, many leaders fly by the seats of their pants and talk themselves into (or find themselves talked into) making impulsive, high-risk decisions.

RISK
CHANGE
GROWTH

Decisive Behavior Versus Decision-Making Skills

There is a difference between decisiveness and decision making. **Decisiveness is a behavior** that demonstrates an individual's ability to quickly select a choice from options and then confidently move into action. If decisiveness is the end result of preparation, it is fantastic, but if it is an impulsive reaction to gut or intuitive instincts, it can be a concern because it means you are likely acting with unconscious competency. With decisiveness, there may or may not be a rigorous assessment of the information, options, or risks.

Decision making, alternatively, is a leadership skill. It is based on the ability to consciously question, analyze, and integrate information and insights into a set of best choice trade-offs and then to make a rational selection with a well rounded understanding of the risks and consequences.

Analytical Rigor is about making decisions with conscious competency and eliminating, whenever and wherever possible, unconscious decisiveness.

On the other extreme are the leaders who require ongoing discussions, comprehensive analyses, and multiple approvals for every initiative under consideration, because if any risk is taken and a mistake is made, they fear someone's head will roll—theirs!

Leaders and teams are often challenged or intimidated by decision making and problem solving because they don't have easy-to-use tools to facilitate the process. They need to find a *balanced approach with an appropriate amount of rigor,* not too little and certainly not too much. The **Analytical Rigor** model provides this balance.

What Planet Are We On?

As mentioned, a diagnostic tool I was exposed to just prior to moving to Canada was the MBTI, or Myers-Briggs Type Indicator personality assessment.

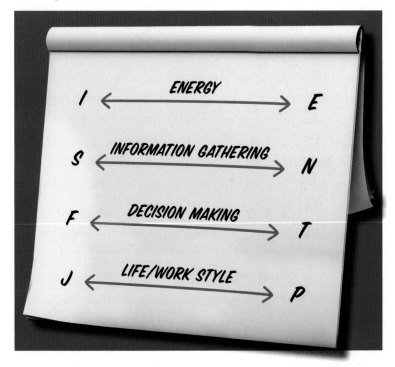

Taking this personality assessment revealed to me how I was hardwired as well as what my natural preferences were in critical areas, making my world much easier to understand and navigate. Even more valuable were the insights I gained once I learned my supervisor's type and how we dramatically differed in our preferences.

He was an ISTJ, which meant he had preferences for being an introverted, sensor, thinker, and judger.

I was an ENTP, with preferences for being an extraverted, intuitive, thinker, and perceiver.

Educated and enlightened by this information, everything began to make sense in a whole new way. Because he was an IS, or introverted sensor, he needed me to share information with him up front, often a day or two before we met to discuss issues. He preferred working alone initially to thoroughly review the details and to reflect on the material. By contrast, as an EN, or extraverted intuitive, I preferred to lay it all out and discuss it in real time together.

Fortunately, we were both thinkers (Ts) who were objective about the facts and circumstances, so we connected well around the decision-making process. The biggest revelation for me was in understanding why he annoyed me with his never-ending deadlines and due dates. He was a judger (J) who planned and organized everything in advance, while I was a perceiver (P) who wanted to go with the flow and work on my own timetable, not his!

He used to call me "Chief Head in the Clouds" because NTs love ideas, concepts, and new innovative strategies. I used to call him...well, "Chief" of something else.

Learning how and why our approaches differed was so impactful that I decided to build on this experience and have my entire Canadian division assessed so we too could understand more about each other.

Incredibly, I learned that I was leading an ISFJ (introverted, sensing, feeling, judging) organization! These individuals were quiet and detail oriented, influenced by subjective circumstances and personal values in terms of how they made decisions, with a clear desire to efficiently organize their time and efforts.

Once I realized they were my complete opposite in every way, I understood why this experience felt so challenging and foreign for all of us!

Why Analytical Rigor Was Created

Analytical Rigor was *created out of necessity* during my first general management assignment in Canada. The division I was leading had access to significant amounts of data but demonstrated only a limited ability to frame it into a clear story with appropriately displayed information *to guide meaningful business discussions.*

Much of my time was initially spent asking questions and working with the team to transform raw data into structured information so we could start to analyze it for insights. Each of my direct reports had the same challenge, so I realized we had a divisional learning opportunity that could impact both performance and productivity.

Meanwhile, the largest brand in our portfolio was stagnant, missing market growth opportunities due to an apparent misunderstanding of the dynamics at play in the business. This brand had (2) different product lines. When I asked how the business was performing, I was given charts that showed a flat sales trend.

When I asked for the information to be broken out visually by the (2) different lines, a completely different story emerged. One line was growing exponentially while the other was in slow decline. A significant investment opportunity was being completely missed, contributing to the division's lingering poor performance.

I was a young, direct, and outspoken American woman in Canada, a relatively reserved and extremely polite country. Most of my team was quiet, partly driven by personality styles and partly out of fear surrounding the potential changes that were required to turn the business around.

They had feelings of anxiety about what was going to happen, whereas I had feelings of anxiety about what we were missing and needed dialogue, engagement, and answers.

During a meeting, frustrated by how difficult it was to get the critical information visible and on the table so we could really talk about it, *I spontaneously mapped out the following picture:*

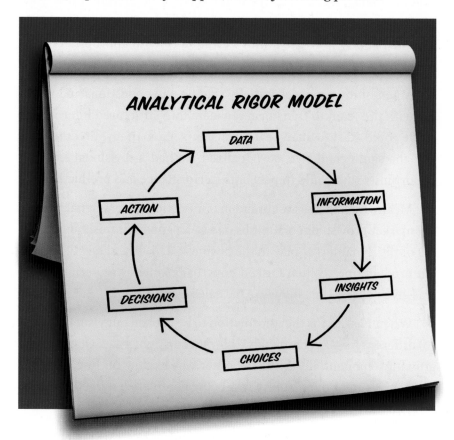

With this, the conversations in our division started to change.

Why Your Team Needs Analytical Rigor

Analytical Rigor provides you and your team with:

- A *disciplined structure* for conducting conversations

- A *sequential and progressive road map* that eliminates frustrating circular discussion loops

- A dynamic process inviting *meaningful participation* from team members in their areas of strength and preference

- A balanced, collaborative approach that *consciously avoids* personality dominance, overthinking, and impulsivity

- *A transparent lens* for decision making and issue processing

The Benefits of Using Analytical Rigor

The benefits of using the **Analytical Rigor** model center around taking complex, controversial or confusing business issues and breaking them down into simple and sequential points that flesh out the major considerations, leading to aligned forward action.

Beyond securing alignment on business issues, using **Analytical Rigor** with your team and organization has impactful benefits:

- It creates an *open and inclusive* environment

- It provides opportunities for applying *learning agility* in real time

- It reinforces a *cultural discipline* to "doing things around here" in a consciously competent way

Determine Who Will Make the Decision before You Rigor It!

Always clarify up front who the decision maker will be before initiating the **Analytical Rigor** process. Remember the RACI framework mentioned in Chapter 2? Determine who has the "A" for accountability and encourage the decision maker to declare how he or she would like to use the **Analytical Rigor** model. Will it be implemented formally and fully or will certain areas be staged? Use the flexibility of the tool along with the clarity of the decision maker's request on how best to use it to ensure up front expectations are aligned and a productive team experience results.

What Type of Tool Is Analytical Rigor?

Simply put, Analytical Rigor is a process facilitation model. It enhances your team's performance by providing a structured road map to productively engage and align diverse personalities in conversations on important issues! Thus, it can help you:

- Facilitate decision making and problem solving

- Structure discussions on change initiatives

- Brainstorm to socialize ideas or structure negotiations

What Skills Does Analytical Rigor Develop?

Analytical Rigor is a comprehensive leadership learning and development model that integrates the following skills, tools, and concepts during its utilization (each is discussed in more detail as the (7) steps of the model unfold later in this section):

- *Framing* information (putting a clear story together)

- Pattern recognition (*identifying* insights through trends)

- MBTI hardwiring (*leveraging* diverse style preferences)

- Scenario planning (*envisioning* a range of outcomes)

- *Teaming* skills (a weigh-in/buy-in process for alignment)

- Divergent/convergent *thinking* (expand/narrow options)

- Strategy and execution (up front *planning* and rollout)

- Conscious competency (*avoiding* impulsivity)

- Performance evaluation (*defining* success)

- *Creating* a learning environment (transparency)

- Leadership style diversity (*facilitating* with flexibility)

Individually and together, these skills and capabilities prepare you to work through the dynamic challenges of business today.

When to Use the Analytical Rigor Model

Analytical Rigor can be used to make a breakthrough difference in your performance and productivity when:

☑ **You fear that an impulsive decision will be made**

☑ **You have too many or too few options on the table**

☑ **Team discussions are chaotic and undisciplined**

☑ **Team members have strong opinions causing gridlock**

☑ **The decision significantly affects resource allocations**

☑ **You want to socialize an idea and get early input**

☑ **You are designing a new process or preparing its rollout**

☑ **Your change initiative has multiple work-streams**

☑ **Team has similar personalities; group think concerns you**

☑ **You have complicated options and need team alignment**

More Rigor, or Rigor Mortis?

Organizations that become well versed and disciplined in using **Analytical Rigor** may occasionally find themselves asking whether they are using it too much. Be mindful about using **Analytical Rigor** to address a challenge that simply shouldn't be on the table at all right now! Remember that, as a leader, your altitude needs to be focused on the prioritization of initiatives and the allocation of resources. If you attempt to rigor initiatives that are not appropriate priorities, you will find frustration and resentment within your team even if you attempt to invest in discussing them with greater productivity using **Analytical Rigor**. Be certain your issue is a confirmed priority; then **Rigor it!**

Where to Use The Analytical Rigor Model?

While the **Analytical Rigor** model can be applied in virtually any setting, team environments typically benefit the most because of the need to debate complex issues, make interactive trade-offs, and align resources around decisions. ***Securing alignment between parties is a natural outcome of utilizing the Analytical Rigor process.***

Two individuals discussing a decision, process, or potential negotiation could also benefit from **Analytical Rigor**, but it would be impractical to utilize this model in an audience setting, given the large number of participants.

How to Practically Utilize The Analytical Rigor Model

There are no rules here. **Analytical Rigor** can be *utilized formally, informally,* or in a *staging process* as discussed in the following pages.

Creating Breakthrough Progress

Analytical Rigor can be used to create a breakthrough in progress when there is a logjam or stalemate on an issue being discussed. For example, if you find yourself in a meeting that gets underway with an agenda yet at some point in the process it becomes clear that there is confusion, multiple opinions in terms of how to go forward, and/or a team leader who is struggling to figure out how to bring the topic to some form of clarity or closure, consider this a potential entry point for **Analytical Rigor**. Even late in the game, this model can provide structured perspective on where the team is in the deliberation process and how it can get refocused with traction.

Assess where the conversation is at this point using the model as a guide. Determine what is known and what is missing, then go back and create forward momentum based on the gaps in the sequence. **Analytical Rigor** can break through the confusion and help you move forward with a road map even if you didn't start with one.

Formal Process

To formally implement **Analytical Rigor**, take a straightforward decision (versus a large or complex one) and walk through each of the steps with your team to gain tangible experience on how the model works. Go slowly and be methodical so that you can explore the various elements that are integrated within the model. Talk openly about each step as you work through it so the team makes both a verbal and visual connection to the approach and methodology.

Next time, on a more complicated issue or decision, you will have the confidence to apply the model, having worked through the pieces on this simple practice run.

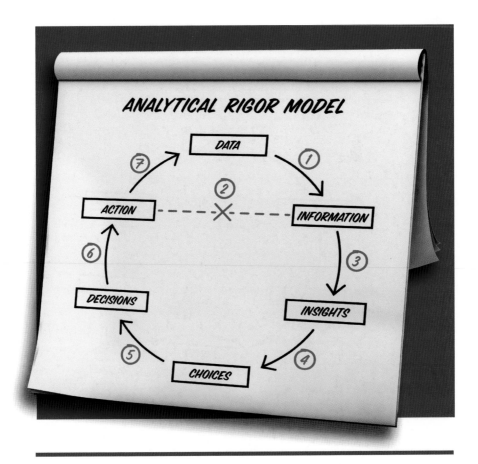

Informal Process

Assuming your team has secured a solid base of experience with the model, in the middle of a discussion, challenge yourself and your team to assess where you might be in the **Analytical Rigor** process and begin to consciously guide the conversation. You might have already intuitively clarified your insights but need to come up with additional choices. Rigor this using divergent and convergent thinking to identify alternative options.

Or perhaps you have made a decision and want to ensure you are completing the rigor process by specifically discussing the implementation plan and how communication will be rolled out. Up front utilization is always preferred, but covering your bases with an informal rigor check-in in a specific area of focus is also a good practice!

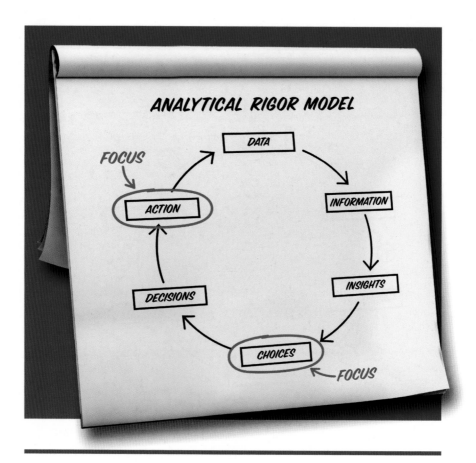

Staging Process

There are *(2) ways* in which the **Analytical Rigor** model can be used with a staging process approach.

The first staging approach relates to using the model as a way to *increase meeting productivity.* As a team leader, request that the data/information framing work takes place in advance of the meeting as a "homework" phase. The background analysis or report can be sent out a few days prior to the meeting to give participants time to read/prepare for the discussion. It might also be worthwhile to request feedback on the initial information sent out prior to the meeting so that you can confirm that the appropriate lens has been used and that it was appropriately reviewed by the meeting participants. If there are questions or suggestions, they can be addressed or prepared prior to getting the team together.

The value of the team meeting is in discussing the insights and choices. This is where interactive engagement can fully leverage the diverse talent as well as the various thinking styles on the team, thereby most productively using your blue dollars.

Depending on how you have chosen to make your decision (i.e., by team leader, by vote, etc.), you may leave the execution (decision and communication) to the person with the "A" for accountability, come back for another session, or make the decision then and there.

The second staging approach acknowledges that some business decisions have *long time frames* and multiple issues to be worked through. In such cases, you might tackle an early stage of the project with **Analytical Rigor** (i.e., data/information framing) in one meeting and agree to come back in several subsequent meetings to discuss insights and choices. You also may have a project that requires data/ information gathering on an organizational level *requiring weeks or months.* The interactive stage for insights/choices may also carry over for weeks or months, depending on the size of the investment decision.

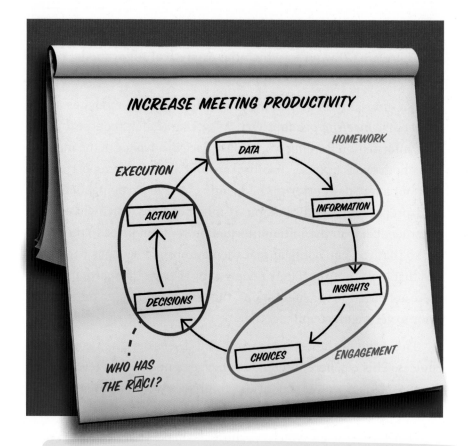

You don't need to take on the entire **Analytical Rigor** process at one time. Instead, work iteratively through larger-scale initiatives. In some cases, you may find yourself using the model several times during a project's life cycle in both a larger and smaller staging format to gain maximum performance and productivity.

However you choose to use **Analytical Rigor**, remember to clarify (3) things up front:

1. Who is the decision maker?

2. How will the decision be made? By the leader? By vote?

3. How will you utilize the process? In staged pieces, or will you embrace the entire process today?

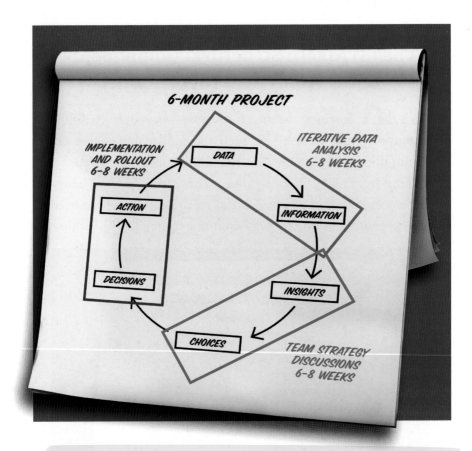

6-MONTH PROJECT

IMPLEMENTATION AND ROLLOUT 6-8 WEEKS

ITERATIVE DATA ANALYSIS 6-8 WEEKS

TEAM STRATEGY DISCUSSIONS 6-8 WEEKS

DATA

INFORMATION

INSIGHTS

CHOICES

DECISIONS

ACTION

Regardless of your specific approach, **Analytical Rigor** will improve your decision-making process because the issues will be well thought out and the options broadly considered before you take action. Most importantly, because the process is transparent, it provides both a learning opportunity and a way to visibly secure alignment prior to execution. Your productivity and performance will inevitably increase due to higher-quality communication.

Don't Travel without It!

If you were on a desert island and needed to conduct business, you would definitely want Bayer® Aspirin and the **Analytical Rigor** model with you!

The (3) Macro Structural Components of the Analytical Rigor Model

Take a *learning versus a leaping approach*. Avoiding impulsivity and working through the model means you are committed to being consciously competent in your decision making by making it transparent. This also creates a learning environment in which decisions can be visibly processed and pressure tested, thereby building capability in others.

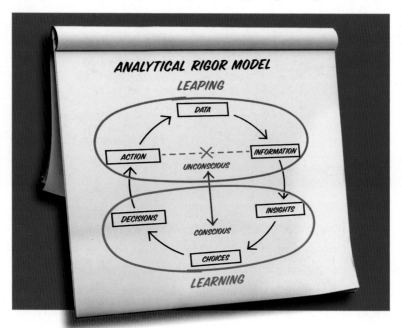

Creating weigh-in and buy-in opportunities for your team. The initial components (right side) of the **Analytical Rigor** model focus on information gathering and identifying insights through weighing in on the details and expressing your personal thoughts and ideas. The later components (left side) of the process are about getting buy-in and alignment around the decision so you can collectively communicate with those who are impacted, put the decision into action, and measure its success.

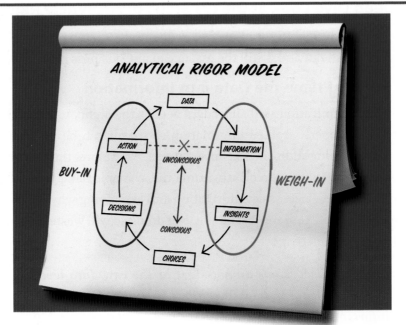

Moving from strategy to execution. The first part of the process is about understanding where you are and ideating on where you can go and why (strategy). The second part of the process is determining the action steps on the ground regarding how you get there (execution).

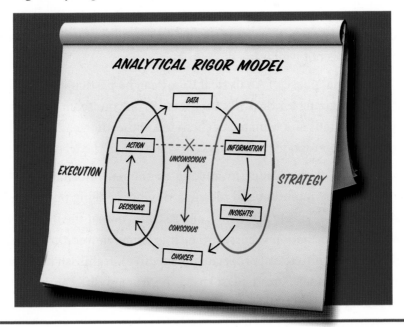

A Deep Dive Look at the (7) Steps of Analytical Rigor

The **Analytical Rigor** model is a sequential, (7)-step process that can help flesh out and distill the essence of any business challenge.

Step 1: Frame the Data into Information

A communication skill all leaders need is the ability to transform data into properly framed information so that it can be practically used in meaningful business conversations. Therefore, the first step in **Analytical Rigor** is to clearly frame the available data, grounding your team in the necessary information and explaining why it is relevant to the context of the discussion. Not doing so will waste time and hold back productivity.

> *Business discussions do not start at the raw data level with detailed spreadsheets; they start at the framed information level with context.*

This means starting with reports that provide background or historical perspective and charts that are organized into meaningful structures with time periods, basic trends, subheads, information columns, and percent changes compared to previous time periods of relevance as appropriate. The material needs to tell a story. If it doesn't, and I need someone to walk me through a chart or report in painstaking detail, it is not well framed.

This initial phase of **Analytical Rigor** can be particularly important and energizing for the MBTI sensors (S) on your team who gravitate to the details and want to get anchored in the information, as long as they don't get too fixated on the data or stuck in the weeds.

The role of the leader in looking at framed information is to understand the intention and meaning of what is being put forth, to assess what if anything is missing, and to confirm that the interpretation of the information is correct (i.e., it is being viewed through the right lens and with the appropriate perspective). If this isn't the case, your role as leader is to request that it be framed differently before proceeding to discuss the insights it reveals.

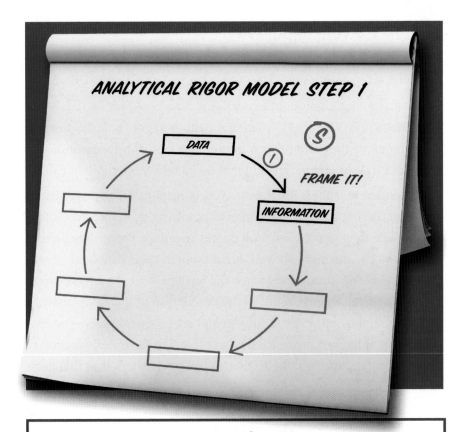

Frame It for Me!

As a GM, one of my favorite phrases was "Frame it for me." This applied to both reports and verbal communication. I would ask my team to start a discussion by reminding me where we were when we last met on this issue, where we were now, and where they suggested we go next (note the use of **The Progressive Mindset** model in this approach). I would encourage them to remember that I was not living in their world of details and that they needed to anchor me back to a previous set point of reference and then lead me forward. If they didn't, I would become frustrated and either take over the meeting with a barrage of framework questions to get oriented, wasting valuable time, or I might even stop the meeting and ask them to come back when they were more prepared. Framing the context of the discussion up front is critical!

Step 2: **Avoid Impulsivity!**

The second and perhaps most critical step in the **Analytical Rigor** model is to avoid impulsivity!

Leaders with significant expertise (or big egos) immediately believe they know what to do without needing to get "bogged down in the details," or they trust that a limited amount of information is all they need to leap into action and make a gut-driven judgment call.

Often, these leaders are unconsciously responding to an emotional trigger. Perhaps they've seen pieces of information like this before and believe they know how it all comes together. Since they believe they know the business so well, it isn't worth their time and energy to entertain long discussions when the answer is so patently obvious. They don't want to get caught in the perception of low-level analysis paralysis, so they opt to be indulgent and act on their entrepreneurial leadership behaviors or position power to make the quick decision to move forward, rationalizing to themselves and others that this decision is relatively low risk.

Data Can Mislead!

A related watch-out to ensuring that your controller/CFO is meeting your needs at the right altitude is the concern that data can be creatively framed and presented to make multiple points. It is critical that you know the right lenses to look through so you can assess the information for the appropriate insights. For example, earlier in *Leadership Rigor*, I explained how looking at our Canadian brand on a combined, (2)-product-line basis showed a flat sales trend. This was technically correct, but it did not reveal the dramatic differences in performance of the (2) contributing lines and the alternative investment strategy that would better serve the division's growth.

Make sure you understand how to look at data/information so that you are putting yourself and your team in the best position to reveal meaningful trends and insights. They are likely hidden in plain sight!

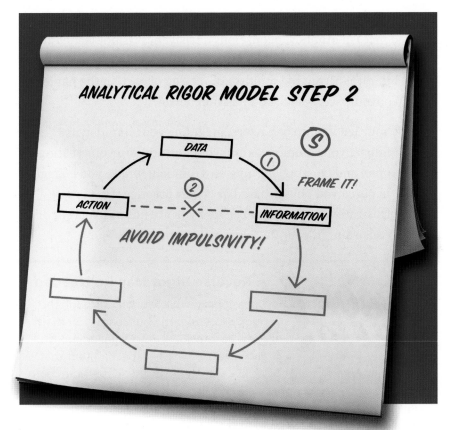

It is important to *avoid impulsivity* for several reasons:

- Decisions made unilaterally without input from and alignment with the broader team are likely to be perceived as higher risk, to have less buy-in, and to cause resentment among team members because they were not involved in the process.

- Impulsive decisions are usually made with unconscious competency, when executives' intuitive instincts tell them what is right. In all likelihood, they are probably correct, but because they have not made their thinking visible, they deny aspiring leaders in their organization the opportunity to gain insights and learning on the decision-making process and experienced leaders an opportunity to contribute.

  Remember, your job as a leader is to be disciplined in utilizing conscious competency in order to build capability (and confidence) in others. Unconscious decisiveness is not leadership because it does not come from the mindset of serving others but rather from the mindset of serving oneself in the name of convenience, speed, and position power.

- Your leadership behaviors, including your impulsivity, impact your employees and your culture. Are you creating an open and trusting learning environment, or are you engaging in perceived power-based or covert practices that create frustration and anxiety because you are not transparent or consistent in your decision-making processes?

A Reverse Rigor May Be Needed

Occasionally, while working through the rigor process with your team, you may need to break off into smaller groups and invest time on a specific item that requires more homework or data analysis. In this case, you can choose to **"reverse rigor"** as a smaller group and go back up a step, coming back together again as a larger group once additional information is provided to assess insights and choices.

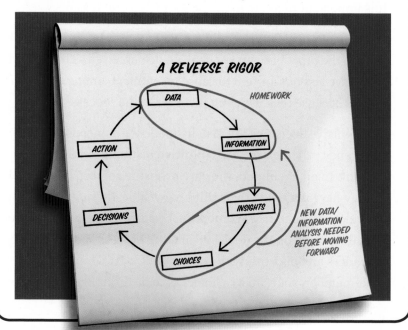

MBTI Profiles Embedded in the Model

Those who are familiar with the MBTI profile assessment for decision making will notice how the **Analytical Rigor** model naturally includes these various preferences. As data/information is gathered, the sensor (S) profiles are naturally engaged. Moving into the insights and choices stimulates the engagement of the intuitives (N), who are future focused on possibilities. As you narrow the possible choices, the thinkers (T) select from the various options based on their objective assessments. The feelers (F) come into play as you consider how your ultimate decision will emotionally land on others and how best to communicate your action plan with empathy and compassion.

Does Your Chief Financial Officer (CFO) Really Understand the Business Dynamics?

In my experience with both large corporations and small to mid-sized businesses, the ability of your financial controller/CFO to frame data into meaningful information is one of the critical determinants of a business's success. Without the perspective of knowing and understanding what is relevant and why, you will be continuously challenged with struggling through low-altitude data and conversations.

The problem for the team leader and organizational leader occurs when the controller/CFO is brilliant with the numbers and spreadsheets but is unable to communicate them appropriately for the required strategic and operational level business discussions.

If you are temporarily hypnotized and settling for "brilliance in data," **pinch yourself and raise your expectations** to brilliance in framed information and insights to accelerate your performance, productivity, and profitability. The difference will be game changing for both you and your team/organization!

Step 3: **Ask Clarifying Questions and Seek Insights**

With impulsivity under control, skillfully framed information in hand, and the certainty that you do not have an incorrect bias or missing elements, you can now ask clarifying questions to confirm that you understand the dynamics at play, begin to identify or recognize patterns and trends, and create various hypotheses about what might be going on as well as what might be possible.

This is where intuitive team members (N in their MBTI profile) will thrive as they start to ask probing questions that may reveal a sequence or pattern to what is being looked at or discussed. Insights may emerge for team members as they start to put information together in new ways. As a consequence, new possibilities and options may surface for consideration.

An example of what turns up during this phase is that someone might notice a downward trend compared to what occurred in a previous time period. In a moment of insight, another team member

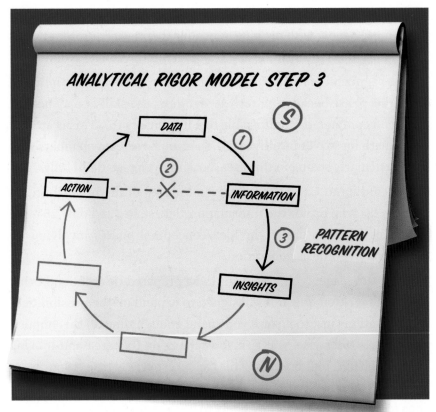

might realize there were two fewer shipping days last month, which explains the troubling variation.

You may also see trends that show dollar growth versus previous time periods even though units are the same. The insight could be that the company took a price increase at this time last year.

These examples are extremely basic, but the idea is to have the numbers, reports, and framed information tell a story that can prompt insightful questions that in turn reveal a deeper understanding of the dynamics at play.

In this part of the process, you might also be asking questions such as, "What if we did this instead of that?", "What if that isn't the reason this is happening?", and "What else might be happening here?"

Generating hypotheses provokes the team to look at the dynamics of cause and/or effect. Leaders often see the effect and think it is the problem they are solving for when actually it may be a symptom and not the root cause. Investing time to differentiate and explore these areas more deeply with probing questions that reveal different trends can change both the altitude and trajectory of the conversation.

Be cognizant of the fact that most teams want to quickly move on from this phase because pattern recognition, the skill at play here, is neither a common or comfortable one for sensors (S). This is an area of strength for MBTI intuitives (N), so if you have team members who are particularly strong in this area, be sure to engage them fully.

According to U.S. MBTI data, almost 75% of the population are sensors (S) who prefer the information/data stages and only 25% are intuitives (N) who prefer the idea/conceptual phases involving insights and hypothesis generation.

As team leader, you may want to be prepared up front and bring in a set of written questions designed to expand on the possibilities/ considerations just to ensure you spend enough time on this important phase. Otherwise, you risk shortchanging this area and moving to the decision step too early. This can be especially true if your team has more members who are detail or fact based than intuitive and idea focused, which is highly likely to be the case.

Of course, too many idea-focused participants can keep a conversation going on for an extended period of time with no closure, so this is something for the team leader to watch out for as well.

What Problem Are You Really Solving For?

One of my CEO clients had a problem with low morale across his entire sales organization. We used the **Analytical Rigor** model to facilitate a discussion on the concern with his leadership team. Within minutes, the team impulsively rushed into group think and definitively concluded the salespeople needed more training. Their solution was to resend training decks and clarify them with more detail.

I was taken aback by how clearly this was a real-time example of impulsivity at work. I pointed this behavior

---

out and challenged the team on whether the need for more training was a validated problem or just a hypothesis. To open up their thinking a bit more, I asked what else was going on with the sales organization in terms of processes and people in the last year in order to more specifically frame the context of the data/information we were working with.

I learned that the roles of the district managers (DMs) had recently changed, altering their authority to make decisions and take independent action at the field level.

With this new information on the table, I asked what morale was now like for the DMs in particular. Not good, the team confirmed. These individuals no longer felt they had flexibility for decision making, and they were passing their negativity on to their direct reports.

Their most pressing problem, the leadership team now realized, was not necessarily training and it was not potentially a pervasive problem across the sales organization. The information/insights discussion using the **Analytical Rigor** model revealed that connecting with the DMs and working with their concerns on roles and responsibilities was important to consider as well. This was a breakthrough for the leadership team, and it happened as a result of working through the stages of **Analytical Rigor**.

As team leaders, we need to ensure that we are solving the right problems. We do this by looking for the root causes of issues, by not being impulsive, and by remembering to ask what has changed recently, who was affected by the changes, and what the emotions are around the changes.

Remember, business is simple and people are complicated. In the **Analytical Rigor** process, you will be well served by using your emotional intelligence and personal power as you navigate your use of this model.

Step 4: Create Choices for Consideration

Once you reveal illuminating insights based on the potential root causes at play, you can start to identify various choices in how you might move forward. In doing this, it is helpful to use *the divergent and convergent thinking approach* first mentioned in Part 2.

To briefly recap, divergent thinking is a broadening process in which you eliminate filters and limitations and brainstorm about choices that are possible options based on the insights revealed.

There should be limited rules here initially; the idea is to cast a wide net and allow natural links to new choices to result from a previous choice put forth.

The goal is to see what possibilities are revealed, so let this naturally unfold for a while with group input.

When this step is complete, group and consolidate your outputs where necessary so that you have a final set of options.

Next, define criteria or go/no-go filters to look through so that you can start the convergent process of narrowing your options into a smaller subset. Some examples of your go/no-go criteria might be:

- ☑ **Investment requirements**
- ☑ **Pricing ranges**
- ☑ **Financial returns**
- ☑ **Technology requirements**
- ☑ **Timing considerations**
- ☑ **Geographical limitations**
- ☑ **Knowledge available now/in-house**
- ☑ **Talent currently available and on board**

Moving between divergent and convergent thinking can provide you with a thorough and disciplined approach for optimizing your options for decision making.

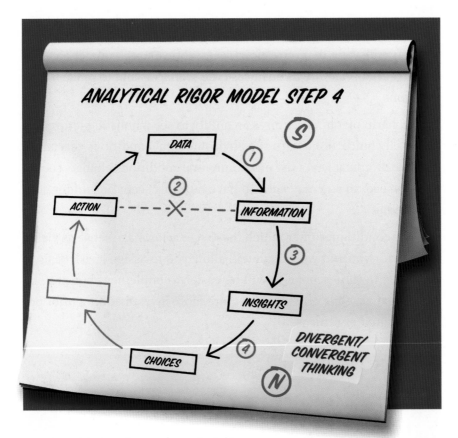

ANALYTICAL RIGOR MODEL STEP 4

An additional step to include in your approach is to look at your choices and see if there is a potential sequence of how these options might unfold. Many times, these are solutions for different phases of the challenge. You might also notice that there is overlap and that you don't really have (3) to (4) options; perhaps you really only have (2) to (3). Further consolidate via sequencing and get yourself focused on those few highly leverageable and impactful ideas.

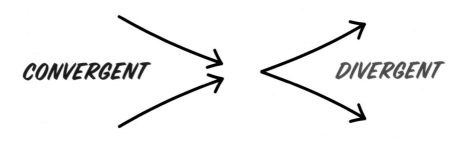

Step 5: **Evaluate Choices and Make a Decision**

You and your team are now ready to evaluate your choices in terms of their viability as business case scenarios and to make a final decision.

Scenario planning requires an ability to see a holistic picture of a potential choice along with the environmental conditions that make it viable or unviable. As the environmental conditions change, so will the scenario, so you may need to have multiple scenarios under consideration.

The conditions under which these scenarios make sense as viable options for you and your team will allow you to assign a risk basis to each one. Certain scenarios will be easier to implement but provide limited gains, while others will require more investment but offer potentially greater returns.

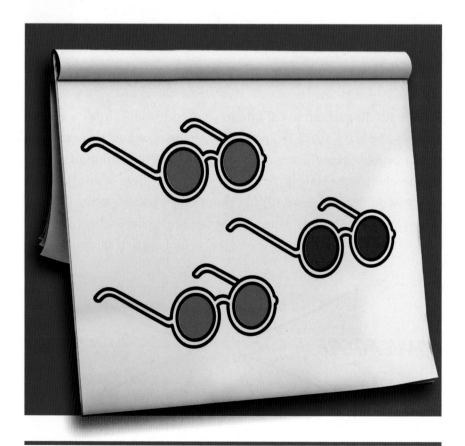

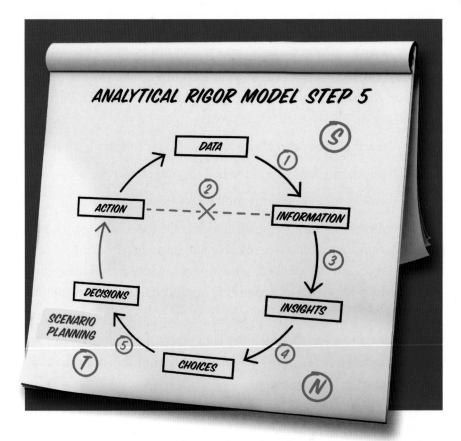

ANALYTICAL RIGOR MODEL STEP 5

DATA
INFORMATION
INSIGHTS
CHOICES
DECISIONS
ACTION
SCENARIO PLANNING

In some cases, you will grapple with a short-term fix versus a longer-term solution and may want to think about how to stage/phase your scenarios. Perhaps you can sequence your choices and choose a longer-term solution with a pilot execution phase to test the waters. These can all be put on the table as options.

Depending on how you agreed up front to handle the decision-making process before you and your team engaged in the **Analytical Rigor** discussion, you will now make the final selection from your scenario options.

RIGOR IT!

Step 6: Move into Action with a Plan for Executing

The "what you are going to do" decision has now been made, either by choosing from one of your potential scenarios or by sequencing the scenarios you identified. The next step is to develop your execution plan, which has (3) parts:

1. Determine your targets for success (*expectations*)

2. Decide who does what by when (*accountability*)

3. Develop your communication plan (*messages*)

Setting expectations for performance is the role of the leader, and these expectations need to be clearly agreed upon up front so that measurements can be tracked, adjustments made, and contingency plans can be put into place, depending on the changing conditions.

Outlining who does what by when clarifies the roles and responsibilities and ensures accountability is in place. Depending on the resources that are needed or available, **The Accountability Conversation** may need to be initiated.

The final essential step in the execution plan is ensuring clarity and closure on the communication plan. The (3) cascading messages you want to deliver as a team about your decision are as follows:

- The purpose

- The outcome

- The aspirational impact

Remember that the communication phase needs to be focused on the people directly and peripherally affected by this decision. How you make them feel and how the decision messages land on them is an important up-front consideration (align your intentions and your impact!). Your messages will be well served to include both visionary leadership language and affiliative language, and you might want to take the time to check in with your team members who are MBTI feelers (F) to ensure your communication is appropriately empathetic and compassionate.

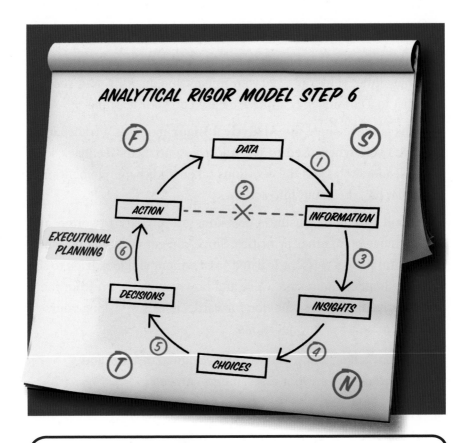

ANALYTICAL RIGOR MODEL STEP 6

RIGOR ALERT!

Contingency Planning

For the scenario you select, you may want to develop a contingency plan that maps out how you would move forward should the environmental conditions change. For example, perhaps you assume a slow-growth environment for one of your marketplace investments. If growth starts to accelerate at a faster rate, your investment choice may be locking you into a lower-level of returns. Changing your approach to take advantage of the higher-growth marketplace may require an investment change. The contingency planning target needs to determine what the growth rate change needs to be to signal this investment change.

Don't skip or move too quickly through this part of the process. A smart decision and skillfully developed action plan, if poorly communicated, will not result in a successful outcome!

Step 7: **Generate New Experiences and New Data**

Once the execution plan is in motion, you will be generating new data that allows you to analyze your impact and quantify your success or adjust to a contingency approach based on your learning.

This is ideal, since the **Analytical Rigor** model is a transparent iterative cycle when used to its fullest potential. Its feedback loop allows leaders to assess the decisions taken and the implementation plans that have been put into action.

Yet all too often, business decisions are quickly forgotten and leaders move on to other priorities. Since you get what you measure, it is helpful to do a "lessons learned" assessment and look back to see what the impact and results were and how you can learn from them and improve the process moving forward. Do this by asking yourself and your team a few key questions:

- In tracking your results back to original insights and patterns, were your assessments correct?

Shortcutting "Rigor it!"

One of the watch-outs you will want to be mindful of as you become more skilled at using the **Analytical Rigor** model as an individual and a team is to avoid dropping back into unconscious competency and either shortcutting your rigor efforts or just paying them lip service and not really doing the work. The true benefits lie in working through the process.

When you fail to do this, (2) things happen. The first is that you risk not getting the best thinking and potential solutions out on the table for consideration. The second is that you potentially shut down the learning of others who can benefit from participating in the more structured format. Stay consciously competent; **Rigor it!**

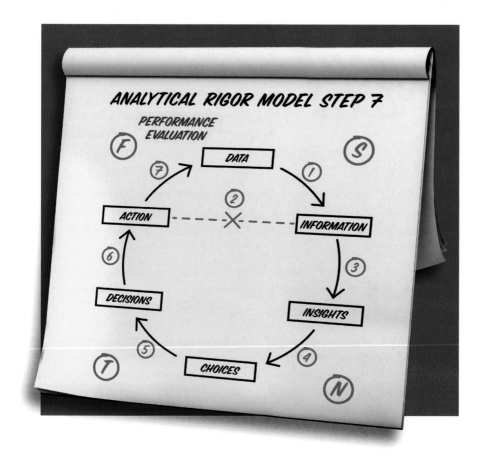

- Did the conditions under which you made the initial decision change, and did you adjust to them in a timely way?

- In the event that you needed to move into your contingency plan, did you follow the adjustments originally identified? Were they successful?

Quite simply, the **Analytical Rigor** model's sequential and integrated framework for dynamically engaging and aligning your team's thinking with a simple approach allows you as a team leader to have an enormous and lasting impact on your team's performance and productivity!

Facilitating the Model with the Appropriate Leadership Styles

Facilitating an issue-processing or decision-making discussion with the **Analytical Rigor** model will require you to reach into your leadership style toolbox and pull out all of your skills.

In step 1, your **directing style** can help shape and set the framework for how you want to see the data presented. Providing suggestions on the lenses to look through and the structure of the reporting can accelerate the preparation process.

Step 2 is to avoid impulsivity by jumping into a **pace-setting leadership style** because you believe you see the immediate answer and are compelled to move into immediate action planning with an urgent goal to achieve. This can seem self-indulgent, task oriented and potentially unreasonable to your team members who need more clarity on working through the pieces of the process to feel that it is achievable.

In step 3, when the framed information is available for discussion, you will have an opportunity to use your **coaching style**, asking questions to draw out potential insights as a critical part of the process. You may also want to use silence to create space and let both introverts and intuitives start to see the patterns emerge.

In step 4, when you are applying convergent as well as divergent thinking approaches, you will be well served to use your **participative leadership style** to engage the broad group and ensure you hear from everyone during this important weigh-in process.

Step 5 will provide an opportunity to use your **visionary leadership skills** for the first of two times in the **Analytical Rigor** process. Here you will want to pressure test the choices under consideration with your current strategy or operational plan to ensure consistency. Do they fit with where you are going and how you believe you can create competitive advantage with your team/organizational talent and resources? Those potential choices that fit with the direction can stay in the mix while those that don't will likely be tabled for now.

In step 6, when a final choice has been selected and the go-forward decision is clear, you will be wise to call upon your **affiliative leadership skills** as you and your team develop the communication messages that will be rolled out to announce your decision. Consulting your feeling (F) preference team members here can be of great value, as they will naturally be concerned about how your messages will land on others.

In step 7, once your action has been implemented, you will again want to alert yourself to utilizing your **visionary leadership skills**; this time they involve consideration for whether the action you have taken is working as expected and whether you need to adjust your strategic/operational plan based on the in-market learning you have received from the new data being generated.

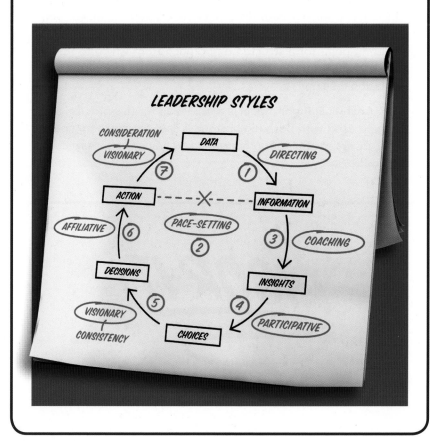

"Big Data" and Predictive Analytics Still Require Thinking!

The excitement around the concept of "big data" and its role in identifying business insights has never been greater. Our technological capabilities for collecting huge amounts of data have exploded in recent years, yet ironically, our ability to extract valuable insights still depends on our ability to think in a structured, methodical way with rigor!

I recently attended a CEO roundtable conference where big data was the discussion topic. I was struck by how timely and relevant the **Analytical Rigor** model is and how it can help CEOs/business leaders participate more consciously in this exciting dynamic today.

The biggest struggle the speakers identified was accepting the fact that even big data does not reveal anything unless you first know what you are looking for. In other words, data is a starting point for a structured approach from which to frame information, extract insights, and develop choices for smart decision making.

The **Analytical Rigor** model is a road map for this process and can be used with both big and small data to create competitive advantage for your organization by helping you make better decisions!

"It doesn't matter which side of the fence you get off on sometimes.
What matters most is getting off. You cannot make progress without making decisions."

— Jim Rohn

"Vacillating people seldom succeed. Successful men and women are very careful in researching their decisions and very persistent and determined in action thereafter."
—L.G. Elliott

"I don't think leadership demands 'yes' or 'no' answers; I think leadership is providing the forum for making the right decision, which doesn't demand unanimity."

— Arthur Ochs Sulzberger, Jr.

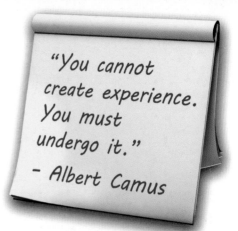

"You cannot create experience. You must undergo it."

– Albert Camus

THE *TENSION* TO RESOLVE:
Becoming a Practitioner and a Philosopher

Thus far, Part 2 of *Leadership Rigor* has explored the challenges of leading teams. It examined the role of team leaders and their (3) main areas of focus: delivering the work, developing the individual players, and developing the team as an entity.

It also covered the importance of creating healthy team dynamics, which begins with building trust and learning to engage in productive conflict with courageous conversations in a carefrontational way.

By now, one thing should be abundantly clear: if the members of a team can't say what needs to be said and openly debate issues to secure alignment with one another, no team can fully realize its potential and unleash the value of its diverse talents.

The concept of the team leader toolbox was presented along with the principles for running the operations of a team so that performance and productivity can be achieved at a level of excellence.

The team leader, Part 2 emphasized, must begin to work across the interfaces of the organization at the right altitude, securing cross-functional alignment, appropriately prioritizing and utilizing resources, and working closely with stakeholders to manage the development of his or her personal and team reputation.

This section also covered the important topic of networking and explained how it assists team leaders in facilitating progress both within and outside their organizations.

The signature model presented in Part 2 was **Analytical Rigor**, a dynamic and integrated process facilitation model for making decisions and productively engaging in complex or critical discussions.

At This Point in the Journey...

As a functional team leader with a proven track record of performance, it is probably clear to you which areas of the team leader role are most fulfilling and which are less attractive based on your professional interests and personal preferences.

Perhaps the technical expertise area of your profession energizes you most. While your leadership skills are solid and you enjoy working with your team to build their technical capabilities, the time required for leadership development is significant and not as satisfying to you as developing and applying your functional expertise.

Alternatively, perhaps you have thoroughly enjoyed the opportunity to grow and develop individual team members and are increasingly interested in advancing their leadership skill sets as well as your own, convinced that through this focus, you can contribute to accelerating organizational performance and productivity for the future.

You Have Now Arrived at the Second Tension...

The question you must ask yourself is, what is next for your career progression?

Do you want to continue in your current functional role and further build your technical expertise, or do you have ambitions for advancing into expanded leadership roles at the organizational level?

308

The first path leads toward being a thought leader or functional/technical expert where greater depth in your professional knowledge is your preferred direction and there is less passion to take on organizational level challenges or to invest significant time in developing the leadership capabilities of the future talent bench.

The second path chooses organizational leadership where leading the growth of the enterprise as a whole and developing the leadership capabilities of the future talent bench is in fact your primary focus.

Resolving This Tension through Transcendence

Assuming you are a talented executive performing well in your current role, your organization will have a natural desire or genuine need to invest in the acceleration of your growth. If you are only marginally interested in this path, be honest about it. Taking on a role that you do not have passion for will limit your growth and more than likely hold back the growth of your talent bench.

> *Throughout **Leadership Rigor**, you have had to make choices in service of your personal and team's growth. Now you must make a choice in regard to your organization's growth. So, what will it be?*

Assuming you do wish to advance and lead at the organizational level, you will need to embrace what is referred to in **Leadership Rigor** as being both a practitioner and a philosopher.

The **Practitioner Drives Performance** on the Ground

The practitioner is a strong technical expert who has reached a level of excellence in his or her functional area and has sufficiently crossed the knowing-doing gap in becoming a team leader.

Consciously competent or consciously incompetent and working to apply the fundamental leadership models and frameworks on a day-to-day basis in real time as best they can, practitioners continuously seek opportunities for facilitating interactions to enhance the performance and productivity of their team's technical skills to deliver the work product. They are primarily focused on producing high quality tangible outcomes or completed tasks.

Practitioners have a passionate desire to continue to increase their technical skills and expertise, always wanting to be on the cutting edge of what is next, new, or breakthrough in their industries. They enjoy their professional roles and are willing to share, teach,

Your Career Timeline

If you are not interested in further career advancement at this time for either professional or personal reasons, this is a conversation you need to have with your supervisor so that expectations are mutually aligned. Do not signal insincere and inconsistent interest out of fear that your career will stall. Instead, consciously step on and off your development path in a transparent and authentic way.

coach, and train others into higher levels of their own technical expertise. They view their leadership skills primarily as an aid to support the expansion of their technical resources, project portfolios, and priority initiatives. Building a team of high-quality professional experts is exciting and fulfilling. The experience they seek is being at the top of their technical games through innovation, execution, and excellence in all that they do.

The key limitation for practitioners is that they confine their focus to tasks and work products. Their teams are a means to facilitate the work product execution, and while they are willing to invest in training, it is in service of technical proficiency or functional expertise and not necessarily with a view toward broader leadership skills and behavioral competencies.

> *The "content of the work" is their preferred altitude, and tangible work product outcomes are their priority.*

They are potentially solid team leaders, though they may not have the desire, bandwidth, or skill set to lead at higher altitudes or the broader organizational level.

The Philosopher Develops the Leader Within

Philosophers are leaders who have reached a level of conscious competency in their leadership practices and who believe their purpose is to inspire the accelerated growth of the next generation of leaders as well as participate in shaping the future of their enterprises. These individuals actively seek to advance the learning and development of others within as well as outside their organizations for several reasons. First, they genuinely enjoy it; second, they recognize its need and value in terms of securing the longer-term performance and productivity of their enterprise through a strong leadership bench; and third, they understand that to be an organizational leader, cascading their experiences and insights through engagement and storytelling is their responsibility as well as their opportunity to shape the future and its leaders!

Philosophers are passionate about developing motivated, high-potential talent into confident and consciously competent leaders. Their focus is on *"context, purpose, and meaning,"* assisting emerging leaders in understanding themselves as well as the altitude and landscape of their current and future roles. They are outstanding relationship builders with strong personal power, and they leverage both formal and informal coaching and mentoring approaches to engage and partner with aspiring leaders in their development.

Philosophers are highly emotionally intelligent and generously use compassion and empathy to create and hold a safe space for emerging leaders to be vulnerable in as they explore, stretch, and find their own unique leadership voices. They ask powerfully reflective questions and challenge aspiring leaders to articulate their developing beliefs and philosophies based on their ongoing learning and experiences. They are patient in terms of understanding that the internal growth process for a leader takes time and can move at variable rates depending on the individual. *As long as progress is being made, philosophers remain engaged facilitators to the growth process.*

Philosophers understand the struggle of creating a personal story as a leader, of intimately digging down deep within and allowing their truth to be exposed so they can emerge with confidence and strength, capable of living their principles and character with credibility. Philosophers to varying extents have already traveled this journey and can serve as guides for aspiring leaders so they too can travel their unique leadership paths with mentorship and compassionate understanding.

Philosophers have a clear enterprise mindset when it comes to leadership, and they work relentlessly to recruit, develop, and retain high-potential talent for the future of their organization. They hold a longer-term vision for the growth of their enterprise and know that they need partnerships, collaborations, and talent around them to realize this future. After all, the ultimate performance of the organization will be built upon the shoulders of the leadership talent potential that can be realized.

Your Philosophies

One of the exercises I assign my coaching clients is to write down (3) to (5) philosophies on business and life that guide their approaches and choices as leaders. This is an incredible way to develop clarity and to focus on what is important, and it helps them consciously tap into where their practical wisdom comes from. Armed with their philosophies, they are able to more impactfully tell the stories of their learning and experiences as they help others to grow and develop.

Your Choice Is...

While advancing in our careers is something most of us aspire to, developing others is not of interest to everyone. Many individuals prefer to focus predominantly on the technical aspects of their jobs, comfortably remaining practitioners with technical expertise.

As a team leader, are you now willing to evolve your focus and play more of an organizational leadership role that includes technical expertise but also a significant commitment to developing others, or is your preference to exclusively pursue a thought leadership role through your professional expertise and knowledge?

Leading at the organizational level requires letting go of the day-to-day "doing/technical role" and firmly elevating your altitude to the managing and leading levels. It means making room for the philosopher approach, investing time in developing others, and having less focus on all the details and nuances of the specific work product.

The (2) roles are clearly different: the practitioner primarily serves the work product and process, and the philosopher primarily serves the people and the enterprise. So, the question is, will you give full voice to both your leadership capabilities and your technical abilities to embrace the role of consciously developing others on their professional and personal leadership journeys?

Depending on the culture of your company, it might not be possible to hold an organizational level leadership position and only focus on technical skills. In fact, an increasing number of companies, seeking to transition into performance-based enterprises, are emphasizing both technical and leadership skill requirements for their individual, team, and organizational leadership roles.

Desire and willingness to lead are, of course, the first steps. Leadership, remember, is also a skill-based profession, so your capability to perform in the role must be considered as well.

Obstacles to Overcome

It isn't easy to become both a practitioner and a philosopher. It requires you to manage through challenging obstacles, from overcoming resistance to taking risks to being willing to be vulnerable.

Leaders Wanted (and Desperately Needed)!

As mentioned previously, the current state of leadership development is a major CEO concern domestically and globally. Many team leaders in organizations both large and small are being named to their positions lacking many if not most of the leadership skills discussed in *Leadership Rigor*. Since far more leadership positions are available than qualified leaders to fill them, reluctant or unproven leaders are being put into roles where they are asked to develop both teams and individuals without having first fully developed or demonstrated their own leadership capabilities. **Rigor it** with accelerated learning and development!

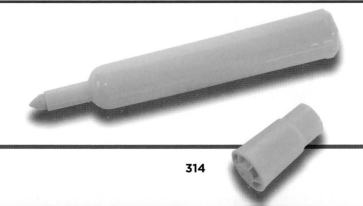

▶ Overcoming Resistance

Practitioners will need to overcome their resistance to investing time in coaching the behavioral aspects of performance. They will also have to resist the temptation to work at lower altitudes since they are no longer problem solvers but rather process and people solvers. Finally, they must resist holding on to the facilitation function in their leadership roles. In other words, they need to learn to trust and let go so that others can step into the spotlight and learn to lead.

Philosophers will need to overcome their tendency to jump into advisory roles with prescriptive actions based on their own experiences and remember to actively listen to the fears, concerns, and challenges of emerging leaders by creating safe space and using questions to guide their process forward in their mentoring roles.

They will also need to resist the urge to protect aspiring leaders from occasionally falling short or failing in their efforts. Failing, learning, and recovering are all natural parts of the leadership growth process that the philosopher can be there to coach and mentor through.

▶ Taking a Risk

Both practitioners and philosophers must risk the investment of up-front time and energy without knowing whether it will pay off in the realization of either potential technical or leadership skill capability. Give trust, believe, and make the investment!

Your personal risk on the career front is an important consideration. For example, if you decide to be a thought leader (a practitioner only), will you be limiting your longer-term organizational growth and earning potential? If you pursue being a philosopher and a practitioner, will your technical skills erode, leaving you vulnerable in your functional area of expertise?

While both choices represent potential risks, you need to embrace the reality of the road you emotionally feel called to choose and give your full efforts to creating the most fulfilling career for yourself.

The bigger risk is taking what you believe is the so called smarter path if it does not match your inherent motivations. Here, the risk of true failure is higher because you are out of alignment with your authentic self.

In addition to not realizing your own potential, you may also unnecessarily hold back the development of others and contribute to slower growth for your organization because of your decision to serve your egotistical self instead of being true to your real passions.

▶ Being Vulnerable

As either a practitioner or a philosopher, being vulnerable means sharing the real stories of your own growth and development journey. Be willing to admit your mistakes, embarrassments, and regrets as well as to highlight your proudest moments. You will build trust through the story of your struggle. It may feel risky to share your experiences, whether they are successes or failures, but don't let your ego hold you back; you don't have to look good or sound all-knowing. You only need to speak authentically from your heart and experience.

How to Confirm Your Role as a Practitioner

Those who are drawn to the practitioner role are well served to consider the following questions, as they will shed light on the probable long-term outcomes of this decision:

- If I pursue thought leadership, will I limit my promotability or future compensation?

- Will I limit my access to organizational resources?

- Will I be able to lead a company in the future or be named to an executive leadership team?

The most important decision you can make is to follow your heart with respect to your professional desires. If you are excited about knowledge/expertise and not energized by people development, honor that. Leadership is a service to others, and if you cannot passionately serve in the area of leadership development but can passionately serve the technical advancement of knowledge, then serve in that capacity. Your future is limited only by your own mindset.

Thought leadership and technical knowledge are in demand in all marketplaces and organizations. You will want to make sure that your particular organization acknowledges professional/technical expertise as a development track so that your potential expectations regarding salary and promotional opportunities are in alignment with the reality of your career aspirations.

Given your thought leader status, it is likely that the dedication and availability of resources allocated to you will be indirect or shared as opposed to direct, given your more exclusive technical focus. This may not be a concern for you and might in fact be preferred, given that your highest priority is to have access to smart individuals to advance the work as opposed to being responsible for engaging in soft-skill behavioral and leadership development needs.

The aspiration to lead a company as a practitioner with primarily technical knowledge/expertise can lend itself to a start-up venture, private company, or a new targeted project within a larger organizational infrastructure. What you may need to be prepared for in pursuing this ambition is being able to only champion the initiative through certain phases of its life cycle. For example, once the technical start-up phase is complete, a scale-up approach that requires additional people resources as well as organizational infrastructure may be necessary. This, in turn, may call for both a practitioner and philosopher approach to manage the next growth phase.

Alternatively, you may find yourself on an executive leadership team as the chief innovation/technical officer or in another individual contributor technical role contracting with outside consulting resources, a capacity that is more likely to fit your professional goals and personal temperament.

What Fear Is Holding You Back as a Philosopher?

Those who believe they are drawn to the philosopher approach need to rigor the following questions to determine whether they are truly prepared for what this role requires:

- Can I share my experience in a way that provides relevant learning?

- Can I balance listening and providing appropriate coaching?

- Can I articulate how and why I take action? In other words, am I a consciously competent leader?

Welcome back to the world of learning where leadership is a practice! You too will continue to grow, needing only to be a few steps ahead of those you are leading to have a meaningful impact.

Captain's Log – *USS Enterprise*

I would not consider myself a big *Star Trek* fan, but I often find myself whispering familiar phrases when I observe the seemingly innocent but unconsciously incompetent behaviors of my clients. These comments sound like, "Coach's log aboard the *USS Enterprise* mindset...Please remember that the role of the leader is to create context and meaning as well as to explain the 'why' when it comes to communication."

In a recent leadership journey I was facilitating, (1) of (3) teams I was working with held a powerful discussion regarding talent recruitment and the challenges of finding experienced candidates.

We all struggle here, yet a big part of this team's challenge was its collective mindset. Technical expertise was its most important consideration, and as a result, it often found only a limited number of qualified candidates.

Instead of expertise or technical performance exclusively, I challenged the team to widen its lens to the potential these candidates had in quickly learning these technical skills. In determining that potential, I asked this team to consider a concept included in Part 1 of **Leadership Rigor,** *learning agility.*

The concept resonated. After the workshop, an inspired participant did some online research and found some articles on agility that he attached to an FYI email and shared with his colleagues in that specific workshop. The organizational leader, who was also copied, earnestly forwarded these articles on an FYI basis to the other (2) groups engaged in the journey whose workshops were held on different days and who did not have access to the same conversation on this topic.

My observation? The organizational leader sent out the articles with no context, no explanation, and no insights on why this material was relevant or how it might be used to improve the organization's performance and productivity regarding recruiting or interviewing. This individual is a skilled practitioner who had not yet fully embraced the role of being a philosopher.

The receivers, who likely did not know how to use this information because no context or explanation accompanied it and the topic was not discussed in their session, likely discarded it.

Swing and a miss! This is an example of the practitioner genuinely looking to share knowledge to advance his organization's capabilities without taking the time to include the philosophical framework to shape it into learning, growth, or development.

Communication must always be framed so that it is able to stand alone. The organizational leader must learn to be both a practitioner and a philosopher!

You already know and have all that is required here! It is your collective experience to date that has prepared you to step into this role, and it is your desire to play it that already makes you a successful philosopher. You can lean into the models and frameworks in **Leadership Rigor** for structure, support, and language to make your actions understandable to others, but the core of your philosophies comes from your real life experiences and insights already learned. Lean into storytelling and let the lessons of your experience emerge naturally through questions and the context surrounding your discussions.

Being unrehearsed, spontaneous, and authentic is your best approach. Be fully present, engaged, and responsive to the needs of aspiring leaders. Remind yourself of your emotional intelligence skills and self-manage your potential impulses to give advice before fully listening, hearing, and understanding. Let your personal power and emotional intelligence guide the process, and don't feel compelled to overengineer anything.

Becoming Both: What's Needed to Resolve the Tension

Those who feel drawn to become both a practitioner and a philosopher will be well served to pragmatically consider what it is *they really need* versus what they *think they want* to achieve this goal:

- Do I need an established relationship in place?

- Do I need a request that taps into my comfort zone?

- Do I need to plan out my sharing up front?

Optimal conditions will never be in place, but coachable moments present themselves every day. If you are waiting for trust to build before you get into action, forget it! Trust will naturally accelerate when you step into your vulnerability and share your experiences.

> *Though it sounds counterintuitive, your comfort zone expertise may come off as preachy and your natural discomfort as more authentic, so be careful about what you think is important here. Your impact might run contrary to your intentions.*

Let go of your desire for planned sharing, too, for it is the **spontaneous coaching moment proximal to an observation or an event** that serves to impact and influence people the most. For example, the greatest gift you can give someone who is genuinely interested in learning about leadership is the knowledge of how they make you feel, the impact they have on you, and what their message "says" and "does not say." Often, this can be a sobering piece of learning or a positive reinforcement and confidence builder.

Occasionally, you will have the opportunity to really change the course of an aspiring leader's future by tapping into your **veritas** and **gravitas.** For example, if an individual is communicating with sarcasm, inappropriate body language, or passive-aggressive behavior and you can "call them out on it" and explain why it is negative, the impact on their leadership growth can be tremendous. Real-time feedback on "what it is like to be with you" or "the impact you have on others" is rarely given but desperately needed. Without it, individuals unconsciously move through their worlds, continuing to make the same mistakes and stay stuck. Take the time to listen, notice, and comment. Consciously choosing to be both a practitioner and a philosopher in these moments can be a game-changing experience for the aspiring leader.

The Service You Provide

The service you provide if you choose to be a thought leader and *practitioner only* focused on your expertise is that of being an industry *specialist*. Your deep skills are likely to separate you from your peers, and your organization benefits from having your problem-solving contributions and expert perspective within the enterprise, assisting in *creating technical competitive advantage.*

The service you provide by being both a *practitioner and a philosopher* is that of an *enterprise level generalist.* Having built a solid technical skill foundation, you now choose to maintain the status of your knowledge with continuing education along with an

The Warrior and the Wizard

Be mindful about the leadership style and the flexibility you will need to demonstrate as you evolve into being both a practitioner and a philosopher who is capable of leading at the organizational level.

Often, we begin our careers as warriors, focused on the goals, tasks, and deliverables we must complete. Passionate and motivated to succeed, we may not let anything get in our way, including whiny people or organizational distractions. As we move through our roles, we potentially leave a few hurt feelings and dead bodies in our wakes, but alas, the mission is always accomplished!

The warrior in us has emerged and stays strong, thanks to continued challenges, obstacles to overcome, problems to solve, and heroic opportunities to show the world who we are and how great our performance is.

Here's the problem: low-level, individual, task-driven leadership approaches can be good in war or at crisis time, but in generally stable team and organizational settings, the warrior is always more of a liability than an asset.

Ideally, the wizard within us emerges as we realize that the purpose of our leadership role is to call forth with our personal power the potential and capability from the talent we have in our organizations. Asking the provocative or reflective questions, clarifying the choices that lie ahead, confirming the emotional dynamics at play, and then stepping back and letting ownership for what is next rest on the shoulders of the aspiring leader is the work of the wizard.

Wizards are wise in that they help to narrate the journey for the traveler. They point out paths that are available as well as the potential requirements for navigating the terrain, but they always stop short of offering the solution or a preferred choice. Advocating for the strengths they see, supporting the premise that there are no right or wrong choices, just different options with varying levels of risk, is the role of wizard energy—of the philosopher—in the organizational context.

Create a safe space for learning, stand back, and watch the transformations unfold in others before you. Rigor your own leadership through the influence of your **Wizardship**™!

intensifying focus to lean into and share your leadership and business wisdom in order to accelerate the learning and growth of others.

Your contribution is one of continuing to build organizational momentum in creating a scalable and sustainable enterprise for the future. You are a nurturer of others and their learning curves; you are beginning to experience the higher altitudes of leadership and in so doing are making a contribution to *creating a cultural advantage for your organization.*

Both services are critical to the organization. Knowing which you are personally more motivated to take on and then consciously following your passion allows both you and your organization to reach your true potential!

The New Perspective You Take On

Regardless of how you choose to resolve this tension, the new perspective you take on is authentically stepping into your unique leadership practice with greater confidence based on aligning who you really are with your true aspirations and strengths.

Making the decision to be a specialty expert who is on the cutting edge of making things happen technically or acknowledging your passion for building the organization's capabilities and talent bench in order to grow and compete in the future creates energy and momentum for both you and your organization. You can now passionately focus your attention without regret or second-guessing, thereby truly experiencing who you are and what your real contributions and service can be.

Being a practitioner feeds the solidification of your experiences, philosophies, and professional expertise on the ground, while being a philosopher feeds the development of the leadership intangibles that are nurtured and grown with time, space, and patience.

Demonstrating a balanced capability and a commitment to becoming both a practitioner and a philosopher is how you transcend and resolve this tension with rigor and advance into leading at the organizational level!

"Personal Leadership is not a singular experience. It is, rather, the ongoing process of keeping your vision and values before you and aligning your life to be congruent with those most important things."
— Stephen Covey

RIGOR IT!

"Mountaintops inspire leaders but valleys mature them."
– Winston Churchill

PART 3:
LEADING
ORGANIZATIONS

Advancing into a leadership role at the organizational level can feel like going from piloting the Boeing Dreamliner to becoming an astronaut operating a space station. Both roles require skills for flying but at completely different altitudes and in extremely different conditions of complexity and ambiguity.

In business, a major difference between organizational leaders and team/functional leaders is the disciplined focus and skills required to frame the broader *"context and perspective"* on the issues and challenges for their respective audiences versus being concerned with the content elements only.

Being consciously competent at all times is also now the expectation the organizational leader must step up to given that the work at this level is integrated, systems based, and requires working collaboratively with highly competent functional leaders.

The requirements for leading at this level include creating a performance-based organization, developing a leadership team and talent bench, and ensuring that the operational platform is running productively today as well as being viable for the future.

Part 3 of *Leadership Rigor* covers these topics and introduces the final signature model, **Organizational Excellence**, that provides leaders with a road map for customizing their action agenda in the (6) critical areas CEOs and their leadership teams must own.

Part 3 also outlines the final tension you must resolve in your own personal *Leadership Rigor* journey: deciding whether you will be the entrepreneurial or the enterprise leader for your organization. This choice determines the role you will actively play and the role you will flank yourself with to ensure balance and long-term sustainability and scalability for your organization.

The most compelling organizational leaders to follow are those who are able to learn, grow, and evolve in real time with vulnerability as well as authenticity. They are ready to go first to show their teams the way forward, and they are willing to advance the journey forward when others want to turn back. They **Rigor it!**

Aspire to lead at the organizational level? Turn the page, and let's begin the next phase of your journey!

The Fundamentals of Leading Organizations:

CHAPTER 1:
Shaping the Leadership Roles

CHAPTER 2:
Shaping Your Operational Platform

CHAPTER 3:
Shaping Your Future Landscape

"As we look ahead into the next century, leaders will be those who empower others."

– Bill Gates

CHAPTER 1:
SHAPING THE LEADERSHIP ROLES

Holding a position is different from playing a role, and the risks for getting this wrong as well as the rewards for getting it right are enormous. At the organizational level, leaders must appreciate that how they play their role influences the environmental dynamics they establish as they shape the conditions for performance and productivity for their enterprise.

The Fundamentals Explored Here Include:

   I.   The Role of the CEO

   II. Being the CEO of Your Organization

   III. The Role of Your Executive Leadership Team

   IV. Delivering Executive Team Performance

I. The Role of the CEO

In business, holding the position and title of CEO is perceived to be the crown jewel of status and accomplishment, often accompanied by a complete set of perks and trappings that others envy. In your own company, you are likely viewed in the same light as the *local rock star or celebrity*. Not surprisingly, the CEO is typically someone who is admired and whom others are proud to say they know personally.

On a purely social level, where most people have an outsider's view of the business world, those who wear the mantle of CEO are exalted or treated with deference. At intimate gatherings, CEOs may enjoy ego-boosting adoration based on their perceived social ranking. CEOs may even receive the occasional compassionate comment about how hard it must be to make decisions all day long and carry the "weight of the world" for their organizations on their shoulders.

Playing the actual role of CEO, however, can be a *polarizing* experience. While many CEOs are admired for their skills and styles, others are resented for their tactics or selfishness and may be justifiably questioned regarding their competence or moral compass. Those who are business insiders know that the title can mean nothing and that the role of the CEO is greatly influenced by the man or woman who serves in it. Depending on how well we know you, for example, we may either be amazed at your energy and capacity for all that you do or wonder just what it is that you do all day long!

Your true value as a CEO is determined by *what you create, build, and shape* in those around you. To play the CEO role at the level of *Leadership Rigor,* you must be ready, willing, and able.

Can You Answer "Yes" to the Following (3) Questions:

1. Can You Play at the Required Altitude?

2. Can You Be a Consciously Competent Leader?

3. Can You Lead a Performance-Based Organization?

Question 1:
Can You Play at the Required Altitude?

For serious players, the game begins and ends here. If your *altitude is too low,* you compress your organization's capabilities and severely limit your line of sight for the competitive horizon. You simply cannot be prepared for or take advantage of what you cannot see!

Low-altitude CEOs fail to invest sufficient time in establishing priorities, sequencing critical workflow, and allocating resources for the organization's growth agenda because they are doing and managing the work of others several levels below them. The impact is the creation of a leadership void across the enterprise.

The challenge for these CEOs is to raise their altitude and work *on* their business rather than *in* their business. If they don't, as I've asked before, who will?

On the other extreme, CEOs who move through their organizations at *too high an altitude* appear inaccessible except for when they personally need something and choose to helicopter down into the details, typically causing disruption and resentment.

These CEOs might be informed about what is going on, but they are not actively engaged in or part of it. They are passionate about their own agendas, but *they are out of touch* with the true emotional energy and needs of their organizations.

Being popular, well liked, or visible does not ensure that a CEO is connected. Emotionally connecting requires using your leadership currencies of communication and relationship building in a meaningful and purposeful way so that the people in your organization feel seen, heard, and understood.

> *The challenge for all CEOs is to create an authentic level of intimacy with their organization by playing at the altitude their role requires. This means being focused on the business and emotionally connected to their people!*

Question 2:
Can You Be a Consciously Competent Leader?

Leading with rigor means that you think about what you do, why you are doing it, and how you can best do it so that your intentions and impact are appropriately aligned.

To be an influential CEO, you must be highly skilled at being consciously competent for several reasons. First, you are now leading leaders who are likely to be professionally accomplished in their own leadership practices, so the bar for providing them with advanced learning and growth is higher. Second, you are the ultimate role model for the organizational behaviors you are championing, so *you need to be alert to and aware of how you show up in all circumstances.*

Being a consciously competent leader does not mean you are perfect. It does mean being aware of your choices in each situation, including your language (verbal and body), your emotions (and moods), your use of personal power over position or expertise power, your emotional intelligence, and your open expression of vulnerability.

You will make mistakes. Being consciously competent, however, will prevent more mistakes from happening and will shorten the recovery time between your mistakes and the appropriate corrective action you take.

Always appreciate that your leadership "position" has tremendous perceived *gravity*. Be mindful of your impact, whether you are making an apology, losing your temper, or simply making facial expressions. As CEO, you need to always "walk your talk." If you expect your organization to display emotional intelligence through self-management, it must start with you. The consciously competent CEO is a visible and consistent role model!

Question 3:
Can You Lead a Performance-Based Organization?

Saying "yes" to this game-changing question will transform the DNA of your organization. Perhaps you believe that you already run a performance-based organization. My first response is, really? My second is, good for you, if it's really true!

The **Leadership Rigor** criteria for performance require that:

- *Expectations for results are known and visible* (formal written goals)

- *Expectations for behaviors are known and visible* (formal written values and competencies)

- All leaders competently and consistently *coach performance* **with open and direct feedback** (both positive and corrective)

If you claim, "Yes, we do this" to these (3) statements, congratulations; you are halfway there! The second part of this question, which will validate your approach as a performance-based organization, is this:

Are you practicing consequential leadership?

Consequential leadership consistently recognizes and holds accountability for **both positive and negative performances** with specific and tangible actions.

As leaders, we have a tendency to acknowledge and reward the positive while tolerating the negative. In performance-based organizations, there is a fair and equal emphasis on addressing both!

If you are playing at the altitude your role requires, are consciously competent, and are running a performance-based organization that is practicing consequential leadership, congratulations! You are playing your CEO role at the level of **Leadership Rigor.**

If you answered "No" to any of these questions, targeted opportunities for becoming a performance-based organization with consequential leadership practices exist and await your attention.

As CEO, remember that *your fingerprints are on everything* in your organization. If you like what you see, keep doing what you are doing and look to continuously raise the bar where you can.

If you don't like what you see, *objectively ask yourself* what you are creating and what you are tolerating.

Practicing Consequential Leadership Requires:

- **A Performance** Management Framework
- **Performance-Based** Compensation Plans
- **Performance** Feedback Tools

These initiatives include basic concepts, philosophies, and behaviors.

A Performance Management Framework **Includes:**

- ☑ Annual performance goals that are aligned and cascaded (corporate, team, and individual)

- ☑ Performance goals that include expectations for both results and behaviors

- ☑ Expectations for organizational values that are "known and lived"

- ☑ Quarterly performance-based coaching conversations

- ☑ Regular employee-driven 121s for feedback and insights

- ☑ Calibrated performance reviews across the organization for consistency

- ☑ A new employee on-boarding program

- ☑ A formal performance improvement process (PIP) to coach performance gaps

- ☑ A succession-planning process that is formally defined and consistently utilized

- ☑ Defined action plans to develop successor talent in critical roles

- ☑ Technical and behavioral competency expectations for each progressive job level

- ☑ A culture in which demonstrating competencies precedes promotional advancement

---

- [✓] A culture in which career management is mutually owned (talent and enterprise)
- [✓] A culture in which learning and leadership development are emphasized
- [✓] Immediate termination of employees who do not fit with company culture

Performance-Based Compensation Plans Include:

- [✓] Compensation plans containing both fixed and variable components
- [✓] Company performance targets that are achieved prior to full activation of variable pay
- [✓] Variable percentage targets that progressively increase at advancing executive levels
- [✓] Annual raises that are performance based and calibrated across the organization
- [✓] Market-based compensation levels that are benchmarked

Performance Feedback Tools Include:

- [✓] An annual or biannual (360)-degree feedback process
- [✓] Annual performance goals that are linked to (360) feedback learning and insights
- [✓] An annual cultural engagement survey
- [✓] Culture survey results that are linked to team leader performance goals
- [✓] Culture survey results that are linked to the CEO's organizational action agenda
- [✓] Coaching and mentoring relationships that accelerate behavioral performance

II. Being the CEO of Your Organization

Your employees are *watching and listening* to everything you do and say as the CEO, but understand that they are doing so *from their viewpoint.* They are asking themselves important questions about you that you need to be mindful of as you communicate and build relationships with them.

Overcome (3) Hurdles to Be Followed as a Leader:

- Making Your Authentic Self Visible

- Sharing the Lenses You Will Look Through

- Creating an Enterprise with Both Architects and Artisans

 **Hurdle 1:**

Making Your Authentic Self Visible

A CEO needs to be both real and credible. Being visibly comfortable in your own skin puts others at ease. Your projection of confidence, approachability, and your use of leadership language, including your body language (smile, handshake, openness), all convey important messages that set the stage for who you will be as a leader.

Taking the time to walk the (4) corners of your office while stopping to ask genuine questions with curiosity will send a message of being an authentically engaged leader. This along with being vulnerable as you communicate will signal your desire to build a trusting and open environment.

Remember that *vulnerability is not about your weakness but rather a sign of your strength.* When leaders are vulnerable, they openly acknowledge what they are good at and where they have shortcomings or need help. Expressing these needs becomes a call to action for members of your organization to step up, fill the gap, and be leaders as well.

"Our leader needs us here! We have to play our part" will be the powerful takeaway from your message of vulnerability.

Vulnerable CEOs will *own and take accountability* for mistakes made on behalf of the organizations they lead *without publicly blaming others.* When a mistake is made, a vulnerable leader quickly admits it, apologizes, and immediately addresses the changes that are required. This creates an environment in which everyone knows that mistakes will happen, and when they do, they will be owned and addressed with consequential leadership. If the CEO actively demonstrates vulnerability, others will follow.

A lack of vulnerability, especially on the part of the CEO, can have enduring *reputational consequences* for you personally as well as for your organization. *First, your weaknesses are already known and visible* whether you openly acknowledge them or not, so be honest and don't pretend to be invincible.

Second, not being forthcoming regarding your own vulnerability will signal multiple potential messages, including that you are either unconsciously incompetent with significant blind spots and are therefore an emperor without any clothes or that you arrogantly reject acceptance or ownership for your growth areas, thereby limiting your ability to establish trusting relationships because you cannot handle the truth.

The question your employees are asking is "Can I trust you?"

Rigor your vulnerability and make your authentic self visible, or be prepared for the reputational consequences!

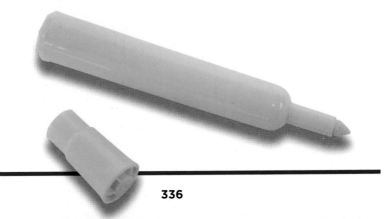

336

Hurdle 2:

Sharing the Lenses You Will Look Through

Having established your authenticity, the CEO role now shifts to expressing your vision and expectations for the organization and your employees. How will you look at the business, culture, and talent? Do you see exciting opportunities for change and growth or opportunities to judge and criticize previous efforts while positioning yourself as the heroic leader who will save the day?

> *The question your employees will be asking is "Can I meet the expectations of this CEO?"*

The Playbook on You

I encourage my CEO clients to give their employees the playbook on how to successfully work with them by sharing up front their work style preferences and philosophies. These insights can relieve the anxiety of trying to figure you out by trial and error.

If you are a big-picture thinker, advise your team that you will show signs of impatience if there is too much detail presented and the issue isn't appropriately framed for your altitude. Let them know that you will flex to their styles as well, but in terms of full disclosure, it is important that they understand your natural hardwiring.

Give your team your philosophies about leadership, business, and how you prefer to communicate and build relationships. Share the stories that have shaped you thus far as a business leader and a person. Be honest about your fears, your struggles, your proudest moments, and your disappointments. Be vulnerable, and invite their vulnerability as well!

Having *empathy and compassion* for the potential anxiety of your employees will serve you well as you introduce your expectations.

You want to *strike a balance* between setting a high bar for being a performance-based organization while establishing an inspiring vision and creating an environment that will be energizing rather than intimidating. This is not an easy challenge to meet!

Expressing your expectations through the following lenses, some of which have already been introduced in other contexts, will help guide the experience you create on your journey to becoming a performance-based enterprise using **Leadership Rigor.**

Lens 1:

Building a Leadership and Learning Culture

Establishing your priority for building individual leadership capabilities within the broader context of creating a learning culture sends a message that behavioral competencies will be as important as technical competencies. It also confirms your commitment to the growth and development of the talent within your organization.

Lens 2:

Having a "We-Based" Enterprise Mindset

Creating a "we-based" enterprise mindset in which leadership is in service of others reinforces the importance of personal power and influence over the use of position or expertise power within your culture. It also puts "I-based," self-centered employees on notice in your organization that you will be team based and collaborative in putting the enterprise needs first versus being focused on the needs and achievements of "superstar" individuals.

Lens 3:

Balancing Risk, Change, and Growth

Without being prepared to take risks and make changes, you cannot expect to grow your business, yourself, or your talent bench. ***Leadership Rigor*** creates change-ready leaders who capitalize on growth opportunities while balancing the dynamics of risk and change.

Lens 4:

Using Analytical Rigor in Decision Making

Encouraging the use of the signature model, **Analytical Rigor**, confirms your commitment to a disciplined and transparent approach toward decision making. This model provides a road map for navigating discussions with clarity and less analysis paralysis or impulsivity, setting a high bar for performance and productivity.

Lens 5:

Using The Accountability Conversation

The competing priorities of business today require that tools for accountability be consciously utilized. **The Accountability Conversation**, presented in Chapter 3 of Part 1, provides a structured up-front approach for aligning expectations, securing resource requirements, and establishing mutually agreed-upon timelines for deliverables. This confirms your commitment to the workload being negotiated and appropriately prioritized in your organization.

 Lens 6:

Developing an Organizational Action Agenda

Organizational Excellence will be covered in greater detail later in the signature model section, but sharing that you will be utilizing this model as a framework establishes your intention to take an integrated business approach with your leadership team and to target your action agenda initiatives at the enterprise altitude level.

Transparency and the Optics

While not all that you do as CEO is visible, what is will be put under both a microscope and a magnifying glass. To avoid misinterpretations you must be aware of "the optics" of how your actions will be viewed.

For example, your use of a corporate jet can send a message of indulgence and entitlement as opposed to productive time management. The story your organization creates may or may not reflect the truth of the situation. Be clear about if and how you want to frame the context of such realities so they do not become distractions of time, energy, and goodwill.

Private business owners may be reluctant to share company financial information with employees. You, as the owner, may rationalize this by thinking, "My finances are none of their concern." Be careful to balance your desire for an "ownership mentality" in your organization with the transparent sharing of information. Your employees must be trusted as mature business professionals capable of understanding how your organization makes money, what drives costs, and whether the company is profitable.

Hurdle 3:

Creating an Enterprise with Both Architects and Artisans

Your expressed language of appreciation for both architects and artisans establishes your cultural expectation for an intentionally diverse *community that embraces inclusion.*

> *The question your employees will be asking themselves is "Will I feel like I belong here?"*

The word *"architect"* acknowledges and appreciates the detail-oriented builders of processes, systems, project plans, and financial details. Without them, you would not be grounded or structured in your business fundamentals.

The word *"artisan"* acknowledges and appreciates the creativity and innovation your employees bring to the business environment. Without them, you would not explore the possibilities of your views in new and different ways, revealing breakthrough opportunities.

You will need both architects and artisans to round out the dynamics of structuring your operations as well as facilitating breakthrough ideas and innovations for your evolving strategies. It is interesting to note that these descriptions can be broadly applied to your MBTI sensors (S) and intuitives (N) as well.

What Employees Are Looking to Confirm in Their Leaders

Character: The beliefs that inspire you on a deep personal level

Principles: The practical philosophies that drive your behaviors

Credibility: The consistency of their experiences with you

III. The Role of Your Executive Leadership Team

As CEO, you want to create and lead a *change-ready* organization capable of seizing opportunities and consistently delivering or exceeding performance expectations.

> *Realizing this goal starts with your ability to shape the development of your leadership team.*

You are the executive team leader and therefore the initial role model for the process that lies ahead, so you personally will set the benchmark for performance.

Welcome to real-life leadership and the pursuit of a performance-based organization! *This is something you create, build, and shape over time.* It is not unlike a sports franchise that builds to competitiveness and dominance under the influence of a new coaching team after multiple seasons of average play.

Be serious about this work and realize that the only way out, once you begin, is to power through it by persevering. There's no turning back. *You've made a choice. Now do the work and work it out!*

The success or failure to build a high-performance leadership team is determined by the vision and persistence of a dedicated CEO. The fact is, most leaders fail! Do you have what it takes to *rigor it?*

Shaping Your Leadership Team Is Tougher Than You Think

Expect the process of building and shaping your team to be frustrating and time intensive. The reality is, it can be so challenging that at times you will question the pace of your progress and consider abandoning your efforts to just focus on the business! Your team members will also push back and encourage you to "give up on these nice-to-have leadership concepts and just drive the business," especially once they start to experience the challenges of leading at this level. In fact, most of your team members, including you, will start to realize *they had no idea what their true role was as a leader.* You will also both question whether they have what is required to succeed as organizational leaders

Let's look at (5) critical steps to build your executive team.

Step 1:
Naming Your Leadership Team

The name you give to your direct reports matters! It sets the tone for who you will be as the CEO, and it defines the scope of the work your team will do together. Among the names you may consider are:

- My staff
- My direct reports
- The management team
- The executive team
- The corporate team
- The leadership team
- The senior leadership team
- The executive leadership team
- The corporate executive team
- The division management team
- The organizational leadership team

Naming a Leadership Team Does Not Make It One!

Be careful not to convince yourself that because you named your direct reports a "leadership team" that they or you have the competencies and capabilities to lead! Teams are built and developed over time; they are not named or announced. **Rigor it** now with the reality of the real work!

You might look at this list and immediately think, "This is nonsense; just pick one and get on with it!" Each choice, however, implies a slightly different scope and meaning.

How you choose to name your team will impact how people interpret *your use of position versus personal power* as well as how you establish the altitude and expectations for the cascading teams throughout your organization.

> *The language you use as an organizational leader shapes your culture, so you need to always consciously consider the direct and subtle impact of your communication!*

Using "the" in your team's name can be appropriate when naming an area of expertise. For example, "The Medical Leadership Team" is an area where "The" is appropriate, as this team is distinguished from "The Supply Chain Leadership Team" or "The Commercialization Leadership Team" within a larger corporate structure. It also implies there is only one of these particular teams.

If you work in a larger global organization, you might choose to include a geographical boundary within the name as well, such as "The Canadian Medical Leadership Team."

Using "The Management Team" when you are the CEO of a small to mid-sized company or a division of a larger global corporation implies two potential takeaway messages. First, this team is going to be focused on managing or running the operations of the business. This would be declaring an altitude that is too low and not focused on priority setting or resource allocation if your goal is to establish **Leadership Rigor** across your organization. Simultaneously, this name implies that levels below this are "only doing what this team decides" because this is "the one and only" management team.

Using "The Senior Leadership Team" or "The Executive Leadership Team" also sends multiple messages. First, the team is focused at the leadership level of the organization. Second, there are other

Titles Matter

As a leadership coach, I often see leaders of private companies mistakenly letting their employees declare their own titles, randomly changing their employee titles to match what they believe is best for establishing credibility with their customers, or recklessly announcing new titles with little regard to the potential creation of overlap in responsibilities or the general confusion that will prevail across their enterprise as a result.

Organizational titles can play one of three roles. One, they either do not formally exist and the organization's culture is egalitarian with a "members of the firm" or "everyone is an associate" mentality. Two, the titles acknowledge and reward levels of progressive achievement technically and behaviorally based on demonstrated competencies (i.e., senior manager, director, or vice president). Or three, titles reflect a level of ownership such as founder or principal.

All of these approaches can work; choose the one that best represents your culture and consistently stick with it because names and titles send messages internally and externally about your organization and your talent. They do matter, so **Rigor it!**

leadership teams in the organization. Third, there may or may not be a unique level called "executive" in this organization.

Some CEOs believe this level of detail is too granular and does not matter. It might not, to them, but it does matter to others in your organization who will pick up on your subtleties and make inferences or "stories" about them whether they reflect your intentions or not.

Each name reflects a subtle but significant difference that helps *shape the culture* of your organization. Make a *conscious choice* and *consider the consequences* so that you are clear on *both the intention and the impact* you want this name to have.

Step 2:
Selecting Your Leadership Team

Selecting your leadership team is an important decision to make as a CEO. You want to surround yourself with team members who embody the values, behaviors, and philosophies you believe in and want role modeled at the enterprise level. These individuals must also be capable of and committed to passionately developing themselves as well as other leaders.

As a leadership coach, I am exposed to a large number of organizations and their leadership teams. I often see (3) different scenarios:

1. There is *no* leadership team in place

2. There is a *faux* leadership team in place

3. There is a *formal* leadership team in place

▶ *Scenario 1:* No Leadership Team in Place

In this scenario, the CEO has a loose consortium of direct reports, with informal, ad-hoc, one-to-one communication being the primary method of interaction. Group communication takes place on an as-needed basis, but there is no formally identified or named team with a clear sense of purpose or a shared action agenda at the enterprise level. The CEO typically thinks each direct report is a strong player performing well, while the direct reports feel connected to the CEO yet disconnected from their other colleagues or a sense of team.

> *The culture of this organization reflects the personality and blind spots of the CEO, who without a formal leadership team is at risk of being an emperor with no clothes who thinks everything is fine but is significantly limiting the potential performance and productivity of the organization despite whether it is currently profitable or growing.*

This individual either doesn't really believe change is necessary or (mistakenly) believes there is an endless amount of time to make changes, operating under the illusion that once this, that, or the other thing is in place, the time will be right to form a leadership team.

This is typically an unconsciously incompetent or consciously incompetent judgment call by the CEO, who is losing valuable time in creating a formal framework for fully capitalizing on the talent across his or her enterprise in driving business growth. Additionally, this also puts the organization at significant risk for a haphazard or confusing transition in the event of a dramatic departure by the CEO.

Today's organizations are simply too complex to be run by a single individual who is merely coordinating activities. Without cohesive and well developed leadership teams in place, organizations are likely *underperforming to their potential.* Typically, these organizations are privately held, so the initial consequences, if any, are mainly limited to financial plus/minus changes in individual or family net worth.

Sequencing Your Involvement in Boards

Whether running a public or private company, CEOs can obtain insight and value from a board of directors or peer advisory board. A board of directors with functional expertise and voting rights can offer formal guidance to CEOs, whereas peer advisory boards can provide general advice more informally. Both can be of great value to the CEO who is charged with strategic and operational decisions in a complex business environment. The one mistake many privately held companies make, however, is waiting too long before forming their own internal leadership teams. These CEOs tend to run their companies with a "spoke in the wheel" approach and seek to supplement their narrow perspective with a peer advisory board or formal board before forming their internal team. Sequencing matters here, and if you have to confirm it with one of your boards, do so, but I am going to guess they will tell you to **rigor it** with an internal leadership team first!

▶ *Scenario 2*: A Faux Leadership Team in Place

Large corporate organizations often have all "functional leaders" formally report to the CEO, including both operational and staff roles. Meetings are held, attendance is encouraged, and the agenda tends to be a laundry list of topics that range from administrative information sharing to rolling out new corporate initiatives. Team members typically do not bring substantial business issues to the table for debate or discussion, and real decisions impacting strategy or operations are not made in this forum. These tend to be *alignment and assignment* meetings for further cascading information or organizing workstreams to support the next wave of corporate initiatives. When meaningful work is required, the CEO typically names a smaller work group to design and develop recommendations or hires outside consultants to guide the process.

Day-to-day critical operational decisions are made in smaller group settings or in one-to-ones with the CEO and the respective functional head, though their outcomes are often not shared or communicated back to the broader team in a transparent and integrated way, leaving little doubt that no real team dynamics exist.

> *The culture of this organization likely reflects the personalities of the functional leaders with some loose corporate alignment. In short, this is an example of a leadership team "in name only."*

Small to mid-sized companies, or functional teams within larger infrastructures, may have a similar approach. *The team meetings are professional but not dynamic or purposeful.* Individuals either wonder why they are here and whether this is a good use of their time, since they all have "real work" to do, or they are engaged passengers on an entertaining bus that is discussing interesting topics they appreciate hearing about, even though they don't understand what they should do with this information.

The team leader typically struggles to unify the team around defined initiatives with shared interests, given that the members behave as individual contributors who are mainly concerned about their personal and functional responsibilities. These individuals enjoy the money, titles, and status that come with being perceived as organizational leaders, but they don't see the value of this team or embrace the shared accountability to create it. The culture of this organization likely favors individual contributors, high achievers, and collaboration on a technical or functional basis only. There is no overarching leadership development occurring, and limited behavioral expectations are in place for leadership performance.

Typically, the leader lacks a clear vision of how to lead the executive team or is too patient in indulging reluctant or practitioner-only team members who need to be removed and replaced with those who want to lead at this enterprise level.

The risk here is that observant high-potential performers who want to advance in the organization will leave because they do not see enterprise value being created at the leadership level.

▶ *Scenario 3:* A Formal Leadership Team in Place

Organizations that have formal leadership teams in place are consciously attempting to operate at the right altitude, doing the work that only they can do. They are taking on the challenge of working together with a shared purpose and are creating both an expectation and accountability for excellence across their enterprises.

These teams tend to be led by passionate CEOs who have the vision to see their organizations performing at levels team members don't yet see themselves at and who hold this open space for them to expand into. Relentlessly optimistic and resilient, these CEOs see the leadership experience as a true journey of growth and development for both the technical and leadership skills of their enterprises, and they invest significant resources to realize the tangible on-the-ground benefits from their efforts.

They realize that winning in the marketplace requires a culture and talent bench focused on performance. They also know it is their job, along with their leadership team, to create the environment in which their talent can perform at its highest level so it can build a scalable and sustainable enterprise with traction and momentum for future growth. They are building a team and leadership culture in which those who aspire to lead at the team and organizational level are identified early and given learning tools with which to accelerate the creation of their own leadership practices.

> *These leadership teams recognize how competitive advantage can be created through their culture and leadership development initiatives.*

They collectively nurture and encourage their expression of vulnerability in service of building trust in their relationships because they realize that productive conflict creates better solutions as well as alignment for the team. Committed to high performance, they lean into peer-to-peer accountability because they appreciate that a shared action agenda they are on point to deliver collectively is required to inspire their enterprise to evolve beyond ordinary to extraordinary.

The Seismic *Shift* in Perspective

The framework shifts dramatically when leading at the organizational level compared with leading a functional team:

- Focus .... my team — *Shift* → the enterprise

- Visibility .... cave — *Shift* → fishbowl

- Altitude .... do/manage — *Shift* → lead

- Solution .... problem — *Shift* → process and people

- Message .... team mission — *Shift* → company narrative

Step 3:
Announcing Your Leadership Team

Making organizational announcements in writing, especially those concerning promotional or position changes, requires thoughtful consideration in order to establish the context as well as appropriately select the language.

Each written communication must be able to stand on its own and be clearly understood. If it cannot, you have not appropriately *"framed and landed"* the communication, which is your role as the leader. Think carefully about what you want to communicate, both in terms of words and in feelings, and make sure your intention and impact are aligned. As the old saying goes, measure twice and cut once.

As you think about announcing the members of your leadership team, which of the *following options* best describes the action you are taking for each individual?

- You are *promoting...* This is a level and scope change.

- You have *selected...* You have made a choice from options.

- You have *appointed...* This individual is needed on the team.

- You have *named...* This individual fills a required post.

Include in your announcement why you are excited about this team by sharing what each member brings to the enterprise level and what your expectations are for them as both functional leaders and organizational leaders.

Also confirm what the scope of work will be for your leadership team and the impact you believe it will have on the current and future landscape of the enterprise.

Step 4:
Engaging the Executive Team in a Leadership Journey

Once you have named, selected, and announced your team, it's time to consider engaging in a leadership journey that establishes your commitment to building a high-performance executive team capable of enterprise-level work.

Let's be clear here; this is not about going off on another (2)-day retreat to discuss strategy and play golf. No, this is a structured learning journey designed and facilitated to build team cohesiveness and behavioral skill sets so you are not only philosophically aligned but also productively using the same language and tools across the enterprise to drive performance. This is critical, because how you engage as a leadership team will affect the evolution of your culture.

Unfortunately, many teams believe that leadership development is a waste of time and money or they arrogantly and ignorantly assert,

"We know what we need to do; we can do this ourselves!"

I wish this were true, but in reality, high-performance teamwork is rare. In fact, most leaders don't know what a high-performance team looks or feels like because they have never been part of one, yet

Is Your Organization "Functionally Dysfunctional"?

Being comfortable or satisfied with your organization can be a sign that you are becoming "functionally dysfunctional." You know that certain things are not being done productively, but you are used to them and know how to work with and around them.

As CEO, your job is to *consistently raise the bar* on performance and productivity expectations. A brief renewal period allows your organization to reset and get ready for what comes next, but don't be complacent and accepting, and certainly don't stop rigoring it!

many boldly declare they have created and currently lead one! As the saying goes, "In the land of the blind, the one-eyed man is king."

This can be especially true for CEOs or business owners of small to mid-sized firms who have *limited or no work experiences at other companies* during their careers. This puts them at significant risk because they don't know what they don't know. ***Their blind spots often prevent them from seeing their real growth opportunities and painfully obvious need gaps.***

Meanwhile, to grow the business, organizations need to bring in new talent. That talent, if strong, will either challenge the low-performance environment or will quietly and gracefully leave without explaining why.

You can color it any way you want, but strong talent today desires

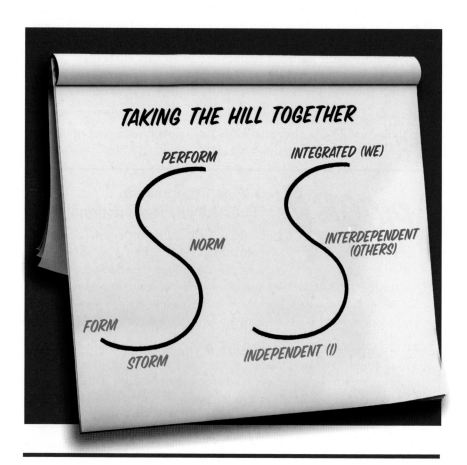

a high-performance culture. If talented individuals are leaving your organization, you need to realistically consider why.

As you consider engaging on this journey, you need to appreciate that building trust and working through your team's barriers and baggage is not a passive process that will naturally occur over time. Team building, like muscle building, requires commitment. There will be breakdowns, healing, rebuilding, and breakthroughs along the way as you become an integrated, high-performance team. The good news is, the harder you work, the more significant the outcomes!

▶ Use a Team Coach to Facilitate Team Building

Partnering with an experienced team coach as you undertake your journey can provide you with important advantages for accelerating your team's growth and development. First, you will have a professional in the room capable of facilitating challenging, emotionally charged, and potentially high-conflict conversations productively.

Second, a team coach can extract and articulate learning insights in real time from the interactions. This can be critical to ensuring meaningful progress when you are dealing at the senior executive level with strong-minded leaders who are likely to be smart, confident, and verbally assertive.

Be sure to choose a team coach who is a competent and experienced business leader in his or her own right so this individual is viewed as a respected peer by your leadership team and not simply a trained workshop facilitator.

Having sat at the executive leadership table myself makes a meaningful difference in my professional credibility and adds to the skills and talents I can bring into the room to facilitate practical and substantial breakthroughs in the leadership journey process. Having the courage to dive deep and say what needs to be said because you have experienced it yourself can be the stimulus for revealing and resolving issues that may otherwise linger for years, causing ongoing dysfunction that limits performance and productivity.

Coaching Is Not Therapy

Coaching is specifically focused on the here and now as well as the real-time impact of your behaviors. Therapy is often a retrospective exploration of what has brought you to this point in time based on reconciling previous exposures and experiences. While both encourage open dialogue and vulnerability, they are very different professions.

In partnering with the right team coach, you as CEO will get to be an active participant, an observer of the interpersonal dynamics, and a co-facilitator where it is appropriate. Being in the mix of the emotions and the dialogue makes you vulnerable and more approachable as a leader. In fact, be prepared, because many of the initial concerns from your leadership team members will focus on your style and impact as well as the relationship baggage they have with you. Working through this first clears a path forward so that your team members can begin to work through their issues with each other.

Facilitating yourself or using an internal HR professional seldom results in the open and honest leadership team dynamics needed to get this high-intensity work done.

Your better bet is to rigor it with an external team coach, who can provide provocative objectivity by saying what needs to be said and going where your team needs to go.

▶ **High Impact Facilitation Accelerates Breakthroughs**

The initial issues that surface on the leadership journey are usually just symptoms of the bigger challenges at play. A skilled facilitator will *separate the decoys from the real obstacles* so that when they are overcome, the breakthrough causes a game-changing shift around your leadership table and ultimately across your enterprise.

High-impact conversations supported by safety and trust in the room will be required to achieve these breakthroughs. Conversations involving productive conflict are particularly positive because they drive acceleration in team performance by getting weigh-in on issues so commitment can be secured. A seasoned facilitator will work with you through these challenges rather than shutting down the dialogue, rescuing colleagues, or taking the conversations offline, all of which stunt the progress of team building and are more likely to happen without an outside team coach present.

You will all be pushed by your team coach to take the *"hot seat"* occasionally and endure the discomfort of having your specific behaviors be the focus of attention. Naturally, these discussions are uncomfortable. While most teams avoid them, high-performance teams and their leaders embrace them out of necessity, realizing they accelerate personal and professional growth. Without reality-based conversations requiring both vulnerability and productive conflict, you are just dancing around the issues, and they will continue to hold you back as a team. The choice is always yours. Choose to **Rigor it!**

Self-Control Is Dangerous!

Self-control is not the same as self-management. Self-control means we ignore, resist, and fight back our emotions. Self-management allows an open flow through which we consciously experience our emotions and learn to appropriately express and work with them. Self-management is healthy; self-control is a time bomb!

Step 5:
"We Don't Need That Touchy Feely B$^&*^#!"

The most frequent comment I hear at the beginning of a leadership journey is, "We don't need that touchy feely stuff and we don't need a team shrink. This is business!"

The thought of expressing vulnerability or talking about feelings with people we work with can send many executives "running for the hills." If they avoid expressing or rarely share their feelings with close friends and family members, they certainly aren't going to share them with the people they work with, right?

Times are changing. To be a successful organizational leader in today's business world, CEOs must be willing to share both their thoughts and feelings as well as express their vulnerability. This isn't an option; it's a leadership requirement!

The critical questions you must honestly assess as CEO as you begin your executive team leadership journey include the following:

- Does your team have a minimal threshold level of *self-awareness* and emotional intelligence with which to start this journey?
  (How long will it take to see progress?)

- Are your team members *open minded*, curious, and willing to commit to this leadership and learning journey?
  (How hard will this journey be?)

- Are your team members *capable role models* who can develop the leadership talent bench you will need in your organization both today and tomorrow?
  (Will the benefits of this work be successfully cascaded?)

These are tough questions. Now that you have selected your team, the journey you are about to embark on will begin to confirm whether your choices were wise. If they were not, this journey will challenge whether you have the patience to persevere over the long haul and the courage to practice consequential leadership!

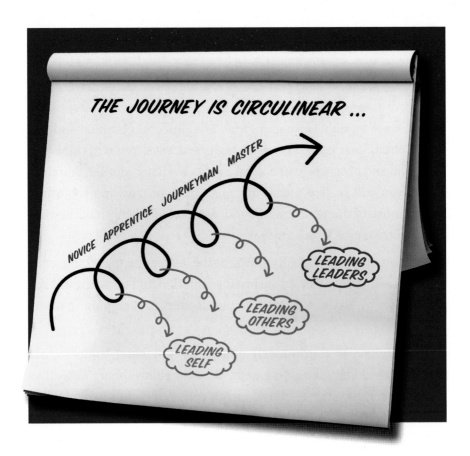

THE JOURNEY IS CIRCULINEAR ...

NOVICE APPRENTICE JOURNEYMAN MASTER

LEADING LEADERS

LEADING OTHERS

LEADING SELF

Peer Relationships and Career Advancement

If you have been self-serving and occasionally disrespectful of your colleagues, you will have less support among your peer group for advancement. In fact, peers who feel uncomfortable with your leadership style may threaten to leave if you are promoted into a supervisory role over them. If the potential loss of talent is a significant enough risk, a less polarizing candidate may be selected over you even if he or she is less technically qualified. Make sure your peer relationships are solid. **Rigor it!**

▶ The Journey Is Both Experiential and Evolutionary

Where you start the leadership journey as a team is just that... *a starting point.* Where you finish is a place you could have never imagined because through the journey's evolution, *the players are transformed* as they learn and grow. The process is gradual and follows a circulinear path. There are highs and lows. You will think you have made no progress, you will take a dip, perhaps another, and then slowly you will realize that your language, your trust in each other, and your use of the tools look, sound, and feel different than they did before. *Progress is being made!*

Discovering who is really sitting at the leadership team table with you is an exciting and often surprising experience. The perceived superstars may retreat, and the reluctant leaders may step up in unexpected ways.

The dynamics continuously change as individual leaders cross their personal knowing-doing gaps, become philosophers as well as practitioners, and start to consciously work with their personal hardwiring as well as flex to the preferences of others. With confidence and clarity taking hold, the team bonds as the individuals begin to **rigor it** together!

▶ Peer Relationships—A Sign and Signal to Watch

Strong peer-to-peer relationships are a visible sign of healthy team dynamics and are required, not optional, for high-performance executive leadership teams.

Consistent signals of respect, connectivity, and authentic communication at the executive leadership team level in turn build trust and confidence across the enterprise.

Be mindful that casually sharing your thoughts on executive leadership team discussion topics with a colleague outside of this team should always be avoided. While seemingly harmless, the impact is that you appear to be *"talking out of school"* and therefore cannot be

We Show Up the Same Everywhere

The behavioral expectations in performance-based organizations are higher than in our private lives, right? After all, at home, we can do anything we want, including losing our tempers or being self-indulgent, can't we?

The truth is, all of our relationships suffer when we fail to lead ourselves; we just may not always be aware of it or understand the eventual consequences.

Listening to each other, speaking openly, sharing how we feel, and dealing with our real issues at home is necessary if we want to have healthy and fulfilling relationships.

As a coach, my clients often share with me that the leadership work we engage in together carries over into their personal lives as well. This isn't surprising, because each of us is an integrated person.

When clients tell me they behave differently in their work environments than they do at home, I know a huge growth opportunity awaits them because we show up the same everywhere! Perhaps you control or self-manage better in one place than another, or then again, perhaps you just think you do!

trusted. Whatever you speak about is irrelevant; what you say puts at risk your credibility and alignment with your peer leadership team.

You must have an enterprise perspective at all times as a member of the CEO leadership team. This mentality requires your conscious awareness in always ensuring the organization's needs are above your own personal or team needs as well as remembering that you are a role model for the organization in a transparent fishbowl in which your every move is openly viewed. This also means that you cascade only agreed-upon messages for the purposes of consistency and alignment with your leadership team as well as always hold confidentiality in the discussions held behind closed doors.

As mentioned earlier in **Leadership Rigor**, peer relationships are so important at the enterprise level that many executive changes are considered in the context of how they will be accepted by other leaders in the organization. A leader who has built trust, credibility, and strong relationships with peers is always better positioned for a promotional opportunity.

▶ Expected Outcomes for Your Leadership Journey

The resultant outcome you should expect is that each member:

- *Demonstrates* a "we-based" mindset and is not self-serving or reluctant to lead

- *Demonstrates* with conscious competency the skills required for leadership at the organizational level

- *Demonstrates* a willingness to be open, vulnerable, and grow by continuously uncovering blind spots (their own as well as their colleagues')

- *Utilizes* personal power to influence across the organization and coaches others to do the same

- *Commits* to holding themselves, the leader, and their peers accountable to being a performance-based organization that practices consequential leadership

Serving at the highest levels of impact and influence through membership on an executive leadership team is an opportunity and a privilege. Individuals who are distracted by the personal pursuits of money, titles, or position power are not well suited for organizational leadership roles.

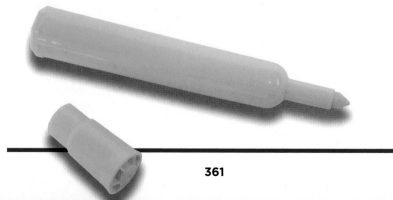

IV. Delivering Executive Team Performance

With your leadership team fully engaged in the learning process of building a cohesive team, it is important to clarify what performance *looks like, sounds like,* and *feels like* at the executive leadership level.

Expectations for the Executive Leadership Team:

- Always Serves the Enterprise First
- Acts as a Performance-Based Role Model
- Is Visible and Vulnerable

Always Serves the Enterprise First

The executive leadership team is unique because members play dual roles. They have functional and enterprise accountability, but their priority in playing this *"interface role"* must be to align with the CEO at the enterprise level first.

There will be times when members of the leadership team have to make choices or decisions that do not favor their functional areas. The maturity and poise they display here will be a sign of their ability to perform as organizational leaders at the enterprise level.

Acts as a Performance-Based Role Model

As CEO, how serious you are about being a performance-based organization that practices consequential leadership will be visibly determined by the way you work with the members of your leadership team. If you tolerate unproductive behaviors, the message of tolerance will be sent across the organization. If individuals are held accountable, that message will be equally clear.

Is Visible and Vulnerable

You and your leadership team members need to take the time to engage with both internal and external stakeholders in meaningful, respectful, and visible ways.

Initially, visibility equals leadership. Those who are most visible are assumed to actively be playing leadership roles, but this favorable perception can quickly fade to frustration if it becomes apparent that someone is a *"fly-by leader"* or a highly social individual who engages in unproductive chit-chat that distracts from productivity. You want to strive for "engaged visibility" where you are seen, heard, and mutually exchanging thoughts and ideas with others in meaningful ways.

Being vulnerable is about being authentic, asking for help, and apologizing for mistakes. Leadership vulnerability is a strength that creates a safe space for your organization to work in. It must, however, be actively demonstrated and encouraged by you and your leadership team if it is going to get real traction in your culture.

Performance at the Executive Leadership Team Level:

- **Be Present and Engaged at the Right Altitude**

- **Role Model the Behaviors of a Leader**

- **Deliver On-the-Ground Results**

Be Present and Engaged at the Right Altitude

Being present means *actively paying attention and appropriately interacting.* If team members are physically present but do not facilitate dialogue, share learning, or ask insightful questions about priorities and resources, they are not delivering against the performance expectations of an organizational leader.

Remind yourself frequently that what you and others verbally communicate is only one of the two conversations that is always taking place. ***The other conversation is what your body language communicates, and this is the one that has the most influence.*** If you roll your eyes, fall asleep, look down, or otherwise ignore the dynamics of the room, you send a message of being disengaged and disinterested.

If you are an introverted leader, push yourself to use some extraverted energy as you interact because your internal processing and quiet nature may be misunderstood. Stay alert to entry points for making contributions, presencing yourself, and being heard.

> *As an organizational leader, remember that your mere presence may unintentionally intimidate others based on your position power unless you consciously and proactively utilize your personal power to create a safe environment and confirm your approachability.*

Calibrating your performance at the right altitude establishes how productively the organization around you operates. Your primary role as a leader is to prioritize initiatives and allocate resources (people, time, and money). Operating at this level ensures that your direct reports can manage and do their jobs *without* you compressing them by dropping down into your comfort zone and interfering with their growing space.

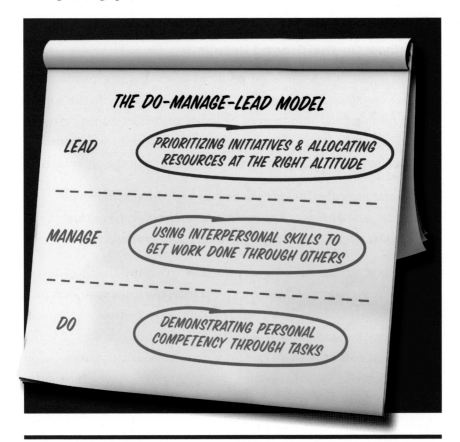

THE DO-MANAGE-LEAD MODEL

LEAD — PRIORITIZING INITIATIVES & ALLOCATING RESOURCES AT THE RIGHT ALTITUDE

MANAGE — USING INTERPERSONAL SKILLS TO GET WORK DONE THROUGH OTHERS

DO — DEMONSTRATING PERSONAL COMPETENCY THROUGH TASKS

Role Model the Behaviors of a Leader

Organizational leaders must be consciously disciplined role models for the values, behaviors, and culture of the enterprise. This means they proactively and appropriately use the language, models, and frameworks the organization is investing resources in to improve performance and enhance productivity.

> *As you engage in role modeling specific behaviors, name them and intentionally talk about their value. In so doing, you will be demonstrating the practitioner and philosopher approach developed in the previous section in real time for your talent bench.*

You may occasionally ask an aspiring leader to share the stage and role model with you to broaden the community involvement and facilitate the cascading effect of building **Leadership Rigor** across your enterprise.

Deliver On-the-Ground Results

The leadership team is on point to guide the organization towarddelivering collective results. Working together with an *"enterprise first mindset,"* you need to calibrate priorities, adjust resource allocations, and track performance targets so revenues and profits are delivered to ensure the growth and sustainability of the organization.

> *Results may also include the delivery of process improvements, new business initiatives, or talent objectives that increase organizational performance and productivity.*

While making trade-offs on priorities to ensure the most favorable return, members of the executive leadership team must be mindful of both **ROI (return on investment)** and **ROR (return on resources)**. The first reflects the use of green dollars while the second is the fully loaded cost of both green and blue dollars. Performance-based organizations are also disciplined at tracking **ROR2**, which can also be referred to as your return on resources and rigor!

Accountability at the Executive Team Level:

- Performance and Productivity at the Right Altitude

- Peer Group Communication Is Aligned

- Messages Are Cascaded with "The Why"

Performance and Productivity at the Right Altitude

The leadership team must consciously apply discipline to avoid the trappings of efficiency and effectiveness instead of the real targets they are accountable for, which are performance and productivity!

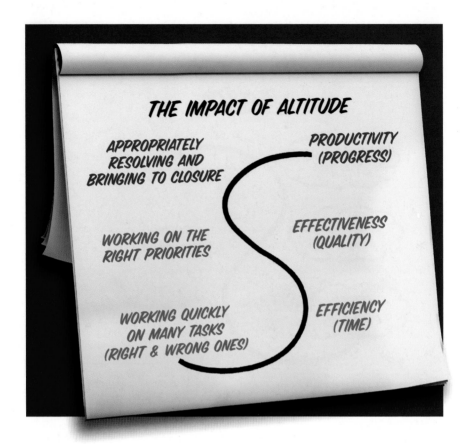

The time and energy you as CEO and your leadership team invest now to coach and develop your direct reports will ultimately pay off with productive returns for you later, if you pay it forward. If you alternatively choose to put minimal time into coaching and development, rationalizing to yourself and others that you will embrace this later on down the road, you are deluding yourself and going nowhere.

You will never feel ready to invest time you don't believe you have, so you will be always caught in a stuck system. The change must come from your mindset. Your job as the CEO or leadership team member is to coach and develop others, preferably with passion and from the heart. *Only an investment in your people will unlock the stuck system,* so train, coach, or hire those with the right skills and remove those who don't have them.

Meanwhile, *your personal bandwidth* can only be expanded by working smarter (time management, energy management, prioritization) and by developing your team to give you greater lift so that you can all perform at the right altitude.

In Part 1 of **Leadership Rigor**, it was established that influencing others through your personal power has more impact than leveraging position power, but what about using expertise power at the organizational level?

The expertise senior executives amass over the course of their careers is a source of pride. They are **master problem solvers** who can quickly *assess* a situation, *diagnose* the problem, and *prescribe* an immediate solution. Yet at the executive leadership team level, leaders are no longer in the problem-solving business. **They are now in the process- and people-solving business!**

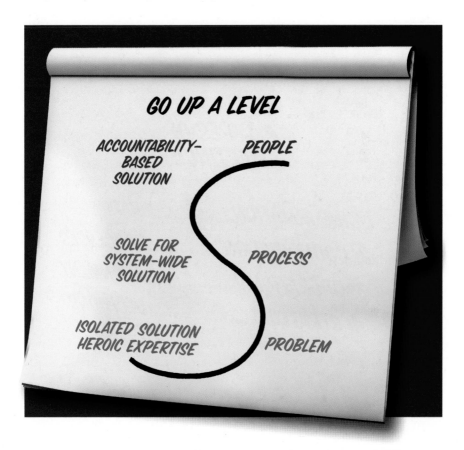

When you engage in solving situational problems, you are working at the lowest level of **Leadership Rigor**. You are telling, directing, or micromanaging for a fast and efficient solution by *indulging in expertise power flexing*. As a result, your altitude is too low, and ultimately you compress the growth of your team.

One of the hardest **Leadership Rigor** challenges at the organizational level is to act with conscious discipline and resist the lure of heroic leadership or situational problem solving by using expertise power. Instead, choose to *go up a level in altitude* and coach your team to solve the problem by working through a *process or people lens.* This reflects appropriate accountability at the leadership team level.

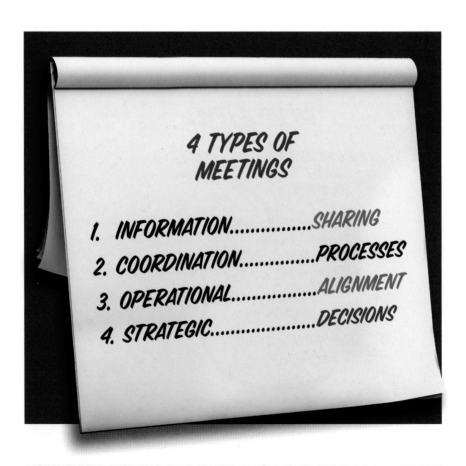

▶ Meeting Management at the Executive Team Level

When you ask organizational leaders about their time pressures, one of the most significant culprits is *"meetings."* They are either in one now or running to one next. The question is whether these are *"spends" or "investments" of time and energy?*

Leadership Rigor urges leaders to apply conscious discipline toward performance and productivity by making smart investments with their resources (people, time, and money).

> *Meetings, the ultimate utilization of people and time, cost blue dollars to the tune of many thousands per hour, yet we collectively and unproductively conduct them every hour on the hour!*

> *A productive meeting is defined as focusing on meaningful progress and tangible outcomes with the right agenda items, for the right amount of time, with the right people in the room who demonstrate emotionally intelligent behaviors.*

Emotionally Intelligent Meeting Behaviors

Be conscious of how you show up (self-awareness and self-management) and what it is like to be with you (social awareness) as you participate in meetings. If you are introverted, push yourself to engage. If you are extroverted, remember to bottom line your comments. Indulging yourself by repeating what has already been said just to hear yourself talk is frustrating for others. It is refreshing, though rare, when leaders say they have nothing further to add!

Staying at the right altitude (details or big picture) and balancing between an abrupt close and "beating a dead horse" are emotional intelligence reminders for the meeting facilitator or team leader.

Let's take another look at the (4) types of meeting approaches first introduced in Part 2 and consider how they contribute to performance and productivity at the organizational level:

- *Information*..... general sharing

- *Coordination*....process orientation

- *Operational*...... trade-offs and alignment

- *Strategic*........... decisions on external initiatives

Information sharing. The majority of team time is typically spent in the information sharing meeting format. As mentioned, these detailed updates on specific projects are *an indulgence* for the team leader and may not be relevant for other participants. These types of meetings do not tap into the collective insights and talent in the room to move the business forward. Unfortunately, teams spend between 40%–70% of their time here, which is why executives complain that meetings are frustrating and a waste of time.

Leaders may justify holding information sharing meetings out of a desire for "whole team inclusion" or efficient "face time." These are good intentions but do not have a good impact. These leaders need to consider more productive formats for achieving their objectives.

One **Leadership Rigor** approach to information sharing is *the disciplined roundtable update* on (1) to (2) priorities that are broadly relevant and that focus on progress, challenges, or where an individual needs assistance from the specific colleagues around the table that can be highlighted and followed up on later. In this format, time is strictly limited to (1) to (2) minutes per person, depending on team size. This approach provides an opportunity to practice communication skills, especially bottom lining. Long stories or detailed questions are a self-indulgent use of team time, and leaders need to exercise discipline and discretion in actively managing this.

If a critical issue arises during the roundtable, the leader can either choose to address it with more time on the agenda that day or defer to an appropriately planned follow-up meeting.

Another productive use of an information sharing format is to engage in a best practices discussion. Sharing outcomes and insights learned from previous experiences on the team can be of practical use, but leaders should frame the discussion at the appropriate altitude for group relevancy in an effort to maximize productivity.

Coordination of processes. Coordination meeting formats are best utilized when instructions on processes and timelines need to be discussed to ensure clarity and collective alignment on the sequencing of deliverables.

High-performance teams establish an annual coordination meeting calendar; this eliminates wasted hours debating, discussing, or redoing work that is relatively consistent on an annual basis. After all, the budget planning cycle and performance reviews come the same time each year, yet many executives struggle with finding the time to work on them as if they are a surprise!

Additional processes that can be productively discussed in coordination meeting formats include calibration of raise/bonus payouts, succession planning, and quarterly board meetings. The leadership team must decide when in the year these topics are best placed on the action agenda for preparation, review, discussion, and alignment.

To continually improve performance, you might build into your annual process calendar "a lessons learned and best practices discussion" so you can identify and incorporate necessary changes for increased productivity.

Operational alignment. Operational alignment meetings include discussions and debates on managing the trade-offs associated with conflicting priorities, investment decisions, resource allocations, and timeline projections as well as overall performance expectations.

Meeting Time Allocation Inversion

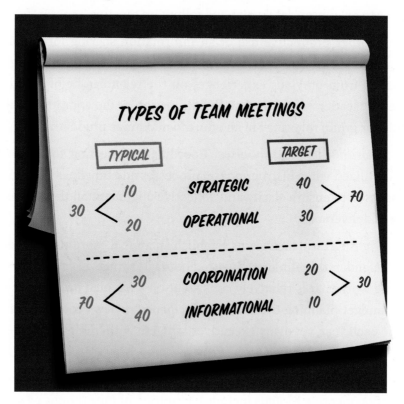

Most teams are *inverted* in terms of appropriate meeting time allocation. If I were to draw a line separating low-level activity from higher-level productivity, it would become clear that teams spend about 70% of their time in low-level activity meetings.

Ideally, the distribution is the opposite, with high-level initiatives receiving 70% of the meeting time. The takeaway? ***Rigor your meeting formats with conscious discipline and practice!***

The altitude of these conversations focuses on whether resources are being appropriately applied to secure the lift, return, and outcomes you budgeted for and planned to achieve at this point in time or whether operational adjustments need to be made.

> *The leadership team needs to spend the majority of its time together discussing what is or is not working, why, what needs to change, and how to move forward.*

Strategic initiatives. Strategic initiative meetings focus on driving the business forward by defining where the business can create competitive advantages in the marketplace and why your organization can win with your specific resources and capabilities.

How you get there requires execution through operational choices. The executive leadership team needs to target working predominantly at the strategic and operational levels, with functional teams working at the operational and coordination levels. Information sharing should always be minimized in meeting forums.

At times, teams may engage in all (4) formats during one meeting with different topics. The challenge is using the discipline of **Leadership Rigor** to maximize team meeting productivity with high-value topics versus consuming time with low-level activities that can be shared in more limited or passive ways, if at all.

> *Performance and productivity for the leadership team means establishing the right priorities, working at the right altitude, appropriately allocating resources, resisting the use of expertise power, and conducting meetings with high-engagement formats while minimizing time spent with low-level information sharing.*

Peer Group Communication Is Aligned

Leadership teams have *the challenge of making choices* on the basis of risk, change, and growth when multiple paths have equally reasonable rationales and justification.

Executive leaders are supported by their functional teams in assessing and analyzing options related to critical decisions that need to be made at the enterprise level. In turn, functional teams not only expect their leaders to represent their points of view but also to persuade their leadership team colleagues to agree with them!

As an organizational leader, however, you must listen openly to the views of your peers, take a position on the issue at hand, and *rigor the options collectively* so a decision can be made that is in the best interest of the enterprise. That ultimate decision then needs to be appropriately framed and communicated back across the organization and specifically to all functional teams involved.

Sometimes the leadership team decision will not line up with your personal or functional team's point of view. It is now when you go back and communicate with your functional team that your alignment with your leadership peer group is most critical. You must represent the enterprise by communicating the decision in the context of the leadership team's altitude and landscape as well as its assessment of the risk, change, and growth considerations.

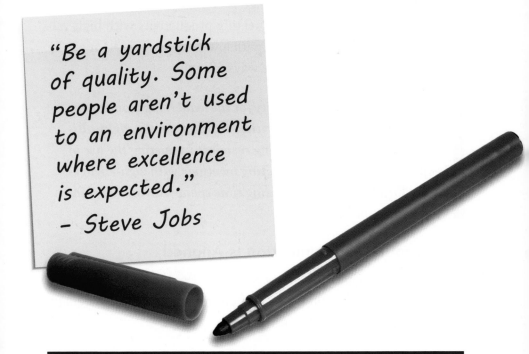

"Be a yardstick of quality. Some people aren't used to an environment where excellence is expected."
— Steve Jobs

Here is an example of how this might sound:

At our leadership team meeting, we discussed the Genesis project you all passionately worked on, and we were impressed with and appreciate your analytical insights; thank you again. We debated the opportunity from multiple angles, and I shared the persuasive arguments you put forth in our pre-meetings. While the case was compelling, we collectively chose to pass at this time.

The reason **why** we made this decision was that the window of opportunity for creating competitive advantage was believed to be too short. Next generation technologies are too close behind this choice. We did not believe the risk we would need to take would provide us with the longer-term growth platform needed to sustain success.

We remain committed to innovation and want to now accelerate our exploration of the Nexus project.

I know this news is disappointing, and I too feel disappointed that the work we put into this project will not get a chance to debut in the marketplace.

We do have several exciting opportunities in the pipeline, so we need to put this disappointment behind us and turn our focus toward our next chance to make a technological breakthrough. As a company, we continue to be passionate and optimistic about this development area, and I am confident that with the talent in this room and across our organization, our future vision will be realized together!

Alignment at the leadership team level is not about "agreeing to the outcome" but being "in agreement with the outcome" as you go forward.

Messages Are Cascaded with "The Why"

Depending upon their impulsivity, executives can spend significant amounts of time making (or not making) decisions, but they often invest little or no time in considering how to appropriately communicate their decisions so they land with the intended impact on those who are affected, including both internal and external stakeholders.

Communication, when delivered well, builds strong and trusting relationships. Done poorly, it damages relationships by eroding trust and confidence and diminishes credibility for the individual leader as well as the executive leadership team.

> *Communication from the leadership team must always clarify "the why."*

Framing the context of why a decision was made and how it was arrived at helps to gain alignment with and confidence in the decision. Transparency builds trust, and your communication approach is a demonstration of your commitment to transparency.

Always plan to tell those who are directly affected first about any changes or decisions you have made. News and rumors travel at lightning speeds, creating emotional turmoil and distractions that can impact performance and productivity.

Appropriately coordinating your communications and carefully cascading your messages maintains organizational focus and reinforces leadership team credibility.

At the organizational level, shaping your role as CEO and establishing a strong leadership team sets the stage for what follows in the next chapter: focusing on the business and shaping your operational platform for both today and tomorrow. ***Let's get to work!***

RIGOR IT!

"Great leaders are almost always great simplifiers who can cut through argument, debate, and doubt to offer a solution everyone can understand."

— General Colin Powell

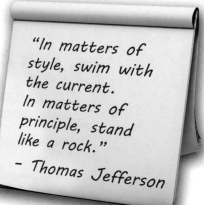

"In matters of style, swim with the current.
In matters of principle, stand like a rock."

— Thomas Jefferson

CHAPTER 2:
Shaping Your Operational Platform

To capitalize on *risk, change, and growth* at the organizational level, you must have an operational platform in place for your business that you can evolve over time to optimize your performance and productivity.

This platform includes how you internally organize (structure and processes) and utilize your resources (people, time, and money) so that your go-to-market strategy is successfully supported.

The Fundamentals That Shape Your Operational Platform:

I.   Life Cycle Dynamics

II. Your Business Model

III. Your Structural Design

I. Life Cycle Dynamics

Understanding life cycle dynamics is critical in business, because where you are in a particular cycle will affect the options available to you as well as the risks involved in making certain choices. Acting early, late, or not at all can affect your chances of success and your risks of failure.

Life cycle Dynamics **We Must Be Mindful of Include:**

- **The Life Cycle of the** Marketplace

- **The Life Cycle of Your** Organization

- **The Life Cycle of Your** Leadership Pipeline

The Life Cycle of the Marketplace

Understanding the risks, challenges, and growth opportunities in the external environment is critical for shaping your operational platform. The marketplace dynamics determine the conditions you must compete in and make choices around. For example, you need to know whether your marketplace is emerging, growing, approaching maturity, stable, or declining. Depending on the life cycle stage, you will encounter different barriers to entry or require varying levels of investment for success.

The Power of Sequencing

Organizational-level work is systems based and integrated. Everything you do is connected to an appropriate first step and a resultant next step in an ongoing "precursor and consequence" series.

Getting the sequencing right is important for organizational leaders because it can create synergy and momentum; the consequences of not getting it right are wasted resources and lost opportunities.

When you are **unconsciously competent** at sequencing your actions, you might find yourself saying, "We were lucky; everything just fell into place and it all worked out."

When you are **unconsciously incompetent,** you trap yourself in a series of bad decisions, causing ongoing starts and stops that you need to go back and correct, sometimes again and again.

Frequently, I see variations on a common theme, such as hiring several different individuals for the same position over an (18)–(36) month period. The root cause of this is a combination of not being clear on the life cycle stage of the organization's culture (the type of role that is needed now) and the failure to establish a sufficiently clear position profile up front to ensure hiring the right talent.

Another example involving the impact of sequencing focuses on the timing of organizational changes and talent development. One extreme occurs when organizational leaders want to accelerate structural changes in their organization in an effort to grow faster but their talent does not yet have the capability to take on the new roles. Here, the illusion of time saved is lost during an extended training/on-boarding or development phase. Alternatively, leaders may believe they need to wait years before their talent is ready and may consequently hold back structural changes, missing the opportunity to catapult their team capabilities ahead by placing high-potential leaders in new roles earlier.

Rigor it with sequencing and conscious competency!

These *marketplace conditions* will also certainly challenge whether your product or service offering support levels are adequate. New offerings launched by competitors could diminish your visibility or share of investment voice. Market *pricing pressure* may require you to "price match at a lower level" compared to your original target expectations, thereby decreasing your margins to remain competitive.

Or perhaps the marketplace is *undergoing consolidation.* To stay competitive, you may need to adjust your customer target to a smaller niche focus or internally streamline your cost of doing business to compete with larger players who have deeper investment pockets.

If you are unable to appropriately compete in the marketplace with the current conditions, you must adjust or you will fail. As an organizational leader, it is your job to understand the marketplace life cycle and the conditions for competing in it.

The Timing of Innovation

Consider life cycle dynamics and entry point timing with your innovations.

Being a first mover into the marketplace with something new is taking a high-risk, high-reward position. It's definitely worthwhile if your organization is a start-up and your product offering is a breakthrough. The attention and short-term business revenue burst can potentially accelerate the life cycle development of your organization by attracting funding and talent to fuel growth.

If you are a mature organization looking to drive incremental innovation, being a fast follower with a "better" proposition and more significant resources to invest in building your market presence may be a better choice.

If you are a relatively risk-averse company, you might be a reactive laggard to the marketplace with a "me too" offering (assuming you have either a strong brand or an enterprise reputation to support it). If you are too late, however, you will risk spending time and money to get to market but might lose the chance to successfully penetrate because others have already secured strong positions, leaving you with only a price/value entry point to the market that can hurt your profitability.

The Life Cycle of Your Organization

Leaders also need to manage the life cycle dynamics of their organizations. This means consciously anticipating the changes required at each stage and proactively putting the foundations in place to minimize the pains, where possible, of the natural evolutionary process.

A newly created organization is in the *start-up phase* of its life cycle. Driven by a compelling idea and limited resources, its challenge is to develop its *proof of concept* and demonstrate that it can consistently deliver its product or service. The focus is on developing its core capabilities in a cost-effective way and solidifying the core customer base that will provide initial traction and momentum for further expansion.

The start-up phase evolves into the *stabilization phase.* Here, challenges are worked through and the organization reaches a dependably steady state where revenues can start to cover the cost of doing business. The goal is to break even and turn the corner toward profitability.

With a stable foundation, the next challenge in the life cycle is *expansive growth* with the goal of building a scalable and sustainable enterprise. This requires additional resources and will need to be sequenced properly to ensure the growth trajectory is in line with profitability to fund that growth (or to secure outside investors).

This growth stage of life cycle management includes increasing both scope and depth of internal capabilities (talent and processes), accelerating the innovation pipeline, and actively nurturing your reputation with stakeholders to ensure you are appropriately meeting or exceeding their expectations.

In the *mature stage* of your life cycle, the challenge is to maximize your profitability and minimize your cost structure while anticipating entry points to further transform and evolve your business. Protecting the stability of your base business through geographical expansion and incremental innovation is your priority. If this is poorly managed, you run the risk of your business going into decline and not being able to remain competitive. The consequence is that you will either go out of business or suffer the pain of a radical transformation or turnaround process.

It is in the mature stage of an organization's life cycle that it is most vulnerable to a disruptive innovator or low-cost provider that suddenly steals market share and leaves you to manage at a higher-cost structure with declining sales. Be proactive in managing this risk, because if you are caught by surprise, you will be forced to make urgent decisions with a blunt instrument as opposed to finer adjustments with more finesse.

Rigor the risks and manage them accordingly!

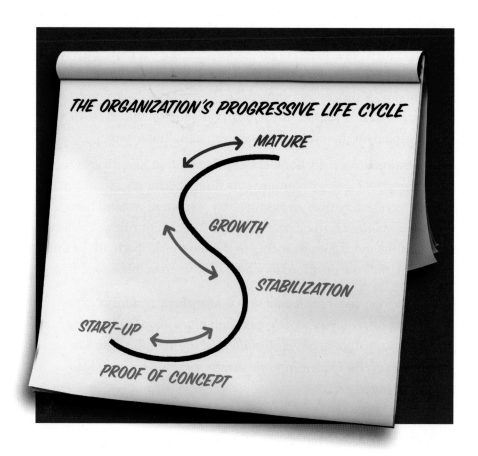

The Life Cycle of Your Leadership Pipeline

Corporations large and small are increasingly devoting time and energy to succession planning and leadership development to ensure they have the talent in place to secure their growth strategy targets as well as the ongoing viability of their organizations.

The reality is, organizations can no longer just develop a job description and hope to fill a position externally based on the required technical skill sets alone. They now need to have an enterprise leadership perspective that nurtures and develops talent within the broader organizational context of culture, strategy, and performance. This means that recruiting talent, or more appropriately *acquiring* talent, is about selecting candidates based on an integrated skill set for both current technical and future leadership capabilities.

This shift in the marketplace is reflected in how organizations are adjusting their risk, change, and growth equations regarding talent. Today, performance-based organizations are relying more on a readiness-based set of criteria and competencies when it comes to talent selection for critical roles compared to yesterday's experience-based approach. For this reason, consciously shaping the life cycle of your leadership talent pipeline has never been more important.

Traditionalists, Baby Boomers, and Generation Xers all grew up in corporate structures with progressive linear pathways for advancing their careers. Executives started at entry levels and worked their way up by *"punching their tickets"* through a series of roles to validate their qualifications for advancing to the next level, patiently waiting their turn until the position for which they were in line opened up.

> *Today, readiness for leadership is less about technical experiences or seniority entitlement and more about possessing the appropriate behavioral skills and the genuine desire to play an active leadership role versus merely holding a leadership position.*

Having emotional intelligence, learning agility in acquiring and applying knowledge quickly, and a passion for developing talent while demonstrating maturity that transcends age and experience are the new mandatory leadership requirements!

> **Leaders must also consciously place the right challenge at the right time with the right aspiring talent so that both the organization and the talent are well served.**

What this looks like today may be surprisingly different from historical approaches. Both the skill sets and temperaments required for specific business challenges must be considered before naming talent to a role. For example, the skills and temperament needed for a turnaround assignment are different from those needed for a growth phase or the integration of an acquisition.

Remember, as CEO, your job is to manage risk and change in service of growth. Choosing the "next in line" talent if this individual does not have the ability to take on the risks and changes you need will limit your organization's growth. By the same token, a high-risk candidate who initiates change too quickly can also negatively affect growth. This is always a balance, so **Rigor it!**

Marketplace Talent Dynamics

Challenges for organizational leaders:

- (4) generations currently in the workplace
- Economic volatility that is pushing out retirement timelines
- High unemployment and underemployment
- Work and life choices that are changing career life cycles
- Diversity and inclusiveness as mainstream requirements
- Pressure for naming women to highly visible leadership roles
- Leadership gaps as the #1 concern among CEOs
- Technology natives advancing social and digital platforms
- Leadership development as a required retention strategy
- Culture as a competitive advantage in the pursuit of talent
- Flextime choices that are changing the workplace

Matching Temperament to Challenges

Appropriately matching a leader's temperament to the business challenge is an important consideration for overall success.

My own temperament, for example, is well suited to the turnarounds, *transformational* changes, and start-up initiatives common in the corporate world. I have been described as a creative, high-energy solution seeker who recognizes patterns quickly, is comfortable with change and ambiguity, and is able to structure chaos with a simple and straightforward communication style that inspires teams to take on high-risk challenges and be disciplined on processes and analytics.

Accordingly, throughout my business career, I have been asked to lead businesses that have become operationally sloppy, that have suffered a devastating product loss that threatened their viability, or that needed a strategic game plan to support an investment.

Individuals with more moderate temperaments usually do well managing steady *growth* or expansion over the mid to long-term if the internal and external conditions are favorable. They often have low to moderate risk profiles, a desire for significant clarity before taking action, and a patient profile for orchestrating change. Typically, these leaders try to minimize disruption to the status quo without losing opportunities. They also often choose to forego an opportunity rather than accept the potentially necessary disruption in order to protect against the downside risk.

Temperaments that can orchestrate a large, complex, and integrated initiative to facilitate an organization's movement from one life cycle stage to another are well suited to the middle range of the life cycle challenge, managing *transitions.* Examples may be leading a merger, a restructuring, or a technological platform change.

Here, the challenge is change management within an otherwise stable business environment that requires managing the expectations of internal stakeholders for on-time deliverables.

As a leadership coach, I often see organizations face the challenge of a life cycle change with leaders whose temperaments do not fit. The risk is that an organization will only manage the challenges its leader can handle. If a change in the business model, structural design, or strategy is required but the leader isn't capable of navigating through these initiatives, the organization will not take the necessary steps and performance will suffer. In public companies, the outcome is replacing the leader with a player(s) who can execute the required changes.

In the private sector, outcomes can be more variable. In a family business, you might see a slow, almost imperceptible decline in competitiveness that continues until a generational change in leadership occurs and new ideas and approaches are infused. Alternatively, the business may be able to withstand the ups and downs of inconsistent performance because owners subsidize the variability. Ideally, leadership will seek external advice through the challenges that lie ahead.

In leadership roles today, age and experience matter less than temperament, emotional maturity, or the personal power to handle the conditions in which the work must be performed.

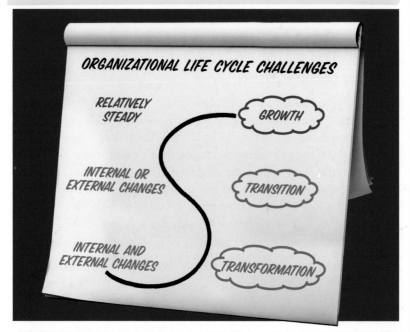

Life Cycle Signs and Signals

Demonstrating **Leadership Rigor** with respect to identifying potential life cycle changes competitively underway means looking for the signs or signals of a shift and assessing the potential implications (positive opportunities to seize and negative threats to protect against). Here are examples to look for:

- New technology introductions

- Globalization and international expansion

- Patent loss and genericization

- Commodity pricing wars

- Board-led changes in CEO (or membership)

- CEO retirement and new leadership appointed/named

- Acquisitions or mergers

- Going public (IPO)/Taking a company private

- Establishing a board of directors

- Restructuring or implementing a new business model

- Significant layoffs or hirings

- Changing headquarter locations

- Closing or opening plant sites

- Changes in ownership

In managing the risk, change, and growth equations for your organization, be careful about pushing, holding back, or denying the natural evolution of life cycle dynamics. Each stage needs to be met with the proper readiness. If you fail to meet these needs, either with the right leadership, appropriate organizational capabilities, or relevant offerings for the marketplace, you risk loss. This may be the loss of talent that does not want to wait for his or her next role, loss of an opportunity you did not see, or the loss of sales because you did not evolve to your customers' needs.

If you doubt this, think about Kodak, Blockbuster, BlackBerry, JC Penney, and the many family/private businesses that had no successors and/or underestimated the marketplace changes.

II. Your Business Model

The second variable that shapes your operational platform is your business model, or how you create value and make money by the way you go to market with your offerings.

One of the most breakthrough business models in operation today is Amazon. Initially underestimated as merely an online book distributor, Amazon has created a technology-driven distribution and logistics business model that ultimately has little to do with books and everything to do with on-demand access to and fast delivery of all products with a point and click.

> *Business models work at the intersection of creating value (a differentiation that people care about) and making money in the marketplace (prices people are willing to pay and most importantly that an organization can ultimately make a profit on).*

Notice the use of the word "ultimately." In many cases, business models are up front or back ended in terms of their profitability. For example, your smartphone offers numerous free entry-level applications in the hopes that you will fall in love with them and upgrade to a pay version with expanded bells and whistles.

Businesses can sell their products and then sell their services as an incremental option like Apple does (i.e., Apple Care), they can sell products and provide free services as a value-added proposition, or they can sell baseline services and add incremental services for a fee.

How you decide to organize your offerings and price your approach is unique to your business. The key message in **Leadership Rigor** is to consciously choose to develop a business model that you can scale and sustain profitably. You don't want to risk going out of business while you wait for your ship to come in!

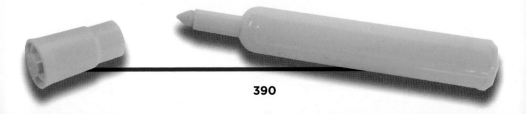

Pricing and Positioning the Business Model

Depending on your business model, the value proposition of your offerings may be *premium* priced, *value* priced, or *commodity* priced.

In business models that sell products, such as the consumer packaged goods industry where I spent most of my healthcare career, value is created through a strong brand that has equity beyond that of the physical product only. For example, you can buy generic aspirin or Bayer® aspirin. You will pay more for the aspirin made by Bayer, so how do you justify that cost to a consumer?

In some cases, the cost is justified by the trust consumers have always had in the brand and its well regarded reputation of a hundred-plus years. Others recognize the value in the innovation and research that went into creating the brand and that it continues to bring to the marketplace. Or perhaps your physician recommended the brand by name and you believe in taking exactly what she says out of fear that another product may not have the same quality standards.

Justifying a higher cost for any product is a challenge in today's marketplace, and with side-by-side comparison pricing of private label brands in this industry, it is especially difficult. Having the right perspective and lens when you create your pricing model is critical.

My own business model offers a range of coaching and facilitation services in the form of an engagement that can include one-to-one coaching sessions, (360) interviews, workshop facilitation, custom-designed leadership programs, culture survey development, competency model development, talent management initiatives, and regular email/phone exchanges as needed by the client. Because I provide these services in an engagement package, clients will occasionally try to break down pricing into an hourly rate and attempt to negotiate but I do not negotiate on price nor do I price my services by the hour.

> *In terms of framing the value of my engagement services, I often ask leaders to benchmark the investment relative to the compensation and/or organizational influence of the executive(s) involved.*

Does this individual or team have a broad impact across your organization? Can the performance and productivity greatly affect the organization's success? If this executive or team were maximally successful, what would the financial impact be? If this executive or team were only marginally successful, what would the consequences be? If an executive(s) were terminated due to poor performance, requiring a severance package and the hiring of a retained recruiter to find a replacement as well as a sign-on bonus, what would the total cost be?

Considering the investment in a coaching engagement through these lenses often completely changes the context and perspective of the discussion with the client.

Vistage Board Selection and the Business Model Criteria

As chair of a Vistage peer-to-peer private advisory board in New Jersey, I have the opportunity of selecting a small number of highly qualified CEOs and business leaders to engage with each other in an intimate setting. These CEOs are interested in growing both their own businesses and their personal leadership capabilities as well as contributing their insights and experiences to the growth of their peers. To make the board as provocative and challenging as possible, I consciously select members with diverse business models.

Around the table sit CEOs from businesses that focus on products, services, sourcing, investment, franchise, contingency, turn-key manufacturing, and full-service vertical integration as well as brokers, holding companies, and advisory/consulting models.

While this diversity expands the global view and appreciation of businesses across industries and sectors, the challenges and opportunities around the table tend to be similar as they all filter through the **Organizational Excellence** areas of focus that are presented in the next section of *Leadership Rigor.*

My business model is also defined by intimacy level, or what I call "boutique intimacy," since I mainly work with high-potential talent and/or senior-level organizational leaders and their executive teams. This target audience is relatively small and highly specialized.

> *The leaders of the organizations I choose to work with must be willing to hold a vision of excellence for themselves and their teams that can withstand the potential pushback, challenges, and questioning that cause most leaders to retreat from rather than power through to reach their potential.*

My goal is to make a meaningful impact on the ground (OTG) by facilitating breakthrough levels of performance and productivity. For this to happen, I must be selective as a leadership performance coach with respect to the clients I invest my time in working with as well as when choosing which initiatives to pursue and over what time period.

Another part of the business model design is to integrate and monetize your pillars so they all feed into each other and offer a maximum return on your resources and rigor (I call this "ROR2").

For example, in my business model, my coaching practice helps to drive my writing and workshop content design. Vistage, my private CEO peer advisory board, serves as a forum in which I can test material I am developing for my leadership journey clients or vice versa.

Finding a way for your business activities to be highly integrated helps to further drive your performance and productivity, so **Rigor it!**

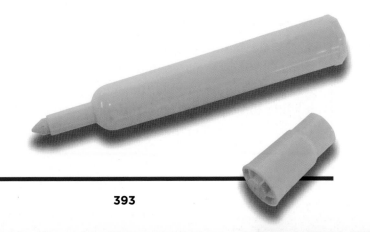

III. Your Structural Design

The final variable that shapes your operational platform is the structural design of your organization. This design needs to reflect both an assessment of the life cycle stages you are dealing with and the business model you are using in your go-to-market approach.

> *Your structure enables function, and the function you are going for is a viable business model that reflects an understanding of the life cycle dynamics at play while delivering performance and productivity at the enterprise level.*

Your organizational structure sends impactful messages that are consciously intended as well as subject to variable interpretation. You must be mindful of what you are creating and how you are communicating around your structural decisions so that the company narrative is clear.

Open Office Structures, Spaces, and Power

In business, "structures" are both tangible and intangible. Organizational charts are intangible, but your office space and design tangibly express power through structure.

The move toward open and collaborative office spaces today sends a clear message of personal power over position power. It also encourages creativity and collaboration while requiring a high level of emotional intelligence to ensure performance and productivity. A heightened sense of self-awareness, self-management, and social awareness must be in place given the open conditions and potential impact on others with respect to noise, distraction, and disruption.

Companies that are turning to open space environments as a way to drive cultural dynamics are using structure to enable function. Culturally, this expresses "how we do things around here" in a whole new way!

Creating a new structure within your organization, whether it's a new division, a new team, or a new position, generates an expansive *positive energy.* You are exploring new possibilities and preferably dedicating incremental resources to an initiative rather than trying to get more productivity out of existing resources that may already be too stretched.

Restructurings, on the other hand, whether you refer to them as "downsizing" or "right-sizing," radiate a "concerning" and often *negative energy.* The driving force can be strategically motivated by external competitive circumstances, internal life cycle or business model evolutions, or an operational cost savings requirement.

Because organizational structures are integrated systems of work-flow, when they change, they profoundly affect people's emotional energy. The inevitable *"How will this affect me?"* questions include:

- Will I have a job?

- Will I be demoted?

- Will I have to work for someone I do not like or respect?

- Will my power be taken away?

- Will I still have access to certain people?

- Will I philosophically agree with the new approach?

Structures are both tangible and intangible representations of position power. Your organizational chart could just as easily be titled "Your Implied Position Power" chart. For this reason, any changes made to structure need to be consciously considered in terms of the downstream consequences experienced by those affected either directly or indirectly.

When referring to your operational platform and the (3) pieces that comprise it—life cycle, business model, and structure—it is the business model that you primarily support, with adjustments made to reflect the life cycle dynamics and structural application of your resources to drive performance and productivity in the market.

Structural Models in Organizations

When it comes to structural choices an organization can make, there are no right or wrong answers, *just better or worse timing.* All the design approaches can work, and each serves a purpose. The question is, are you clear about your specific purpose and are you consciously using structure to productively achieve targeted goals? Likewise, are you consciously competent in terms of knowing what the triggers are that call for a structural change to be made again?

Well designed organizational structures lay the foundation for facilitating performance and productivity across the enterprise. Structural designs that do not work well increase complexity and administrative burden, create duplication, and decrease morale and productivity.

> *The choice you make on structure will depend on the conditions you are operating within (life cycle dynamics/business model) and the culture you are creating as well as the technical and leadership skills you are trying to build.*

The most significant impact of your structural choice will be around decision-making rights and who will be given what authority or accountability.

Let's take a look at the most common structural options you as an organizational leader can consider utilizing:

- *Centralized and decentralized* (as well as a hybrid of both)
- *Geographical* (global, regional, and local)
- *Integrated teams* (and matrix formats)

Note: Depending on your industry or sector, formal/informal networks, centers of excellence, or communities of practice may be additional "structrural" considerations to rigor.

▶ Centralized and Decentralized Structures

The centralized and decentralized structures reflect significant differences in control and decision-making approaches.

The centralized model is a "headquarter" or "home office-based" hierarchical structure with *progressive vertical authority in function.* Here, functional heads have ultimate authority for decisions.

The decentralized model is one in which intact divisions or cross-functional *teams are co-located and have independent localized decision-making authority.* Individuals in this model might have direct reporting lines to an onsite leader as well as a matrix or dotted-line reporting structure to a functional headquarter leader for skill and career development, especially in larger corporations.

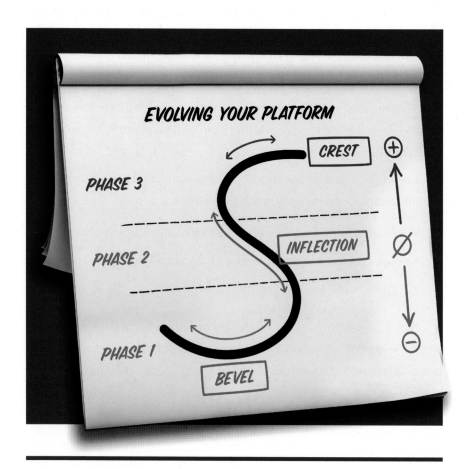

These are basic definitions for the purposes of framing the context that you as an organizational leader need to be thinking about as you rigor the structural considerations for your enterprise.

Before making structural changes, it is important to consider the timing and organizational readiness for these decisions. For example, you may be personally attracted to speed or control as a leader, but you will be well served to think in terms of where your organization is in its life cycle and where you are with your current talent capabilities before making structural decisions. Objectively ask yourself, is your organization ready to decentralize, or will this introduce chaos?

Operationalizing Your Platform

Once a structure is chosen to support the business model, the executive team must ensure that the platform is operationalized to enable performance and productivity that creates lift.

The questions to address are:

- Is there role clarity (for individuals and teams)?
- Are expectations for performance and accountability clear?
- Are leaders engaged in their role of coaching for performance?
- Are decision rights defined (transparent process and tools)?
- Are processes in place to enable workflow?
- Are key performance indicators (KPIs) defined and tracked?
- Is the altitude right for prioritizing and allocating resources?
- Are meetings productively focused on high-value coordination and operational trade-offs?
- Are compensation plans aligned with platform goals?
- Is there enough communication taking place?

With these elements defined and in place, organizations can move through the bevel, the inflection, and toward the crest in driving the business forward.

Centralized Advantages and Disadvantages

A centralized structure:

- Offers greater oversight to decision making

- Facilitates learning (talent reports to functional head)

- Makes it easier to develop functional excellence

- Offers consistency in approach (valuable during large-scale change-management initiatives)

- Makes geographical expansion easier to manage

- Makes cultural changes easier to make and monitor

- Can be less expensive

However, it may:

- Limit collaboration, given centralized silos

- Be slower (based on enterprise size and agility)

- Offer fewer talent development opportunities in functional leadership roles (vertical hierarchy)

Do you need to stay centralized, or will this slow down longer-term growth and market development potential? What are the cost implications of choosing one type of structure over another?

Your structure needs to clarify how work gets done and who holds accountability for deliverables and decision making. If your current structure does not have sufficient clarity around these areas, address this immediately. Lack of role clarity in a confusing structure is a *prescription for a prolonged loss of productivity* due to the wrong efforts, no efforts, or duplicated efforts and frustration for your talent.

Decentralized **Advantages and Disadvantages**

A decentralized structure:

- Ensures decision making is closer to customer needs

- Accelerates leadership development (more roles)

- Promotes cross-functional team-building skills

- Increases customization of offerings to market needs

- Increases speed to market/geographical expansion

However, it may:

- Offer less oversight to decision making/risk taking

- Have higher costs due to duplication of roles

- Make cultural consistency more challenging

- Make performance and productivity gaps surface slowly

Be mindful not to fall in love with a structure that does not make sense for your current business model, life cycle, or talent capabilities. What could be good from a general marketplace perspective or in theory on paper may not work from a practical standpoint in your unique organizational circumstances. Yes, you can make it work, but at what cost of resource investment, including your own time as a CEO or executive team member? Will your structural choice provide you with the right *ROR2 (return on resources and rigor)?*

Don't assume the answer is "yes." **Rigor it**, and be certain!

■ The hybrid structure

Some organizations will use a hybrid model in which their front-end commercialization (marketing/sales) is decentralized, providing the benefit of speed and creativity at the market interface, but back-end functions (finance, HR, and IT) are centralized for cost containment, effective process management, and control. This hybrid approach can also be an interim step when moving from one approach to another or a sustainable way to structure your organization.

The potential operational challenge in this hybrid approach is the business tension and philosophical differences between a "marketplace/customer-driven mentality" versus an "internal/cost-management mentality" that can affect investment priorities and decisions. Of course, the *Leadership Rigor* approach would suggest an **Operational Excellence** integrated philosophy so that divisiveness is not an issue and an enterprise-based mentality prevails, but this will take conscious discipline and practice to achieve!

What Drives Your Choice of Geographical Structure?

Leaders need to define what drives their structural design formats. For example, your global structure might be an outgrowth of your decision to drive strategy consistently in all your markets. Your regional structure might be an outgrowth of your intention to drive targeted investments and profitability as a geographic portfolio. Your local structure might be a signal of speed and empowerment as you try to build a first-time presence in the market. Being clear on your intentions will ensure that there is alignment with the various teams who will be interfacing to get work done and that there are no passive or active resistances due to power struggles.

The Matrix—Magic or Mayhem?

Global organizations often use a matrix structure approach in which dual reporting lines (global/regional or global/local) create both direct and indirect supervisors with varying degrees of authority who can add to the challenge of communication and relationship building. If you are developing a matrix structure, be conscious about role clarity and accountability in decision making and select leaders who are capable of exercising high levels of personal power and emotional intelligence to align resources and drive cohesive performance rather than those who incite divisiveness through power struggles.

▶ Global, Regional, and Local Structures

In today's economy, leaders need to consider if and how they will structure expansions regionally and globally. Will they have boots OTG? Partnerships? Will they outsource their presence?

In large corporations, a global footprint is designed through a common culture and seamlessly integrated processes. Such organizations are likely to refer to themselves as *"One (insert company name)"* because they painstakingly develop a consistent feel to their global and regional structures while attempting to take advantage of local diversities and varying business conditions in legal and ethical ways.

Global structures are similar to centralized models, and regional/local structures tend to mirror a decentralized approach on a geographical basis. The challenge, as with all structures, is ensuring role clarity and decision rights between the local, regional, and global organizations. Each group will naturally strive for and seek maximum power and autonomy. The role of leadership is to define role clarity, decision rights, and the desired outcomes for the structure in terms of performance and productivity so that resources are appropriately focused and utilized across the organization.

▶ Integrated Team Structures

Team structures are broadly prevalent in progressive, performance-based organizations. Whether the teams are functional, cross-functional, matrix, or geographical in design, collaborative work is required in today's business environment.

The value of a team structure is diversity, broad expertise, integrated ownership and accountability for performance.

A team-based structure requires leadership talent, established processes for collaborative work across the organization, and a culture with defined expectations for performance that includes both results and behaviors.

Organizational leaders need to be careful not to casually define "teams" or, worse, use team labels inappropriately when the dynamics are not in place to support performance (i.e., no team leader, no formal members, no defined scope of work).

The fact is, teams are not named; they are built! It takes time and effort to build a high-performance team, and organizations need to account for this when they are creating structural designs to support their platforms and business models.

"The greatest danger a team faces isn't that it won't become successful, but that it will, and then cease to improve."

– Mark Sanborn

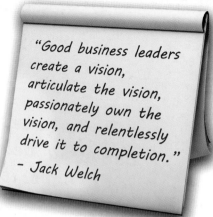

"Good business leaders create a vision, articulate the vision, passionately own the vision, and relentlessly drive it to completion."
– Jack Welch

CHAPTER 3:
Shaping Your Future Landscape

As CEO, leading your organization includes shaping its landscape, and this requires you to have a continuous, dynamic, and iterative approach of asking yourself, "What's next, and where do we go from here?"

Invest Your Time and Energy in (3) Fundamental Areas:

    I.   Imagine It!

    II.   Rigor It!

    III. Design and Create It!

I. Imagine It!

As a leader, *you must have both* the capacity to dream big and a process for indulging your creative imagination. This includes how you personally engage as well as how you engage with others in this future-shaping process.

Invest and Indulge in Reflection Time

Getting into action and making things happen on the ground (OTG) has had a big emphasis throughout **Leadership Rigor.**

When it comes to creating your future landscape, however, you need to stop the action and get into reflection!

Reflection is a powerful yet underutilized leadership capability. Because it lacks immediate outcomes, reflection is seldom prioritized as a productive use of an executive's time; yet without it, CEOs typically stay in the same action patterns and repeat mistakes because they lack perspective on what is working and what needs to change.

Reflection stops the noise, creates space, and results in new insights that spark previously unseen opportunities.

This *"alone time"* activity is most powerful when it involves daydreaming or letting your mind wander. It might include writing, drawing, or doodling words that have resonance for you.

Holding your energy in the quiet space of reflection so that ideas can surface takes discipline and practice. Not every reflective experience provides a breakthrough idea, but the blue-sky thinking and conceptual ideation process can create entry points for *the emergence of an idea* that may simply have needed incubation time.

Natural Wonders

While attending an insight and intuition class in Costa Rica, I learned a powerful technique for reflecting and then stimulating creativity. The facilitator had each participant privately ask himself or herself a question and then take some time to be with nature to discover the answer. As we walked around and experienced our surroundings, we were encouraged to notice what caught our attention and what we were sensing.

This was extremely powerful for me, as I had just left my corporate job and was engaging in a year of adventures to figure out what was next in my professional life. One consideration I was entertaining at the time was taking on a CEO position with a small pharmaceutical company.

As I walked around and asked myself what was next, I spotted a huge branch overhanging a small still pond. At the end of the branch was one large leaf gently twirling in the breeze. I was surprised at how clear the message was for me to *"turn over a new leaf"* and try something completely different as opposed to returning to the same type of industry role. The stimulation of nature can be surprisingly impactful, so **rigor it** with nature!

Engage in a Well-Rounded Life

Insights and creativity can come from anywhere. An executive who travels the world and has varied interests as well as a wide circle of friends can bring more diverse knowledge and life experiences to his or her business-building efforts than those who grind out (12)–(14) hour days in their office cave and work every weekend.

Pay Attention

Many leaders, lost in their own thoughts, simply forget to pay attention. They disregard environmental signs and symbols passing in front of them, at times missing blatant opportunities for connecting the dots or creating new insights.

What exactly is an insight? An insight is a "connected link" whereby pieces of information come together to form a new perspective. Think of *"in*formation" as being *organized data* and *"in*sights" as *organized information* that creates a new view.

Insights are incredibly valuable, and while some people are naturally gifted at putting things together (pattern recognition), **the practice of identifying business insights** can be strengthened by a dedicated focus to pay attention, look for, and find potential connections.

Listening is an important part of paying attention. Taking the time to listen to the advice, challenges, and questions of your employees, advisors, and friends can provide a road map to new opportunities.

Write It Down

You will not remember your random thoughts and ideas, so write them down, then periodically review your notes. Check whether you are writing things over and over. If you are, this is a sign of something important making its way into physical form that needs to be cultivated. After all, ideas need incubation time to fully develop.

Creativity, Seriously!

According to a recent IBM research study, creativity is now the #1 required leadership skill for CEOs when it comes to future success.

The dynamics of the business world continue to change, and the skill sets required now are those of a different and unique executive. Beyond a comfort with ambiguity, an ability to order chaos, and a propensity to strategically link disparate thoughts into coherent patterns with insights, today's leaders must imagine, create, and rigor new approaches and solutions rather than simply relying on old ones. The pace of change, disruptive technologies, and the new economic realities have completely changed the game and therefore the skill sets of the successful players of the future.

You may be surprised by how many times you write down a concept and then...**Bam!**...a breakthrough insight or fresh perspective shines through and you see a connection you did not recognize before.

Take a Shower and Sleep on It

Great ideas often come in the shower because we allow ourselves to daydream or relax as we enjoy a few peaceful moments with our eyes closed. Likewise, breakthroughs can occur while we sleep if we set up the conditions for success.

Here is a challenge: ask yourself a question as you go to bed. Don't torture yourself by thinking about it as you lie there. Simply ask the question and then let yourself fall asleep. Giving your subconscious mind the challenge will be enough. Either that night or shortly thereafter, your mind will process an answer. Keep a notebook and pen by your side. Be prepared to rigor it in the morning, but write it down if it wakes you up!

Be Provocative with Your Leadership Team

To stimulate your leadership team's focus toward future growth, ask provocative "what if" questions that are expansive and that encourage divergent thinking skills, such as:

- What if we doubled/tripled the business in (5)–(10) years?

- What if we had unlimited financial resources?

- What if we had unlimited people resources?

- What if we had unlimited time for product development?

- What if we acquired our #1 competitor?

- What if we only focused on building _____?

Notice that these powerful questions are focused at a "leading altitude level" regarding resource allocation (i.e., people, time, and money) and prioritization. These are the variables at play for placing your bets on the areas you want to invest in for growth.

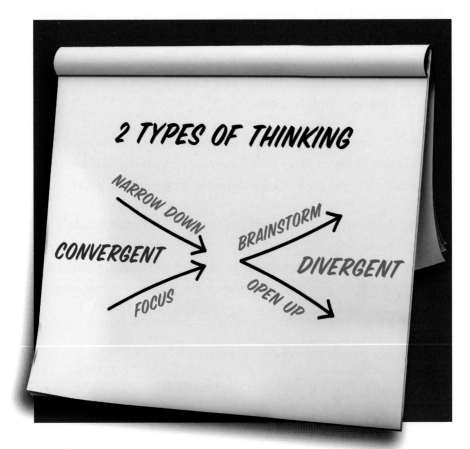

2 TYPES OF THINKING

NARROW DOWN
CONVERGENT
FOCUS

BRAINSTORM
DIVERGENT
OPEN UP

Our job as leaders is to ensure that the future landscape for our organization is secured. In the "imagine it" stage, we must be patient, playful, and comfortable with the ambiguity that is a precursor to the clarity we seek. You must have an open and beginner's mindset as you engage in the iterative and continual process of shaping your future.

Remember Your (2) Types of Thinking!

When we are reflective, we create space in our minds and open ourselves up to new ideas and possibilities. This is an example of divergent thinking. Paying attention and focusing intently is an example of convergent thinking. Leaders need to be consciously engaged in both approaches as they envision the future.

II. Rigor It!

Imagining your future landscape can be an exciting process that generates big, creative, and interesting ideas. Not all ideas, however, are good business opportunities.

> *Leaders need to rigor through the challenging process of differentiating between ideas that have real potential and those that are not right for their organization now or, perhaps, ever!*

The future needs to be well thought out and appropriately assessed. The balance, of course, is in knowing how much you need to *rigor it* before getting into action and not impulsively acting too quickly or being unable to act at all because you are overanalyzing.

Here are (3) resource areas to help you assess the future:

- Rigor it with...*structured* planning tools

- Rigor it with...*staged* in-market testing

- Rigor it with...*trusted* advisors who provide objectivity

Structured Planning Tools

You already know about the power of the **Analytical Rigor** Model in decision making, so let's look at some additional tools you can integrate into your organizational planning process.

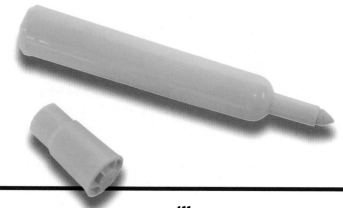

Dashboard of Leading and Lagging Indicators

To effectively rigor your ideas, it is important to confirm whether the environmental conditions are favorable or unfavorable to your next possible moves.

> *Specifically identifying the leading and lagging indicators (leading indicators can validate your initial interest and confirm that entry points exist for traction, whereas lagging indicators are a measure of the longer-term momentum that you can establish) and then tracking on an ongoing basis how best to consciously navigate through the risk, change, and growth dynamics in a disciplined way is an important step in the planning process.*

Leading indicators to watch can be economic, political, legal, or regulatory changes that open up or shut down new pathways for growth or innovation in your business. You will want to understand the drivers in each area and what you can do to influence them.

In the pharmaceutical industry, for example, being aware of a pending change in regulations can provide greater clarity about a drug's development and approval path, allowing a go/no-go decision to be made more quickly versus investing at risk and not knowing whether the development plan will be sufficient to gain approval.

Changes in political leadership or economic stability can also affect your business choices. A geopolitically unsettled area, for example, might preclude you from international expansion given the environmental volatility, difficulty in placing talent, and risk of business disruption.

At the operational level, a leading indicator could be the trial rate of a new product. Usage behavior, a mid-term indicator, needs to be tracked over time. Loyalty, depending on purchase cycle time, may be a lagging indicator you will learn about later in your market launch initiative.

Lagging indicators might also be your referral rates, employee retention rates, or cross-utilization of related services by customers as they require experience and perceived loyalty to be in place first.

Organizational Planning Approaches

Business planning encompasses a wide spectrum of approaches. On one extreme are large corporations, which often have well designed processes for assessment and documentation yet are not always proficient in putting their plans into operational action OTG. On the other extreme are small to mid-sized organizations, which often have no planning process, no formal budget (revenue/spending targets), and no written strategy yet often move into action quite impulsively. *Both can benefit from a dose of Leadership Rigor!*

> *The most valuable part of the planning process includes openly discussing, actively debating, and collectively answering the critical business questions of what, where, why, when, how, and by whom.*

Once you have invested time in the dialogue and debate with your team, you can make the final decisions, commit to them in writing, communicate them through action plans with timetables, and hold accountability for deliverables.

Planning is a living and breathing process. You don't want to simply abandon plan A this month for plan B next month. Commit to plan A with trigger points that will signal an adjustment is necessary along with a potential link to plan B as a contingency plan based on learning and insights as progress unfolds.

The (4) stages of planning leaders must rigor if they want to shape their organizations' future landscape are scenario planning, operational planning, strategic planning, and contingency planning.

STEEP Analysis

A STEEP (Social, Technological, Economic, Environmental, Political) Analysis can help you determine inputs for scenarios. Take a look at the social, technological, environmental, economic, and political changes that can affect the context of your business decisions.

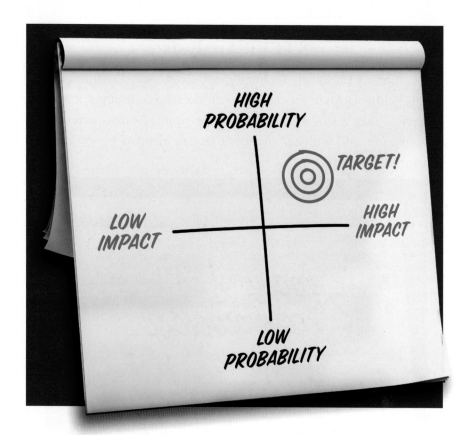

▶ Scenario Planning

Scenario planning involves focusing on what the world you are competing in might look like under different *macro conditions.* These are not blue-sky considerations; rather, they are intended to identify the full range of reasonable possibilities and the occasional *"black swan"* that could be a game changer for your business.

Once you determine the various scenarios, assign each of them a probability and impact score. Some are high impact and low probability; others are high probability and low impact. Your goal is to decide which scenario is most likely to materialize and then to anchor onto that choice for your strategic planning phase. Don't just dismiss the other scenarios, however, because they can inform your contingency planning later.

▶ Operational Planning

Having an operational plan means that you have an **up-front budget** that itemizes projections for revenue and investment expectations by month, quarter, and the full year. As CEO, you have **defined objectives, goals, and targets** that you specifically invest your resources against. You are tracking performance milestones to ensure you are on target for meeting your expectations by month/quarter and are **prepared to adjust both your resources and priorities** as appropriate.

In large corporations, once an operational plan is set with top-line revenue and bottom-line profit targets, the executive leadership team is challenged to deliver or adjust *with performance consequences.* Delivery of either the top or bottom line may be prioritized if the plan cannot be reached based on changing market conditions.

For example, if you are launching a new product and are investing to achieve distribution or market share, you might see an opportunity and choose to drive the top line with incremental investments that cause you to fall short on the bottom-line profitability. Alternatively, you might choose to pull back investment levels if your launch is not going well due to an increased competitive response, missing your top-line projection but protecting your bottom-line profit delivery.

These are business choices that need to be made consciously and with alignment against organizational priorities and governance bodies if you are working in a large organizational structure, as they will likely have a corporate as well as a team/personal impact on performance targets and executive compensation.

Private small to mid-sized companies that don't answer to a board or external investors are likely to have less rigor around their performance targets at the operational level and might "let the chips fall where they may" in terms of sales and profit short of violating a banking covenant. Since many of these private companies also do not have variable incentive compensation programs in place, there is little alignment between the *performance (both results and behaviors)* of employees and their potential rewards. This is another reason to link compensation to operational planning objectives; it ensures that corporate objectives are met. This requires integrated planning, so **rigor it** with linkages!

▶ Strategic Planning

Strategic planning is about creating competitive advantage in the marketplace; it is not about what you are going to do internally to run and grow your business. That is your operational plan. Herein lies the initial confusion for most business leaders and their organizations.

> *Strategy is focused on creating differentiated value for your clients. It is about winning in the marketplace and validating that win with metrics such as market share, independent survey rankings, or other objective formats.*

Strategic planning is not something most organizations do well, assuming they do it at all. Perhaps the organization does not have a process it is guided by, the leadership team is unwilling to make

Variable Compensation Plans

Variable compensation plans, based on "pay for performance" principles, provide strong alignment between an organization's operational goals and its annual employee goals. If the organization succeeds, high-performing individuals also succeed, and those who are not at the highest end of the performance curve are compensated fairly based on the level of their performance.

This is in stark contrast to the old school "peanut butter" bonus approach where there is an even spread across the board regardless of performance or, worse, a purely discretionary allocation based on subjective measures that are not transparent.

If you want to create growth and secure alignment between the enterprise and your employees, make sure your operational plan and incentive compensation plan are linked. This will contribute more to shaping your future than anything else you do.

choices or trade-offs and wants to maintain a purely entrepreneurial approach remaining open to any and all opportunities without discipline, and/or the organization does not understand its business well enough to create a strategy (i.e., it may not have a strong enough operational plan in place).

What I often find is that CEOs and business executives need to work on their operational planning process first and that they confuse their lack of an operational plan with a lack of strategy. Both are important, but there is a sequence for developing them.

▶ Contingency Planning

Developing contingencies is a critical part of the overall planning process. Opportunities will arise and risks will materialize, so be ready to exercise organizational and leadership agility to appropriately respond to them. Leaders are well served to plan in advance for how they will handle both of these potential realities, yet most fail to do so and are caught off guard and unprepared to take action.

In planning for *downside risks,* rigor the following questions:

1. If **revenues start falling** short of target, what is your predetermined "go to" plan for making up the gap?

2. If **profit** targets are not on track to be met, what are your priority spending cuts to protect the bottom line?

3. If one of your low-probability **competitive threat** scenarios materializes in the marketplace, what is your predetermined response plan?

In planning for *upside opportunities,* rigor these questions:

4. If **revenues are stronger** than expected, how will you utilize the incremental profit? Will you invest, reward, or return to the bottom line?

5. If the product/service revenue **mix is different** from original expectations, yielding higher margins, what is your promotional and/or inventory response plan?

6. If a **new opportunity** presents itself, how will you assess the go-forward investment? Will you table a current initiative or invest at risk and take a lower profit return this year? What are the conditions that will drive your choice?

Many leadership teams do not plan for or anticipate risks. When they materialize, teams are thrown into a tailspin of random cuts or need to ask their larger corporate entities for "relief in the form of revised goals due to external circumstances." Surprisingly, this is also true for upside chances that provide incremental opportunity.

High-performance leaders and teams plan and anticipate so they have options to go to; they are able to deliver against their original commitments on a consistent basis or exceed those expectations because they are prepared to capitalize on their opportunities and proactively mitigate their risks. Rigor your plan with upside and downside contingencies!

"War Gaming" Your Possibilities

To assess the impact of your scenario plans on your current business, you might engage in a "war gaming" process. This approach includes creating teams for each scenario and asking them to develop a theoretical business plan and market strategy that can be visualized, challenged, and debated. The resulting insights and approaches help prepare you for the possibilities that can materialize in the marketplace. This can be particularly valuable if the scenarios involve "game changing" dynamics to the marketplace that have upstream and downstream consequences, such as preemptive launches or unexpected superiority claims that significantly differentiate the competitive products, leapfrogging disruptive technologies, or corporate mergers of competitors now wielding increased scope or resources.

Staged-in Market Testing Approach

As an organizational leader, you want to *learn about the strengths and weaknesses of your business opportunities at the lowest levels of investment and risk.* To do this, you must learn how to pressure test your initiatives before overcommitting your resources. How do you stage the learning process and rigor it appropriately?

Consider these approaches before a full go-to-market launch:

- ☑ **Customer/client feedback**
- ☑ **Proof of concept**
- ☑ **Prototype**
- ☑ **Pilot test**
- ☑ **Scale-up test**
- ☑ **Test market**
- ☑ **Regional rollout**

Customer Feedback

Connecting to the needs and insights of your current and/or prospective customers will always be an important part of your planning approach. Access to customer feedback can be formally gained through *quantitative or qualitative research* techniques (product concept tests, marketing mix models, market structure studies, focus groups) or informally obtained through outreach conversations and networking event connections.

Proof of Concept (with Financials)

A standard part of the corporate approval process for validating an opportunity under consideration is a business case with financial modeling evaluating *potential returns with varying levels of risk and investment.*

Another application of the proof of concept approach in the scientific arena involves preliminary laboratory work in which early-stage profiling demonstrates activity of an ingredient or drug against a target. In the technology or manufacturing sectors, you may have a preliminary program or process design that validates your idea or hypothesis.

Prototype

This approach involves early stage development of an offering that includes a *"physical model,"* an architectural design, or even a rough draft of a services platform to do some preliminary market research and gain insights into potential refinements before investing larger dollars in a pilot or scale-up test.

Pilot Test

In this approach, you test the validity of your offering and identify where it exceeds or falls short of expectations in a *small, well-controlled environment.*

Scale-up Test

After a pilot test, a scale-up test allows you to see if you can deliver on expectations with a *larger number of customers or increased production size.* You are assessing whether what works on a small scale has any limitations or red flags before you roll out and risk further investment costs associated with full-scale production.

Test Market

This is an opportunity to gain market-based experience at a fraction of the cost. The advantage of a test market is that it provides *real-world conditions.* The disadvantage is that the market you select may have idiosyncratic or regional considerations that may not be consistent on a broader scale.

When a test market is considered, you may want to do a matched comparison—(2)-markets with similar specifications—so that you can better control for the conditions that may affect outcomes and readability. In some cases, you may opt out of a geographical approach and instead do a test in a chain of stores or (1) distribution channel before taking your product more broadly into the marketplace.

Regional or Country Rollout

The regional or country rollout is the *largest opportunity to pressure test* in real market conditions while minimizing exposure. |If successful, the national or global rollout can follow.

Not all of these approaches for how to rigor opportunities through testing and learning need to be completed, and they do not necessarily need to be staged in the order presented here, though they are sequenced for increasing risk and investment level.

Trusted Advisors Who Provide Objectivity

Shaping your future landscape requires an assessment of multiple opportunities that may involve talent acquisition, business model changes, investments in emerging technologies or markets, and partnerships or collaborations. Utilizing a range of objective and specialized advisors to assist you in appropriately assessing and rigoring your future options is an additional avenue to consider prior to making significant resource investments.

Some initiatives may not lend themselves to being tested or planned for but rather *the go/no-go decision is a judgment call* based on perceived opportunity and risk management. In these cases, checking in with and gaining insight from a variety of sources may provide you with informed objectivity that allows you to pressure test your ideas with rigor.

These optional resources could include:

- ☑ **A special team**
- ☑ **Trusted advisors**
- ☑ **A board of directors**
- ☑ **Peer advisory groups**
- ☑ **Industry subject matter experts**

A Special Team

Assigning a small group of well respected, credible voices to assess a potential initiative is a smart move. This may be a combination of *insiders and outsiders* who know your culture and capabilities and can provide a measure of validation to your own judgment as to whether the idea can work and identify less obvious risks or opportunities for your consideration.

Trusted Advisors

Whether this is your legal counsel, financial advisor, or leadership coach, carefully selected trusted advisors (this concept was fully explored in Chapter 3 of Part 1) can provide you with objective and informed perspectives.

A Board of Directors

Whether formally in place with decision-making authority or semi-formally in place with more of an advisory role, a board of directors can be invaluable in assisting with risk assessments and opportunity validation.

Peer Advisory Groups

If you are a leading-edge small to mid-sized business leader, you might want to be part of a peer advisory group such as Vistage with access to and intimate relationships with (12)-(16) CEOs who can listen to your ideas, challenge your assumptions, and provide you with insights, experiences, and perspectives.

Industry Subject Matter Experts

Successful business leaders stay on top of their respective industries and have relationships with the thought leaders who are driving innovation and change. As you explore opportunities, seeking counsel with the experts in your industry under confidentiality agreements can help secure your confidence in shaping your future landscape.

III. Design and Create It!

Leading at the organizational level requires an architectural perspective. Shaping the future of an enterprise is an ongoing and iterative process much like building a house and making it a home. The foundation must be in place first, and then the process of creating your framework begins.

In *Leadership Rigor,* designing and creating your future landscape is about embracing and embedding the **Organizational Excellence** Model into your enterprise. This model sets your leadership team's action agenda in both the short and longer term, so let's take a closer look at how this powerful signature model works.

"A vision without execution is an hallucination."
— Thomas Edison

> *"We are what
> we repeatedly do.
> Excellence then,
> is not an act
> but a habit."*
> *— Aristotle*

THE *SIGNATURE* MODEL
Organizational Excellence

Organizational Excellence, the third signature model presented in **Leadership Rigor**, outlines a sequential and integrated road map for the work of the CEO and his or her executive leadership team. This template for shaping the future with a customized action agenda is expressly suited for enterprise-level work.

As with the **Progressive Mindset** and **Analytical Rigor** Signature Models, the case will be made for why, what, when, where, and how this model can be used to deliver enhanced performance and increased productivity.

The Macro Business Challenge

Surrounded by complexity and ambiguity, business leaders today have unlimited opportunities and challenges to face but limited resources (people, time, and money) to leverage. How can leaders best prioritize and establish the right action agenda for their work at the organizational level?

Many executives believe it all starts with vision and strategy. "Let's figure out where we want to go and make a concrete plan to get there. The rest will fall into place, right?"

Not exactly!

As both a leadership performance coach and a business executive who has significant experience developing strategies in large corporations, I have seen CEOs attraction to strategy as their highest priority derail their future by distracting them from focusing on the underlying forces and dynamics at play in their organizations that require their attention first.

Having worked personally with over (25) CEOs and hundreds of executive clients in my first (7) years of leadership coaching, a clear theme has emerged and been repeatedly validated regardless of business size, industry, life cycle stage, or whether the business is publicly or privately held. *That is, the work of CEOs and their executive teams centers on the (6) critical areas shown below:*

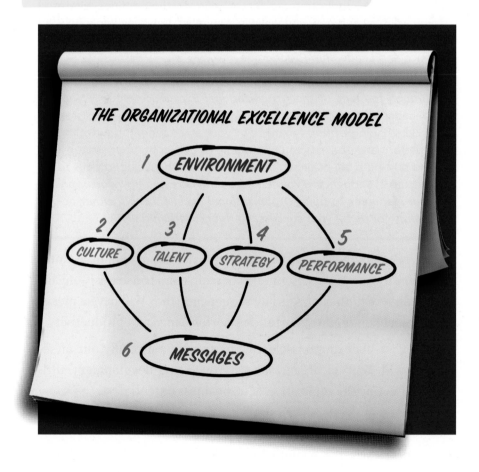

Strategy at the Organizational Level

As mentioned previously in *Leadership Rigor,* strategy is a misunderstood concept. What is often needed when initially seeking a strategy, especially for small to mid-sized companies, is an annual operating plan that documents the company's financial projections and conceptually frames the rationale for its current investment priorities to drive growth and profitability. This operational plan must be in place first.

A strategy (or strategic plan) is a mid- to longer-term approach for creating competitive advantage in the marketplace in a targeted way that can be measured. If it is not competitive and measurable externally, it is not strategic. Simply put, strategy defines where you will play and how you will win. You must, however, know how to play first. This is where the concepts of **Organizational Excellence** and *Leadership Rigor* come into play!

Strategy is actually fourth in the priority sequence when looking through the lens of the Organizational Excellence Model. What precedes your ability to design and execute your strategy is an understanding of the dynamics of your environment, developing a performance-based culture capable of delivering your strategy, and putting a talent bench in place that has the required skills to execute it. *Sequencing your choices for where and how you apply your resources to build Organizational Excellence will either accelerate or derail your success, so rigor it sequentially!*

These areas represent the foundational components of an integrated enterprise. If the CEO and leadership team consciously engage in each area with the appropriate sequencing, they will have a meaningful impact on their organization's performance and productivity.

Likewise, focusing on selective parts only, especially out of sequence, will limit an organization's growth and development, ultimately affecting the realization of its business potential.

Why You Need the Organizational Excellence Model

While clearly the evolution from leading yourself to leading a team represents a significant transition, leading at the organization-

THE ORGANIZATIONAL EXCELLENCE MODEL

CONTEXT — ENVIRONMENT

CONTENT — CULTURE · TALENT · STRATEGY · PERFORMANCE

COMMUNICATION — MESSAGES

al level requires *a transformational change* in your perspective. The **Organizational Excellence** model provides structure and support to (3) mandates that capture the rigor required at this level of leadership:

1. You must work at the *integrated enterprise level* to build leaders and teams that can sustain and scale your business.

2. You must consistently demonstrate the *conscious discipline to work "on the business"* and not be lured into working "in the business" because enterprise-level initiatives can only be driven by the CEO and his or her leadership team.

3. You must appreciate that the *sequencing of your actions* is important and that it *has consequences.*

Unfortunately, organizational-level work is not initially understood or appreciated by most executives, especially those whose experiences have been limited to working in one or two small to mid-sized firms or in technical/functional areas of larger organizations. These executives have likely had little to no outside formal leadership development exposure and often admit they are products of their limited environments and the styles of their predecessors.

The **Organizational Excellence** model provides a framework for naming your specific leadership accountabilities at the enterprise level and provides perspective on what working "on the business" looks, sounds, and feels like.

Moving up the Solutions Curve

Working at the right altitude has been emphasized throughout *Leadership Rigor.* At the organizational level, moving up the solutions curve is a way to consciously master this challenge. For example, solving a specific problem is always the lowest-level solution. To leaders, it can be painfully obvious what the solution to a problem is, and they typically want to jump in and use their expertise power to be smart and efficient and just solve it. Indulging themselves here, unfortunately, compresses organizational growth and learning.

A better approach, assuming your involvement is actually needed at all, is *to take your altitude up a level* and coach for an enduring process solution at the enterprise level so that additional organizational time is not wasted in the future on similar problems.

Your highest-altitude solution, as a leader, targets the people level. At this level, leaders ask who should be on point with what expectations and resources to solve this problem. Framing the challenge in an **Accountability Conversation** is a great reinforcement to your performance-based cultural approach.

When focused on being people solvers, leaders play their roles at the right altitude, demonstrate trust in their talent, and challenge other leaders to step up, play bigger, and grow faster.

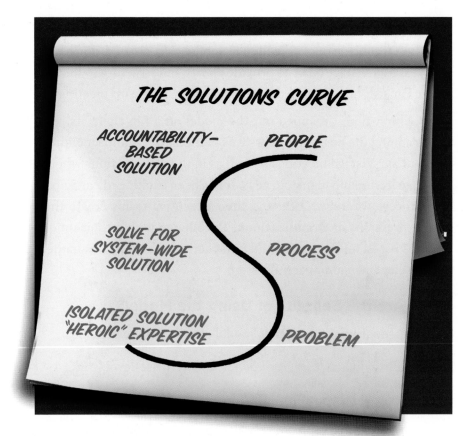

Why the Model Was Created

No official playbook exists that explains how to lead at the organizational level. Many executives are still just beginning to fully understand that running the technical operations of their business is only a part of their leadership role and that delivering performance at the enterprise level requires a broader perspective on how people and organizations work, change, and thrive.

Organizations are made up of people, emotional beings with feelings and needs, so ego, power, money, status, recognition, purpose, meaning, security, ambition, voice, influence and achievement are important motivations for leaders to understand. Business challenges can appear relatively straightforward in comparison to understanding the complexities of human interpersonal dynamics. This is why working to master the (2) currencies of leadership, communication and relationships, is critical for success at the organizational level.

The **Organizational Excellence** model was created during my first year as a Vistage chair to provide clarity and structure to the topics we consistently discussed in our monthly CEO board meetings.

The first time I mapped out the model on a flip chart, its resonance among the board members was immediate. Its impact endures today in our Vistage meetings as well as in the organizations where I facilitate leadership team journeys. It has been exciting to participate in a process whereby CEOs and their executive teams create their own expressions of **Organizational Excellence** within their unique cultures based on the clarity and perspective offered in this model's simple, elegant, and impactful design.

What Are the Benefits of Using the Model?

The **Organizational Excellence** model offers (3) main benefits:

1. It provides an *integrated view* of enterprise-level work.

2. It provides you and your team with a *common language.*

3. It provides a *sequenced road map* to prioritize initiatives.

Perspective, language, and prioritization can significantly accelerate the impact you have on your organization's future growth and development. The tangible outcomes will be greater performance and productivity!

What Type of Tool Is Organizational Excellence?

The **Organizational Excellence** model is an *enduring architectural design tool* that can support the development of your annual or multi-year enterprise action agenda. Its simple framework can also guide the creation of your company narrative, the evolving story of how you are building capability in each area and striving toward your own unique and ongoing expression of **Organizational Excellence**.

Integrating this model into your enterprise can be a driving force for conscious discipline in becoming performance-based.

What Skills Does the Model Develop?

The **Organizational Excellence** model further accelerates your proficient utilization of the (2) currencies of leadership, communication and relationship building.

Communicating the meaning and context of your overall approach with the **Organizational Excellence** model as well as each area of your leadership action agenda is what your employees want to hear. Being clear and purposeful in articulating what you will do, why you are doing it, and how you will do it builds trust and confidence.

Your *relationship-building* skills will be continuously tested at the organizational leadership level. The interpersonal value equation is constantly in flux, and every interaction you have will either add equity to or take equity away from your relationships.

Your credibility as a leader is critical, and having it or not having it is what either makes you effective or renders you unable to lead. With credibility in your relationships comes trust, confidence, and, importantly, goodwill. If you are going to challenge your employees to engage in risk, change, and growth initiatives to achieve **Organizational Excellence**, you must have relationship credibility.

> *All leaders are in the communication and relationship business—in other words, the people business. Everything we are accountable for as leaders is accomplished through others. Your personal ability to master this reality and successfully cascade it to your executive leadership team will accelerate your organization's success.*

In addition to these fundamental skills, the **Organizational Excellence** model also provides an opportunity for your executive team to further enhance their skills in leadership development, succession planning, and operational excellence as they apply themselves to the *"book of work"* within each section of the model.

When to Use the Organizational Excellence Model

Practical applications for using the **Organizational Excellence** model can be found across your enterprise. As initiatives are begun, updated, or completed, framing them in the context of the model will ensure transparency and a focus on the consistent delivery of your action agenda. On a monthly, quarterly, or annual planning basis, the model can be used to ensure a balanced approach to your resource allocation or to validate and/or correct an unbalanced approach.

Most organizations have long lists of performance-based goals focused on sales, financials, manufacturing targets, customers, R&D, and technology initiatives. What most fail to develop are cultural, talent-based, strategic, environmental management, and messaging goals. The **Organizational Excellence** model can *ensure your focus is conscious and by design* in terms of appropriately applying resources for delivering performance and productivity at the enterprise level.

Where Is the Customer in This Model?

Everywhere! By establishing a commitment to **Leadership Rigor** and using the **Organizational Excellence** model as a framework, you are fundamentally creating a culture of change-ready leaders who are in service to others. The expectation of utilizing the leadership currencies of communication and relationships as a performance-based organization in which results and behaviors are equally important is an orientation that is completely customer focused, *both internally and externally!*

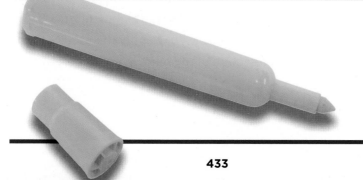

Where to Use the Organizational Excellence Model

While opportunities for reinforcing the model exist everywhere, utilizing it in the *(4) high-visibility forums* listed below will provide you with both traction and momentum within your enterprise:

- Town hall meetings

- Leadership team meetings

- Planning sessions and workshops

- Cultural engagement surveys

Town hall meetings, where your entire community gathers to learn what is happening across the enterprise, are an ideal forum for utilizing the **Organizational Excellence** framework to formally identify in which of the (6) areas your discussion topics reside.

Leadership team meetings can be structured using the **Organizational Excellence** model as an agenda outline. This gives you and your team consistent visibility to the enterprise priorities and resource allocation needs while ensuring focused alignment at the right altitude.

Planning sessions and workshops where annual or multi-year time frames are discussed are also prime places to apply the **Organizational Excellence** framework. These forums are focused on high-level goal setting, and addressing each of the (6) core areas can ensure a well-rounded discussion.

Finally, designing and then debriefing your cultural engagement survey results within the **Organizational Excellence** model framework provides a transparent annual benchmark for tracking performance strengths and opportunity gaps over time with the audience that matters most here, your employees!

How the Organizational Excellence Model Is Designed

This is a simple design with unique enterprise applications:

- (3) *levels* (context, content, and communication)

- (2) *interfaces* (environment and messages)

- (4) *sequential content areas* (culture, talent, strategy, and performance)

- (3) *couplets* with enterprise applications (leadership development, succession-planning, and operations)

The (3) Levels

The (3) levels of the **Organizational Excellence** model define the interactive and dynamic nature of the roles CEOs and their leadership teams need to take ownership of and accountability for:

- *Level 1* is the environmental *context* within which the enterprise operates. This level provides visibility to the internal and external conditions affecting risk, change, and growth that leaders must navigate. CEOs and their leadership teams have the highest altitude and broadest landscape view; it is their role to identify, interpret, and share what they see, explain how it affects the business environment, and convey why specific choices will best position their enterprise for success moving forward.

- *Level 2* sequences the *content* areas for achieving **Organizational Excellence** and underscores the pervasive impact of culture on all aspects of the enterprise. As CEO, how you shape your culture will set the stage for the talent that will join and stay, the strategy you will be able to execute in the marketplace, and the overall performance you will be able to deliver.

- *Level 3* is the critical role of *communication* both internally and externally. The messaging from the leadership team must be con-

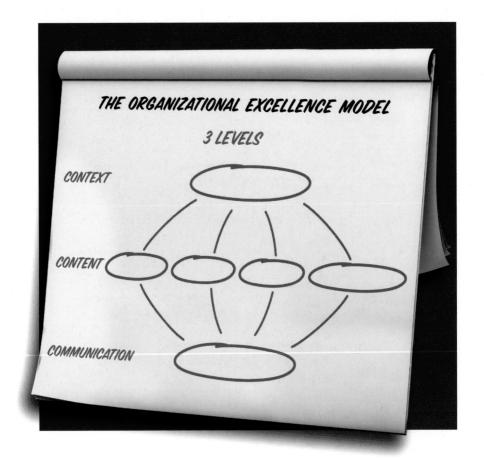

THE ORGANIZATIONAL EXCELLENCE MODEL

3 LEVELS

CONTEXT

CONTENT

COMMUNICATION

sistent, clear, and appropriately framed to land with the intended impact. Performance and productivity on the ground (OTG) will not have traction or momentum without communication that can be understood and acted upon.

"The greatest leader is not necessarily the one who does the greatest things. He is the one that gets the people to do the greatest things."
– Ronald Reagan

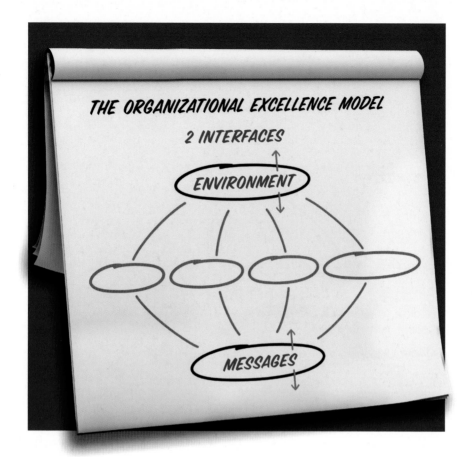

The (2) Interfaces

The (2) interfaces of the model are the *environment and messages.* Both represent areas where internal and external exchanges take place.

Organizations are living, breathing entities. Your ability to read and then shape the external environment as well as be appropriately proactive or responsive with your impactful communication messages establishes confidence in and credibility for you and your leadership team across your organization and your business community.

The (4) Sequential Content Areas

Each of the (4) sequential content areas of *culture, talent, strategy, and performance* has an integrated and comprehensive book of work associated with them. The role of the CEO leadership team is to ensure that:

- *Priorities* are established

- *Resources* are dedicated

- *Forums* for engagement around decision making are set up

- *Processes* required to facilitate workstream progress are in place

- *Expectations* and accountability for the deliverables are clear

- *Coaching* for performance is ongoing and consistent

- *Metrics* for tracking results are in place

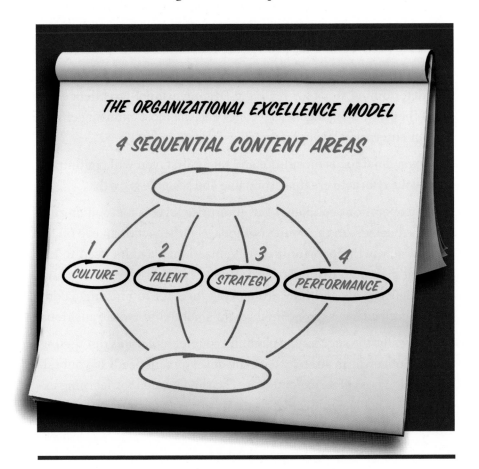

The (3) Couplets

There are (3) couplets with significant enterprise applications.

Culture and talent are the leadership development couplet that focuses on the traction and momentum of the embedded behavioral capabilities of your organization.

Talent and strategy are the succession-planning couplet that focuses on identifying future critical roles given your longer-term growth expectations and the talent and skills that will be required to get you there. Also included is a structured process for managing talent development with expectations for job rotations, exposures and experiences as well as training, coaching, and mentoring. The gaps in your talent will be identified here should you need to hire externally.

Strategy and performance are the operations couplet that focuses on the technical capabilities of your organization, including your platform, structure, and business model to execute your go-to-market strategy both today and for the future.

Culture and talent, your leadership development couplet, are the rate-determining steps for realizing **Organizational Excellence** because they have the longest lead times and the most enduring effects on your enterprise-level performance and productivity.

If you don't focus on culture and talent first, you will continually lag in your efforts to create sustainable and scalable growth.

The operations couplet at the enterprise level is focused on running the business in the context of today's targets with an eye on tomorrow's growth opportunities. Organizational leaders need to ensure that their mid- to longer-term strategy is tethered to their annual performance goals and they are moving together in unison, making the required changes to set the stage for smooth life cycle transitions.

Critically, the succession-planning couplet integrates discussions on your longer-term strategy with the development needs of your talent bench who will be executing it. The time needed for learning experiences is not insignificant; this needs to be regularly discussed on a formal basis and proactively led by CEOs and their leadership teams.

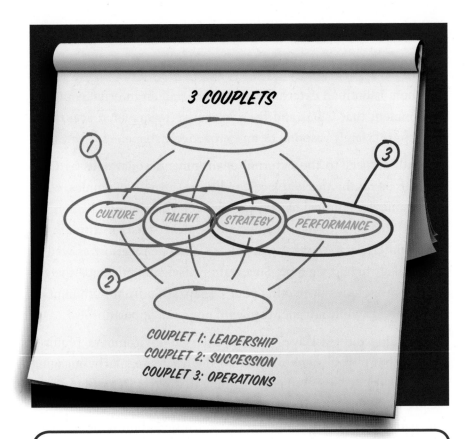

3 COUPLETS

CULTURE · TALENT · STRATEGY · PERFORMANCE

COUPLET 1: LEADERSHIP
COUPLET 2: SUCCESSION
COUPLET 3: OPERATIONS

The Growth Challenge for CEOs

CEOs must pursue (2) paths to ensure the future growth of their enterprises: *First is being ready for growth; second is consciously choosing how best to grow.*

Many CEOs spend time asking theoretical questions about pursuing new products, new geographies, or acquisitions but invest little time rigoring the answers within their organizations. They also delay hiring talent and building the skill sets of their current bench for the future growth they expect. So, when opportunities present themselves, these CEOs are not prepared to take advantage of them.

CEOs must clearly understand their organizational culture (who we are and how we do things) to assess whether a growth opportunity is a current fit and if the executive team has the technical and leadership capabilities to deliver the enterprise through the stages of that growth opportunity. **This requires sequencing and preparation!**

Ensure culture and talent (leadership capability) are in place first!

A Deep Dive into the Model's (6) Areas:

The Environment (Context and Interface)

There is both an external marketplace and an internal company environment that CEOs and their executive teams must accurately read, appropriately respond to, and proactively shape.

With respect to the external environment, your focus as CEO needs to be on the marketplace conditions (growth dynamics, competitive moves, political landscapes, financial barriers, and emerging trends). You need to feel, see, hear, and make sense of through informed interpretation what you believe is happening now as well as what's likely to happen next. Successfully navigating through the environment includes protecting your organization from imminent or future threats while advancing toward potential opportunities.

"Reading the tea leaves" on the external environment requires reaching out to your network of trusted advisors regularly, engaging with industry experts, and creating time to discuss, debate, and synthesize the information you acquire into actionable insights. Reflection, pattern recognition, integration, and anticipation skills are critical for external environmental leadership.

Internally, your leadership role is to create the conditions of *safety and space* in the environment so that there is accelerated learning and growth for your talent as well as OTG performance and productivity.

"Safety" means that appropriate risk taking is encouraged. It also means accepting that mistakes will be made and that everyone needs to own, respond, and learn from them. Safe environments openly invite individuals to voice and presence themselves even when bringing up challenges or concerns.

"Space" means playing your role at the right altitude and consciously creating room as well as the expectation that others will take ownership, accountability, and the reins of empowerment versus waiting for these to be given.

▶ What Your Environment Says about You

The look, sound, and feel of your environment will create initial perceptions about your culture (i.e., open or closed, organized or chaotic, friendly or cold).

Ask yourself whether an executive interviewing for a leadership role in your organization would be inspired when entering your environment. Would new entry-level employees, possibly Millennials, be energized by what they see, feel, and experience?

Your environment is not only about your office location, floor plan, and furniture, though such elements are telling. It is about how people are *greeted and treated.* Are visitors made to feel welcome and comfortable, or are they treated as an intrusion into someone's busy day? Rigor the experience of your environment!

The Consequences of a False Start

Leading your organization through a cultural change initiative is one of the hardest and longest challenges you can take on as a CEO. It can be a game changer to your future and one of the most all-around rewarding experiences you can have as a leader, but it requires *revisiting, recalibrating, and realigning* around potentially new or modified beliefs and behaviors.

If you start this intense work and then stop a cultural change initiative for whatever reason, you will lose your credibility as a leader and send the message that you lack vision, commitment, and persistence. Starting and stopping will leave your employees wondering whether any of the initiatives you take on are really important or whether they can get away with not putting in too much effort, considering whatever is now or next on your agenda in the context of "this too shall pass."

The Culture: #1 in the Content Sequence

Defined broadly as *"how we do things around here,"* your culture reflects the behaviors, language, symbols, tools, and processes your employees use every day. It is the powerful combination of what you create and what you tolerate.

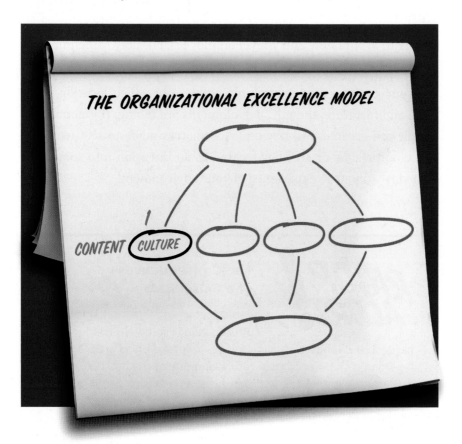

Advancing into becoming a performance-based organization typically requires a cultural change initiative that will not happen passively. You and your leadership team must be consciously disciplined in actively creating and shaping it.

Unfortunately, most leaders *ignore, underestimate, or arrogantly pay lip service* to the importance of their organization's culture. These leaders typically wait too long to get started on cultural initiatives in the mistaken belief that other business priorities are more important.

This is a bad decision! These leaders don't understand what is involved, how long it takes, and what is really at stake. This is also why high-performance teams and performance-based organizations are so rare!

When these leaders finally begin their cultural work, often because morale has fallen, growth has stalled, great talent cannot be retained, general confusion has set in, or perhaps the lightning bolt has finally hit them, they underestimate the personal effort required to be the champion and role model for this intense initiative as well as the time it takes for the expected changes to take hold.

Feeble and fleeting attempts by weak leaders are why most cultural change initiatives fail and consequently why organizations not only do not reach their true potential but ultimately stagnate or fall into decline!

If an organization is not growing at or above the market, lacks accountability, or is unable to recruit and retain a strong talent bench, it is in cultural trouble. In the corporate world, this usually results in the CEO being replaced. In small to mid-sized private or family owned businesses, this situation can and does continue for decades, generations, or even indefinitely.

Don't let this happen in your organization. Embrace a cultural change initiative that has a strong leadership vision and commitment to excellence. In other words, **Rigor it!**

▶ Why Is Culture So Challenging and So Important?

The **Organizational Excellence** model begins with the environment, because without first establishing the internal conditions of safety and space, cultural change cannot take hold or gain traction in your enterprise.

A company's culture does not change because leaders make announcements, requests, or proclamations. You cannot simply sit at your desk, make a list of (5) values, and then draft an email or PowerPoint presentation announcing your new culture.

Cultures change because leaders utilize the *influence* of their *personal power* and apply their *visionary leadership* skills to make a compelling case for *why change* is necessary. They honestly describe what the change will be, how it will be supported, and what the consequences will be for being or not being a role model for the culture. They then have the conscious discipline to consistently practice and apply the skills and tools required to give their cultural changes traction and momentum.

> *Cultures align around common values (shared beliefs) and are strengthened when there is accountability for demonstrating the behaviors associated with those values.*

Values and Shared Beliefs Impact Culture

If you believe that being a hard-driving achievement-based individual who gets things done at all costs is what will get you ahead, and if getting ahead is all that matters to you, you will behave in accordance with that belief. You will passionately pursue your work and overcome any and all obstacles (including people) because you believe the ends justify the means. *In a culture that rewards delivering results at all costs, you will be a high performer.* For those who do not share these beliefs, this will likely be a toxic culture with unacceptable behaviors.

Perhaps you believe, as the CEO of a private business, that you have an obligation to your employees based on their loyalty to you and your family over the years or generations. The fact that a number of employees do not have the skills or passion to deliver against performance expectations causes frustration and resentment across your organization, yet you continue year after year to encourage their development, giving them feedback and hoping for eventual change, because you value harmony and believe your culture is built around caring for each other. Besides, they will likely retire in (5) years anyway.

This belief is supported by your behavior of tolerating underperformance. While many employees will stay because your organization is a "kind and comfortable" place, those who want to be part of a growth-oriented and performance-based culture will be unfulfilled and will leave.

As the leader, remember that your fingerprints are on everything. **What you create and what you tolerate form the basis of the beliefs and behaviors that define your culture and ultimately determine your performance.** If you are satisfied with your performance, great! If you believe your organization can be better and achieve more, consider your culture first and embrace sequencing. In other words, **Rigor it!**

AS CEO, WHAT ARE YOU...

CREATING

CULTURE

TOLERATING

▶ Designing Your Organization's Cultural Footprint

Cultural change is hard. People often want to keep things the same because "the same" is familiar and comfortable. They might passively resist specific changes or, depending on their confidence level and the power they perceive they may lose, attempt to convince you that your efforts to change are overblown, unnecessary, or that you are closer than you think to already achieving what you want in an effort to stop or slow you down.

Pay attention to those who resist change and try to determine if their reluctance is rooted in personality hardwiring, fear-based obstructionism, or just a fundamental lack of understanding the potential benefits at stake. With exposure and education, these individuals will either become a force for positive change or will remain a passive-aggressive blockade to the growth and development of your enterprise, which is something you will absolutely need to address with definitive action if being a performance-based organization is your goal.

Notwithstanding the potential reluctance around you, seriously reflect on whether you personally have the vision, conviction, and persistence to take your organization to another level. Over time, will you get caught up in complacency yourself? Do not start what you do not have the heart and stomach to finish!

When designing your cultural footprint, there are multiple elements to consider, from your company's values to how your organization makes decisions or encourages the use of power.

■ Your company's values

Your values need to be thoughtfully designed to clearly express the *unique emotional energy and personality* of your organization as well as the non-negotiable behaviors that support your organization's performance at its highest level. Your values represent the essence of your organization's spirit and help to define who would be

The Inspirational Influence of Values

Values are the emotional blueprint to the beliefs an organization holds and the behaviors it expects. They are either inspiring to you as an individual or they are not. Google any company and look at its values; you might be surprised at what you find. Some leading companies merely offer a generic list of words such as "honesty," "integrity," "trust," and "teamwork" that can be applied to anyone.

Instead, why not consider developing a simple but powerful sentence or more expansive statement of beliefs such as the following:

- "We believe we are on the face of the earth to make great products."

- "We believe in the simple, not the complex."

- "We believe in saying 'no' to thousands of projects so that we can really focus on the few that are truly important and meaningful to us."

- "We believe in deep collaboration and cross-pollination of our groups, which allows us to innovate in a way that others cannot."

- "We don't settle for anything less than excellence in every group of the company, and we have the self-honesty to admit when we're wrong and the courage to change."

Want to join the company with these values? These are (5) of Apple's (7) values as articulated by CEO Tim Cook. Your values articulate both the expectations you have as well as the experiences you are creating within your enterprise.

Striving for Mediocrity

In organizations that have yet to actively engage in or consciously define their cultural footprint, CEOs and their leadership teams will likely hire talent because the candidate has the necessary technical skills they desperately believe they need now to drive the business, even when the cultural fit of the individual is questionable. The "consensus" approach is usually to worry about that later!

The consistency in the outcome is amazing: continuous turnover in critical positions and CEOs who continue to think the problem is finding the right talent!

The problem is that the organization lacks a clearly defined culture upon which to build its version of performance-based **Organizational Excellence** and keeps meandering through a unconsciously incompetent pursuit of mediocrity.

Get off the treadmill going nowhere. Instead, rigor it with your cultural footprint going forward!

a good cultural fit with your enterprise because they share the same beliefs.

Values are timeless and enduring. While they do not change over the course of an organization's life cycle, what does change is how these values are expressed in the context of the changing business conditions. For example, having a sense of urgency in 1995 might look different from having a sense of urgency in 2014. Both imply speed, but the response times might require a new interpretation given today's tech-driven marketplace.

Tell the Story of Your Values

Your values are not just words or phrases on mugs or wall posters. Your expectation needs to be that they will be lived in real time OTG every day! To socialize your values appropriately, take the time to ensure that each member of your leadership team can "tell the story of your values." *In other words, make sure all team members can consistently tell a short and clear version of exactly what your organization is expecting from each value, not a random personalized interpretation.* For example, if "being passionate about our ideas" is a value, the consistent story you might tell is the following:

"In our organization, we thrive on new ideas. We want everyone to develop ideas, and we want them to be passionate about communicating their ideas to others so we can all consider the potential business opportunity these ideas can create. Being passionate means that we expect individuals to have a strong reason and clear rationale for why their ideas make sense. It means they can explain how the company can benefit from their ideas, and they have a next-step action plan for how to make their ideas work! This is what we mean by being passionate about our ideas."

> *It is the role of the CEO and his or her leadership team to establish the values, role model how they are lived, communicate the expectations around why they are important, and be clear about the consequences of not being in alignment with them.*

When your values are successfully embedded within your culture, you as CEO can be confident that even when you or your leadership team are absent from the room, your values will be a reference guide to your organization in terms of how best to make decisions and move forward. Some employees might even ask themselves, "What would so and so do?" This, of course, is an unconscious way of consulting the values since the individual being referenced is likely a positive role model for the company culture.

Organizations that apply as much rigor to ensuring that potential new hires align with their cultural values as they do to attempting to validate their technical skill sets are far more effective in developing and retaining a strong talent bench for the future than organizations that overlook this. In the long run, in high-performance organizations, cultural fit is simply more important than technical capabilities. Technical skills can be developed; values are either an authentically shared connection or a personal disconnect.

Understanding this in the interview process is critical because shared values are the underpinning of a highly engaged and inspired community of employees. Individuals who do not embrace and live your company's values will cause problems by engaging in potentially disruptive behaviors that become resource distractions. Failure to immediately address this will communicate that you are tolerant of your values not being upheld and are willing to prioritize technical competency over behavioral competency. You must promptly exit people who do not exhibit or, worse, who openly violate your company values. *This is work that only leaders can do!*

■ How your organization makes decisions

Decision making is more than just determining what action to take. It is your organization's process for framing challenges, inviting alternative ideas, and debating options as well as engaging in a structured learning process for developing business judgment.

In other words, your decision-making process helps define your culture. Are you transparent and inclusive, utilizing tools such as the **Analytical Rigor** model, or are decisions made behind closed doors with outcomes delivered in an email, team meeting, or town hall forum? Does the CEO make all the critical decisions alone, or does a highly functional leadership team collaborate in the process?

All of these are cultural messages. Ask yourself whether your decision-making process is consistent with the values you have established and the culture you are creating.

■ How your organization holds accountability

Larger corporations are fixated on creating "cultures of account-ability." Frustrated when leadership teams make commitments and then don't deliver against them, senior executives often believe they need to take a firmer stand on holding people accountable (often out of fear for their own jobs).

My concern as a leadership performance coach is that these executives typically believe they can demand and delegate new requirements from 30,000 feet without role modeling and living these accountability behaviors personally. More importantly, these executives often appear unaware that the real lack of accountability lies with them. They ultimately are responsible for putting people in these roles and appropriately setting the expectations as well as coaching or empowering them for performance.

When people don't deliver, you as a leader need to take a close look at why, because to some degree, and perhaps a large degree, you are part of the problem. These individuals either *don't have the skills* (they need you to coach, train, or remove them from the role), they don't have the bandwidth (they need your help prioritizing or securing additional resources), they *don't understand the request* (your communication is an illusion), they *don't understand their role* in delivering the request (role clarity is muddled or nonexistent), or they *are consciously or unconsciously trapped* (you have fixed the game and they rightly or wrongly believe that they cannot succeed).

It is common for corporate executives to lose their jobs because they "overpromise and under deliver" on their financial goals more than once. If, however, during the annual planning process, an executive looks to negotiate a lower number with solid analytical justification and it is not approved, who is to be held accountable if the target is not reached?

This is where the game might appear to be fixed. Corporate leaders are at times forced into chasing what can't be achieved, having backed themselves into a corner by originally committing to unrealistic numbers over the mid to longer term, and are now locked into target levels that, based on the trajectory of the current business performance, they cannot reach. This is, unfortunately, their own doing, if early in their tenure they made lofty and heroic commitments that appeared to be far off in the distance but actually came around quicker than they expected, with all-too-realistic consequences.

Under performance pressure, these executives might then "force" unrealistic expectations on their teams and set up a "fall person" whom they can sacrifice if the deliverables are not met. In such situations, the game is definitely fixed. Everyone loses, including the leaders, the talent bench, and the broader organization, and all because unrealistic expectations were accepted instead of appropriately challenged!

This represents a lost opportunity to have held **The Accountability Conversation** up front, before unrealistic commitments were

proposed or agreed to. It also demonstrates that the accountability challenge is twofold: first, a culture of accountability must be shaped and nurtured through the "way we do things around here" at all levels, including consistent role modeling by CEOs and their leadership teams, and second, your organization needs to have a clear understanding of what accountability looks, sounds, and feels like. Without language, tools, practice, and time, you simply cannot expect a new set of behaviors to snap into place, and the consequences in large organizations can be significant and swift.

Leadership Rigor has already presented (2) tools concerning accountability. One, of course, is **The Accountability Conversation**, in which leaders negotiate expectations, resources, and mutually agreed-upon deliverables up front.

The second is **The Progressive Mindset** model, which outlines how holding accountability starts with setting expectations and then requires the supervisor to be and stay engaged by coaching for performance throughout the process to ensure accountability.

The third tool you need to imbed in your culture is peer-to-peer accountability. Ask your employees to challenge each other on personal behaviors that may be unproductive, unrealistic expectations that set the team/organization up for failure, or on missed deliverables that hold back organizational performance and productivity. The use of courageous conversations when trust is in the room, conflict is embraced, pink elephants are named, and personal power is leveraged in service of your commitments to each others' growth are the building blocks of an accountability-based culture!

■ How your organization encourages the use of power

The use of power is a strong cultural signal. When I was a young executive working at a large consumer packaged goods healthcare company, senior leaders sat on the highest level floors lined with special carpeting and were armed with executive assistants sitting outside every office to ensure entry was "by invitation only." Bathrooms and dining areas were private. Conference room meetings had protocols regarding who sat where as well as who spoke when. When you were invited, or more likely summoned, to the offices of a senior leader, it was perceived to be "an event." Leadership aspirations for young executives centered on getting promoted as quickly as possible, getting an office with a window, and getting that new business card with a title that declared to the world how important you were. This was position power at work in Corporate America!

Today, as explained in the previous chapter, the walls are literally coming down. Open floor plans have senior leaders sitting with and among their employee community. Fewer power symbols signal a difference in level or responsibility. Informal engagement and collaboration are encouraged. In short, we are living in a professional fishbowl environment. Even titles are increasingly focused on common language such as "associates" and "members of the firm" rather than hierarchical titles that distinguish perceived rank, though this is still evolving.

The consequences of this shift cannot be underestimated, including the significant shift in how we now communicate and build relationships. For Traditionalists, Baby Boomers, and Generation X employees, this is a significant change with historical reference points for comparison. To Generation Y and "Generation Z" or "Next" employees, this is all completely natural and as expected.

Organizations adopting this new open-environment approach believe they win on several levels. First, costs are lower, driven by fewer build-outs and simpler, more agile office space reconfigurations. Second, this shift provides an opportunity to consciously invite openness and team collaboration for accelerating innovation as well as to create increased transparency that evolves and shapes the power dynamics at play in the culture.

With these environmental changes, the concept of position power dramatically diminishes. The visible symbols projecting "I am different, important, and powerful" start to fade. How the interpersonal behaviors of executives will continue to evolve will be interesting to watch.

As Part 1 of *Leadership Rigor* explained, position power is weak and unlikely to yield significant impact with respect to real influence. It is the selective use of expertise power and the full utilization of personal power that progressive and enlightened organizations today want to develop.

Look at your environment and ask yourself how power is communicated and expressed. Is position power symbolically in place? Is this consistent with the culture you are trying to create?

■ How you use language, processes, and models

Some organizations are overly dependent on formalized systems and processes that limit their freedom to operate. Other organizations appear to have few or no formal processes, with people "doing their own thing" and using different approaches on similar tasks, causing a duplication of effort and a lack of resource optimization.

> *Culture is shaped as much by your processes and systems (or lack thereof) as anything else.*

In an organization practicing **Leadership Rigor,** making statements like "Let's have an **Accountability Conversation** on that initiative" or "Let's rigor that decision" or "Are we playing at the right altitude on this problem?" are clearly understood, culturally based calls to action that quickly shift behavior and focus without a significant amount of conversation time required.

Using the same models, language, and processes across your organization creates a common culture that accelerates your performance and productivity.

■ How you use control and empowerment

The leadership styles used by the CEO and his or her executive leadership team have a strong cultural influence. Positive role modeling of visionary, coaching, affiliative, and participative leadership styles can create an expectation for their cascading use across your organization. If leaders relentlessly pace set, with one impossible-to-reach goal after the next, or are highly controlling, doing or directing the work and not trusting the skills of their talent bench, they send a strong cultural signal for adopting this style of leadership behavior as well.

The risk and resultant consequence is that high-potential employees won't want to work in low-altitude environments with highly controlling, micromanaging, or pace-setting senior leaders who are not appropriately focused "on the business." These employees understand that such low-altitude leadership styles prohibit them from getting enough experience working "in the business" and developing their own skills. This can delay their growth and development and cause them to exit, fast.

Environments that empower and provide space for creativity, decision making, and learning, while exciting for some talent, may actually be intimidating for others. Creating a high-performance culture will require all of your employees to ultimately align with, support, and openly embrace your environment and your values. Those who do not feel comfortable in such an environment will not be a long-term cultural fit.

■ How communication impacts culture

The one thing most individuals say about their organization's culture is that there is never enough communication. Everyone wants more, and they want it to be consistent, clear, and meaningful.

While leaders often repeat themselves (4), (5), and (6) times and think that's sufficient, the "rule of (8)" I was introduced to over (15) years ago challenged this perception. It suggested that until we hear a message (8) times, we are unlikely to remember it.

> *Today, research indicates that technological advances along with the pervasiveness of social media and the increased pace of life mean we need messages to be communicated upward of (15)–(18) times to break through, land, and be recalled.*

As a leader, be mindful that this is not about you and your boredom in delivering messages; it has everything to do with the number of times you need to communicate something to ensure it is heard and retained by others. If employees do not get the message, they are unlikely to comply, not necessarily out of conscious resistance (though there may be some of this) but rather because you literally do not penetrate the environmental noise level, appropriately frame the delivery so it can be heard, and check to be certain that the communication lands and is understood. Delivering on the currency of communication with messages that are heard is the responsibility of the leader!

■ How long "culture change" takes

In my professional experience as a leadership coach and transformational change agent on the front lines of business, (3) to (5) years is the average time it takes for a culture to start to sustainably evolve, assuming dedicated and consistent efforts, though in special circumstances, a profound impact can occur in as few as (18) months.

Let me explain a bit further, because the words "culture" and "change" alone are challenging. In combination, they become increasingly complex.

Changes occur in systems, not independently; this is especially true at the organizational level. If we are changing a technology process such as an enterprise resource planning (ERP) system or redesigning our sales force from geographical to key account coverage, we affect not only those on the front lines of the change but also those upstream and downstream in the process.

On the technical operational side, it's fairly straightforward to map out the specific changes on paper. Implementing them through people takes more time and effort. Any transition involves a learning curve, slow initial progress, the challenges of mistakes, and general frustration until skills and competencies are strong enough that the belief of "I hate this" goes away and the new realization of "I think I am finally starting to get this" settles in. The length of this process varies based on individual adoption preferences and the conscious discipline of the leader to operationalize the interpersonal changes OTG with role clarity, communication, and support as well as enabling processes to facilitate the changes being requested.

Now let's take a look at the culture, the "how we do things around here," which includes "the collective everything." When you want to change the culture of an organization, you are really taking on a lot. However, not taking it on will doom most of your talent, strategy, and performance initiatives because they cannot be supported, adopted, and maintained within the current culture.

As an example, when I was asked to become general manager of a Canadian consumer healthcare division in Toronto, it took me only a few weeks to realize that the organization was running a "push" strategy. It was offering retail trade customers price deals to stock their warehouses with product to "make the division's numbers" and then running deeply discounted price promotional events with consumers to pull the product out, making more room for the next push of inventory load. This was a good deal for everyone but the company. Not surprisingly, the division missed its budget every year!

To turn this around, we needed to change our mindset, our behaviors, and our overall approach, in other words our culture, into an integrated business-driven culture that balanced a consumer-focused, pull-driven approach with a fair and reasonable partnership with our retail trade. This required transparency, sharing the truth about where we were in the marketplace, and assessing our skills and capabilities. It also required a new way of doing things, including processes, decision making, and performance expectations.

The cultural change was transformational in the first (12)–(18) months because we were working with a burning platform: the division had not made its budget in (5) years; the GM had been fired, and I, an American woman brought to lead the division forward, had boldly declared a transformational turnaround would take place including becoming a performance-based organization by aggressively taking on culture and talent as the first steps.

You Can't Wait This Out!

Many large organizations design cultural change initiatives with their HR departments, get training lined up, and roll the changes out across the entire enterprise before the CEO and executive leadership team fully understand, embrace, and demonstrate competency in practicing these changes themselves. As a result, though they "come down from the top" with posters and laminated cards, these changes have limited credibility and little long-term traction because the executive leaders aren't competently or consistently using them with their own teams, let alone role modeling them for the broader organization. ***The result is that organizations become skeptical of cultural change and think they can just "wait it out."***

To combat this, I confirm and openly communicate at the start of all leadership journeys I undertake in partnership with a CEO that no one can wait this out! This change is happening, the CEO is committed, and every individual must decide whether he or she is on board or not. Self-selection out is always an option that is important to verbalize and put clearly on the table up front. If an individual chooses to stay and doesn't emotionally get on board, selection out by the CEO leadership team will likely occur, and this possibility needs to be stated upfront as well.

This announcement calibrates the room at the beginning of the journey and sets a high bar for the initiative to be taken seriously. Without this type of clear messaging, cultural change may never get traction.

Over the next (18)–(36) months, the cultural changes gained traction and my leadership team became more confident and competent business professionals. We exceeded our budget for each of the (5) years I was GM, and we became a recognized and respected high-performance division within our global corporation.

The Talent: #2 in the Content Sequence

To deliver performance and productivity at the level of **Organizational Excellence**, you need to have the proverbial "right people on the bus, sitting in the right seats." The men and women who engage in the work of your organization on a daily basis, if selected with conscious discipline and developed to be leaders, are absolutely your greatest asset. As such, throughout **Leadership Rigor**, they are referred to as your "talent."

> *Your talent chooses to bring their unique capabilities, creativity, and emotional energy to your business every day through their passionate commitment to growing a sustainable future for your enterprise in which everyone can professionally and personally thrive.*

As a leader, it is important to understand that *talent is an enterprise asset.* The CEO and leadership team must have a clear and vested interest in the development of all talent across the enterprise and not just those in their direct reporting line or whom they formally or informally mentor. Skill and capability building take time, and your bench of talent needs to be deep if your organization is to grow and develop over the mid to longer term. Many organizations I initially start working with are severely limited in their growth trajectory due to a lack of bench talent. They have more opportunities than they have people ready to seize them!

Your talent assets appreciate or depreciate based on how well and how quickly you develop them. If you consciously and consistently invest in both skill and experience building, you will benefit from an earlier as well as a greater overall lift contribution from your bench. If you do not, you will erode your talent's value by delaying their potential contributions and compromising the longer-term growth potential for your organization.

THE ORGANIZATIONAL EXCELLENCE MODEL

CONTENT

2

TALENT

Leaders often complain about the talent costs associated with hiring, training, relocating, or expatriating. Here's the **Leadership Rigor** take on this: if your talent is an asset, the associated expenses are better referred to as investments.

When you invest in your talent, you are placing a bet on future return. The time frame for realizing this return can be variable. One thing is for sure: if you don't invest early and often in the growth and development of your talent, you delay at best and at worst never get the return you would like to see, which is your talent bench ultimately assuming the leadership roles for which you initially hired them.

Today's talent increasingly knows its value, which means high-potential and high-performance individuals are more vocal about requesting investments in their skills and capabilities. Additionally, "aspiring high potentials" are actively seeking more meaningful work, career advancement clarity, unique opportunities for accelerated growth, technical and leadership-oriented training and development, pay-for-performance incentive compensation, and earlier involvement in organizational decision making.

Accordingly, talent management at the enterprise level covers a broad and integrated range of initiatives. In the most progressive organizations, CEOs and their leadership teams actively engage in and collectively drive the "talent development process" with additional support from outside experts such as leadership coaches, learning professionals, and organizational design specialists.

Human resources (HR), depending upon its role and the size of the organization, may or may not be at the table. If HR is not present, a chief learning officer (CLO), chief talent officer (CTO), or outside leadership expert will likely be present.

Don't Get Faked Out During the Interviewing Process

Hiring talent is one of the most difficult challenges leaders face. While recruiters claim to preselect qualified candidates and resumes position everyone as accomplished superstars, the reality is that most hiring is about 50/50 at best in terms of securing qualified solid performers. (Forget about hiring a superstar!)

Why is this? There are several factors to be conscious of.

First, we want to anxiously fill the void and pain of the empty spot as soon as possible. If our impatience gets the best of us, we settle early.

Second, most of us actually believe what we read on resumes and hear from candidates and recruiters. Unfortunately, both parties have a vested interested in selling us, so they are not quite as credible as they would like us to believe. That being said, we do our homework and ask our behaviorally based interviewing questions to convince ourselves that these candidates have in fact done before what we are looking to have them do now in our organizations.

The problem, in today's world, is that everyone is a great storyteller and reasonably well prepared for the interview. Having merely sat in a meeting room and listened to a few high-level discussions can provide a smart candidate with enough perspective to "fake it" during an interview if the interviewer is not savvy.

These well prepped individuals have the language and apparently can speak it, but have they crossed the knowing-doing gap and truly delivered what they are talking about? Probably not, but most of us don't know the difference, and we typically hire these individuals once we've heard what we want to hear.

What we need to do is begin using a "contextual interviewing process." Here we create a go-forward scenario and ask candidates to walk us through how they specifically would handle it. We might create some hurdles or obstacles and ask them to role play in real time how they would address them. If they have real experience, they will be able to walk us through their approach and thinking, regardless of whether they are introverted or extroverted. If they claim they need time to reflect, we can give them a few minutes to process the question before proceeding with the conversation. This approach can dramatically minimize the fake out, so rigor it with contextual interviewing techniques!

The big takeaway is that today, HR no longer exclusively owns talent development. In the most progressive organizations, talent is now a high priority and hands-on initiative of the CEO and executive leadership team. The talent development process is also consciously cascaded throughout the organization to the next levels of leadership and functional teams.

Talent development is a comprehensive area. CEOs and their leadership teams need to understand their "book of work" and ensure that the processes, practices, and philosophies that will allow their enterprises to create and deliver their **Organizational Excellence** action agendas are in place for the talent content area.

The Talent Development Book of Work Includes:

- ☑ The performance management framework
- ☑ Recruiting, hiring, and retention practices
- ☑ On-boarding practices
- ☑ A career management philosophy
- ☑ A succession-planning process
- ☑ High-potential programs
- ☑ Cross-functional training
- ☑ Competency models and frameworks
- ☑ Individual development plans
- ☑ Leadership development programs
- ☑ Learning programs (technical and behavioral)
- ☑ Coaching and mentoring programs
- ☑ Internships and special assignment rotations
- ☑ Stretch assignments for accelerated growth
- ☑ Recognition and reward programs

As a leadership performance coach, I typically create (3)- to (5)-year plans with CEOs and their leadership teams to develop their talent development foundation on these initiatives as they evolve into performance-based organizations practicing **Leadership Rigor.**

It is important to note that here, too, is an integrated and sequential approach similar to the overall **Organizational Excellence** philosophy. Leaders who pick and choose initiatives in a random and inconsistent way will not realize the benefits of a comprehensive talent development approach.

Remember that behavioral and leadership skills can be learned. If you currently have strong technical talent, making the investment in leadership and behavioral development initiatives through your talent development approach can create enormous value for individuals and the organizations that employ them.

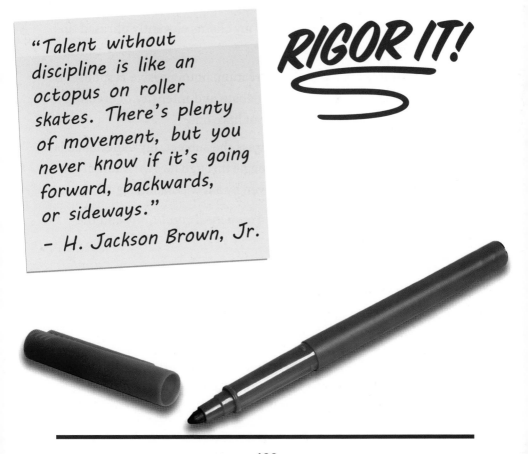

"Talent without discipline is like an octopus on roller skates. There's plenty of movement, but you never know if it's going forward, backwards, or sideways."
– H. Jackson Brown, Jr.

RIGOR IT!

The Strategy: #3 in the Content Sequence

In the **Organizational Excellence** model, strategy is defined as identifying where you can play to create competitive advantage and win in the marketplace. This is a simple concept, yet it encompasses a number of elements leaders need to consciously understand.

First, "strategy" is not just a cool word to use; it is a specific type of plan and approach. Just because you verbally use (or overuse) the word does not mean you are smart, are using it correctly, or even understand what you are saying. As a leadership coach, this is one of my critical concerns, given that most of my clients are "leaders of leaders." A lack of clarity in the language you use can propagate misunderstandings across the enterprise. To lead at the organizational level with rigor, you need to be clear and disciplined about your concepts and language.

Second, strategy is as much about what you say "no" to as it is about what you say "yes" to. (One of my clients elegantly phrased this as "an integrated set of choices.")

Third, strategy is a proactive creation, not a passive response. If you have not labored through the debate and intensity of creating a strategic plan, chances are you do not have one.

Finally, while many books address the subject, my experience is that each organization needs to struggle through its own internal process to develop a strategic plan driven by a few core elements:

- ☑ An assessment of the *environmental conditions* and the competition
- ☑ An internal review of current *organizational capabilities* and skill sets
- ☑ Identification of *innovation/opportunity gaps* (both in current and adjacent spaces)
- ☑ A *critical review* of whether current offerings (i.e., products or services) have a clear and sustainable differentiated position in the marketplace

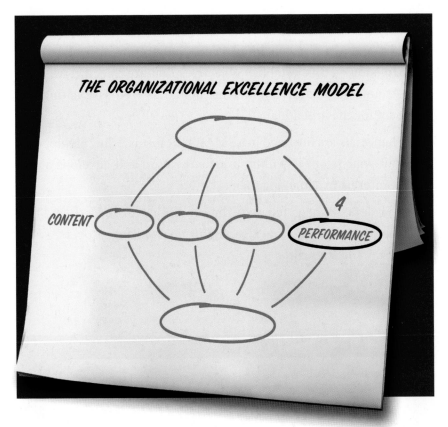

THE ORGANIZATIONAL EXCELLENCE MODEL

CONTENT

4

PERFORMANCE

☑ *Financials:* Revenue, COGS, margin, expenses, and profit

☑ *Manufacturing:* Forecasting accuracy and inventory turns

☑ *Sales:* New customers, product line sales growth, distribution, number of cross-selling outcomes, and conversion rates (i.e., cold/warm leads to proposals to booked business)

☑ *Marketing:* Share, trial, repeat, loyalty, advertising, and promotional effectiveness (traditional and digital)

☑ *New business development:* Target identification, business cases, new client presentations, proposals, and closure rates

☑ *Human resources:* Recruitment, retention, turnover, diversity candidates, high-potential pipeline progression, critical role succession planning, and employee engagement

▶ SMARTER Objectives

Most goals are not well defined and are therefore difficult to measure. To address this, establish objectives that are **S**pecific, **M**easurable, **A**ttainable, **R**ealistic, and **T**ime bound as well as **E**xciting and **R**esonant for the individual.

When goals are outlined in a SMARTER format, they are not only clear but your talent is willing to take them on and develops a passionate interest in achieving them.

As leaders, we need to create the conditions for success, and that includes participating in a meaningful goal-setting process, so be SMARTER and **Rigor it!**

▶ Practicing The Accountability Conversation

Establishing performance expectations and targets with the consistent use of **The Accountability Conversation** will increase the performance and productivity of your organization.

Tracking individual and team utilization metrics through (360)-feedback tools as well as your annual cultural engagement survey can provide ongoing visibility to this area to confirm traction.

▶ Utilizing Analytical Rigor in Decision Making

Establishing performance expectations around the appropriate and consistent use of the **Analytical Rigor** model, the signature model presented in Part 2, will drive adoption and lead to increased performance and productivity in your decision-making process.

On a practical level, since **The Accountability Conversation** and **Analytical Rigor** model are visible in the context of meetings and discussions, feedback can be integrated into coaching sessions, a plus/delta assessment at the end of team meetings, and the performance management coaching process on an informal basis as well.

▶ Cultural Engagement Surveys and Action Plans

Performance-based organizations not only want to hear from their talent community about issues, concerns, and opportunities but they also listen and take action!

Developing your annual action agenda based in part on the feedback from your cultural engagement survey results is a best practice for achieving **Organizational Excellence**. Whether holding others accountable or ensuring that the decision-making process is more transparent, performance-based organizations track and measure so they have visibility regarding what is or is not working and then use conscious discipline to encourage changes and make adjustments.

You will also want to hold your leadership team accountable for cultural engagement scores based on their team and functional area improvements as part of their performance management objectives.

▶ (360)-Degree Performance Feedback

Participating in a (360)-degree feedback process can give you insight into "what it is like to be with you and how you show up" from the perspective of various stakeholders including your supervisor, peers, customers, and direct reports in a safe and confidential way. It can also make your own view of yourself more transparent.

Progressive organizations not only engage in (360)-feedback assessments with their executives to help uncover blind spots and growth opportunities but they also set performance expectations for changes based on the feedback and continue to reassess and track progress.

Off-the-shelf (360) formats are great, but custom designing a (360) format that addresses your culture, your values, your language, and your leadership models is extremely powerful. It takes an investment of resources, but the experiential outcomes are impactful because the customization allows for faster adoption of the feedback and therefore enhanced performance and productivity!

▶ Competency Models and Frameworks

A competency model outlines the progressive technical skills and leadership behaviors expected to be demonstrated OTG at various levels across your organization. Linking career advancement to the demonstration of targeted competencies required for a specific level or position is a best practice for ensuring the right people are in the right roles and providing appropriate lift across your enterprise.

Designing and actively utilizing a clearly documented competency model is a "must have" for performance-based organizations practicing both **Organizational Excellence** and **Leadership Rigor**. This demystifies the "black box" that many organizations create because they have not taken the time to describe the competencies that are critical to performance in their enterprises.

Once defined, these competencies can be incorporated into the performance review process, career management discussions (see "Individual Development Plans" next), job profiles/descriptions, culture surveys, succession planning, and (360) assessments. This transparency builds trust and confidence with your talent so they can play a conscious role in managing their career aspirations.

▶ Individual Development Plans (IDPs)

The individual development plan, or IDP, is *the link between feedback in your direct reports' annual performance reviews and their mid- to longer-term career management aspirations.* This document highlights their demonstrated strengths, encouraging continuity as well as suggesting new areas for applying their strengths, and identifies areas for development, encouraging skill building or increased demonstration of core capabilities that are necessary for their current role or future aspirational roles. Engaging in a quarterly coaching session with each direct report to discuss their IDP and share positive and constructive feedback is highly recommended.

▶ Coaching Engagements

Providing external leadership coaching to individuals is a vote of confidence and encouragement for their future development. Behavioral changes take time, leadership skills can be learned, and creating a safe space to practice and develop new language and approaches can accelerate performance levels. For highly motivated individuals, utilizing the services of a coach, especially one who is engaged in other aspects of your cultural development or leadership framework, can accelerate the time to visible performance OTG.

▶ Mentoring Programs

Mentoring programs *can create powerful connections between more and less experienced colleagues in your organization* who can share insights on company culture, processes, technical skills, career development, and relationship dynamics. This is an opportunity for both parties to learn, but it is recommended that mentoring programs be formally structured with purposeful executive matching, established rules of engagement, and targeted deliverables versus random or informal conversations.

▶ Pay-for-Performance Incentive Compensation Plans

Aligning organizational objectives with an individual's performance goals is best accomplished through a variable incentive compensation plan that rewards various levels of performance.

Most larger corporations already use this approach to link short- and long-term rewards to short- and long-term performance, serving their purposes for both individual accountability and talent retention, but small to mid-sized businesses and especially private companies with closely held ownership seldom fully utilize this tool.

The fundamental approach to getting started with this type of plan includes separating compensation into (2) components, a fixed salary and a variable bonus based on performance targets tied to individual, team, and organizational goals.

An example is an executive with a $100,000 salary and a 25% variable bonus target. While the salary is fixed with a guaranteed payout, the $25,000 is at risk pending the delivery of targeted objectives. An example of a targeted objective would be to secure product distribution in (10) new accounts in the coming year. The variable component might be an all-or-nothing approach in which the executive achieves the goal and gets the full payout or one that is scaled to performance.

For the scaled approach, an executive might be required to secure a minimum of (5) accounts to be "bonus eligible," and for each account between (6) and (10), a $5,000 bonus award is granted. An upside kicker to further incentivize employees might be to say that for new accounts in the (11)–(15) range, an additional $2,500 will be provided per account, which provides an upside target greater than 100% of their total compensation plan. Some organizations may even have an upside approach in which rewards are granted for all distributions above (11) without a cap.

There are a number of ways to design pay-for-performance plans. This example reflects a simple approach that requires a slightly new structural approach each year as the goals change. The key takeaway is that the organization achieves its focused goals first (i.e., a minimum of (5) accounts are closed) and the sharing of the upside goes to both the individual and the organization. Risk and reward must occur on both sides of the equation, with payouts happening in alignment for both the upside and the downside.

> *In initially making the change to a pay-for-performance approach, you will need to potentially benchmark your salary/compensation levels externally to be fully informed as you make your adjustments to the new approach and decide how to adjust your fixed/variable splits.*

What you might face in smaller or mid-sized organizations is initial pushback from your talent based on concerns about income risk and potentially "not being whole" in the first year as the new approach gets underway. You may also have pushback from senior executives, especially in your sales functions, who do not want to perform against targets you set for them when they have been comfortably deciding each year how much effort they want to apply based on the amount of money they want to make (and in so doing have been leaving you vulnerable to their efforts and without any leverage for accomplishing your targeted corporate growth goals).

Of all the performance measures available to the organizational leader, linking objectives to financial rewards may be the most important, so rigor it with consequential leadership!

▶ Being Recognized as a "Best Place" to Work

Being recognized by outside third parties as "a best place to work" can enhance your company's reputation, be a source of pride for your employee community, and therefore assist in your talent recruitment and retention efforts. Often, this requires meeting criteria such as flextime benefits, job sharing, extended maternity/paternity leave, training and development, and so on. If these are in sync with your organizational philosophies, this might be worthwhile to pursue.

Remember that tracking and measuring performance can only occur if targets have been established. Likewise, performance targets can only be reached if they are coached and developed over time. This is the role of the CEO and leadership team.

The Messages (Communication and Interface)

As an organizational leader, you must learn to be a master communicator. In the **Organizational Excellence** model, remember that messaging, like the environment, is an interface. You must therefore actively engage in messaging out into the external marketplace, which includes customers, stakeholders, and competitors, as well as into your own internal enterprise community. How you frame and deliver your messages will affect your reputation and credibility both individually and organizationally.

The critical elements of building your message platform as an organizational leader include:

- What content to message about

- How to stylistically deliver those messages

- When and where (i.e., in what forums) to deliver the messages

▶ What Content to Message About

The **Organizational Excellence** Model is itself *a road map for developing the content elements of your message platform.* As you and your leadership team develop a focused action agenda that reflects your overall enterprise priorities in each of the (6) areas (environment, culture, talent, strategy, performance, messages), this agenda can be used as a practical communication outline for messaging.

Letting your organization know that you will be engaging in the structured use of the **Organizational Excellence** model is an important first message to establish because it will bring people in at the beginning and create excitement around the journey.

Start by introducing each area of the model and what initiatives might be explored without overpromising and raising expectations beyond the true intention and capability of the leadership team (i.e., in year (1) of this process, you are not likely to launch a new talent development program, new performance review process, career

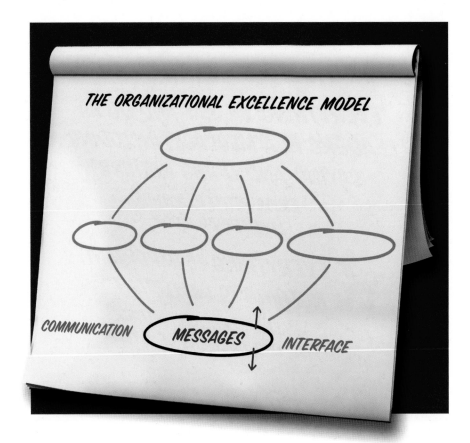

THE ORGANIZATIONAL EXCELLENCE MODEL

COMMUNICATION   MESSAGES   INTERFACE

management process, and succession-planning model, but that could reflect your (3)-year plan).

When I start working with an organization as a team coach, I begin with culture, not surprisingly, and launch a number of foundational initiatives. For example, clarifying the values, engaging in a cultural survey to understand the critical issues, and assessing the overall environmental conditions created by the CEO and leadership team might be the basis for creating a year (1) action agenda.

This does not mean that organizational goal setting is ignored, growth initiatives are not pursued, or hiring new talent is avoided; it simply acknowledges that the organizational change process cannot be taken on for everything at once (remember sequencing!). The first goal is to establish traction; without this, there is no long-term momentum and forward progress.

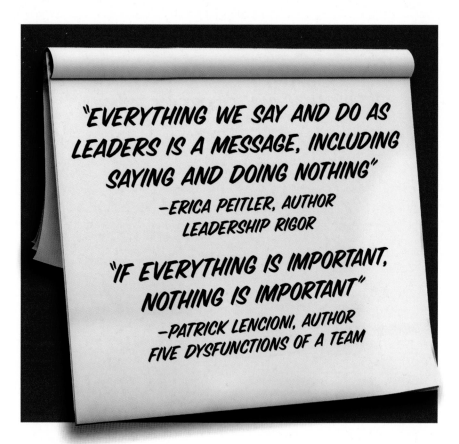

"EVERYTHING WE SAY AND DO AS LEADERS IS A MESSAGE, INCLUDING SAYING AND DOING NOTHING"
—ERICA PEITLER, AUTHOR
LEADERSHIP RIGOR

"IF EVERYTHING IS IMPORTANT, NOTHING IS IMPORTANT"
—PATRICK LENCIONI, AUTHOR
FIVE DYSFUNCTIONS OF A TEAM

Many of the small to mid-sized companies (or functional/divisional teams in larger organizational structures) I work with are being introduced for the first time to these **Leadership Rigor** and **Organizational Excellence** model enterprise concepts (i.e., competency models, variable incentive pay models, talent development initiatives, performance-based review processes with calibration).

> *They often initially believe they are doing some version of these things, but in reality they come to realize that they are unconsciously incompetent in these areas with an occasional unconscious competency thrown in for good measure.*

The most successful companies and their leaders accurately assess that they are really at the starting point with these initiatives and are up front in communicating this to their organizations. They then invite their organizations to begin to consciously walk through the building process and commit to the time and effort it will take. The leaders become advocates for and believers in the end game of developing an organization anchored in excellence and driven by performance, and they embrace the concept of **Leadership Rigor**!

Regardless of how far along you are in the process and your current level of commitment, as CEO or part of the leadership team, you need to consistently message on the (6) critical areas of **Organizational Excellence:** environment, culture, talent, strategy, performance, and yes, messages.

◼ The Environment

Messaging about the environment includes addressing what *trends and competitive moves* you see taking place, how these color your *optimism or caution* with respect to how you are going to market with your business model, and what impact, if any, this might have on your longer-term strategy.

◼ The Culture

Messaging about culture means *reinforcing the core values* of the company by relating them to your day-to-day business activities. Though your values will not change over time, you must continuously frame how they apply to the context of today's challenges.

Share insights that you and your leadership team have identified from the latest culture survey and what your go-forward action plan is, including challenges and new practices you may be looking to put into place (i.e., **The Accountability Conversation**, the **Analytical Rigor** model for decision making, or a new competency model).

◼ The Talent

It is always important to *acknowledge* the new talent you recently hired or new positions being created to add value to your organization. *Recognizing special project initiatives* or new team leaders who have been appointed through structural changes to your platform are important messages to share so that everyone understands what changes are underway and who is involved. It is also important to **celebrate achievements or milestones** (i.e., years of service, anniversaries) within your talent community.

◼ The Strategy

As mentioned, this is an area many executives avoid talking about because they lack the words or conceptual clarity about what their strategy is and may feel uncomfortable about being put on the spot with potential questions from their talent. As an organizational leader, you must address this and work to clearly establish your strategic messages.

You must ultimately have a strategy (or be developing one) that can be communicated as part of your **Organizational Excellence** action agenda. Be honest about where you are and what needs to be done next. When your talent understands your strategy, they can make contributions and ensure alignment with the direction. In the absence of this, you might be wasting resources or ineffectively utilizing them.

◼ The Performance

Your organization will always want you to provide updates on the scorecard that tracks your progress to your goals, and this is the area you are most likely to be comfortable communicating about with respect to content. Your bigger messaging opportunity here lies in linking today's performance to your organization's longer-term goals and strategy. Consider using **The Progressive Mindset** model to communicate your performance in the context of where you were, where you are now, and where you are going next.

◼ The Messages

Link together what you say with what you want your team to hear and the takeaway impact you hope to have on them. Don't shy away from this. On the contrary, "Tell them what you are going to tell them, tell them, and then tell them what you told them." Remember, communication is often an illusion, and you need to repeat your messages upward of (8) times if they are to land and be recalled! Always create the overarching context and seek to inspire action by how you communicate. In other words, **Rigor it!**

▶ How to Stylistically Deliver Your Messages

In addition to using **The Progressive Mindset** model to frame where you are going and what is next, consider using one of the most powerful communication tools ever created, the story.

As mentioned earlier in *Leadership Rigor*, storytelling is a way to engage your audience in a plot, convey who the characters are and what they are going through, and resolve the tension with an insightful ending that delivers an inspiring takeaway message. Some leaders are natural storytellers who use drama, humor, and suspense to rally their audiences. If this is a style you excel at, use it where appropriate to deliver your messages.

One story all leaders must learn to tell, whether they like storytelling or not, is the *company narrative.* This story, unlike any other, tells about the ongoing journey of your organization, including who it is, where its roots came from, what makes it unique, and how it developed into the company it is today.

> *The narrative is your chance as a leader to tell the story that captures the pride and the struggle, reflects on the wins and the losses, and reminds everyone of the original dream and where you are now and where you are going.*

As a leadership performance coach, I am always looking for leaders who have the confidence to tell their company narrative and do so in an inspiring way. The ability to tell this story is part of what separates great employees from future leaders. Recognizing the power and impact of your company narrative is an important part of becoming a master communicator.

▶ When and Where to Deliver Your Messages

As CEO, you need to consider both the forums and the frequency of your communications. You need to create what I referred to earlier as rhythm, a consistent frequency for communication forums that keeps the momentum going and ensures that you don't lose focus or connectivity with your organization.

Part 2, Leading Teams, covered the importance of creating rhythm with regularly scheduled one-to-ones and team meetings. In leading an organization, you now need to consider the rhythm for important communication forums and interactions such as:

- ☑ **Town halls**
- ☑ **Cultural surveys**
- ☑ **Leadership team meetings**
- ☑ **Budget planning meetings**
- ☑ **Performance management coaching sessions**
- ☑ **Year-end performance reviews**
- ☑ **Roundtable sessions/small group sharing discussions**
- ☑ **Annual business meetings**
- ☑ **Annual volunteer community/charity events**
- ☑ **Learning workshops**
- ☑ **Succession-planning workshops**
- ☑ **Career management and IDP discussions**

At the organizational leadership level, you need to *create an annual calendar of events,* ensuring that your rhythm and sequencing make sense and that you are creating enough space for preparation and dialogue while avoiding the disaster of having everything occur all at once. Performance and productivity are dependent on good planning and sequencing at the CEO leadership team level.

The company town hall is *one communication forum to over-emphasize* as you initially work to launch your **Organizational Excellence** journey. Town halls can be held as frequently as monthly, though holding them less often than quarterly is not recommended. They provide an opportunity for the CEO and leadership team to connect, review progress against goals, tell the evolving company narrative, outline progress on the journey of **Organizational Excellence**, and recognize outstanding accomplishments to celebrate together. While the CEO and leadership team should initially lead these meetings, over time they can evolve and develop into forums that other departments and teams can lead and own.

Your town hall forum helps to create a strong sense of organizational community within your business environment while allowing for the delivery of direct and consistent messages from the CEO and leadership team versus a more diluted messaging process that may lose some of its impact in translation.

▶ Remember Intimacy When Framing Your Messages

Last, despite the altitude of your role and the scope of your responsibility, it is important for you as an organizational leader to create intimacy in your communications.

One forum that lends itself well to intimacy and accelerates relationship building is the *roundtable format* with small groups of employees. This forum allows you and your talent to go deeper into areas of importance and to collectively feel the energy around issues that may not be as palpable in a larger town hall setting.

A valuable way to stay intimately connected to both your larger community of employees and the external communities in which you live and work is to organize *volunteer initiatives.* Whether you and your colleagues build a home with Habitat for Humanity or work in a soup kitchen, choosing meaningful ways to express your company values in service of others is a great way to reinforce your leadership roles and build a sense of intimate community outside the office.

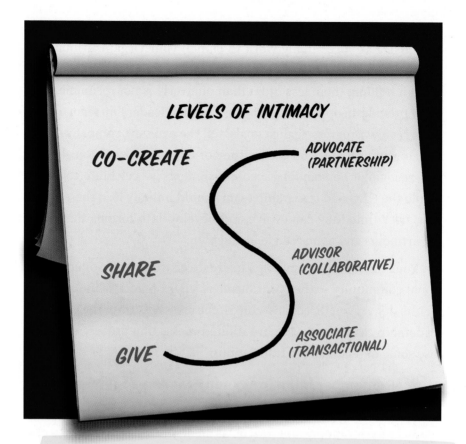

When scheduled events take place that contribute to the growth and learning of your organization, take the opportunity to make a personal appearance. For example, if you as CEO invest in a learning workshop for leadership development, it is highly impactful to hear directly from you why this is important, how it contributes to the organization's future, and what your personal expectations are for the participants.

Meanwhile, asking for input and honest feedback through cultural surveys and (360)-feedback tools sends the clear message, "I am listening; I want to hear from you, and I care about what you think."

The feedback you receive will be both *gratifying and gut wrenching.* What's most important is that you openly acknowledge the importance of the messages you receive and that you and your leadership team make a clear commitment to understand and address them.

Taking action visibly, consistently, and with conscious competency is important for your credibility as a leader. Those companies that do a survey and don't fully acknowledge, share, or act on the results send a message of "We really don't care what you think" to their employees and will not get honest engagement in the future.

> *Being a master communicator means linking all the pieces together to support the company narrative for your* **Organizational Excellence** *journey. Your cultural survey results, ensuing actions, and retesting process will demonstrate your* **Leadership Rigor** *for creating and sustaining a genuinely performance-based organization.*

Armed with an understanding of the CEO and leadership team roles, business platform constructs, and how to shape your future using the **Organizational Excellence** model, you now have a final tension to resolve and a choice to make. The question is, how will you choose to lead and be the architect of your organization?

Ready to resolve this final tension and make your final choice? Rigor it forward to the closing section!

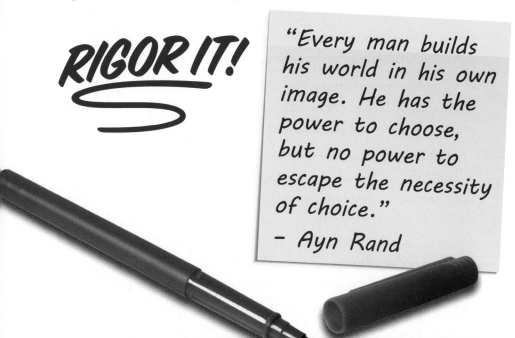

RIGOR IT!

"Every man builds his world in his own image. He has the power to choose, but no power to escape the necessity of choice."
– Ayn Rand

"Whatever you are, be a good one."
– Abraham Lincoln

THE *TENSION* TO RESOLVE: Being an Entrepreneurial or an Enterprise Leader

Thus far, Part 3 of *Leadership Rigor* has explored the role of the CEO and the executive leadership team and how leading at the organizational level requires a different orientation with respect to complexity and conscious competency. Because you are now guiding strong functional leaders, you must diligently maintain your altitude and focus "on" the business and not allow yourself to be indulgent and drop down "into" the business where you cause compression that hijacks your organization's performance and productivity.

Creating the environmental conditions of success includes ensuring that there is safe, empowering space for your teams to operate in, and this is work only you and your leadership team can do.

Leading a performance-based organization with *consequential leadership* that is both positive and constructive, taking your executive team on a development journey of **Leadership Rigor,** shaping your operational platform, and investing time on your future landscape all require patience, commitment, and persistence. ***Growth does not occur without taking risks and making changes.*** Likewise, performance and productivity come from conscious discipline and practice.

The *signature model* presented in Part 3, **Organizational Excellence**, outlined the road map for CEOs and their leadership teams to follow in creating their future action agenda. To briefly summarize, if you are not actively engaged in shaping your environment, culture, talent, strategy, performance, and messaging, you are not playing your role at the organizational leadership level. These (6) areas are non-negotiable priorities the CEO and leadership team must own.

In performance-driven organizations, more than any other factor, the culture a company creates directly impacts the talent it can attract, develop, and retain, which ultimately determines its leadership potential for the future. If the culture is not inspiring, no title or amount of money will retain talent in the long run. Alternatively, if your high-achieving talent does not align behaviorally with your culture, you must swiftly acknowledge that these individuals are not a fit and they must leave, either voluntarily or at your request.

In short, do not underestimate your work as a cultural architect and leadership role model. This is not soft stuff you can delegate, push aside, or wait to act upon. It is the hardest and most impactful part of shaping your organization's current and future success, and it needs to be embraced and respected as an essential business priority if you want to lead and do so with rigor!

You Have Now Arrived at the Final Tension...

Assuming you have fully embraced what needs to be done thus far to lead your organization forward, you have now reached the third and final tension on your **Leadership Rigor** journey:

> *How will you personally choose to play your role in being the architect of your organization's future? More specifically, will you be an entrepreneurial leader, or will you be an enterprise leader?*

Your role as CEO is to advance your organization toward reaching its full potential—in all measurable ways! For this to happen, you must consciously choose the leadership role you will play so that you can create a balanced energy in your organization whereby both skill sets exist and contribute in meaningful and productive ways.

There are no right or wrong answers here. The (2) styles, however, are vastly different. To determine which type of leader you most naturally are, take a moment to thoughtfully consider your hardwiring preferences and reflect on how you can best create value for your organization by leveraging your strengths and self-managing your potentially disruptive or non-productive behaviors.

The Entrepreneurial Leader

Entrepreneurial leaders, for the purposes of our discussion here in *Leadership Rigor,* are characterized as being creative, innovative, idea-driven, on-the-ground situational deal makers.

These individuals are at their best when they have complete freedom to operate unencumbered by rules or processes and are only accountable to their own desires, beliefs, and ideals. Speed of action on their own timetable is important to them. As such, they move through the world with *gut-driven intuitive decisiveness,* preferring to answer mainly to their own good judgment or the input and advice of a small, select group of trusted advisors. They productively deliver on their own personal expectations (which may be stated or unstated), often with their own versions of *heroic outcomes and more than occasional "rule-breaking" techniques.* They avoid being involved in processes that restrict them or team environments that can slow them down due to their negative perception and fear of "group-think" or "management by committee" philosophies.

> *Entrepreneurial leaders exude a strong sense of "Don't worry; I know what I'm doing. Look at who I am and what I've already accomplished." Infectious passion, significant achievements, a healthy ego, in some cases a potentially arrogant disposition, and relatively successful historical risk taking provide these leaders with loyal followers who want to be part of the perceived magic.*

These followers admire their leaders' ideas as well as ideals, though working for them can be a challenge. The fast-moving, ever-changing, impulsive approaches of the entrepreneurial leader can create either *chaos and confusion* due to limited communication alignment or unrealistic and likely unstated expectations for how others need to perform. The end result is usually initial disappointment on the part of the leader and/or his or her loyal subjects followed by a heroic effort to make miracles happen and save the day, either independently or collectively. *An emotional rollercoaster!*

The challenge with entrepreneurial leaders is that they often (perhaps even always) believe they alone know best and are the smartest person in the room. If you are one of them, you are likely a "spoke in the wheel" leader within your organization, individually reaching out to those you need something from but rarely proactively involving others in the transparency of your thinking process. You take input and seek counsel mainly on your own terms, and you make most, if not all, of the critical decisions yourself.

Not surprisingly, your operating paradigm is *"Trust me; I've got this figured out."* Without a doubt, you passionately believe you have the company's best interests at heart, especially when it is your own company. The challenge is that you may not as confidently trust others or be willing to let go of the decision-making process and share in direction setting or managing the operations of the company. This might be especially true in family or small businesses where there is a generational legacy at play and the business tends to be run by a family member, regardless of capability, qualification, or readiness.

With this approach, your ability to run your organization is limited by your own personal bandwidth. Only what you can physically, intellectually, and emotionally take on is completed. The downside to this style is that the business can only reach a certain size without causing unmanageable growing pains for you and your organization.

Being smart, entrepreneurial leaders will always convince themselves that they know what to do and how to do it. *They are usually only half correct, however.* They often know what to do but do not understand the steps, sequences, or implications of how to do it and either do not have or do not trust others around them to assist. This is why they can stay stuck at a certain size or life cycle phase with their business, continuing to spin their wheels unsuccessfully or, worse, why they are surprised when their talent slowly starts to leave, typically out of frustration at not being transparently engaged in the business and/or at not growing quickly enough.

The Enterprise Leader

Enterprise leaders, for the purposes of our discussion here, are characterized as being structured, disciplined, team oriented, actively engaged in developing people and progress, as well as process oriented in their approach to the overall business. They consciously attempt to establish the right altitude for the work of their leadership team and look to *create lift while minimizing compression* so they can collectively achieve maximum impact from applied resources across their organization.

Focused on and concerned with the broader, longer-term view of the business, enterprise leaders ground themselves in **Organizational Excellence** initiatives using the framework as a guide. They see themselves as leaders of leaders, yet they operate with a presence and style that appreciates their team members as peers working together. In addition to operationalizing their business model for continuous scalable and sustainable growth, *they work to instill a leadership philosophy across the organization* as they actively shape their performance-based culture and build bench strength for the future.

> *Enterprise leaders are champions of growth, both for the business and the talent that drives it. They are intent on increasing organizational bandwidth to its highest level of integrated capabilities.*

Enterprise leaders are planners who are seldom caught unprepared. They realize that capitalizing on growth opportunities requires both up-front preparation and timely response, so they proactively bring in new talent on a regular basis so they can take on more complex challenges as they arise. They have a conscious understanding of what life cycle stage their organization and marketplace are in and they attempt to evolve at an appropriate pace to ensure smooth transitions, limited disruptions, and an overall lower-risk approach to growth and change.

Enterprise leaders will likely have a documented operational business plan and appreciate strategy as an ongoing conversation with an identified set of targeted initiatives to create competitive advantage within the marketplace over time. *These leaders are future focused.* Not surprisingly, they engage in collaborative structured planning and budgeting processes for making smart investments over a shorter to longer-term time frame.

Enterprise leaders *advocate for team and leadership development* across their organizations, understanding that business today is too fast moving and too complex to be limited to only a few decision makers. Consequently, enterprise leaders support the process of transparent and conscious decision making through the use of tools like the **Analytical Rigor** model and **The Accountability Conversation** and embed them culturally within their organizations.

Enterprise leaders are focused on and motivated by their scorecards for performance and productivity. They actively set, track, and measure their collective goals. If adjustments need to be made based on milestone achievements or misses, they are proactive in realigning their resources and priorities for ensuring a favorable *ROR2* (return on resources and rigor).

The operating model of enterprise leaders is "let's engage together." They are fundamentally team players who realize the "sum is always greater than the parts" and are therefore *looking for integrated performance and productivity at the organizational level.* They want to create value and shape the future by developing leaders across their organizations. Enterprise leaders are also looking to make their organizations more streamlined, transparent, productive, and easier to work in and across through resource management (people, time, money) and the prioritization of initiatives.

The downside to being an enterprise leader is potentially two-fold. These leaders can overengineer processes and slow down their organizations, causing "work-arounds" for increased speed, thereby defeating their original intentions for streamlined productivity.

The second downside can be a slower and lower-risk profile regarding investments in innovation due to both increased visibility to the "real risks" based on rigorous analytics as well as a desire to secure internal alignment with their teams and stakeholders before taking action, which may include the need for staging multiple conversations to build confidence, all of which can take time.

Two Different Approaches to Growth

As a company naturally progresses along its growth curve and reaches a level of critical mass, it risks hitting a plateau beyond which it struggles to break through. CEOs and their leadership teams must address the question of how to take the business to the next level in top-line revenue growth, bottom-line profitability, or preferably both areas. The challenge lies both in what to do and how to do it. As you might imagine, the entrepreneurial leader and enterprise leader have different approaches.

The entrepreneurial leader might either be comfortable with the status quo, choosing to milk the business for now, or might address this challenge with an impulsive reaction such as an attempt to expand the business into new growth areas or to sell the business and start something completely new. Entrepreneurial leaders may also reluctantly consider hiring a consultant to offer recommendations, but since they do not create this plan themselves, they may or may not trust the recommendations to be the right way forward.

The real risk for entrepreneurial leaders is that without a solid handle on the operations and performance metrics of their business,

which is often the case, the changes they make are likely to be un-consciously competent at best and potentially unconsciously incompetent. As a result, they will often guess at a series of solutions with a hit-or-miss gut-driven mentality and struggle to get out of the bevel and through the inflection point to make progress because they don't understand the root cause of the change that needs to be made. Instead of slowing down to learn more, they want to leap from one quick-fix solution to the next based on their own judgment or assessment.

The enterprise leader, on the other hand, when faced with the challenge of a plateau, tends to have a more consciously competent approach to what is working or not working as well as why this is the case. The systems, structure, and team capabilities that have been created across the organization can now be put to work to provide **Analytical Rigor** and collaborative support to develop a range of viable alternatives on what the problems are as well as what the potential solutions might be.

Unlike entrepreneurial leaders, enterprise leaders do not depend solely on their own ideas; they have the ability to tap into a broad range of talent across their organizations and into the power of collaborative and disciplined teamwork, which often results in the best solutions. Given their altitude and access to a greater bandwidth of talent, they can use processes and people to figure out both what to do next and how best to do it. They will **Rigor it!**

Stop Throwing Spaghetti against the Wall!

Staging your learning so that you minimize costs and risks is a consciously competent approach for launching a new product or initiative. Each step provides insights for you to modify or adjust as you potentially optimize your offering. Unfortunately, many small to mid-sized business owners act with unconscious incompetency or conscious incompetency by impulsively engaging in random tactics without appropriately assessing their marketplace. As a result, they find themselves confused about how to effectively launch a new product or service successfully. Believing they are smart enough to just figure it out in real time, they move from one approach to another without a grounded understanding of why they are doing what they are doing and what exactly they are looking for. In addition to not solving their problem, they frustrate and confuse their talent, who are likely trying to make the process transparent and iterative so that learning can inform the process. Stop the insanity. Instead, rigor it with conscious competency!

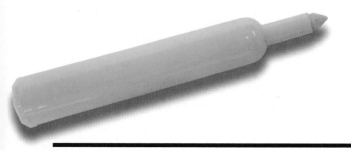

By now, you probably have a pretty good idea of which type of leader you are more likely to be in terms of your natural hardwiring.

Again, there are no right or wrong answers. While most leaders believe they have hybrid characteristics of both styles, *every leader definitely has a preference.* Be honest with yourself. The entrepreneur is most excited about the chase, the kill, the win, the deal, and the innovative breakthrough. The enterprise leader appreciates the complexity of running an integrated organization and is excited about creating both operational and **Organizational Excellence** through systems, processes, people development, and structures.

> *In the end, these are really (2) different approaches. Each is uniquely suited to a time, place, or life cycle stage for the company or marketplace, and knowing as well as understanding how best to apply your strengths or step back and let others take the lead is an important consideration for you regardless of the role you choose.*

Keep in mind that, as the CEO or business owner, you will always have informed access to all aspects of the business. By acknowledging your primary emphasis and strength, you can optimize your energy and contributions to their highest levels and minimize either your disruptions or distractions so that you can unleash the full potential of your organization in becoming performance based.

Regardless of which type of leader you are, own and focus on your inherent strengths while flanking your other side. If you are an enterprise leader, you may need to hire a *chief innovation officer (CIO) or head of business development* to ensure that your organization is focusing on innovative solutions, technology applications, partnerships for growth, targeted acquisitions, and product design—the ideation areas where breakthrough opportunities incubate.

On the other hand, if you are an entrepreneurial leader, you can hire a *chief operating officer (COO) or operations manager* to ensure that your *systems, processes, and procedures* are in place to secure knowledge management, consistent applications, increased productivity, and performance oversight so growth and investment momentum can be realized.

Adopt the necessary yin to your natural yang and ensure that your organization has the benefit of both energies and capabilities so that it can realize its growth potential.

Obstacles to Overcome

Both entrepreneurial and enterprise leaders must overcome certain resistances that are inherent to their temperaments and that have implications for their organizations.

▶ Overcoming Resistance

One of the resistances an entrepreneurial leader must overcome is how to appropriately handle talent without seeming extreme or inconsistent. For example, some entrepreneurial leaders, especially small to mid-sized business owners, are slow to eliminate underperforming talent due to loyalty, tenure, or fear about whether the decision will be seen as fair and reasonable. *This slows progress in their organizations as they hold on to underperforming talent for prolonged periods, potentially years or decades.*

On the other extreme, entrepreneurial leaders might also struggle with rapid turnover in talent and have little patience for the training and development of new employees, mainly because they themselves are unconsciously competent and don't know how to break the learning down and assist others in their learning curves.

> *The impact is that individuals without the ability to completely fit the profile and hit the ground running independently and immediately will be challenged to prove themselves in entrepreneurially-driven organizations.*

Enterprise leaders will likely be more objective, patient, and balanced when it comes to talent development within their organizations. They realize that talent is not always a fit and they are able to emotionally separate performance standards and organizational needs from the challenges of appropriately and fairly terminating, if necessary, long-tenured and loyal employees. They are also relatively clear on the up-front time, effort, and commitment required to train and develop strong talent. They have a structured talent management philosophy and well-established processes including formal on-boarding, a (90)-day probationary period, regular coaching sessions, and documented competency expectations as well as structured performance improvement plans. This ensures that underperforming talent is not tolerated for prolonged periods of time or prematurely asked to leave.

One of the resistances enterprise leaders must address concerns *their handling of the risk, change, and growth equation.* Enterprise leaders will smartly want to pursue maximum growth at the lowest level of risk or change. They understand the challenges they face, will quantify the risk/return ratios, and will make judgment calls in collaboration with their teams, understanding there are known and visible consequences to both success and failure. Yet here in the world of the enterprise leader, we often see *how temperament plays a role.* Does the enterprise leader have a transformational change temperament (with a high risk tolerance) or the temperament of a transitional/growth leader (with a lower risk tolerance)?

The profile of the leader will likely affect the approach, and here is where a strong leadership team can push or pull on the dynamics required to do what is best for the organization.

> *Well-balanced enterprise leaders and their teams will map out plans and contingencies for the risks taken to mitigate possible surprises. They will also ensure that they understand the consequences of not taking action and remaining on the sidelines.*

Entrepreneurial leaders will also face a challenge on the risk, change, and growth equation, especially because personal and family net worth are often involved. The issue here is whether they have the capability, resources, and patience to fully assess the risks so that they understand what the real growth opportunities are versus relying solely on their gut instincts. The higher risk for the entrepreneur is not having mapped out the risks and calculated their financial impact, leaving this individual somewhat in the dark and potentially blind-sided by an unforeseen outcome that would likely have been more visible to the enterprise leader.

▶ Taking a Risk

The risk of letting go of a significant piece of the business and investing in a high-level executive to do part of what you as CEO believe your role is can be uncomfortable. The bigger and more dangerous risk, however, is not fully leveraging your strengths and complementing your weaknesses, which will ultimately hold back your organization's growth.

Before taking this risk, consider the effect it might have on your organizational culture. "The way we do things around here" is already in place, and your organization is functionally dysfunctional around your current structure, processes, or lack thereof. As you consider putting either more structure and processes in place or trying to streamline processes that have become burdensome in order to open up the innovative creativity of your organization, be conscious about your communication messages.

Ensure that you are proactively setting the stage, making the case, and sharing **The Progressive Mindset** of where you were, where you are, and where you are going with this new approach. Share the rational for your choices and frame it within the context of the organization's life cycle. This is important whether you are an entrepreneur or an enterprise leader, as communication is a currency you must continue to master!

▶ Being Vulnerable

Acknowledging that you're either an entrepreneurial or enterprise leader is not an admission of failure or weakness.

On the contrary, playing to your strengths while flanking your weaknesses is enlightened leadership in today's complex business environment. While you cannot give to others what you don't personally have, you still need to provide it for them! Your organization needs both processes and structures as well as innovations and creativity to grow. Denying your organization either of these will cause your business growth to slow or stop and your talent to disengage or leave. Remember, it is not all about you, the leader; you are in service to others here, to your organization as an entity!

The life cycle phase your organization is in will in part inform what type of changes need to be made and when.

> *As CEO, you can be egotistical about this and stand in your arrogance, righteousness, or ignorance, or you can stand strong in your role and do the work that only a CEO can do, providing the supplemental leadership that your organization needs for ultimate sustainability and growth.*

Resolving the Tension

Acknowledging what type of leader you are will give your organization what it needs to succeed without allowing your ego or personal shortcomings to deprive it of the capabilities required to appropriately meet marketplace demands for competitiveness and growth.

> *Both the entrepreneurial and enterprise leaders can hold their organizations back, either by not structuring people and processes appropriately or by failing to infuse innovation and risk taking.*

The Service You Provide

Make a personal choice and create an organizational balance between enterprise business stability and entrepreneurial innovation. In so doing, you will become an enlightened leader who can appreciate the contributions of both sides and who enables your organization's performance and productivity by providing access to both talents and energies.

The CEO must be the ultimate steward of the business. Understanding how you are hardwired and knowing whether the life cycle of your company is consistent with your strengths is critical to your future success. Being proactive versus responsive or reactive can also minimize the frustration and lost resources your organization can suffer during a potential transition involving a change in leadership.

Embrace the concepts and language presented throughout *Leadership Rigor.* Know your strengths and plan for serving the needs of your organization's growth and sustainability, not your own ego.

The New Perspective You Take On

Your legacy as an enterprise leader is that the business continues to flourish and perform under the leadership of your solid talent bench; your legacy as an entrepreneurial leader is that the business is smoothly transitioned to the next generation or ultimately sold at a great profit for your shareholders, demonstrating a productive investment.

Clearly, to achieve either legacy, as well as your own potential as a leader, you must be disciplined and consciously **Rigor it!**

> "The final test of a leader is that they leave behind in others the conviction and will to carry on."
> – Walter Lippman

THE END!

> "Entrepreneurship is living a few years of your life like most people won't, so you can spend the rest of your life like most people can't."
> – A student of Warren G. Tracey

About the Author

Erica Peitler is an accomplished leadership performance coach and high-impact facilitator who creates the conditions for change and growth with her clients so that they can take the evolutionary or transformational steps toward achieving their full potential as individual leaders, high-performing teams, and organizations operating at a level of excellence. A straightforward communicator and conceptual thinker, Erica brings a fast-paced creative approach to the leadership development initiatives and journeys she leads with an overarching desire to take her clients where they need to go and experience what they need to experience in order to break through barriers, let go of baggage, and get to "what is next" in their personal and professional pursuits.

A pharmacist and internationally respected business leader with over (20) years of experience as a transformational change agent, Erica has an extensive background in Operational/Divisional leadership as an executive VP/General Manager, responsible for Board-Level strategic planning initiatives as well as Chief Scientific Officer roles.

Erica was recognized by *New Jersey Biz* magazine as one of the 50 Best Women in Business in 2013 and in 2014 has been elected to sit on the boards of two large, privately held companies. In 2011–2013, she served as the chair of the University of Connecticut School of Pharmacy board and is a member of the Executive Women of New Jersey (EWNJ) and the Healthcare Women's Business Association (HBA). In addition, she is the chair of a Vistage private advisory board where she facilitates provocative debate and dialogue with (15) to (18) CEOs each month centered around how to grow their businesses as well as providing leadership and business coaching.

Over the last (7) years, Erica has built a thriving coaching and consulting business working with over (25) CEOs and hundreds of mid- to senior-level executives in large corporations as well as small to mid-sized businesses. As an author and speaker, Erica educates, entertains, and enlightens her audiences on the challenges of change and growth as a leader with realism and humor based on her own journey and hard-earned lessons. Her first book, *Open Up and Say Aaah!,* is a precursor to *Leadership Rigor,* providing readers with an opportunity to explore the current realities and potential changes they must make in themselves first before being able to experience the fulfilling careers, relationships, and lives that they seek.

Her signature leadership team journeys, which are modeled after the *Leadership Rigor* approach, are creating game-changing experiences for the brave leaders who dare to consciously practice these principles with discipline and deliver their organizations to their true potential for breakthrough performance and productivity.

Erica lives in Morristown, New Jersey, with her partner Mollie and their yellow lab Jazz.

Index

Index

Index

Index

Index

Index

Index

Index

Index

Index

G

Gates, Bill
  empowerment quote, 327
Generalists vs. specialists, 67
Geographical structure, 401, 402
Gift of feedback, 7, 10, 15, 39
Givers of trust, 36, 190–191
Global community as stakeholder, 260–261
Global organizational structure, 402
Goals
  accountability culture, 452–453
  BHAG (Big Hairy Audacious Goal), 203
  integrated performance as, 245–247
  operational planning, 416
  Organizational Excellence, 433, 434
  pace-setting leadership style, 73–74
  performance-based organizations, 331, 334
  personal vs. organizational, 22
  SMARTER, 473
Goleman, Daniel
  Emotional Intelligence, 29
  interpersonal interactions, 201
  outstanding soft skills quote, 101
Good to Great (Collins), 203
Gravitas
  charisma versus, 18
  as leadership skill, 18, 20
  leadership voice, 119
  as relationship building block, 12, 15, 18, 258
Green vs. blue dollars, 98, 249–250, 365–366
Growth
  business as pursuit of, 267, 386
  CEO leadership, 339, 440
  enterprise vs. entrepreneurial leaders, 495–497, 500–501
  gift of feedback, 7, 10
  leadership as facilitation, 54, 200, 311
  organization life cycle, 383
  quote by Abraham Maslow, 69
  quote by Jack Welch, 177
  quote by James Cash Penney, 154
  stretch assignments for, 465
  (360)-feedback tools, 475
Gut reaction. See Intuition

H

Hallucination quote by Thomas Edison, 424
Handshake, 83, 335
Hardwired. See Knowing oneself
Head of business development, 498
Health as discipline, 54–58
"High potential" leaders, 22
Hiring via contextual interviewing process, 463–464
Human resources (HR)
  as metric, 472
  talent development process, 463, 465
Hybrid organizational structure, 401

I

"I" vs. "we"
  See also "We" vs. "I"
  faux leadership team, 348–349, 361
  individual-first perspective, 65–66
Ideas socialized, 76–77
IDPs (individual development plans), 476, 485
Ignorance, 63–64
Illusion of communication, 14
Imagination, 405–410
Impact
  intention and, 37–39, 81, 126, 299, 351
  language of leadership, 344, 345
  opening of meeting, 239
  probability and impact, 415
Impulsivity avoidance. See Analytical Rigor
Inclusion. See Diversity
Incompetence.
  See Conscious incompetence;
  Unconscious incompetence
Indicators, leading and lagging, 412–413
Individual development plans (IDPs), 476, 485
Information meetings, 369, 371–372, 373
Information via framed data, 285–286, 290, 305
  See also Sharing knowledge
Initiative as leadership skill, 20
Innovation
  chief innovation officer (CIO), 498
  enterprise leaders, 495
  open office space for, 455
  Progressive Mindset model, 159
  timing of, 382

Index

Index

Index

Index

Index

Index

Index

CEO guidance, 347
future envisioned, 423
Vistage as example, 392, 393, 423
Peer group
career advancement and, 358
leadership team relationships, 359–361, 374–377
peer-to-peer accountability, 454
as stakeholders, 257–258
Peitler, Erica
everything a message quote, 481
Penney, James Cash
growth is work quote, 154
People
blue vs. green dollars, 98, 249–250, 365–366
as resource to be managed, 95, 98
Perceivers (P)
knowing-doing gap, 171
MBTI hardwiring, 26
Performance
compensation and, 334, 416–417, 477–478
integrated performance, 245–247 (*See also* Integrated performance)
metrics, 248–250 (*See also* Metrics)
operationally driven, 248–252
Organizational Excellence, 426, 438, 439, 471–478, 483
performance management framework, 333–334
as results and behaviors, 19–22, 224, 339, 471–472
team development, 224–225
Performance-based organizations
See also Organizational Excellence; Productivity
CEO leadership, 331–332
compensation, 334, 416–417, 477–478
competency models, 475–476
consequential leadership, 188, 331
development over time, 342
"hot seat" conversations, 355–356
leadership skills emphasized, 314
leadership team journey, 352–356
performance feedback tools, 334
performance management framework, 333–334
priorities of, 21, 22, 490
ROR2 (return on resources and rigor), 365–366, 393, 494
talent and culture, 490
talent selection, 385, 457, 465

team organization structures, 403
Personal power
charisma, 212–213
creating moments, 52
for cultural change initiative, 445
enterprise mindset, 339
leadership team, 344, 361
in networking, 263
open office spaces, 394
Organizational Excellence, 456
philosopher leaders, 312
power model, 44–46
trusted advisors, 117, 121
two-way street, 129
Personal preferences
CEO informing employees, 337
communication preferences, 264
facilitators of progress, 113
knowing oneself, 23–27 (*See also* Knowing oneself)
language of appropriate response, 72–73
temperament and challenges, 387–388
Philosophies
CEO transparency, 337, 341
conscious competence, 78
guiding leadership, 313
hybrid organizational structure, 401
leadership philosophy across organization, 493
operational excellence, 245–252
philosophies of engagement, 190–193
practitioner and philosopher, 307–324
team leadership styles, 196–200
Pictures
Analytical Rigor conversation, 273
anchors for instruction, 79
dashboard of indicators, 412–413, 471–472
Progressive Mindset model, 131–132, 135, 136
quote by Walt Disney, 132
team journey stages, 135
visionary leadership style, 74, 202
Pilot test, 420, 421
Pink elephants
hunting continually, 209–211, 226
issue raising, 111, 119
naming, 209–210
peer-to-peer accountability, 454
Planning
See also Analytical Rigor

Index

Index

Index

Index

Index

Index

Index

Index

RIGOR ALERT!

Putting Rigor OTG (On the Ground)

Putting Rigor OTG (On the Ground)

Putting Rigor OTG (On the Ground)

Putting Rigor OTG (On the Ground)

Putting Rigor OTG (On the Ground)

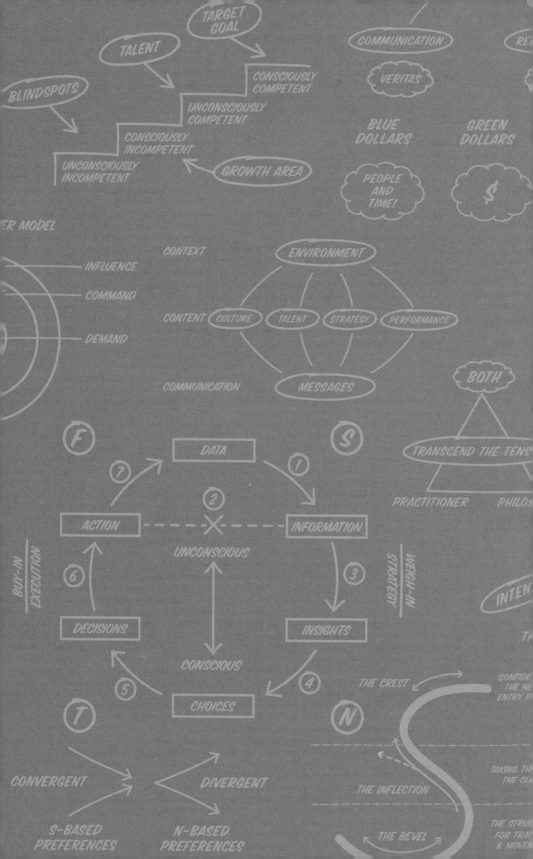